Epistemic Cultures

KARIN KNORR CETINA

Epistemic Cultures
How the Sciences Make
Knowledge

Harvard University Press

Cambridge, Massachusetts

London, England

1999

Library of Congress Cataloging-in-Publication Data

Knorr Cetina, K. (Karin)
    Epistemic cultures : how the sciences make knowledge / Karin
Knorr Cetina.
        p.   cm.
    Includes bibliographical references and index.
    ISBN 0-674-25893-2 (cloth : alk. paper). —
    ISBN 0-674-25894-0 (pbk. : alk. paper)
    1. Knowledge, Theory of.   2. Science—Philosophy.
3. Science—Social aspects.   4. Scientists—Interviews.
I. Title.
Q175.32.K45K57   1999
121—dc21   98-30277

For Margarete Zetina

Acknowledgments

This book would not have been possible without the generous help of the physicists and molecular biologists who welcomed me and my co-workers into their experiments and laboratories, gave us their time, and taught us everything about their work. My greatest thanks go to Peter Jenni, spokesman of ATLAS, who was also the one who got us started in UA2; together with Luigi DiLella, spokesman of UA2, Peter has survived and supported several generations of field ethnographers (Michael Polgar, Detlev Nothnagel, and Luc Gauthier). My thanks also go to Pierre Darriulat, who, at an early stage, was the first to allow us in—even though, as he told me at the first contact over the phone, he did not think this research would lead anywhere, he believed that UA2 was an open environment and that it should depend on participants what they did with us. These participants, to stick with physics, proved invaluable in letting themselves be "ethnographed." We could do practically all the observation and interviewing we wanted, everywhere; Polgar and Gauthier also participated in wiring and shift-taking.

I cannot here thank all the members of UA2 and ATLAS who contributed to this project over the years—they are too many. But I want to express my special thanks to Andy Parker for hours and hours of explanation, interpretation, and frank comments on everything. I and my co-workers have also learned about many important aspects of these experiments from Torsten Åkesson, Giuseppe Battistoni, Christopher Booth, Allan Clarke, Cornelis Daum, Nino Del Prete, Friedrich Dydak, Kevin Einsweiler, Chris Fabjan, Daniel Froidevaux, Fabiola Gianotti,

Claus Gössling, John Hanson, Sten Hellman, Karl Jakobs, Joe Incandela, Eike-Erik Kluge, Michael Levabvre, Lucie Linssen, Livio Mapelli, Karlheinz Meier, Marzio Nessi, Aleandro Nisati, Horst Oberlack, Trivan Pal, Chara Petridou, Hattie Plothow-Besch, Giacomo Polesello, Alan Poppleton, Jörg Schachter, Hans-Wolfgang Siebert, Ralf Spiwoks, Emmanuel Tsesmelis, Toni Weidberg, Jörg Wotschack, Darien Wood, and, in recent times, particularly from Hans Hoffmann—among many others. Finally, I have to thank Ugo Amaldi (DELPHI), Jack Steinberger (ALEPH), and H. Rikaczewski (L3) for enlightening me about the organization of the LEP experiments.

The list of molecular biologists who helped in this project is shorter, in my case, but no less distinguished. Personally, I have first to thank Peter Gruß, leader of the group in Heidelberg and Göttingen, who made it possible for us to study two molecular biology laboratories. In addition, I have learned invaluable things from Rudi Balling, Kamal Chowdhury, Hans Schöler, Ernst Böhnlein, Andreas Püschl, Michael Kessel, and from Daria.

I should also thank here my co-workers, mentioned before, and above all Klaus Amann, whose help in regard to investigating and understanding the molecular biology laboratories was invaluable. Chapters 4, 6, and 9 were written in collaboration with Klaus Amann.

My debts to colleagues in sociology, anthropology and science and technology studies are no less great—there have been innumerable occasions on which someone proved exceptionally helpful in commenting on a talk I gave, in adding an idea, in pointing out some literature I should read. Clifford Geertz, Michel Callon, Piet Hut, Norton Wise, Michele Lamont, Gerald Geison, Natalie Davis, and Andor Carius in Princeton were exceedingly helpful during my stays there. Don Campbell, Randall Collins, Luc Gauthier, Rob Hagendijk, Bettina Heintz, Barbara Herrnstein Smith, Stefan Hirschauer, Wolfgang Krohn, Günter Küppers, Jens Lachmund, Bruno Latour, John Law, Martina Merz, Nils Roll-Hansen, Sharon Traweek, Sherry Turkle, and Peter Weingart contributed ideas and suggestions, in response to papers presented or in conversation. This list must surely be appallingly incomplete, and I want to apologize to and at the same time thank all those I omitted.

Last but not least, I should say that this book really only began in

Acknowledgments

Princeton during my stay at the Institute for Advanced Study in 1992–93, which gave me the time to start some serious writing. I have to thank the School of Social Science for inviting me and for helping pay for my stay, and the Mellon Foundation for providing additional grant money. The research has been made possible by two generous grants from the Deutsche Forschungsgemeinschaft, which let itself be convinced that much longer than two years was needed for completing the project. And which waited patiently for the results. Also contributing to the effort were, of course, my department, the Faculty of Sociology at the University of Bielefeld, and, even more so, its Institute for Science and Technology Studies.

It remains for me to thank Ms. Gisela Diekmeier, who knows best what it meant to finish this book for publication; it is she and not I who really got it ready for publication. And thanks to Agnes, Fanny, Anna, and Dietrich Knorr for supporting me through seemingly endless periods of writing and rewriting, during which I proved insufferable, and for letting me be absent so often to do the research.

Contents

A Note on Transcription — xv

1 Introduction — 1

1.1 The Disunity of the Sciences — 2

1.2 The Cultures of Knowledge Societies — 5

1.3 Culture and Practice — 8

1.4 The Structure of the Book — 11

1.5 Physics Theory, and a First Look at the Field — 14

1.6 Issues of Methodology, and More about the Field — 17

2 What Is a Laboratory? — 26

2.1 Laboratories as Reconfigurations of Natural and Social Orders — 26

2.2 From Laboratory to Experiment — 32

2.3 Some Features of the Laboratory Reconsidered — 43

3 Particle Physics and Negative Knowledge — 46

3.1 The Analogy of the Closed Universe — 46

3.2 A World of Signs and Secondary Appearances — 48

3.3 The "Meaninglessness" of Measurement — 52

3.4 The Structure of the Care of the Self — 55

3.5 Negative Knowledge and the Liminal Approach 63

3.6 Moving in a Closed Universe: Unfolding, Framing, and Convoluting 71

4 Molecular Biology and Blind Variation 79

4.1 An Object-Oriented Epistemics 79

4.2 The Small-Science Style of Molecular Biology and the Genome Project 81

4.3 The Laboratory as a Two-Tier Structure 84

4.4 "Blind" Variation and Natural Selection 88

4.5 The Experiential Register 93

4.6 Blind Variation Reconsidered 108

5 From Machines to Organisms: Detectors as Behavioral and Social Beings 111

5.1 Primitive Classifications 111

5.2 Detector Agency and Physiology 113

5.3 Detectors as Moral and Social Individuals 116

5.4 Live Organism or Machine? 120

5.5 Are There Enemies? 123

5.6 Physicists as Symbionts 126

5.7 Taxonomies of Trust 130

5.8 Primitive Classifications Reconsidered 135

6 From Organisms to Machines: Laboratories as Factories of Transgenics 138

6.1 A Science of Life without Nature? 138

6.2 Organisms as Production Sites 144

6.3 Cellular Machines 149

6.4 Industrial Production versus Natural (Re)production 153

6.5 Biological Machines Reconsidered 155

Contents

7 HEP Experiments as Post-Traditional Communitarian
Structures   159

7.1 Large Collaborations: A Brief History   159

7.2 The Erasure of the Individual as an Epistemic Subject   166

7.3 Management by Content   171

7.4 The Intersection of Management by Content and
Communitarianism   179

7.5 Communitarian Time: Genealogical, Scheduled   186

8 The Multiple Ordering Frameworks of HEP Collaborations   192

8.1 The Birth Drama of an Experiment   193

8.2 Delaying the Choice, or Contests of Unfolding   196

8.3 Confidence Pathways and Gossip Circles   201

8.4 Other Ordering Frameworks   210

8.5 Reconfiguration Reconsidered   214

9 The Dual Organization of Molecular Biology Laboratories   216

9.1 Laboratories Structured as Individuated Units   216

9.2 Becoming a Laboratory Leader   221

9.3 The Two Levels of the Laboratory   224

9.4 The "Impossibility" of Cooperation in Molecular Biology   234

10 Toward an Understanding of Knowledge Societies:
A Dialogue   241

Notes   263

References   299

Index   321

A Note on Transcription

By conversation analysis standards (e.g., Sacks, Schegloff, and Jefferson 1974: 731–734), the interview data presented in this book are fairly roughly transcribed. There is no indication of overlapping words, interruptions (usually), new beginnings, or the length of pauses, and vocal aspirations, "latching," and prolonged syllables are not transcribed. I believe, however, that the transcriptions are adequate for the level of analysis attempted here, and that this rougher style of transcribing is easier to read for the audience to whom the book is addressed. The following conventions were used in the transcription of direct quotes:

()   Single parentheses indicate that the transcriber was not sure about the words contained within. Empty parentheses indicate talk inserted in or before passages relevant to the case presented.

(())   Double parentheses indicate comments by the transcriber.

/   A slash indicates an interruption.

. . .   An ellipsis indicates words trailing off.

In the notes and in Chapter 10, I have summarized comments made to me about the work I am describing in this book and presented them, along with my responses, in dialogue form. These sections are not to be considered "interview data"; they are, instead, paraphrased retellings of the arguments and ideas that may be heard when sociologists, philosophers, and scientists of many kinds get together to talk about their work.

Epistemic Cultures

1

Introduction

This book is about epistemic cultures: those amalgams of arrangements and mechanisms—bonded through affinity, necessity, and historical coincidence—which, in a given field, make up *how we know what we know*. Epistemic cultures are cultures that create and warrant knowledge, and the premier knowledge institution throughout the world is, still, science.

In this book I analyze knowledge processes in two sciences; I explore epistemic features such as the meaning of the empirical, the enactment of object relations, the construction and fashioning of social arrangements within science. Though I analyze science, the notion of epistemic cultures brings into focus the question of knowing in other areas of expertise. By many accounts, contemporary Western societies are becoming (or have already become) "knowledge societies." They run on expert processes and expert systems that are epitomized by science but are structured into all areas of social life. These processes and systems pose questions to the social scientist: How do they work? What principles inform their cognitive and procedural orientations? Can we simply extrapolate from other forms of social order to learn what we need to know about the organization, the structures, the dynamism of knowledge systems? In the landscape of contemporary social science, the functioning of expert systems is by and large an empty space. By examining the notion of epistemic cultures in two sample cases, I hope to provide pointers for drawing the contours of this uncharted area.

By taking epistemic cultures as the theme of this book, I am placing

1

emphasis on two problem areas: one concerns our present lack of understanding of the contemporary machineries of knowing, of their depth, and particularly of their diversity; the other concerns the transition of contemporary societies to knowledge societies, of which epistemic cultures are a structural feature. In the next sections, I consider each problem in somewhat more detail. The rest of Chapter 1 briefly discusses culture as practice and then lays out the structure of the book and the domains of knowledge studied.

1.1 The Disunity of the Sciences

Culture is very likely a permanent feature of the evolution of all human life. Yet there is equally likely no one universal human culture, characterizing all human beings in the same generic way at all times and places. The concept of culture is usually used to refer to specific historical forms, such as the state ("national culture"), the economy ("market culture"), or the business firm ("organizational culture"). Cultural specificities arise and thrive, one assumes, when domains of social life become separated from one another—when they "curl up upon themselves"—for a period of time. In other words, they thrive in internally referential systems—for example, domains in which participants orient themselves more toward one another and previous system-states than toward the outside. Science and expert systems are obvious candidates for cultural division; they are pursued by groupings of specialists who are separated from other experts by institutional boundaries deeply entrenched in all levels of education, in most research organizations, in career choices, in our general systems of classification. Yet the idea of knowledge-related cultures is not part of our common vocabulary; in the past, terms such as *discipline* or *scientific specialty* seemed to capture the differentiation of knowledge. The notion of a discipline and its cognates are indeed important ones in spelling out the organizing principles that assign science and technology to subunits and sub-subunits. But these concepts proved less felicitous in capturing the strategies and policies of knowing that are not codified in textbooks but do inform expert practice. The differentiating terms we have used in the past were not designed to make visible the complex texture of knowledge as practiced in the deep social spaces of modern institutions. To bring out this texture, one needs to magnify the space of knowledge-in-action, rather than simply observe disciplines or specialties as organizing structures.

The present study is an attempt to enlarge this space; in replacing notions such as discipline or specialty with that of an epistemic culture, I want to amplify the knowledge machineries of contemporary sciences until they display the smear of technical, social, symbolic dimensions of intricate expert systems. The book continues work begun by studies of contemporary scientific laboratories and experiments in the late 1970s,[1] with one difference. Many of the earlier studies were interested in how knowledge is produced in science. They challenged realist explanations of natural scientific knowledge, insisting instead that a social scientific account of science that brought into focus the origin of knowledge in laboratory practice was both warranted and feasible.[2] In this study, I am interested not in the construction of knowledge but in the construction of the machineries of knowledge construction. This approach should create no further scandal, but it deepens the split with traditional notions of knowledge.

Magnifying this aspect of science—not its production of knowledge but its epistemic machinery—reveals the fragmentation of contemporary science; it displays different architectures of empirical approaches, specific constructions of the referent, particular ontologies of instruments, and different social machines. In other words, it brings out the *diversity* of epistemic cultures. This *disunifies* the sciences; it runs counter to an assumption generally associated with the work of the Vienna Circle of more than fifty years ago, particularly the argument for the unity of science.[3] The thesis that there is only one kind of knowledge, only one science, and only one scientific method has been challenged in the past on the grounds that the natural scientific approach is not applicable to the human sciences and their distinct goal of understanding actors' meanings in concrete historical situations.[4] However, few analysts have looked beyond this bifurcation, to suspect ontological difference and methodological divergence also among the natural sciences (for one such suggestion see Suppes 1984). Today this suspicion is more frequently articulated and listened to (e.g., Hacking 1992a, Dupré 1993; Galison and Stump 1996). Nonetheless, the image of a unified natural science still informs the social sciences and contributes to their dominant theoretical and methodological orientation. The debates raging over realist, pragmatist, skepticist, or perspectival[5] interpretations of science all tend to assume science is a unitary enterprise to which epistemic labels can be applied across the board.[6] The enterprise, however, has a geography of its own. In fact, it is not one enterprise but many, a whole landscape—or market—of independent epistemic monopolies producing vastly different products.

Two of these monopolies are analyzed in this book. Both are vanguard sciences at the forefront of academic respectability, both intense, successful, heavily financed—but both are also differently placed on the map of disciplines. One, experimental high energy physics, tries to understand the basic components of the universe. Commensurate with the scale of the technology used for this goal, experimental high energy physics requires a specific form of scientific inquiry, the large transnational collaboration.[7] Besides building up an understanding of the deepest components of the universe, high energy physics also builds "superorganisms": collectives of physicists, matched with collectives of instruments, that come as near as one can get to a—post-romantic—communitarian regime. I compare the communitarian science of physics with the individual, bodily, lab-bench science of molecular biology. The contrasts are many: one science (physics) transcends anthropocentric and culture-centric scales of time and space in its organization and work, the other (molecular biology) holds on to them and exploits them; one science is semiological in its preference for sign processing, the other shies away from signs and places the scientist on a par with nonverbal objects; one (again physics) is characterized by a relative loss of the empirical, the other is heavily experiential; one transforms machines into physiological beings, the other transforms organisms into machines. Using a comparative optics as a framework for seeing, one may look at one science through the lens of the other. This "visibilizes" the invisible; each pattern detailed in one science serves as a sensor for identifying and mapping (equivalent, analog, conflicting) patterns in the other. A comparative optics brings out not the essential features of each field but differences between the fields. These, I believe, are far more tractable than the essential features; in fact, one might argue that they are the only tractable elements available to us.

The present study is a first attempt to address the epistemic disunity of contemporary natural sciences in their machineries of knowing. But this book can also be located in the context of a broader question, one that is more in the background than the first but nonetheless informs the present work.[8] This is the question of the current transmutation of modernity into new institutional forms—forms interstitched with knowledge systems and processes.

1.2 The Cultures of Knowledge Societies

There is a widespread consensus today that contemporary Western societies are in one sense or another ruled by knowledge and expertise. A proliferation of concepts such as that of a "technological society" (e.g., Berger et al. 1974), an "information society" (e.g., Lyotard 1984, Beniger 1986), a "knowledge society" (Bell 1973, Drucker 1993, Stehr 1994), or a "risk society" or "experimental society" (Beck 1992) embodies this understanding. The recent source of this awareness is Daniel Bell (1973), for whom the immediate impact of knowledge was its effect on the economy, which resulted in such widespread changes as shifts in the division of labor, the development of specialized occupations, the emergence of new enterprises and sustained growth. Bell and later commentators (e.g., Stehr 1994) also offer a great deal of statistics on the expansion of R&D efforts, R&D personnel, and R&D expenses in Europe and the United States. More recent assessments have not changed this argument so much as added further arenas in which the impact of knowledge is identified. For example, Habermas (1981) argued that the lifeworld is "technicized" through universal principles of cognitive and technical rationality in his description of the spread of abstract systems to everyday life. Drucker (e.g., 1993) links knowledge to changes in organizational structure, management practices, and education, and Beck (1992), describing ecological risks resulting from the alliance between science and capital, depicts transformations of the political sphere through corporate bodies of scientists. He and Krohn and Weyer (1994) also argue that the application of scientific findings before they have been fully explored erases the boundary between the laboratory and society. On a global scale, several authors point out (Smith 1990: 175; Quinn 1992: 229) that the power of the nation-state is undermined not only by multinational corporations and a capitalist economy, but also by transnational social units whose ties are based upon technologically usable knowledge. Lash and Urry (1994: 108) use the concept of (electronic) "information structures" to refer to the "arteries" of economic production systems that operate on a potentially global scale. Finally, Giddens, who focuses more on the microscale of things, extends the argument to the self and the life span. Arguing that we live in a world of increased reflexivity mediated by expert systems, Giddens points out that today's individuals engage with the wider environment and with themselves through information produced by specialists, which they routinely interpret and act on in everyday life (e.g., 1990, 1991: chap. 5).

The good news about this literature is that it recognizes the thick interweaving of (professional) knowledge and other aspects of social life. The bad news is that the concepts used so far remain eclectic; the authors pay scant attention to the nature of knowledge processes and knowledge cultures, and they tend to see knowledge as an intellectual or technological product rather than as a production context in its own right. The most consistent and powerful line of reasoning is still that of Bell and his followers, for whom the transition to a knowledge society is essentially an economic dynamic. In a nutshell, the argument is that knowledge (defined, for example, as "a set of organized statements of fact or ideas" in Bell 1973: 41) has become a productive force replacing capital, labor, and natural resources as the central value- and wealth-creating factor. According to these ideas, it is knowledge that makes our society "post-industrial" or "post-capitalist," fundamentally changing the nature of production systems, the nature of work, and the demands on the work force and on work-related items (Drucker 1993: 45; Lash and Urry 1994).

Among those who consider the role of knowledge in current society more from a sociological (rather than an economic) angle, it is Giddens who goes furthest in articulating knowledge as a determining factor in what he calls "reflexive modernization"—a stage of modernity based on the reflexive ordering and reordering of social relations in the light of continual inputs of knowledge (1990: 17). Giddens sees society as permeated by "expert systems," which he defines as "systems of technical accomplishment or professional expertise that organize large areas of the material and social environments in which we live today" (1990: 27). The advantage of the notion of an expert *system* over some of the other concepts is that it brings into view not only single knowledge products or scientific-technical elites but the presence of whole contexts of expert work. However, Giddens treats these "systems" much as other theorists treat knowledge in general—in terms of their technological or interpretive output. The systems themselves remain black-boxed; they are alien elements in social arrangements, elements that are best left to their own devices. The received assumption here is that expert systems run on principles having to do with the technical content of expert work, and differing from principles manifest in other spheres of social life.

These theories of social transformation tend to follow what Dennett (1987) calls the "design strategy" of interpretation in regard to knowledge. From the design stance, one ignores the details of the constitution of a particular domain; on the assumption that the domain is designed to produce a particular outcome, one considers only its output and its particular relevance to one's purposes. Modernization theorists tend not to address the question of how the knowledge processes they incorporate into their arguments work, which structures or principles adequately describe this working, or how the notion of knowledge dealt with in these systems ought to be specified. What they are interested in, on the whole, are the transformative effects of these systems' outcomes on other social spheres, on personal life, industrial organization, market expansion, etc. Thus knowledge contexts retain their aura of difference simply because they remain uninterrogated—as they did, until recently, even in the specialty devoted to them, in science studies. If the argument about the expanding presence of expert systems and knowledge processes in contemporary Western societies is right, however, the design stance defeats the intention of understanding this particular development. Not only does the expansion of expert systems result in a massive increase in the technological and informational products of knowledge processes. It also amplifies the processes themselves, and knowledge-related contexts and structures. A knowledge society is not simply a society of more experts, more technological gadgets, more specialist interpretations. It is a society permeated with knowledge cultures, the whole set of structures and mechanisms that serve knowledge and unfold with its articulation.

The traditional definition of a knowledge society puts the emphasis on knowledge seen as statements of scientific belief, as technological application, or perhaps as intellectual property. The definition I advocate switches the emphasis to knowledge as practiced—within structures, processes, and environments that make up *specific* epistemic settings. If the argument about the growth of expert systems is right, what we call "society" will to a significant degree be constituted by such settings. In a knowledge society, exclusive definitions of expert settings and social settings—and their respective cultures—are theoretically no longer adequate; this is why the study of knowledge settings becomes a goal in the attempts to understand not only science and expertise but also the type of society that runs on knowledge and expertise.

Epistemic cultures are the cultures of knowledge settings, and these appear to be a structural feature of knowledge societies. But it would be wrong to understand knowledge societies as homogeneous and one-dimensional, which they are not. The linkage of knowledge and society in one concept conceals the complexity of current transitions and the possible contradictions posed by knowledge and expertise. I cannot in this context pursue the various sides of the phenomenon of the knowledge society any further, since it is a matter for a properly detailed analysis in its own right. Epistemic cultures, one must stress, are but one aspect of this phenomenon. While I will come back to the idea of the knowledge society in the final chapter, what I want to do in the rest of the book is to make the idea of epistemic cultures plausible. This can only be done, I assume, by a substantive analysis of such cultures, during which all other issues must be pushed to the sidelines.

1.3 Culture and Practice

Turning from these general sociological issues back to epistemic cultures, I want to say something about how I understand the notion of culture. *Culture,* as I use the term, refers to the aggregate patterns and dynamics that are on display in expert practice and that vary in different settings of expertise. Culture, then, refers back to practice, in a specific way. To bring out the differences between related ideas, consider how practice has been addressed in earlier studies of expertise.

The genre of studies of knowledge that took practice as its organizing theme was created in the late 1970s and early 1980s. The studies differed widely, but they were united by a common focus on contemporary science as produced in contemporary settings, for example in scientific laboratories. *Contemporary* here stands for observable knowledge processes. Although the focus on science-as-practice has been extended to historical cases (studied, for example, through laboratory notebooks), the distinctiveness of the approach rested, originally, on the applicability of direct observation to contemporary knowledge systems.[9] *Practice* served as a contrasting term for these studies; one investigated scientists at work as opposed to the history of ideas, the structure of scientific theories, or the institutional settings of science. Beyond foregrounding such differences, the notion of practice foregrounded the acts of making knowledge. In other words, practice was interpreted within an action-theory framework, or, as Pickering calls it, within a performative idiom (1995: chap. 1; Alexander 1992).

The action framework helped studies oriented toward scientific practice to bring out the shaping and "intervening" (Hacking 1983) features of knowledge work. If one approaches practitioners as actors, one zeroes in on the active, agency-related components of knowledge processes, pushing the results of these processes as they relate to "nature" out of view. Other things are pushed out of view by an action-theory framework: the orientations and preferences that inform whole sequences of action, the structures built from combinations of such sequences, the ways in which the actors themselves are configured. The action-theory framework offers little purchase for establishing the patterns on which various actions converge and which they instantiate and dynamically extend. It shines the analytic torch upon the strategies and interests and interactional accomplishments of individuals, and sometimes groups. While this yields important insights into how agents generate and negotiate certain outcomes, it offers no dividends on the machineries of knowing in which these agents play a part.

Practice, of course, can also refer in a more generic way to just those patterned, dynamic sequences which are the ingredients of such machineries.[10] This notion of practice shifts the focus away from mental objects, such as the interests or intentions that inform concepts of action, and toward the reordered conditions and dynamics of the chains of action of collective life. If one defines practice in this way, the notion of culture follows. Culture in this book foregrounds the machineries of knowing composed of practices.

But the notion of culture also adds something to the idea of practice. In the literature, the term *culture* enjoys a varied range of associations, of which three seem particularly relevant to the present effort. The first is that culture, as already indicated, implies ruptures in any uniformities of practice; these ruptures are important because they suggest the existence of different technologies of knowing serving different substantive, technological, and economic ends. A second association the term *culture* sometimes has is that of a certain richness of ongoing events; in this sense it means a thick growth of variegated patterns piling up on top of one another. Knowledge systems, in particular, appear like density regions of the social world; if knowledge is constructed it is deeply and intricately constructed, involving multiple instrumental, linguistic, theoretical, organizational, and many other frameworks. Third, culture, in recent writings, is strongly associated with the symbolic-expressive aspects of human behavior.[11] This symbols-and-meanings conception of culture is best exemplified by Geertz' (1973: 89) influential definition of culture as "a historically transmitted pattern of meanings embodied in symbols, a system of inherited conceptions expressed in symbolic form by means of which men communicate, perpetuate, and develop their knowledge about and attitudes towards life." Today's culture analysts are divided on what the "symbolic" stuff of which culture is comprised amounts to—shared beliefs and values? expressive rituals? the meanings expressed in much of our behavior? But most analysts nonetheless remain united in viewing culture as a concept that sensitizes us to the symbolic components of social life, which have been investigated in recent years with growing interest and success.[12]

The notion of culture, then, brings to practice a sensitivity for symbols and meaning, a third element that enriches the idea of epistemic machineries. I take the position that signification and the behavioral text of practice cannot be separated, and that views of culture that ignore the conduct of experience are just as limited as views of practice that squeeze symbols out of the picture. In this book, symbolic structurings will come into view through the definition of entities, through systems of classification, through the ways in which epistemic strategy, empirical procedure, and social collaboration are understood in the two fields investigated. I will also briefly return to the meanings of culture in the final chapter.

1.4 The Structure of the Book

I now want to lay out the structure of the book and to say something about the areas of science investigated and the methods I used. As indicated before, the present work will not be concerned with the production of knowledge but with the machineries deployed in knowledge production. The shift in focus is worth emphasizing; earlier studies linked an intense interest in knowledge production to the pursuits of scientists and other actors—to scientists' rhetoric, their power strategies, their economic moves, their laboratory decisions, their communication, and above all their (proof, existence, validity, replicability, and other) interpretations and negotiations (see for example Knorr 1977; Latour and Woolgar 1979; Knorr Cetina 1981; Collins 1981, 1985; Zenzen and Restivo 1982; Pickering 1984; Pinch and Bijker 1984; Lynch 1985). The present study looks upon scientists and other experts as enfolded in construction machineries, in entire conjunctions of conventions and devices that are organized, dynamic, thought about (at least partially), but not governed by single actors. Epistemic subjects (the procurers of knowledge) are derivatives of these machineries. In fact, a variety of substrates could realize epistemic subjects: the thinking and intuiting brain we suppose when we link scientific progress to "genius," "brilliance," or (mental) innovation, or embodied persons inhabited by skills and socially featured as individuals, or social collectives, or the discourse that runs through an experiment and constitutes the workbench of a lab. The substrates are variable; their variability, transformation, and constitution is what leads one to think about the construction of the construction machineries.

In this book, I shall see the producers of knowledge, the scientists and experts, as derivative and focus on the practices that are constitutive of epistemic subjects and objects alike. This has the disadvantage that I will have nothing more to say about the tactics of manufacturing single scientific results, which early studies attempted to describe. I will have something to say, however, on the architecture—and the diversity—of the manufacturing systems from which truth effects arise—on the empirical strategies of these systems, on their configuration of objects, technologies, and epistemic subjects, on the role of the laboratory, etc.

The first point (the empirical machinery) will be the topic of Chapters 3 and 4. Chapter 3 will focus on physics' semiological and fictional ontology of objects; the transposition of physics' work into an alternate reality of signs and simulations. The chapter runs through the "liminal" (concerned with the limits of knowing), recursive epistemology that in experimental high energy physics (HEP) corresponds to this alternate reality. It offers a picture of what it means, in HEP, to work empirically, of its understanding of measurement, of the means deployed to reach truth effects in a universe of signs and fictions, and of the reflexive turn toward the self (the experiment) that accompanies the reduction, in this field, of the empirical. Chapter 4 inspects the contrasting case of molecular biology—its commitment to embodied experience, its disinterest in self-understanding, and its substitution, for the latter understanding, of principles of "blind" variation and "natural" selection. If Chapter 3 shows what it means when the empirical business of science is transposed into an alternate reality of signs and simulations, Chapter 4 shows what it means when the opposite occurs—when natural objects are enhanced and set up as a selection environment for experimental strategies.

In brief, then, Chapter 3 and 4 address questions of the configuration of the "reality" investigated in molecular biology and high energy physics (e.g., the semiological-theoretical versus experiental construction of data) and present the empirical machinery operating in these sciences. Chapters 5 and 6 continue this investigation by looking primarily at the technological machinery—for example, at the ontology of instruments in these disciplines. They compare the reconfiguration of machines in high energy physics with the reconfiguration of life in molecular biology. Chapters 7–9 extend the ontological inquiry to the social machinery. They raise questions such as, Who are the procurers of knowledge in these fields? What mechanisms sustain them? How is the social made to work in the mega-experiments of high energy physics? Lastly, how does the social in the HEP world compare with the "infrasociality" of molecular biology? In these chapters, I disaggregate the fields into some of their basic elements and forms of order. In other words, I sort ethnographic diversity into theoretical blocks—for example, I sort out the biographical regime of physicists as individual subjects, on the one hand, and the communitarian superordering imposed upon these subjects, on the other. The multiple orderings identified in physics contrast with a more homogeneous social form in molecular biology, whose patterns seem to have been assembled more by affinity than by contrast (see Chapter 9). Not all institutions are theoretically diverse; those which are not deploy their own devices to sustain a homogeneous situation.

There remain Chapters 2 and 10. In Chapter 2 I use the notion of reconfiguration to point out how epistemic dividends accrue from laboratory practice. If we can assume the existence of diverse theoretical registers, we will likely need a strong notion of local contextures—the kind of thing emphasized by ethnomethodologists, symbolic interactionists, and anthropologists alike (e.g., Cicourel 1964; Garfinkel 1967; Geertz 1983; Goffman 1972; Lynch 1991), but adapted to the present domain (see also Ophir and Shapin 1991). The laboratory, in laboratory studies, has been such a notion. It sets the boundaries within which much of scientific practice is not only observed but shaped. Chapter 2 offers an explanation of the usefulness of these boundaries[13]—of the usefulness of places where features of the surrounding order are turned on their head, and where alternate realities can be installed and exploited for the business at hand. Real-time laboratories, of course, are units whose function, size, and internal structures change between fields and over time: The "laboratory" itself, in the previously mentioned sense of a reversal and reconfiguration of the surrounding order, tends to migrate into other spaces; for example, in high energy physics large collider experiments or computer simulations[14] constitute laboratories in their own right (see also Chapter 10). What is called a laboratory by participants (for example, Fermilab or CERN, the European Laboratory for Particle Physics) may be considered by others more a facility or an administrative structure. This use of the term is underscored by distinctions physicists themselves make, as I illustrate later in the book.

Finally, Chapter 10. It wraps things up in the easy format of a dialogue; the chapter expands upon and questions some major tenets of the book. The format also allows me to bring into focus some issues that were absent in earlier chapters but that might be of interest to a potential reader. Wrapping things up does not mean tying them together, or summarizing the book. The present work presents a kaleidoscopic view of the domains investigated, and the last chapter does not break that pattern.

1.5 Physics Theory, and a First Look at the Field

Having gone through what is in the book, it is only fitting that I also tell the reader what is not covered. Some issues stand out; one is more a question of content, while the others are more methodological—they will be taken up in the next section. To begin with the first, any book that includes physics is always expected to address physics theory and its role in experimentation. And this is perhaps not surprising. After all, physicists say they search for the "final" theory of nature, which some proponents claim is within their actual grasp (e.g., Weinberg 1992). The kind of experimental high energy physics studied here is fundamentally implicated in this search. How? Most physicists assume the physical principle of symmetry, according to which the electromagnetic force (which is responsible for electric charges of particles and magnetic behavior) and the weak force (which is responsible for radioactive decay) are transformed from one to the other (this is the fundamental principle on which the electroweak theory of the standard model depends). The two forces are carried by discrete particles; the electromagnetic force by the massless photons, and the weak force by the massive W and Z bosons. The problem is that the symmetry by which the photon, the W bosons, and the Z boson are transformed from one to the other is spontaneously broken at cooling temperatures of the universe, which leaves the photon massless and the W and Z particles with mass.[15] The method by which the bosons acquire mass through spontaneous symmetry breaking is called the Higgs mechanism. It has never been confirmed experimentally, but the Large Hadron Collider, to be built at CERN, is designed to achieve the energy needed for its production, and one of the experiments studied in the present work, the ATLAS experiment at CERN, is designed to search for it.

The Higgs mechanism is one of the remaining puzzles of the standard model. Another missing piece was, until recently, the top quark, the last quark in a family of six. Physics theory postulates that quarks are a class of six elementary particles of fractional charge that connect with all four basic physical forces (the strong nuclear force, which holds them together, forming "hadrons"; the electromagnetic force between elementary particles; the weak force; and the gravitational force, which extends to very large distances). Experiments had, up to the end of 1993, found evidence of only five quarks. All collider experiments running in the late 1980s focused on the search for the top: the experiments UA1 (UA1 stands for underground area 1) and UA2 at CERN, and CDF, (standing for Collider-Detector at Fermilab). The present investigations have focused, during this period (1987–1990), on UA2.

Both experiments studied, UA2 and ATLAS, are thus theoretically motivated. The top quark was just another in the long list of successfully predicted particles; Fermilab claimed to have first evidence for it only in April 1994,[16] and its elusiveness remained a challenge. The Higgs mechanism—more honored than the top quark as a key to the mystery of mass of other particles and as a provider of a new observable particle with its own large mass—has been the main argument for expansion at CERN (CERN is building a Large Hadron Collider or LHC, by using its existing Large Electron Positron ring), and for the Superconducting Supercollider (SSC) in Texas (terminated after several years by the U.S. House of Representatives in October 1993).[17] In fact, experimental efforts in high energy physics today can be broadly classified into two categories: on the one hand, continued "tests" of the standard model, meaning the attempt to produce experimentally the particles and mechanisms predicted by theory and to make precise measurements of their properties; on the other hand, experimental searches for physics beyond the standard model (see also DiLella 1990). These searches too are guided by theoretical models; they include, in the experiments observed, searches for "supersymmetric" particles predicted by a class of theories called supersymmetric gauge field theories.

There is no doubt that elementary particle physics theory determines the searches of high energy physics experiments. There is also no doubt that it *enters* experiments at various points—for example, as perturbation calculations (calculations of the probability that certain new particles are produced when others collide), calculations of higher-order Feynman diagrams (basically the same for more complicated particle reactions and decay processes), calculations of structure functions (which describe the density of quarks and gluons within the proton), and so on (see Section 3.5). Nonetheless, high energy physics experiments do not routinely *do* physics theory. For that part of the research there exist "theorists" (especially "phenomenologists") who make the respective calculations. At CERN, theorists are assembled in a separate Theory Division, which is administratively distinguished from the Particle Physics Experiments Division (PPE). The phenomenologists in this division maintain close contact with experiments (they attend, for example, public presentations of experimental results and experimental talks at conferences), but they are not themselves members of the experiments (see also Galison 1989). Experimentalists sometimes regard these theorists as service providers to the experiments—after all, they have the "task" of making the computations used as inputs in experimental measurements and simulations. Those theorists who work, unrelated to concrete experiments, on more fundamental issues (as on string theories or lattice theories) are sometimes regarded with the usual suspicion that "practitioners" have for (esoteric) "thinkers": experimentalists make fun of theorists' alleged lack of technological know-how, and they mock the speed and ease with which new theories are produced, in contrast with the difficulty of experimental work.

Physics theory, then, is not in this book; it is simply not the focus of it. This book is not about conflicts between quantum and relativity theories, about the Einstein-Podolsky-Rosen paradox, about the particle-wave duality, about the uncertainty principle, about the search for symmetry, about physics theory as language, or about perspectives on physical realism or whether fundamental theories of physics should be considered an illusion. Any number of books on these matters exist, as an (incomplete) survey of just a few publication years shows (e.g., Gibbens 1987; Gregory 1988; Park 1988; Rae 1986; Sachs 1988; Tarozzi and van der Merwe 1988; Selleri 1990; Zee 1989). Some of these books are excellent and the reader should be referred to them. Far less frequently published are books on *contemporary experimental* high energy physics from an empirical and ethnographic perspective; in fact, I know of only one, the pioneering study by Traweek (1988a). Some excellent books on the contemporary *history* of particle physics exist, such as those by Pickering (1984) and Galison (1987; see also Kevles 1987). No one has looked, to my knowledge, at contemporary physics theorizing as *practical work* or at physics' theoretical culture either (the eight books listed above are on the content of theoretical models). Such inquiries, however, are now beginning (Merz and Knorr Cetina 1997), and they are just as relevant as the studies of the experiments themselves.

1.6 Issues of Methodology, and More about the Field

A question usually raised about studies such as the present one is their methodological status and generalizability. Before addressing this, let me say more about the two settings I examine and the special problems posed in one. The present study has been performed in two disciplines, experimental high energy physics and molecular biology. Both studies have been conducted (they are still continuing) as field studies involving the unmediated observation, by one or more analysts, of scientific procedure. At CERN, in Geneva, Switzerland, the European Particle Physics Laboratory jointly financed by European countries, we observed the collider experiment UA2 (from 1987 to December 1990) in its upgraded run and analysis stages. We also observed the new experiment, ATLAS, that emerged from UA2 from about 1989 onward. UA2 and its sister experiment, UA1, were originally set up to discover the W and Z vector bosons, thereby testing the electroweak theory. They were also created to explore new energy regions provided by the second hadron collider built at CERN, following a suggestion by Rubbia et al. (1976: 683) to modify the CERN Super-Proton-Synchroton. In a proton-antiproton ($p\bar{p}$-) collider, protons and antiprotons are accelerated and hurled against each other. Thereafter they decay into secondary and tertiary particles that travel through different detector materials before they get "stuck" in the outer shell of a calorimeter. Some of the particles that result from the collision and their properties are of interest to the physicists. Accelerators and colliders—a series of underground "rings" in which particles such as protons and antiprotons are produced, stocked up, and brought to the necessary speed—provide for the original collisions. Detectors provide the apparatus and materials that "intersect" the collider in underground areas. Detectors are "hit" by the particles generated in collisions. They register their traces and transmit the signs of their brief presence. It is these signals (e.g., energy depositions, particle tracks) which are the harvest of a detector. They are recovered offline through computer programs and suitably "reconstructed" and interpreted in terms of underlying real-time particle occurrences and properties of events.

By 1983, the two experiments had identified and harvested the carriers of the weak force,[18] for which the spokesman of UA1, Carlo Rubbia, shared the Nobel prize with Simon van der Meer (UA1 published faster and had a more original detector design; for a summary of events, see Sutton 1984). In the years 1985–1987, CERN upgraded the p$\bar{\text{p}}$-collider complex and the experimenters upgraded their detector to search, among other things, for the top quark. UA2 had less difficulty with this task and was able to collect and analyze a substantial amount of data. Both experiments were phased out by 1991.

Observations for the present study in molecular biology had already started by the fall of 1984. They involved a Max Planck Institute group working on molecular cell biology in Göttingen, and before that a laboratory in Heidelberg, from which the Max Planck group was formed. These observations are also still ongoing, but they now involve other groups. The group observed for the purposes of this book consisted originally of eight scientists but grew to include more than thirty by the end. The citations and disciplinary reputation of the group observed are both high; indeed, it is regarded as one of the world's leading research teams in its field. The leader and several of the key members of the laboratory spent years in the United States before returning to Germany; the group routinely accepted postdoctoral researchers from the United States, Canada, and other European countries, and at later stages also included researchers from the Far East.

The molecular biology group originally worked on transcriptional control mechanisms but has since expanded its work into several other areas. Transcription is the copying of a gene into RNA; the first step in protein synthesis, it is reckoned one of the most interesting and important stages in gene regulation. The core objective of much of this research is to unravel how an embryo uses its genetic information to turn itself into an adult animal. How genes control this developmental process (and are controlled by it) has implications not only for the exploration of cell differentiation but also for the understanding of many diseases, such as cancer.

The comparative approach chosen and the great complexity of the fields investigated implies that the study could not possibly have been done by one person. The study design implies the collaboration of three analysts: one inquirer for each field, more or less permanently placed in the laboratories studied, and one analyst, responsible for making comparisons between the areas investigated. This scheme has been maintained at CERN since the beginning and remained in effect until the end of 1996. In the molecular biology labs, periods of several months of observation were interspersed with retreats from the field for purposes of transcription and analysis from the beginning; after two years of study, the schedule changed from long-term presence to regular visits in the field.

The present study is the outcome of the comparison conducted by myself. It involved, on my part, regular stays at CERN since June 1987, which are still ongoing. I timed these stays to coincide with the regular "collaboration" meetings held by the experiments investigated (periods of several days to one week, at the time every four to six weeks), but I have extended my stays beyond the meetings to periods of up to three weeks, especially in the beginning, during UA2 data runs from 1987 onward. My schedule has the advantage of corresponding with the CERN visits of many physicists who—then and now—are not employed by CERN. These physicists come to CERN regularly for meetings, and for test-beam work, installation, data runs, and other technical activities. I became notorious as a "stranger" whose way of working at least matched the expected pattern of activity. In molecular biology, because of the small size of the group, it was possible to rely to a greater extent on my collaborator, Klaus Amann, who acted as the long-term ethnographer in this field. Fewer visits to this field were necessary (and more, for me, would not have been possible). My previous laboratory and field experience in the biological sciences (Knorr Cetina 1981) also helped. Nonetheless, Amann's primary role as an observer of this field (I focused more on the present data analysis and on interviews confirming and expanding the analysis) needs to be emphasized, as does his contribution to Chapters 4, 6, and 9, on which he collaborated with me. In contrast, the data and materials presented here from the field of physics have been collected only by myself.

Now back to more general methodological questions. Did the kind of investigation undertaken pose any special problems? Consider, first, the size and complexity of the two fields. Molecular biology is a complicated, "forefront" science. It is heavily funded and highly competitive, and it simply moves fast. The problems it poses for the observer have to do with its esoteric, highly specialized procedural knowledge and with its speed—the competence an analyst acquires after some time in the field tends to become quickly outdated as new developments occur. On the other hand, it helps that some principles of the work, including the underlying model of the genetic code, persist, and that molecular biology laboratories tend to be small. They remain, once the technical language and difficulties begin to be mastered, comprehensible to an observer. Also, molecular biology laboratories do not function as "wholes." The work achieved in them fragments into as many projects as there are researchers (see Chapter 9), and only some researchers have a student to supervise or one or two technicians to help. Units of this size are easily followed and offer a natural focus for observation.

This situation differs radically from the one in experimental high energy physics, where the size of experiments alone multiplied by a factor of 15 during our stay in the field. HEP experiments have gone from approximately 100 participants (UA2 had, during our observations, between 80 and 120) to 500 (the Large Electron Positron, or LEP, experiments now running at CERN) and then to more than 1,500 physicists from more than 150 collaborating institutes located all around the world (ATLAS in 1996, whose size increased to approximately 2,000 physicists in 1997/98). Even if, as members estimate, less than half of the participants in an experiment are really "active," the experiment is of a size that no single observer can hope to cover. Add to this the complexity of the field, often labeled one of the most difficult that exists, and the phenomenon that, although experiments break into subgroups (e.g., single detector groups), they do not divide into separate projects that produce and publish experimental results on their own.

How, then, is one to deal, as a student of knowledge cultures, with this overly complex situation? Some possible strategies depend on the cooperation of others. One can put more than one inquirer in the field, not just to cover more ground but to match, if you wish, physics collectives with analysts' collectives (however small), in order for observers to share the information, the control, and the conversation from which physicists draw their strength (see Chapter 7). The "collective" of two observers implemented in this study is not much when compared with, say, 50 or 500 physicists, but it is a vast improvement over one individual. Even a unit of two requires the cooperation of funding agencies, which are not used to financing observer teams. We had that financial support and thus scored one point. We also scored by relying on tape recordings (of meetings, shop talk, etc.); this method is labor-intensive—it requires someone to transcribe the tapes and someone to train the transcribers—but it is nonetheless essential. Only through recordings, for example, can one hope to learn, as an analyst, the grim technical details of high energy physics and to preserve the details of this field well enough for competent analyses. Tape recording, of course, requires the cooperation of the physicists, who must let themselves be recorded. Here too we were lucky. Recording was permitted by physicists from the beginning of our stay—out of sympathy perhaps for sociologists (the poor cousins) who suddenly had to make sense of their difficult science, but surely also out of physicists' awareness of the value of mechanical signal collection and out of an affirmation of the openness and public character of everything they do. This affirmative attitude also existed in molecular biology and was a great asset to us. Openness seems to be characteristic of researchers who are both confident of the positive knowledge in their fields and aware of the essential fragility and contestability of this knowledge, which they do not attempt to hide.

Besides installing a machine-produced record of memory one can, of course, install informants as helpers, as true anthropologists are wont to do. In other words, one can ask physicists for explanations of activities, events, and procedures, and one can use the explanations participants produce among themselves. For example, physicists maintain a life record of the development of an experiment by sending to all institutes brief e-mail summaries of meeting discussions and results—a record that is fragmentary (it is not equally comprehensive and complete in all sub-areas) but nonetheless, on a technical level, better than anything even a group of observers could maintain. Here too we were lucky—all records of this sort plus all meeting transparencies, internal notes, versions of talks and papers, etc., were made available to us from the start, including, when we asked for them, materials not usually available in the public record. In addition, a great many physicists made themselves available over the years for lengthy interviews, which almost always involved technical details (all were recorded and transcribed and now amount to several thousand single-spaced pages). A core group of about ten physicists was questioned repeatedly (at times every few months). I also conducted some interviews with members of CERN's four LEP experiments (not studied here) with respect to these experiments' organization.

Thus, we have enlarged the observer by supplying her with a second observer, with a machine-produced memory, and with native help. An observer, however, also has a few assets of her own. One is the comparative optics mentioned in the beginning of this chapter. As implied before, the advantage of the comparative study of high energy physics and molecular biology is not that we can compare two sciences in order to extract generalizations from the comparison. Rather, the comparative optics served to "visibilize" the invisible—features of a domain were brought into focus through their difference from a comparison domain. In single place studies, expectations raised by everyday knowledge also function as a framework for seeing, but this everyday frame is far less concrete and precise than one trained by the domains one compares. The ability to see is something that one has to learn, as painters like Oskar Kokoschka, who set up a "School of Seeing," know. In the present case, the compared domains functioned as schools of seeing, each respectively, for the analyst who traveled between them. But not only can analysts travel between settings, they also move within them. Doing so opens a window on the contradictions, discrepancies, variations, and *differences* that divide settings. Mobility allowed us to trace the processes by which the social world was *systematically* teased apart—by interests at certain stages, but also by bonds of trust (which exclude those not trusted) and other features—*and* the processes by which this same world was joined together and aggregated.

Let me turn now from space to time and add the obvious point that long involvement with a field helps the observer overcome a field's obdurateness. In my case, the visiting schedule was marked by my frequent (in the beginning, 8–10 times a year; from 1992, 4–6 times) withdrawal from and return to the field. This schedule, if adopted over a period of more than two years, proves constructive rather than disruptive; I recommend it. But one should be aware of the reasons it worked, which I take to be the following. First, the schedule followed the collaboration's own rhythm of meeting and disbanding. Most members of an experiment of this size do not meet face-to-face on a daily basis. Thus, absences are, in a sense, normal, and intermediate communication needs are met through e-mail. A high energy physics experiment today is at least intermittently an e-mail "collaboratory" (Wulf 1993); more precisely, it consists of a center (CERN) that expands, through e-mail contacts, to "outposts," the participating institutes around the world (see Chapter 7). An intermittently absent observer can always link up with the e-mail network, as physicists do. Second, an ethnographer is a life instrument trained up by the field. The on-and-off pace of observations conforms, I suppose to an extent, to the training model of the neurocomputational perspective (e.g., Churchland 1992: chap. 9): it conforms to a schedule of bursts of input followed by hidden processing stages. Perhaps frequent withdrawals from the field sustain hidden processing and, thus, result in learning a field as well as or better than by continuous exposure to it.[19] Lastly, the on-and-off schedule was combined with the presence of a second observer permanently placed in the field, whose goal was to maintain close contacts with participants.

Let me conclude this discussion by returning, once more, to the sciences themselves. Experimental natural sciences of the kind studied deal with their subjects in a deep way. The facts they produce are intricate in the making, the things they handle are handled in detailed and complicated ways, and the processing chains required for the endeavor are infinite and divided into many components and subcomponents. The task of seeing through the thick growth of experimental manipulations in the hope of finding the cultural switchboard that sets the direction of the project is overwhelming. Can one characterize the epistemic machineries of these sciences? What are the limits on such an analysis, even with all the help one can get? Phrased differently, what else, besides physics theory, is not in the book? There are, in my view, at least two kinds of limits to studies of this kind (in addition to the question of generalizability, about which I am optimistic). The first limitation concerns the historical structure of the work observed—characterized by a set of ongoing stories without a clear beginning and ending, perhaps, but with something like a plot development. Collaborations go through several stages whose full story add to the interest. Detectors, until they are built, involve many technical options and a "sifting out" process that should be narrated. The story of the search for a particular particle runs through an experiment from its earliest beginnings, vexing it to the very end. This book, however, is not written as "The Story of UA2," or "The Birth of ATLAS," or "The Path to the Top Quark and the Higgs." If I am not entirely apologetic about this, it is because the story lines in the field were also frequently broken; many times, events did not march in step, sometimes last things came first, and the simultaneity of events was overwhelming. The culturalist genre of description chosen in this book offers an alternative to historical narration, but this is where the second limitation comes into the picture: the present analysis is not, as a survey of a culture might be, comprehensive (covering domains from the cosmology to the economic infrastructure). Rather it is kaleidoscopic. I look at conjunctions of activities by means of a succession of shifts in focus, as someone might turn a kaleidoscope to view various aspects of the empirical machineries, the technological machineries, and the social machineries of two epistemic cultures. There is no pretension that the combination of patterns I discuss somehow adds up to all that could be said about the two sciences' local practices.

What more needs to be added? Surely a word about the generalizability and relevance of the results. Take the case of experimental high energy physics. We studied UA2, besides CDF at Fermilab the most successfully implemented collider experiment in the second half of the 1980s; and we are now studying ATLAS, CERN's presumed "flagship" experiment for the next generation of hadron colliders, which, since the Superconducting

Supercollider will not be built, shares the task of exploring the Higgs mechanism with perhaps only one other smaller experiment, its "sister" experiment CMS at CERN. With respect to generalizability, one can bank on the fact that only two experiments worldwide will monopolize the energy range of the LHC. I believe that the analysis presented in Chapter 3 of the liminal and recursive empirical machinery of HEP and of the semiological and theoretical constitution of its data opens a path to other pp̄-experiments. If detectors in these experiments are structurally alike, their analysis (like the analysis of "life" in molecular biology) should shed light on machine ontologies in other cases.

What about the more sociological question of a collaboration's organization? As indicated in Chapters 7 and 8, some experiments had "strong" leaders—for example, UA1 during its first stage. Would this not alter what I said about the present post-romantic, communitarian organization of massive collaborations? It might, in some cases. On the other hand, it is unclear how much difference one leader, strong or not, makes in solving the problem of managing 1,500 or 2,000 or more collaborators. One assumes that the disappearance of the individual epistemic subject would be felt by participants, that time would still run on a scale that spans generations of experiments, that the mechanisms holding a collaboration together would still include the discursive and temporal devices I put forward, though they might not be based on the same policies of group formation. Nonetheless, what if these experiments were indeed unique? We could still investigate them, I think, as model systems for the cultures of knowledge societies—much as molecular biologists investigate the fruit fly as a model system for (certain aspects of) cell differentiation. The use of model systems is not to be sniffed at. Model systems constitute circumscribed environments in which, as in HEP collaborations, reflexivity is turned into an instrument of knowledge, machines are redefined and recruited into the social world, and the subjectivity of participants is put on the line—and quite successfully replaced by something like distributed cognition. It is precisely such processes, it would seem, which might come to characterize societies that run on knowledge—and HEP experiments offer the captive environments that allow one to study how these work.

2

What Is a Laboratory?

Much of the literature on the history and methodology of science relies on the notion of the experiment as the basic unit of analysis. I want to suggest in this chapter how the notion of the laboratory—beyond its identification as just the physical space in which experiments are conducted—has emerged historically as a set of differentiated social and technical forms, carrying systematic weight in our understanding of science. The importance of this concept is linked to the reconfiguration of both the natural and social orders that, I will argue, constitutes laboratories in crucial ways. Further, I will argue that these reconfigurations work quite differently in different fields of science, generating different cultural, social, and technical stances.[1]

2.1 Laboratories as Reconfigurations of Natural and Social Orders

I want to begin by proposing that laboratories provide an "enhanced" environment that "improves upon" natural orders in relation to social orders. How does this improvement come about? The studies we have of laboratory work (e.g., Latour and Woolgar 1979; Knorr 1977; Knorr Cetina 1981; Zenzen and Restivo 1982; Lynch 1985; Giere 1988; Gooding et al. 1989; Pickering 1995) imply that it rests upon the *malleability* of natural objects. Laboratories are based upon the premise that objects are not fixed entities that have to be taken "as they are" or left by themselves. In fact, one rarely works in laboratories with objects as they occur in nature. Rather, one works with object images or with their visual, auditory, or electrical traces, and with their components, their extractions, and their "purified" versions. There are at least three features of natural objects a laboratory science does not have to accommodate: first, it does not need to put up with an object *as it is,* it can substitute transformed and partial versions. Second, it does not need to accommodate the natural object *where it is,* anchored in a natural environment; laboratory sciences bring objects "home" and manipulate them on their own terms, in the laboratory. Third, a laboratory science need not accommodate an event *when it happens;* it can dispense with natural cycles of occurrence and make events happen frequently enough for continuous study. Of course, the history of science is also a history of lost opportunities and varying successes in accomplishing these transitions. But it should be clear that not having to confront objects within their natural orders is epistemically advantageous for the pursuit of science; laboratory practice entails the detachment of objects from their natural environment and their installation in a new phenomenal field defined by social agents.

Consider an example. Astronomy, by common definition, used to be something like a "field" science. For a long time, astronomers were restricted to observation, even though since Galileo it was observation aided by a telescope. Now, for more than a century, astronomers have also used imaging technology—the photographic plate with the help of which photons of light emitted by stellar bodies can be captured and analyzed. Astronomy thereby appears to have been transformed from a science that surveys natural phenomena into a science which processes images of these phenomena (see also Edge and Mulkay 1976). Further developments of imaging technology since 1976 have resulted in a replacement of the photographic plate by CCD chips (Smith and Tatarewicz 1985). For example, the light of Halley's comet in 1982 was collected by the gigantic 200-inch mirror of the Hale telescope on Mount Palomar and was focused on charge-coupled devices (CCDs). CCD chips constitute a major change in imaging technology. They have digitalized outputs and thus enable astronomers to transfer and process their data electronically. If CCDs are used with space telescopes, they not only improve astronomers' data but they render astronomy completely independent of direct observation of its "field." Once the transition is complete, astronomy will have been transformed from an observational field science to an image-processing laboratory science. And photographic plate astronomy, just like observation through small hand-held telescopes, may become a "backyard" astronomy.

What reconfiguration of the phenomenal field of astronomy is achieved in this process of transformation? The following changes are apparent:

1. Through imaging, the objects of investigation become detached from their natural environment and are made continually present and available for inquiry in the laboratory; through digitalization and computer networks, the availability of the same data is extended potentially to the whole scientific community.
2. With the transition to a symbol-based technology, the processes of interest to astronomers become miniaturized.
3. Planetary and stellar time scales become the time scale of the social order. Astronomers all over the world who are connected to the electronic networks simultaneously and continually process and analyze stellar and planetary responses.

The point is that with these changes astronomy still has not become an experimental science. The processes described all pertain to laboratories; they enable investigations to be performed in one place, without regard to natural conditions (e.g., weather, seasonal changes, regional differences in visibility, etc.), subject only to the contingencies of local situations (e.g., to the resources that scientists can bring to bear on the work; for an initial ethnography of this work, see Gauthier 1991, 1992). In other words, laboratories allow natural processes to be "brought home" and to be made subject only to the conditions of the local social order. The power of laboratories (but, of course, also their restrictions) resides precisely in this "enculturation" of natural objects. Laboratory sciences subject natural conditions to a "social overhaul" and derive epistemic effects from the new situation.

Laboratories not only improve upon natural orders, but they also upgrade social orders, in a sense. This phenomenon has not been considered in the literature. Earlier studies analyzed the social system of science (e.g., Barber 1962; Cole and Cole 1973; Cole 1970; Zuckerman, Cole, and Bruer 1991; Griffith and Mullins 1972; Merton 1965, 1973; Storer 1972; Zuckerman 1967, 1977), or, alternatively, the interweaving of scientific interests with social and political factors (e.g., Barnes 1977; MacKenzie 1981; Pickering 1984; Shapin and Schaffer 1985; Latour 1987; Mukerji 1989; Haraway 1989). But they were not interested in how features of the social world, and more generally of everyday life, are played upon and turned into epistemic devices in the production of knowledge. Yet the social is not merely "also there" in science. Rather, it is capitalized upon and upgraded to become an instrument of scientific work. Laboratory processes align natural orders with social orders by creating reconfigured, workable objects in relation to agents of a given time and place. But laboratories also install reconfigured scientists who become workable (feasible) in relation to these objects. In the laboratory, it is not "the scientist" who is the counterpart of these objects. Rather, the counterparts are agents enhanced in various ways to fit a particular emerging order of what one might call, following Merleau-Ponty (1945: 69, 1962: 57), "self-other-things" and a particular "ethnomethodology" of a phenomenal field. Not only objects but also scientists are malleable with respect to a spectrum of behavioral possibilities. In the laboratory, scientists are methods of inquiry; they are part of a field's research strategy and a technical device in the production of knowledge.

How are aspects of social orders reconfigured? Let me take an example from the history of the medical sciences (Lachmund 1997). As Ackerknecht (1968) and Jewson (1976) have argued, the medical sciences in the late eighteenth and very early nineteenth century were primarily "bedside" sciences. They were practiced by doctors who came to their patients' houses to conduct their inquiry and provide treatments and advice. This situation changed with the advance of a new epistemic culture that emerged in the late eighteenth century at clinics in Paris described by Foucault and others (e.g., Ackerknecht 1968; Jewson 1976). These clinics were at the core of a newly developing clinical medicine. They formed the framework within which different preconceptions of illness and medical procedure were developed and tried out—the arenas in which they were negotiated and implemented. The transition to clinical medicine brought with it a redefinition of illness. Illness was no longer equated with a specific constellation of symptoms—rather, it was seen to reside in bodily "lesions"; the symptoms became the outward signs of these lesions.

What were some of the reconfigurations that accompanied these transitions? Lesions, for example, could only be observed through an autopsy. Detecting them required a dissection room, the kind that had become available at the new clinics. The transition from a bedside medical science to clinical medicine approximates that of a field science to a laboratory science (the term *laboratory medicine* was used for the physiological and bacteriological medicine established in the middle of the nineteenth century). Patients were taken out of their natural setting and subjected to the spatial and temporal discipline of a clinical environment. The dissection room emulated the setting of a laboratory workbench on which objects are taken apart, studied from the inside out, and experimented on. As Lachmund has shown (1997), the new technology of the stethoscope was tested and developed further in the new setting, where it thrived as a means of bridging the gap between anatomical knowledge gained from dead patients and the need for medical treatments applicable to the living (the noises the stethoscope picked up were linked to anatomically defined causes of illnesses, which were directly observable only in the anatomy theater). But the point of interest is how the social order became reconfigured in connection with this process of laboratorization.

Take the case of the medical doctor. With bedside medicine, the social authority of the doctor was extraordinarily precarious. The doctor went to the household of the patient, where he conducted his inquiry amidst a skeptical audience of relatives, neighbors, and, possibly, competing "wise" women and men also called upon to help the patient. None of those present were shy to offer their opinion on behalf of the patient. The whole medical profession was weak, at the time, since doctors failed to adhere to the same medical principles and to consolidate their opinion. Instead, they competed with each other and felt pressured to demonstrate their superior medical skills by offering advice that differed from that of other doctors. This weakness was enhanced by the way the "examination" was conducted, at the bedside of the ill. Doctors had to obtain from the patient a comprehensive account of his/her illness or injury. With the question-answer method they used, the patient's discourse had absolute priority. Doctors had to avoid medical jargon, were not to interrupt the patient, were not to irritate the patient through nonverbal responses (such as frowning, shrugging the shoulders, pacing up and down the room), and had to have the patience to conduct the examination over several days. They had to consider not only the illness, but any circumstantial evidence that could be connected to it. They had to remain aware of the fact that an illness followed its own individual course, which was influenced by the peculiarities of single patients.

Medical historians have called this system of inquiry—which privileged the patient and the lay public—"patronizing"; it was the patient or the patient's household that patronized the doctor and not, as one might expect given the nature of medical examinations today, the other way round. The patient's dominance changed with the onset of clinical medicine. Doctors' power was enhanced by a combination of factors. First, patients had to leave their homes and enter a new setting, where they would be available for continual medical observation and comparison with other patients. Second, patients were primarily recruited from the poor quarters of society; they were in no position to change clinical practice or impose their will on those who ran the clinic. Third, instead of the private, dyadic relationship between patient and doctor, there now existed at the hospital a small public of cooperating doctors and students with which the patient was confronted, and to whose collective judgment he or she had to submit. Collective judgments were often arrived at in Latin; use of the language of learning effectively excluded the patient—as an epistemically relevant agent—from the group that established medical diagnoses.

Medical collectives instead of single doctors, the use of technical devices instead of a shared discourse for conducting a medical examination, communication through a specialized language not understood by the patient, and the possibility of autopsy awaiting the patient—these were the ingredients that went into the remaking of medical doctors. The doctor became a whole new being, aligned with the reconfigured objects (patients) that the clinic created. No longer did the doctor manage complicated interactions with patients and families in familiar social settings; other behavioral possibilities were now in demand. For example, these behavioral possibilities included the capacity to *hear* and classify noises, to dissect organs and see lesions, to operate and develop further technical devices, and to function in medical collectives. Hearing and seeing became privileged senses called upon in medical inquiry, and discursive skills for dealing with patients became devalued.

My point is that scientists have been similarly shaped and transformed with regard to the kind of agents and processing devices they use in inquiry. Just as objects are transformed into images, extractions, and a multitude of other things in laboratories, so are scientists reconfigured to become specific epistemic subjects. As we shall see later, the scientist who acts as a bodily measurement device (by hearing and seeing signals) is also present in molecular biology (Chapter 4). By the time the reconfigurations of self-other-things that constitute laboratories have taken place, we are confronted with a newly emerging order that is neither social nor natural—an order whose components have mixed genealogies and continue to change shape as laboratory work continues.

2.2 From Laboratory to Experiment

What I have said so far refers to laboratory processes in general. I have neglected the fact that concrete laboratory reconfigurations are shaped in relation to the kind of work that goes on within the laboratory. This is where experiments come into the picture; through the technology they employ, experiments embody and respond to reconfigurations of natural and social orders.

Let me draw attention to three different types of laboratories and experiments in the contemporary sciences of particle physics, molecular biology, and the social sciences. In distinguishing between these types, I shall take as my starting point the constructions placed upon natural objects in these areas of science and their embodiment in the respective technologies of experimentation. I want to show how, in connection with these different constructions, laboratories and experiments become very different entities and enter very different kinds of relationships with each other. First, laboratories and experiments can encompass more or less distinctive and independent activities; they can be assembled into separate types, which confront and play upon each other, or disassembled to the extent that they appear to be mere aspects of one another.

Second, the relationship between local scientific practices and "environments" also changes as laboratories and experiments are differently assembled. In other words, reconfigurations of natural and social orders can in fact *not* be entirely contained in the laboratory space. Scientific fields are composed of more than one laboratory and more than one experiment; the reconfigurations established in local units have implications for the kind of relationship that emerges between these units, and beyond.

In the following, I shall do no more than outline some of these issues in a most cursory manner. I shall thereby introduce a first *set of differences* between the sciences of molecular biology and high energy physics, which will be the focus of much detail in later chapters. In this section I want to draw attention to the diverse *meanings* of "experiment" and "laboratory" that are indicated in different reconfigurations (see also Hacking 1992b). I want to indicate the varying significance of laboratories and experiments in relation to each other in three situations, which I distinguish in terms of whether they use a technology of correspondence, a technology of treatments and interventions, or a technology of representation (see also Shapin and Schaffer 1985). The construction placed upon the objects of research varies accordingly; in the first case, objects in the laboratory *stage* real-world phenomena; in the second, they are *processed partial versions* of these phenomena; in the third, they are *signatures* of the events of interest to science. Note that the distinctions drawn are not meant to point to some "essential" differences between fields; rather, they are an attempt to capture how objects are primarily featured and attended to in different areas of research. To illustrate the differences and to emphasize the continuity between mechanisms at work within science and outside, I shall first draw upon examples of "laboratories" and "experimentation" from outside natural science—the psychoanalyst's couch, the medieval cathedral, and the war game.

2.2.1 EXPERIMENTS (ALMOST) WITHOUT LABORATORIES: OBJECTS THAT STAGE REAL-TIME EVENTS

I begin with the war game. The hallmark of a *Kriegsspiel* in the past was that it took place on a "sand table," a kind of sandbox on legs, in which the geographic features of a potential battle area were built and whole battles were fought by toy armies. The landscape was modeled after the scene of a real engagement in all relevant respects, and the movements made by the toy soldiers corresponded as closely as possible to the expected moves of real armies. The sandbox war game was an eighteenth-century invention and was developed further by Prussian generals. Its modern equivalent is the computer simulation, which has become widely used not only in the military but in many areas of science, where real tests are impracticable for one reason or another. Computer simulations are also increasingly used in laboratory sciences to perform experiments. Indeed, the computer has been called a laboratory (e.g., Hut and Sussman 1987); it provides its own "test-bench" environment.

The point here is that many real-time laboratory experiments bear the same kind of relationship to reality as the war game bears to real war or the computer simulation bears to the system being modeled: they *stage* the action. As an example, consider most experiments in the social sciences, particularly in social psychology, or in economics, in research on problem solving and the like. To illustrate, in experimental research on decision making by juries, research participants (often college students) are set up in the way real juries would be in court. They are given information on a case and asked to reach a verdict in ways that approximate real jury decision processes. They may even be exposed to pleas by the mock accused and other elements of real-time situations (e.g., MacCoun 1989). Research on the heuristics of problem solving uses a similar design. Experts, lay persons, or novices to an area are recruited and asked to search for a solution to a simulated problem (Kahneman, Slovic, and Tversky 1982). One difference from the war game in the sandbox is that the experimental subjects in the social sciences are not toys but members of the targeted population. For example, they may be real experts who play experts in the laboratory, or students who are thought to be representative of the jury pool. Nonetheless, social science experiments receive the same kind of criticism as computer simulations do. While the subjects recruited for the experiment may not differ much from the persons about whom results are to be generated, the setting is artificial, and the difference this makes, with respect to the behavior generated in experimental situations, is poorly understood. What the critics question is whether generalizable results can be reached by studying behavior in mock settings when the factors distinguishing the simulation from real-time events are not known or have not been assessed.

Researchers in these areas are, of course, aware of this potential source of error. As a consequence, they take great care to design experimental reality so that in all relevant respects they come close to the perceived real-time processes. In other words, they develop and deploy a *technology of correspondence*. For example, they set up a system of assurance through which correct correspondence with the world is monitored. One outstanding characteristic of this system of assurance is that it is based on a theory of nonintervention. In "blind" and "double-blind" designs, researchers attempt to eradicate the very possibility that they will influence experimental outcomes. In fact, experimental designs consist of implementing a world simulation, on the one hand, and implementing a thorough separation between the experimental subjects and the action, interests, and interpretations of the researchers, on the other.

Now consider the laboratory in social science areas. It does not, as a rule, involve a richly elaborated space—a place densely stacked with instruments and materials and populated by researchers. In many social sciences, the laboratory is reduced to a room with a one-way mirror that includes perhaps a table and some chairs. In fact, experiments may be conducted in researchers' offices when a one-way mirror is not essential. But even when a separate laboratory space exists, it tends to be used only when an experiment is conducted, which, given the short duration of such experiments, happens only rarely. The laboratory is a virtual space and, in most respects, co-extensive with the experiment. Like a stage on which plays are performed from time to time, the laboratory is a *storage room* for the *stage props* that are needed when social life is instantiated through experiments. The "objects" featured on the stage are *players of the social form*. The hallmark of their reconfiguration seems to be that they are called upon to perform everyday life in a competent manner, and to behave under laboratory conditions true to the practice of real-time members of daily life.

2.2.2 LABORATORIES COME OF AGE: THE CONSTRUAL OF OBJECTS AS PROCESSING MATERIALS

Consider now a second example from outside the sciences. In the twelfth and thirteenth centuries cathedrals were built in Paris, Canterbury, Saint-Denis (an abbey church)—and later in Chartres, Bourges, and other places—that were modeled after earlier, smaller churches. They demonstrate a rapid transmission of innovative designs, manifest, for example, in the spread of the flying buttress (see Mark and Clark 1984 for a detailed analysis of this transmission). From structural analyses of these churches, Mark and Clark have argued that "cathedral builders learned from experience, using the actual buildings in the way today's engineer relies on instrumental prototypes" (1984: 144). It appears the builders observed in already built churches wind-pressure damage, cracking in the mortar of older churches, flaws in the original buttressing scheme, light influx, and, generally, how a particular design held up over time.

Given that architectural changes were made to correct problems in earlier designs, a system of surveillance must have existed which permitted the designers to build upon (rather than to deplore, find the culprit of, ignore, or otherwise deal with) past mistakes. Since at the time no design drawings were circulated, the system of surveillance must have rested upon travel between cathedrals and upon a traffic of orally transmitted observations. The observation circuit, together with the actual buildings, acted as a kind of laboratory (Mark and Clark 1984) through which builders experimented. But another point to note is that experimentation in this laboratory consisted of changing architectural designs and building cathedrals. In other words, it involved *manipulation* of the objects under study, a sequence of "cures" classified today as architectural innovations.

Consider now a typical experimental setup in a molecular biology laboratory, such as the ones in Heidelberg and Göttingen where the present research was conducted. These laboratories are bench laboratories; all experimental work is conducted at workbenches, on and around which specimens are stored and manipulated. As in twelfth-century cathedral building, the work in this laboratory is not concerned with staging a reality from somewhere else. The most notable feature of experiments in this laboratory is that it subjects specimens to procedural manipulations. In other words, experiments deploy and implement a technology of intervention (compare Hacking 1983). In this way natural objects are treated as *processing materials* and as *transitory object-states* corresponding to no more than a temporary pause in a series of transformations. Objects are decomposable entities from which effects can be extracted through appropriate treatment; they are ingredients for processing *programs,* which are the real threads running through the laboratory. There is no assumption that the transitory object-states obtained in the laboratory and the manipulations generating these objects correspond or are supposed to correspond to natural events. Consequently, the conclusions derived from such experiments are not justified in terms of their *equivalence* with real-world processes (though there are some experiments in which equivalence plays a role—for example, those which address the origin of life). In addition, the assurances installed with such experiments do not create a separation between experimenter and experiment in the sense discussed before. They are not based on a doctrine of noninterference by the experimenter or on a doctrine of object integrity, which sees experimental objects as not-to-be-tampered-with performances rooted in the natural course of events. How could such a doctrine be warranted if the whole point of experimentation is to influence the materials of the experiment, through direct or indirect manipulation by the researchers?

If we now turn to the laboratories where the manipulation takes place, it should come as no surprise that they are not, as in the first case, storage rooms for stage props. It seems that it is precisely with the above-mentioned processing approach, the configuration of objects as materials to be interfered with, that laboratories "come of age" and are established as distinctive and separate entities. What kind of entities? Take the classical case of a bench laboratory as exemplified in molecular biology (see also Lynch 1985; Jordan and Lynch 1992; Fujimura 1987; Amann 1990, 1994). This bench laboratory is always activated; it is an actual space in which research tasks are performed continuously and simultaneously. The laboratory has become a *workshop* and a *nursery* with specific goals and activities. In the laboratory, different plant and animal materials are maintained, bred, nourished, warmed, observed, and prepared for experimental manipulation. Surrounded by equipment and apparatus, they are used as technical devices in producing experimental effects.

The laboratory is a repository of processing materials and devices that continuously feed into experimentation. More generally, laboratories are objects of work and attention over and above experiments. Laboratories employ caretaking personnel for the sole purpose of tending to the waste, the used glassware, the test animals, the apparatus, and the preparatory and maintenance tasks of the lab. Scientists are not only researchers but also caretakers of the laboratory. As will become clearer in later chapters, certain types of tasks become of special concern to heads of laboratories, who tend to spend much of their time representing and promoting "their" lab (see Chapter 9). In fact, laboratories are also social and political structures that "belong" to their heads in the sense that they are attributed to them and identified with them. Thus, the proliferation of laboratories as objects of work is associated with the emergence of a two-tier system of social organization of agents and activities—the lab level and the experimental level. Experiments, however, tend to have little unity. In fact, they appear to be dissolved into processing activities, parts of which are occasionally pulled together for the purpose of publication. As laboratories gain symbolic distinctiveness and become a focus of activities, experiments lose some of the "wholeness" they display in social scientific fields. When the laboratory becomes a permanent facility, experiments can be continuous and parallel, and they even begin to blend into one another. Thus, experiments dissolve into experimental work, which, in turn, is continuous with laboratory-level work.

But there is a further aspect to the permanent installation of laboratories as *internal processing environments*. This has to do with the phenomenon that laboratories now are collective units that encapsulate within them a traffic of substances, materials, equipment, and observations. Phrased differently, the laboratory houses within it the circuits of observation and the traffic of experience that medieval cathedral builders brought about through travel. At the same time, neither the traffic of specimens and materials nor the system of surveillance is solely contained in the laboratory. If the laboratory has come of age as a continuous and bounded unit that encapsulates internal environments, it has also become a participant in a larger field of communication and mutual observation.

The traffic of objects, researchers, and information produces a *lifeworld* within which laboratories are locales, but which extends much further than the boundaries of single laboratories.

2.2.3   LABORATORIES VS. EXPERIMENTS: WHEN OBJECTS ARE SIGNS

The laboratory as an internally elaborated locale of a more extended lifeworld contrasts sharply with the third case to be considered, where much of the lifeworld appears to be drawn into *experiments* that are no longer merely streams of work conducted under the umbrella of a laboratory but that "confront" the laboratory. In this case objects are not reconfigured as not-to-be-interfered-with performances of "natural" events or as decomposable material ingredients of processing programs, but as *signs*. The case in point, from outside the natural sciences, is psychoanalysis. Freud repeatedly referred to psychoanalysis as analogous to chemistry and physics; he likened the method of stimulating patient recollection through hypnosis to laboratory experimentation (see for example Freud 1947: vol. 10, 131, 320; vol. 12, 5, 184, 186). He also compared psychoanalysts to surgeons. He envied a surgeon's ability to operate on patients in a setting removed from everyday social and physical environments under clinical conditions—a situation Freud emulated by what he called the special, "ceremonial" treatment situation (1947: vol. 11, 477f.; vol. 8, 467). In a nutshell, this ceremony consisted of the patient being put "to rest" on a couch while the analyst took his seat behind the couch so that the patient could not see the analyst. The patient was not to be influenced by the analyst's nonverbal behavior, and the analyst was to remain motionless during the encounter.

Some of Freud's instructions are reminiscent of the rules doctors were asked to follow in bedside medicine (see Section 2.1), but the psychoanalytic encounter always took place at the psychoanalyst's office; the patient's surroundings, kin group, and advisors were excluded from the encounter. The setting at the psychoanalyst's office shared some features with the characteristics of a clinical (laboratory) science. Moreover, the protocol Freud introduced strengthened these features. It immobilized the patient and subjected him or her to a strict regime of stimulus and response in which the doctor dominated. Thus, the ceremony proposed by Freud served a purpose entirely different from that of the rituals followed by the practitioners of bedside medicine. Together with certain rules of behavior the patient was asked to observe in everyday life during the analysis, the special setting Freud created helped to disengage patients from everyday situations by sustaining a new system of "self-other" relationships, which he, as the analyst, developed in his office. One could say that Freud went to some lengths to turn psychoanalysis into a laboratory science.

But my point refers to the kind of activity performed in this setup rather than to the setup itself. In essence, the analyst starts from a series of pathological "symptoms." S/he tries to associate these with basic drives, which, via complicated detours having to do with events in the patient's biography, are thought to motivate the symptoms. "Analysis" is the progression from outward signs (the patient's symptoms) to the motivating forces that are the elements of psychic activity. Unlike the previous type of science, psychoanalysis does not process material objects but rather processes *signs*. The office ritual of the couch and the way inquiry is conducted produces these signs. When they elicit and interpret these signs, psychoanalysts are *reconstructing the meaning and origin of representations*.

Now consider a field in contemporary particle physics, experimental high energy physics. This is a science that indubitably involves laboratories and experiments, in fact, the largest and perhaps the most complex ones in all the sciences. In the collider experiments studied at CERN and described in Section 1.6, detectors register particle traces and transmit their signs to offline operations, where these signs are suitably "reconstructed" and interpreted according to real-time particle occurrences and properties of events. In physics the signs are not words in the usual sense; and the process of producing the signs, as well as the process of reconstructing their identity and origin, is not literary or psychological in character. But these processes nonetheless attach signs to underlying causal events (particle occurrences), within the limits of certain probabilities—as is done in psychoanalysis, where a process exists by which symptoms are attached to basic motivating drives.

In high energy physics experiments, the natural order is reconfigured as an order of signs. In the next chapter, I will say more about the nature of these signs. Signs are incorporated in particle physics experiments in a far more extensive sense than they are in other fields. This is not to deny that all sciences involve sign processes that can potentially be analyzed from a semiotic perspective. Most sciences include a mix of technologies in several respects. For example, HEP experiments may require imitating the energy levels and subatomic activities present in the early universe. The goal of such imitation resembles the goal of the simulation in the social and behavioral sciences. In molecular biology, too, there are experiments whose explicit goal is to recreate and explore naturally occurring phenomena and events—for example, the circumstances surrounding the creation of life. However, such goals are often limited to specific experiments, clearly distinguished from other, more "common" types of work. Sign-creating technologies, on the other hand, in so far as they turn out verbal renderings, visual images, or algorithmic representations of objects and events, seem to be present in all sciences. If for no other purpose, they are needed for the transmission and publication of scientific results. Not all of these technologies produce "inscriptions" (Latour and Woolgar 1979), however; many, like the stethoscope mentioned earlier, involve visual or auditory signs. In addition, the way they are utilized and the degree to which a science depends on them varies strongly across fields.

For the most part, experiments that can be described in terms of intervening technologies process material substances rather than their signatures and representations. They use sign-related technologies mainly to produce (intermediary) end products from experimental processing. Experiments in high energy physics, on the other hand, seem to start with processes focusing upon signs—the point where other sciences leave off. The construction of objects as "signatures" and "footprints" of events, rather than as the events themselves, shapes the whole technology of experimentation. Such signs occur in many varieties and extend far back into the process of experimentation; they cannot be limited to the written traces, which in other sciences signify experimental results.

A more detailed exploration of high energy physics' rather complicated maneuvering in a world of signs will be left to the next chapter. Instead, I want to turn now to the meaning of experiment in high energy physics, as opposed to its meaning in the other sciences discussed in this chapter. High energy physics upgrades some features that are also present in other sciences and sustains them as special characteristics of its pursuits. For example, in excluding whatever material processes lead to the production of signs, HEP experiments rely on a *division of labor* between laboratory and experiment. We encountered a rudimentary version of this division of labor in the distinction between "work on the laboratory" and experimental work in molecular biology laboratories. In high energy physics, however, this loose division between kinds of work, which remain continuous with each other, appears to have been transformed into a new separation between laboratory and experiment—a separation through which the lab becomes technically, organizationally, and socially divorced from the conduct of the experiment. *Technically,* laboratories build, maintain, and run accelerators and colliders, while experiments build, maintain, and run detectors. Experiments process signs. Laboratories become segregated providers of signs—they provide for the particle clashes whose debris leaves "traces" that are the signs of particles in detectors. *Organizationally,* experiments conduct "science," while laboratories provide the (infra-) "structure" for carrying it out—they supply office space, computers, living quarters, transportation, financial resources, and, above all, particle collisions. One laboratory sustains many small-scale "fixed target" experiments, but only a few big collider experiments. Organizationally, most of the researchers and technicians that are part of the "structure" do not have any direct contact with experimenters. Researchers with one experiment often know little about others, even if the others are part of "sister experiments" dedicated to the same goal. Experiments become relatively closed, total units, and laboratories become total institutions.

Consider the reconfiguration this implies of the common, focused, interlinked lifeworld that was the context of benchwork laboratories. As indicated before, experiments in HEP involve huge collaborations; up to 500 physicists from physics institutes all over the world participate in each of the 4 currently running LEP experiments at CERN. Sometimes all physics institutes in a country join one experiment. There are only a handful of large high energy physics laboratories in the world at this point, and hardly more collider experiments. These experiments and laboratories deplete scientific resources; there are few active HEP institutes or working high energy physicists who are not being drawn into one of the experiments and who are not thereby associated with one of the major labs. The external lifeworld that in molecular biology is shared from inside each laboratory is, in particle physics, substituted by internal lifeworlds encapsulated within experiments. This has implications for the notion of a scientific community and for the concept of a scientific field. For example, it is clear that experiments, which are at the same time "collaborations" of physics institutes, also represent a tremendous political force, particularly since core members of collaborations tend to stay together and form the seeds of new collaboration. The political and financial strength of collaborations leads to the curious situation in which experiments "match" laboratories. They become counterparts of laboratories, near-equals that, in some sense, stand almost independent of the terrain of a laboratory. How do experiments play out their political strength? A collaboration conducting an experiment at CERN may simultaneously submit a proposal for a continuation of the experiment at its home base and at another competing laboratory (for a while, this was the case with the SSC in Texas). Collaborations and experiments do not have to be "loyal" to laboratories, though most are. On the other hand, experiments need laboratories just as much as laboratories need good (technically and financially powerful) collaborations and experiments (see Chapters 7 and 8).

2.3 Some Features of the Laboratory Reconsidered

I have argued that the notion of a laboratory in recent sociology of science is more than a new field of exploration, a site which houses experiments (Shapin 1988), or a locale in which methodologies are put into practice. I have associated laboratories with the notion of reconfiguration, with the setting-up of an order in laboratories that is built upon upgrading the ordinary and mundane components of social life. Laboratories *recast* objects of investigation by inserting them into new temporal and territorial regimes. They play upon these objects' natural rhythms and developmental possibilities, bring them together in new numbers, renegotiate their sizes, and redefine their internal makeup. They also invent and recreate these objects from scratch (think of the particle decays generated by particle colliders). In short, they create new configurations of objects that they match with an appropriately altered social order.

In pointing out these features I have defined laboratories as *relational* units that gain power by instituting *differences* with their environment: differences between the reconfigured orders created in the laboratory and the conventions and arrangements found in everyday life, but of course also differences between contemporary laboratory setups and those found at other times and places. Laboratories, to be sure, not only play upon the social and natural orders as they are experienced in everyday life. They also play upon themselves; upon their own previous makeup and at times upon those of competing laboratories. What I said in Sections 2.1 and 2.2 implies that one can link laboratories as *relational* units to at least three realities: to the environment they reconfigure, to the experimental work that goes on within them and is fashioned in terms of these reconfigurations, and to the "field" of other units in which laboratories and their features are situated.

Laboratories introduce and utilize *specific differences* between processes implemented in them and processes in a scientific field. Take the case of the space telescope mentioned earlier, or the recently developed underwater telescope. The underwater telescope does not operate in space or on mountaintops, but three miles beneath the ocean. Unlike previous telescopes, it does not observe electromagnetic radiation but streams of neutrino particles thought to be emitted by components of distant galaxies, such as black holes. Neutrinos are an elusive type of particle that travels easily through the earth and through space, undeterred by cosmic obstacles. The water under which the telescope is built serves as a screening system that filters out unwanted high energy particles that might mask the neutrino signals. Since even several miles of water do not offer enough shielding, however, the telescope, looking *down* rather than up, picks up signals from particles that fly all the way through the earth and emerge from the ocean floor.

The notion of reconfiguration needs to be extended to include issues continuously at stake in laboratories: the ongoing work of instituting specific differences from which epistemic dividends can be derived, and the work of boundary maintenance with regard to the natural and everyday order (see also Gieryn 1983). We need to conceive of laboratories as processes through which reconfigurations are negotiated, implemented, superseded, and replaced. Doing so would imply a notion of *stages* of laboratory processes, which can be historically investigated and which may also be important for questions of consensus formation (see Shapin 1988; Hessenbruch 1992; Lachmund 1997; Giere 1988). But it also implies that we have to expect different *types* of laboratory processes in different areas, resulting from cumulative processes of differentiation. It is the task of Chapters 3 and 4 to begin to describe these differences in the two sciences chosen for analysis here.

3

Particle Physics and Negative Knowledge

3.1 The Analogy of the Closed Universe

I shall now seek to characterize epistemic cultures more systematically, switching from laboratories to laboratory processes and to the ways different sciences understand and enact empirical research. I want to begin with high energy physics; the chapter examines the observable order of HEP's research policies as these are displayed in physicists' experimental activities, in their meetings (where these activities are exhibited among fellow physicists), in their explanations to me (which I draw from for "easy" illustrations not requiring whole transcripts or research histories), and in their conversations.

When defining laboratories I said that the empirical machinery of HEP is a sign-processing machinery. It moves in the shadowland of mechanically, electrically, and electronically produced negative images of the world—in a world of signs and often fictional reflections, of echoes, footprints, and the shimmering appearances of bygone events. In what follows I show how this world that is marked by a loss of the empirical operates in terms of a negative and reflexive epistemics (the notion of epistemics is used here to refer to the strategies and practices assumed to promote the "truth"-like character of results). An analogy appropriately describes the "truth-finding" strategies of experimental HEP, which I want to present up front. This is the analogy of the brain as an informationally closed system. The neurophysiology of cognition is based on theories developed in the nineteenth century proposing that states of arousal in a nerve cell in the brain represent only the *intensity* but not the *nature* of the source of arousal. Maturana and Varela (e.g., 1980) applied these results to the experimental study of perception. They concluded that perception must be seen as a cognitive process that is energetically open but informationally closed. Perception is accomplished by the brain, not the eye, and the brain can only construe what it sees from signals of light intensity that arrive at the retina. In order to form a picture of the nature of the source of these signals, the brain refers to its own previous knowledge and uses its own electrochemical reactions. Phrased differently, during perception the brain interacts only with itself, not with an external environment. It reconstructs the external world from internal states, and in order to accomplish this the brain "observes" itself. Consciousness, according to this theory, is a function of a nervous system capable only of recursive self-observation.

I want to argue that, like the brain, high energy physics operates within a *closed* circuitry. In many ways, it operates in a world of objects separated from the environment, a world turned inward, or, better still, a world entirely reconstructed within the boundaries of a complicated multilevel technology of representation. A detector is a kind of ultimate seeing device, a type of microscope that provides the first level of these representations. The representations themselves show all the ambiguities that afflict any world composed of signs. Yet particle physics is perfectly capable of deriving truth effects from sign-processing operations.

The spotlight in this chapter is on the rough parameters of these procedures to gain access to the world and stability in outcomes. Section 3.2 provides more details of the semiological understanding of inaccessible objects and their variously distorted traces. In 3.3 I discuss the notion of the "meaninglessness" of pure measurement and the practice of molding real "data" from the intersection of theory, detector models, and measured components. Section 3.4 describes the replacement, in these experiments, of the "care of objects" with the "care of the self"—their switch from an emphasis on "observing the world" to an emphasis on observing (controlling, improving, recording, understanding . . .) their own components and processes. Sections 3.5 and 3.6 complete the view of experimental HEP as an internally referential system by describing the turn toward negative and liminal knowledge for epistemic purposes—and by exemplifying relevant strategies such as unfolding, framing, and convoluting. Readers interested in selective differences in laboratory processes between molecular biology and HEP might focus on Sections 3.3 to 3.5.

3.2 A World of Signs and Secondary Appearances

In HEP experiments, natural objects (cosmic particles) and quasi-natural objects (debris of particles smashed in particle collisions) are admitted to experiments only rarely, perhaps for intermittent periods of several months in an experiment that used to last ten and more years and now lasts more than twenty. The proposals for UA1 and UA2, the two large collider experiments at CERN, were approved in 1978, after several years of preparatory work, and both experiments were dismantled in 1991, although analysis of UA1 and UA2 data continued. During the upgrading period in which the detectors were rebuilt, which lasted from the early 1980s to the end, the experiments had four "runs" (data-taking periods) between 1987 and 1990 lasting about four months each. Thus, researchers deal with the objects of interest to them only very occasionally, while most experimental time is spent on design, installation, testing, and other work outlined below.

What is more, these objects are in a very precise sense "unreal"—or, as one physicist described them, "phantasmic" *(irreale Gegenstände);* they are too small ever to be seen except indirectly through detectors, too fast to be captured and contained in a laboratory space, and too dangerous as particle beams to be handled directly. Furthermore, the interesting particles usually come in combination with other components that mask their presence. Finally, most subatomic particles are very short-lived, transient creatures that exist only for a billionth of a second. Subject to frequent metamorphosis and to decay, they "exist" in a way that is always already past, already history.

These phantasmic, historical, constantly changing occurrences can be established only indirectly, by the footprints they leave when they fly through different pieces of equipment. When a detector "sees" or "senses" their presence, it registers their passage through a substance, which used to be a liquid contained in a bubble chamber detector (e.g., Galison 1987), but now is often solid or a mixture of gases. Detectors are made of many subdetectors wrapped in shells around a beam pipe from which the particles emanate during collision. These subdetectors use different technologies, such as scintillating fibers, wire chambers, silicon crystals, etc. The interaction of particles with detector materials, through liberations of electrons and the emitting of light by electrons, results in the first level of particle traces in a series of three levels. The work on this level is done by the particles themselves. The experiment designs and builds the apparatus in which the particles register. Physicists, however, do not start with the particles, they start with representations of the detector, that is, "offline" manipulations of the signals extracted from detectors after data have been taken. This level of representation *reconstructs* the events in the detector and slowly molds these signals into a form that echoes the particles of interest to physicists. ("Online" manipulations are manipulations during data taking.) Finally, the third level involves representations of physics: from the reconstruction of events *in* the detector, physicists create "variables" that are no longer interpreted in terms of the signs that register in detector materials, but are designed and analyzed in terms of distributions and models in physics (e.g., expected distributions for certain kinds of particles).

Step two in particular includes major "chains" of complicated substeps, which I cannot present here in detail. Suffice it to say that physicists' classification of the major segments of these chains as the work of "production" and "reconstruction" indicates their representational concerns, continued in step three through procedures of "choosing the right variables" to represent physics processes. What I want to illustrate further are the complications that arise in collider experiments, particularly those which work from proton-antiproton collisions, from the fact that their signs marking interesting events are muffled and smeared by signs from other occurrences in the detector. In these experiments the universe of signs and traces is overlaid by a universe of simulations and distortions of signs and traces. These effects derive from uninteresting *parts* of events, from other *classes* of events, or from the *apparatus* itself—they refer to the "background," the "underlying event," the (detector and electronics) "noise," and the "smearing" of distributions. All of these phenomena are a threat to the scientists' ability to recognize interesting events. They may falsify the signature of events, misrepresent their character, or jeopardize their identification. They deceive detectors, and hence analysts, about the presence of events, the shape of their distributions, and the identity of the information they provide. They worsen the results and "resist" (e.g., Pickering 1991) physicists' attempts "to get results out," causing infinite problems to researchers.

The most insidious of these antiforces of the experiment surely is the *background:* competing processes and classes of events that fake the signal. The physicists in the proton-antiproton collider experiments observed for this study see themselves as "buried in background": in the words of a participant working on the top analysis in UA2, "The nature of the problem is to deal not really with the signal so much as the background. You have to deal with the horrible case that you didn't want to see." Their task, as they see it, is to get the proverbial needle out of the haystack. The signs of the events of interest are muted by the background. If you think of these signs in terms of footprints, it is as if millions and even billions of different animals stampeded over a trail, and among their imprints one seeks to discern the tracks of a handful of precious animals. In the original collider experiments at CERN, the counter-rotating bunches of protons and antiprotons met every 7.6 microseconds (7.6 millionths of a second). During the upgrading of these experiments, collisions occurred every 3.7 microseconds. Each collision produces an "event": a cascade of new particles that spill out into the surrounding detector. But only very few of these events give rise to the particles physicists define as "interesting." In the search for the Z^0 boson at CERN in the early 1980s, less than one event was retained out of every 10,000,000,000 interactions (Barger and Phillips 1987: 31). In the search for the top quark, during the upgrading of UA1 and UA2, for example, it was expected that approximately 40 top events would appear in six million selected electron triggers (electron candidates), a number already vastly reduced from the number of interactions.

The importance of the background manifests itself in a variety of ways in an experiment. First, the background is from "last year's" or the "last ten years'" physics (events studied at lower energy co-occur with new ones at higher energy). In other fields, topics that are "understood" are black-boxed and set aside or become incorporated into new techniques, but in HEP some of these topics keep popping up as "the enemy"—as the background that has to be dealt with if one wishes to learn anything about "new physics." In this sense, the old physics does lend a hand to the new in the familiar sense (Merton 1973), but it also haunts it. Second, backgrounds are specific to specific detectors. Therefore, the background for a particular class of events needs to be studied and taken care of anew with respect to each detector constellation. Third, the task of dealing with the background, of sifting out "interesting" events from uninteresting ones, penetrates all levels of experimental activities. It manifests itself in the way subdetectors are constructed—not only to receive particles, but also to provide a defense against certain backgrounds. It is embodied in a hierarchy of selections, which started in UA2 with a three-level trigger system (a multistage, electronic threshold-setting process through which only some events in numerous interactions are retained and selected out of the detector), continued through "safe," more precise, additional selections in the filter and production program, and ended with "analysis cuts," which are the selections made by "individual" physicists to separate the signal from the background. The flow of activities in the whole experiment can be expressed in terms of a series of selection processes. Finally, interest in this enemy is shown in the manifold distinctions and classifications applied to the background, and in a vocabulary of killing and suppression that I will illustrate in Chapter 5.

The background may be the most insidious antiforce in the experiment, but it is not the only one. Physicists also have to deal with a wide variety of *noise;* random, unpredictable, and undesirable signals in a detector and in the electronics of the apparatus that mask the desired information. A third category of undesired signal is the "underlying event," the result of hadron colliders producing large, inelastic cross-sections[1]—event-production rates dominated by low-energy particles ("spectator" jets) that do not participate in the interaction proper but nonetheless pass through the detector, where they may overlap with events of interest, make the energy of the initial partons (components of nucleons) uncertain, and add confusing extra tracks. A fourth category of obstacle, "smearing," refers to a distortion of physical distributions that makes these distributions wider. The resolution of a detector refers to the degree to which it can give distinguishable responses to two separate particles of two very small energies, or separate tracks for two particles running through the material closely together. Since this resolving power cannot be infinite, the resulting distributions are wider than they should be for physical reasons alone. A second reason for the smearing of distributions is related to the uncertainty of surrounding processes and quantities in physics. For example, the transverse momentum distribution of a W boson is seen to smear the mass measurement of the W because it is not well known.[2]

A final point to add is that different categories of distortion may also interact with each other and work together to co-produce a particular effect. The background events of a particular type produced in UA2's scintillating fiber detector were called "ghosts"—fake tracks of particles misinterpreted as real tracks. They could be caused by pieces of real particle tracks overlapping with one another or with fake information from cross-talk between layers of fiber. Ghosts could also derive from pure electronic noise or from smearing—smearing "fattened" projections, making the resolution of this detector worse, which meant that they picked up more ghosts. Thus, smearing, noise phenomena, and real particles all contributed to the making and the size of this background. At one time, UA2 was swamped with ghosts—"you end up with 50 real tracks producing 2,000 ghosts"—a problem that was hard to handle not only because of the technical difficulties involved, but also because of the sheer amount of computer time needed to solve the problem.

The term *ghost* is a vivid native pointer to the shadow world of signs and appearances in high-energy collider experiments. Through the anti-forces of the experiment, the world of signs is joined by a level of simulated and distorted signals and their by-products—an extra world that sticks to the surface of valid representations as a coating of paint sticks to the surface of an object.

3.3 The "Meaninglessness" of Measurement

I now want to turn to the "meaninglessness" of measurement, an issue that adds to the picture high energy physics presents of a self-enclosed system and sets it apart from many other sciences. In many fields, measurements, provided they are properly performed and safeguarded by experimenters, count as evidence. They are considered capable of proving or disproving theories, of suggesting new phenomena, of representing more or less interesting—and more or less publishable—"results." This view holds irrespective of the fact that measurements are theory-laden, prone to raise arguments in crucial cases, and sometimes subject to re-interpretation. Within the framework of their dependence on a certain paradigm and tradition, measurements count as self-sufficient quantities; they are granted a powerful role in validating knowledge, and they are considered irreplaceable as witnesses and arbiters in scientific disputes. They provide, one might say, end-of-the-line verdicts; verdicts which experimental work leads to through intermediary and final steps, from which this work takes its clues, and at which point it pauses and starts afresh. In high energy collider physics, however, measurements appear to be defined more by their imperfections and shortcomings than by anything they can do. It is as if high energy physicists recognized all the problems with measurements that philosophers and other analysts of scientific procedures occasionally investigate. As if, in addition, they had pushed one problem to its limit and drawn a conclusion that other sciences have not drawn: Purely experimental data "means nothing by itself." Not only are there few quantities that can be measured relatively directly, but even those are not to be taken as they are. Experimental numbers are dependent upon a particular detector configuration and on the criteria applied in extracting information from the detector. Another detector, another set of criteria, yields other measurements. A UA2 postdoctoral fellow (now a member of ATLAS) reacted indignantly to my insinuation that one might "just measure" the mass of the W: *"You cannot read off a detector how big the mass of a particle is like you can read the time off a watch!"*

The master problem, then, is the detector. As an example, consider the strong force-coupling constant, Alpha S, in effect a measure of the probability of the emission of a force-carrying particle. Alpha S depends on the momentum transferred between two quarks, which in UA2 was assumed to be equal to the squared mass of the W. What one could measure experimentally was the ratio between the number of W plus 1 jet event divided by the W plus 0 jet events. As the physicist who had done this work in his doctoral thesis explained, however, there is a problem:

> As an experimental quantity this number is totally dependent on the detector configuration and on the criteria used in jet-identification. *It is a purely experimental number which says nothing in itself. It is absolutely meaningless.* Because if you took another detector with a greater acceptance, for example, a detector that is almost completely hermetic ((one that covers almost the whole area around the beam pipe such that no particles can escape)), the measured quantity would be much higher. The experimental quantity must be put in relation to theory. If the theory is correct, then one has to find the same Alpha S with the new detector, with a greater acceptance, with the greater value for the ratio.

Thus, what is interesting is not the experimental value, but "the theoretical ratio in relation to the experimental ratio for a given detector configuration." To get this value, one must first determine the experimental ratio described above; second, one had to assemble a Monte Carlo calculation that included all the necessary theoretical calculations *and* simulated the detector. The Monte Carlo also simulated the "fragmentation" (the breakup of quarks and gluons into jets) and the underlying event, etc. From this simulation one obtained the same ratio as the experimental one, in theory. The theoretical ratio was a function of, among other things, the coupling constant. It increased when the coupling of relevant particles increased. The experimental ratio, on the other hand, was a constant. The "real" Alpha S derived from intersecting the experimental value with the "Monte Carloed" curve of the theoretical ratio.

The same procedure, in principle, is necessary to obtain "directly measurable" quantities such as the W mass, as described by a physicist in UA2 and ATLAS who had used the W channel:

> **KK:** ((How do you measure the W mass?))
>
> **JJ:** (()) If one looks at the experimental spectra ((distributions)) of the W mass, one gets an impression of where the W mass lies. But one has to run an MC to describe the data. Because it takes into account not only the decay properties of the W boson, but also *how my detector reacts to it.* One can see the Jacobean peak in the spectrum of the missing transverse momentum, and where it is in the spectrum. But to

know why the peak looks like it does, why it is smeared to the degree it is, and what this means for the uncertainty of my mass measurement, you can only find that out by running an MC.

An experimental measurement in HEP experiments is a sort of *amputated* quantity; a quantity that, without the nonmeasured parts that are missing from it, is not worth much as an experimental result. It is not a final figure that can stand on its own, but a position in a structure of relations to which other positions must be added before the whole becomes useful. With respect to the analogy of the closed universe, this epistemic strategy means that measurements are placed firmly—and obviously—*inside* the ranks and components of the experiment rather than outside of it, as attempted in other fields (see Cicourel 1964, 1974, for the social sciences). They are not cast as external evaluations of internal propositions, but rather as elements and stages that are held in check and turned into something useful only through the interaction of these elements with other features of the experiment.

3.4 The Structure of the Care of the Self

The conception that data are contingent upon the measurement apparatus and are representations of this apparatus (rather than of the world) reveals the detector as a mediating device (Wise 1993) interposed *between* the experiment and the phenomenal word. The detector is the outpost of the experiment; it has to bear the impact of incoming particles that strike its materials. Like the retina, which is hit by the photons that make up raw light and which converts these into the nerve signals that the brain interprets as visual images, the detector is hit by particles and converts their impact into electrical currents and pulses that must be interpreted as physical processes. The analogy between the experiment and the brain as interpreter suggests that considerable internal processing is needed to perform this task. The energy and track reconstructions mentioned before reflect this processing. Reconstructions are based on the premise that one knows the detector and all other components of the measurement machinery. Equally, the idea that measurements must be intersected with detector simulations assumes that the complete measurement apparatus can and must itself be properly understood. HEP collider experiments seek this understanding. They substitute a concern with their own internal production circuitry for a concern with real-time objects, found in other sciences such as molecular biology. To borrow a phrase from Foucault (1986), they substitute the care of objects with *the care of the self*. By this I mean the preoccupation of the researchers with the experiment itself, *with observing, controlling, improving, and understanding its components and processes*. Confronted with a lack of direct access to the objects they are interested in, caught within a universe of appearances, and unwilling to trespass the boundaries of their liminal approach (see Section 3.5), they have chosen to switch, for large stretches of the experiment, from the analysis of objects to the analysis of the self.[3]

3.4.1 SELF-UNDERSTANDING

The "care of the self" becomes obvious, for example, merely by looking at an experiment's expenditure of time. More time in an experiment is spent on designing, making, and installing its own components, and in particular on examining every aspect of their working, than on handling the data. Another indicator is the importance credited to self-analysis in practice and discourse at all points of experimental activities. For example, energy reconstruction is considered a relatively "uncontroversial" step in data processing, but only insofar as one believes that one "understands" the calibrations that go into it. These in turn are part of the "understanding of the behavior of the detector" that comprises a major portion of the care of the self. The detector is an apparatus that is self-created and assembled within the experiment. Nonetheless, the behavior of this apparatus, its performance, blemishes, and ailments are not self-evident to the physicists. These features must be learned, and the project of understanding the behavior of the detector spells this out.

What exactly does one mean by understanding the behavior of the detector? As a physicist working on the inner detector in ATLAS and UA2 put it, it means "knowing when some physics process of some kind happens (in the detector), what comes out of it." To understand means "being able to do a perfect mapping" of it, and "trying to unfold what has happened between an input and an output" of results. Understanding the behavior of a detector begins when the its first components arrive and undergo several stages of test-bench and test-beam studies, all presenting their own difficulties and time requirements. But it involves much more. For example, learning how a calorimeter (which is central to electron identification) responds—that is, learning "what signal you get out of the detector for a given input"—in UA2 required several steps. First, it required an understanding of the basic response of the detector, which entered into the fixed calibration constants. Second, it required an understanding of these calibrations, which meant examining how the detector response changed over time. With regard to these changes, one needed to learn the long-term deterioration of the response, a slow, continuous "aging" process. Finally, it required an understanding of the short-term "instabilities" in the response by which detectors are also affected, the nonuniform "jumps" in the behavior of phototubes, analog-digital converters, and the basic electronic noise. Figure 3.1 illustrates these different levels of understanding involved in learning the workings of a calorimeter.

Understanding thus refers to a comprehensive approach to learning what happens in every relevant part of the material, what happens over time, and why these things happen. This approach is maintained even when understanding is *not* necessary for the successful completion of ongoing work. To provide an example, the organic-chemical structure of scintillators in a calorimeter dissolves slowly over time, which leads to the deteriorating light response that physicists call "aging" of the detector. During the routine measurement of the degree of aging, after the first (1987) data-taking run in UA2, it was found that the light response in certain compartments of the calorimeter had actually changed for the better; the calorimeter had "gotten younger." This was unexpected and seen as a problem that had to be understood. The effect was soon attributed to the fact that the calorimeter had been "packed" into nitrogen during the run, a gas that was used for the first time in the experiment. To understand the problem, test setups were prepared at CERN and independently in Milan.

Both setups found a 6–8 percent gain in the light response of the scintillators over time, which corresponded to the gain found in the experiment. They also found that if nitrogen was switched off, the response returned to normal. This was taken as an important confirmation of what happened in the real calorimeter—its response also returned to normal when two of its slices were tested after the run with the nitrogen

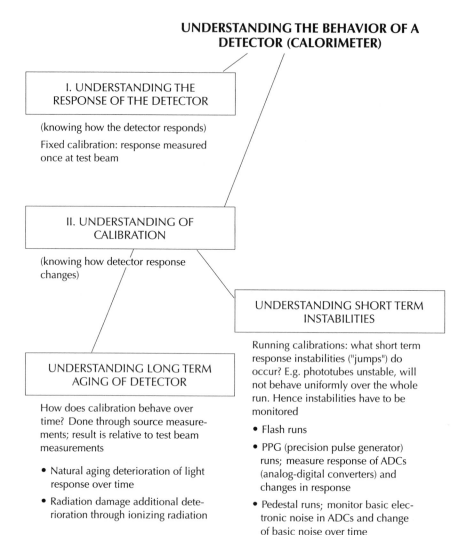

Figure 3.1 Some components of understanding the behavior of a detector.

switched off. It was also decided to use one of these slices and expose it to nitrogen at test beam. Since the test beam could be set to different energies, one could learn more about nonlinearities in the response. Efforts at "understanding" how, for example, the diffused gas became trapped differently in different parts of the calorimeter, continued despite the fact that this knowledge was not needed to start the next run or perform analysis on the data. In fact, it had been decided almost immediately not to use the nitrogen again because of expected nonuniformities in the light gain—signs of which had been seen at the first source measurements of aging after the run (the light gain was high in the hadronic part of the calorimeter, but nonexistent in the endcaps). It was also known that the response would return to normal after the nitrogen was switched off, which meant that the original calibrations that provided the baseline for measurements of changes, and the enormous work that went into them, were not lost. With respect to the afflicted run, its luminosity was such that mass precision measurements of the kind to which an error of 6–8 percent caused by the nitrogen mattered could not be performed—the statistics were too low. Thus, learning exactly the size of the effect of nitrogen on the light gain, for particles of different energy in various regions of the detector at different points in time, was of no relevance to data taking. Nonetheless, participants of the CERN calorimeter group and from MILAN studied the problem well into the summer of 1988; they went to some length to obtain as differentiated and precise a picture as they could possibly produce.

Understanding the behavior of the detector is only one component of the overall project of understanding. All important elements and forces in the experiment are subject to understanding, among them a considerable number of algorithms, especially those dedicated to particle (track) identification. All the track recognition algorithms that had been written for UA2 before the first data-taking period were called "guesswork games." Comments about them ran along the line that "there surely is a lot more understanding to be gained" of what they do and how they perform. Another example of an item to be understood is the background and the "cuts" one needs to deal with the background—variables that separate the signal from the background (see also Galison 1987). In the following excerpt from a conversation, the cuts refer to the top analysis:

> **KK:** Looking in detail means looking at histograms/statistics ((of the cuts))?
> **AP:** () these cuts are foreseen, but you don't know how tight to make them and we don't know what the background would look like in the

top sample yet. We know what the background looks like in the old W sample. So in fact before we can really do a top analysis the very first thing is to select Ws (). And then you can really tune the cuts to select those electrons. But then when you go to the top you are dealing with the softer electrons (). So you have to study how well you are doing, the first step would be to apply the W cuts, we even know that those are probably too hard. So you would have to look at your signal ((asking)) well what happened to the signal as you change the cuts (), what happens if I change this cut and make it bigger and bigger, and what have I learned about the cut and how much signal do I (? . . .). And that sort of thing.

In the following exchange about physics analysis, the need for understanding cuts was summarized as follows:

> **KK:** How did you do this ((making the cuts))?
> **SH:** You have to do essentially a study for every cut you put on. You have to study what effect it has on the background, is it buying you something, and how much? Ideally, you want to *understand* each cut individually.

There were also in UA2 a multitude of special test runs, for example, runs in which the trigger setting was changed so that "minimum bias events," which are used to simulate the underlying event, could be studied. Finally, when something goes wrong, when measurements diverge from expectations and problems occur, then understanding refers to an unfolding (see Section 3.6) of what has happened.

3.4.2 SELF-OBSERVATION, SELF-DESCRIPTION, AND RE-ENTRY

The care of the self has a threefold structure: *self-understanding* (discussed above), *self-observation,* and *self-description* (see Figure 3.2).

Self-observation is a form of *surveillance,* present at many levels of these experiments, but especially at its later stages, and during runs. The most clearly specified forms of self-observation involve increasingly more sophisticated levels of online and offline *monitoring.* "More sophisticated monitoring" means that the computer performed the watching, while humans watched computer messages projected onto screens or checked computer printouts. Hundreds of such messages were displayed

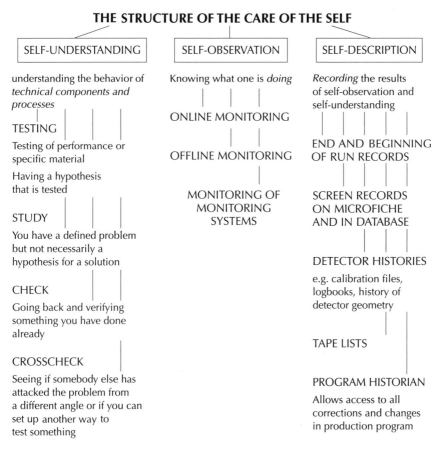

Figure 3.2 The tripartite structure of the care of the self in high energy physics.

on up to ten screens in the "counting room" of the UA2 during data taking. The main messages changed every few moments; they indicated whether the detector was putting something on the tape, which events were being taken, which monitoring tasks were running, and what problems the computer detected. Offline, the data were looked at in a more comprehensive fashion by the production program, which reconstructed every event, while experts looked at varying amounts of the printouts and plots produced by the data. Data-taking efficiency was monitored through a calibration program, performed every few days, that detected dead channels, increasing noise levels, etc. There was also a multitude of special data runs in which some functions were turned off to cross-check these functions against each other. Finally, besides online and offline monitoring there were "checks of the checking system"; different observers watched the same occurrence concurrently and thus were able to detect whether other checking systems worked. They also used special graphic "event display" computers "to see what your experiment is actually doing out there, whether it is doing what you have told it to do, and whether, having told it that, did you really mean something else."

Self-understanding and self-observation are continued through meticulous efforts at self-description, including not only logbook keeping but many forms of computerized recording and track keeping. These efforts generate "histories" of the experiment. In UA2 they included "bookkeeping" information so that people could find their way around the many data tapes: for example, tape lists, records on tapes, and "end-of-run records." To illustrate, the latter alone contained

> The type of record, run number, start time of the run and end time, which tape it was written on, what software triggers and hardware triggers were enabled, number of events in the run, length of tape used, number of words in UA2, which gates, what type of trigger (whether we are running on beam or whether it was a clock trigger), which triggers were enabled at each level, which processing was enabled, which detectors were active, what the pre-scaling factors were on the level 1 triggers, what all the thresholds are in the level 2, what all those parameters were on level 3, etc.

"So in principle we know exactly what was going on online," the physicist coordinating the offline operations said. Besides tape records and equally elaborate run records, there were "detector histories" which included the logbooks physicists keep on all the tests and monitoring tasks they have performed. An important component in relation to detectors was the calibration files—also a record—of the energy scales through which raw signals are transformed into physics quantities and their changes over time. When "running production," one had to know "all the calibration files for all of the experiment at all times." For example, one had to know the pedestal values (the basic noise fluctuations), which changed often and were measured several times daily. They were considered almost as *photographs* of the status of the experiment at the moment the tape was written. Finally, there was the tool called the "historian." This was a program that maintained the main production program, keeping all the old versions on files. As native references to "history keeping" and similar terms suggest, physicists were well aware of the effort they maintain not only to know what they are doing, but also to store this knowledge and keep it available for future reference.

Records such as those described above fulfill many purposes. One is "backtracking" in error searches. Some "old" members of these experiments (in UA2 members who had already participated in it before the upgrade, and in ATLAS those who had worked on UA1 or UA2 before) perform similar functions: they were praised for a memory that, when questions came up, could supply reasons for past technical problems and decisions. Most important, perhaps, and in line with the conception of HEP experiments as internally referential systems, history keeping serves the purpose of re-entering the self-understanding gained through tests, studies, checks, cross-checks, and continuous self-observations into experimental analyses. For example, the understanding physicists acquire about the behavior of the detector re-enters physics analysis in the form of calibration constants, changes and corrections to these constants, quality factors, acceptance calculations, efficiencies, and uncertainties. Re-entry completes a circle, channeling the results of the care of the self back into experimental work.

3.5 Negative Knowledge and the Liminal Approach

Having argued that to assure success HEP experiments turn toward the care of the self, I now want to add that they also turn toward the study of "liminal" phenomena, things which are neither empirical objects of positive knowledge nor effects in the formless regions of the unknowable, but something in between. *Limen* means "threshold" in Latin. The term has been used in the past to refer to the ambiguous status of individuals during transitional periods of time (Turner 1969). I shall use the term to refer to knowledge about phenomena on the fringe and at the margin of the objects of interest. High energy physics incorporates liminal phenomena into research by enlisting the world of disturbances and distortions, imperfections, errors, uncertainties, and limits of research into its project. It has lifted the zone of unsavory blemishes of an experiment into the spotlight, and studies these features. It cultivates a kind of negative knowledge. Negative knowledge is not nonknowledge, but knowledge of the limits of knowing, of the mistakes we make in trying to know, of the things that interfere with our knowing, of what we are not interested in and do not really want to know. We have already encountered some forces of this kind in the background, the underlying event, the noise, and the smearing of distributions. All of these are limitations of the experiment, in the sense that they are linked to the features of the detector, the collider, or the particles used in collisions. High energy collider physics *defines* the perturbations of positive knowledge in terms of the limitations of *its own* apparatus and approach. But it does not do this just to put the blame on these components, or complain about them. Rather, it teases these fiends of empirical research out of their liminal existence; it draws distinctions between them, elaborates on them, and creates a discourse about them. It puts them under the magnifying glass and presents enlarged versions of them to the public. In a sense, high energy experimental physics has *forged a coalition* with the evil that bars knowledge, by turning these barriers into a principle of knowing.

In Christian theology, there was once an approach called "apophantic theology" that prescribed studying God in terms of what He was *not* rather than what He was, since no positive assertions could be made about His essence. High energy experimental physics has taken a similar route. By developing liminal knowledge, it has narrowed down the region of positive, phenomenal knowledge. It specifies the boundaries of knowledge and pinpoints the uncertainties that surround it. It delimits the properties and possibilities of the objects that dwell in this region by recognizing the properties of the objects that interfere with them and distort them. Of course, if one asks a physicist about "negative knowledge" he or she will say that the goal remains to catch the (positive, phenomenal) particles at loose, to measure their mass and other (positive, phenomenal) properties, and nothing less. All else is the ways and means of reaching this goal. There is no doubt that this goal is indeed what one wishes to achieve, and occasionally succeeds in achieving, as with the discovery of the vector bosons at CERN in 1983 (Arnison et al. 1983a,b; Bagnaia et al. 1983; Banner et al. 1983). My intention is by no means to deny such motivations or their gratification, but what is of interest as one works one's way into a culture is precisely the ways and means through which a group *arrives at* its gratifications. The upgrading of liminal phenomena—the torch that is shone on them, the time and care devoted to them—is a cultural preference of some interest.[4] For one thing, it extends and accentuates what I call HEP's negative and self-referential epistemics. For another, the majority of fields, among them molecular genetics, does not share this preference. And, lastly, it is quite remarkable how much one can do by mobilizing negative knowledge.

There are two areas in which the liminal approach is most visible: the area of *errors* and *uncertainties* and the area of *corrections*. Let me start with the latter. The idea of a correction is that the limits of knowing must enter into the calculation of positive knowledge. For example, "meaningless" measurements can be turned into meaningful data by correcting them for the peculiarities and limitations of the detector. "What you really want to know," as a physicist summed up this point, "is, given that an event is produced in your detector, do you identify it." Corrections can be characterized as "acceptances", or as "efficiencies." An acceptance tells physicists "how many events my detector sees of what it should see"; it is the number of observed events divided by the number of produced events.[5] An overall acceptance calculation requires a detector response model: it requires that all the physics processes that end up in a detector are generated, and a full detector simulation is created to ascertain what the detector makes of these processes. In UA2, the detector response model also included such components as a simulation of the underlying event and detector performance measures, such as its geometrical acceptance (which describes how many events are lost through the incomplete coverage of detectors with dead angles and cracks), its resolution (which refers to the smearing of distributions described earlier), and its response curves (which determine the reaction to energy inputs that deviate from those of the test beam used to determine the basic calibration constants). Computing the overall acceptance is a complicated and elaborate effort, which brings together nearly all the results of the self-analysis of the experiment into its final operative stage. A physicist from an outside institute working in UA2 summarized this as follows:

> **KK:** ((How would you characterize the acceptance))?
>
> **NO:** Inside the UA2 apparatus we produce an object we want to measure. To do that we have to exploit to the best of our knowledge how UA2 works. This knowledge is gained by test beam studies etc., it is a complete structure of layered information. () (This information) is the complete opposite of the basic piece of a single efficiency. *It contains all we know and all our bias, both in the experimental set-up and in the procedure of how we analyze this complex structure.* [Emphasis added.]

Acceptance calculations are joined by "the basic pieces" of efficiency corrections, which tell physicists, once they have a particle in the sensitive region of the detector, whether they have *identified it* as the particle they are looking for. Many components of these experiments have efficiencies: triggers, special conditions set, particle reconstruction programs, fit methods, and, above all, cuts. Overall efficiencies are computed from many such components. For example, the paper published on the top quark (Åkesson et al. 1990:182) lists six components to the overall efficiency used to find a W electron as part of the signature of the top quark:

$$E(W) = E(\text{cal}) \times E(\text{v}) \times E(\text{trk}) \times E(\text{Si}) \times E(\text{ps}) \times E(\text{P})$$

where $E(\text{cal})$ = the efficiency for finding an electromagnetic cluster from an electron candidate in the central calorimeter; $E(\text{v})$ = the vertex-finding efficiency (the vertex is the point of interaction in an event and the point where the particle tracks coming from the event should coincide); $E(\text{trk})$ = the track-finding efficiency for isolated high energy tracks; $E(\text{Si})$ = the efficiency of a cut made with the help of the silicon detector to reduce background; $E(\text{ps})$ = the track-preshower matching efficiency for finding the impact point of candidate electron tracks with the position of electromagnetic showers; $E(\text{P})$ = the efficiency of a cut eliminating candidates with an energy greater than 1 GeV in the second hadronic compartment of the calorimeter. In a 1991 study of heavy particle decays in two jets (of particles heavier than the W or Z^0), the overall efficiency investigated included eight components, ranging from the trigger efficiency to that of a mass cut.

Correction factors like efficiencies may themselves be corrected for by other factors—there is, in a sense, a hierarchy of corrections. For instance, if not all particle tracks in a reference sample used to calculate a tracking efficiency are genuine, the efficiency may be corrected by determining, through another detector, the fraction of genuine tracks. Such secondary corrections can be seen as part of the *background evaluation*, a third major correction task in the experiment. A hierarchy of "cuts" (selection procedures) is normally implemented to "get rid of" the background, but the background that appears with exactly the same signature as the signal cannot be removed through cuts. It must be evaluated through other means, such as through Monte Carlo simulations, and then be subtracted from the signal.

Corrections of corrections indicate how the liminal approach extends to self-knowledge—it, too, includes its very own limitations, in terms of which it can and must be specified. Besides secondary corrections, and the original ones, "errors" and "uncertainties" are the other major components of an experiment that exemplifies the liminal methodology. Physicists distinguish between *statistical errors* (the variation obtained from repeated measurements, a new limitation) and theoretical and experimental *systematic errors,* which indicate fundamental mistakes one makes in ones' procedures. If the first is variation due to random error, the second is similar to using a ruler that is too short for measuring the length of an object and will always yield biased results, no matter how many times the measurement is repeated. As one physicist, then a member of the CERN group in UA2 and now a member of an outside institute working on ATLAS, put it:[6]

> The systematic error is just a way to measure our ignorance . . . (it) is our way to try and estimate what we've done wrong. And if we knew what we did wrong we could correct it rather than to allow for it in the error.

I want to illustrate this by an example that also shows how the existence of different theories is transformed into an uncertainty calculation, or into liminal knowledge. Structure functions describe the density of quarks and gluons (collectively called *partons*) within the proton. They are used to obtain the number of expected events produced in a proton-antiproton collision and the kinematics of the collision. Structure functions are based on extrapolations of experimental measurements from low energy fixed target experiments (which exist) through "parametrizations"—that is, through fitting curves that match the available data points. They predict the values of unmeasured densities in HEP experiments. In early 1991, about 45 sets of structure functions were available, involving different assumptions in their calculations (see also Plothow-Besch 1990).

The systematic errors in this case are "uncertainties"[7] deriving from the fact that one cannot say which of these structure functions is correct. They represent, as a senior physicist performing the analysis of structure functions said, different theories:

> One structure function might lead you to this value, another to that, etc. If these values would result from measurements you could construct a broad Gaussian out of this with an average and a sigma. If you treated it as a Gaussian, you would say that there is a 68 percent chance that the real value is within ($\pm$ 1 sigma) . . . But these are not measurement errors, these are different theories, and for the moment we have no way of telling which is right and which is wrong. All of these values are equally probable . . .

Physicists normally select, she added, a number of these functions for their cross-section measurements, regarding the variation between different functions (the spread between the curves) as the theoretical systematic error or the uncertainty associated with them. She made it clear that this procedure must be improved by making it possible for physicists to use *all* the structure functions on the market, provided they were extrapolations from recent data, so they could calculate their uncertainties from the complete set (the program for this became available in 1991; see Plothow-Besch 1990). The point was to enlarge the basis for the uncertainty calculation by taking into account all functions (theories, interpretations) physicists had imagined to this point, and to update the basis with every new interpretation. The interesting point for us is that these practices are an attempt to gather up the dissension in a field with respect to a particular issue and to transform it into a measure of (liminal) knowledge.

To scientists in other fields, the procedure of turning variations between answers into a precise measure of current knowledge limitations is quite stunning. Would sociologists care to consider the variability between different theories on a subject as a source for making a calculation of their theoretical error? Different theories in sociology—or in molecular biology—give rise to scientific arguments, and to the formation of different groupings of scientists divided along their theoretical preferences, but never to error calculations. Would it make sense in these fields to require that the dispersion of different theories should somehow be ascertained so that we would know, if not what is right, then at least how far we might go wrong? Of course, sociologists and biologists do not make primarily quantitative predictions. But this difference is hardly enough to account for the disinclination to exploit liminal phenomena in these fields.

I can only add two further illustrations of the turn toward liminal knowledge in HEP experiments, one concerning refinements between different analyses, the other concerning the kind of analysis that is routinely produced. Refinements between an analysis and a later one—done, for example, after more data have been accumulated in an experiment—frequently involve changes in error and uncertainty calculations, such that a previously large error may be estimated more precisely and become a correction accompanied by a smaller error. Thus refinements bring about shifts in the weight and distribution of liminal items rather than their elimination. As a physicist searching for SUSY (supersymmetric) particles in UA2 put it:

> Some of the things which we just put as large uncertainties we've tried to make more precise estimates of the effects and then, correct for it, and then assign a smaller uncertainty. Essentially, that has been the sense of, besides the increased statistics, of our efforts to improve the precision of the mass measurement.

Furthermore, greater precision with regard to uncertainties in an improved analysis may mean that one identifies *more* of them. In the analysis of the W mass, seven corrections and uncertainties were listed in the original published paper (Alitti et al. 1990). The improved analysis, however, listed ten uncertainties: "Some subtle effects not considered previously are now taken into account," as the presenter of the work at a collaboration meeting said. When I asked participants about this they said "it makes them uncomfortable" to see such a long list of errors. Nonetheless, an improvement in knowledge might just as well be an imaginative extension of the universe of errors and obstacles to knowledge as it might be an extension of positive knowledge.

The type of results routinely produced in the respective experiments, my final point in this section, illustrates a similar epistemic strategy. I am referring to "limit analyses," which identify the boundaries of a region within which a certain physical process can be said to be unlikely. Limit analyses offer ways out of the problem of negative results. If the top that one searches for in the data is not there, it is at least possible to say "up to a mass of 64, or 70 GeV for which we have searched the terrain the top is unlikely to occur." Limit analyses usually produce limits on the number of events. The number of events reflects back almost immediately on the mass.[8] "So if you look for something and you don't see it (in your data) then you find out at which mass would you start to produce large enough numbers of these things so that you *should* have seen them," said a physicist looking for squarks as a function of squark mass. The limit indicates the boundary beyond which this large enough number of particles should have occurred. From the limit, one concludes that the particle one is seeking cannot be lighter (have less mass) than the mass indicated by this boundary. In the search for supersymmetric particles, for example, no events were seen in the data sample. The mass limit was determined by generating an expected signal and seeing how much one could vary the mass of the supersymmetric particles while remaining compatible with the zero events seen in the data.

Limits are perhaps the most frequently produced results of experiments. Even in experiments designed to produce precision mass measurements of known particles, such as the LEP experiments, limits may be the more frequent output; LEP is said to produce "a stream of papers where they put limits on all sorts of things." The point of interest here is that limit analyses are yet another way to mobilize negative knowledge and turn it into a vehicle for positive knowing. The limits experiments produce are the thresholds from which new experiments start their searches.[9]

3.6 Moving in a Closed Universe: Unfolding, Framing, and Convoluting

In this last section of the chapter, I want to bring into focus some of physicists' ethnomethods of moving in an internally referential system and of articulating such a system. I shall use simple examples, limiting myself to the practices of unfolding, framing, and convoluting. By *unfolding* I mean the continuing unraveling of the features of physical and technical objects, of their details, composition, hidden sequences, and behavioral implications, through the reflexive redeployment of the approach to the data points generated. Let me illustrate with an anecdote. In 1989, the head of online operations was worried about the major online computer in the experiment, the device that wrote the incoming data to tape. The computer was old. Would it make it through the next data run or should it be replaced? What the physicist wanted was a curve that unfolded the deterioration of the device:

> I tried to get some data out of Digital, the firm making these computers, by asking them, since it's an old computer of the kind of which they built (a) 100 if they could make a statistical analysis and see what is the uptime ((the percentage of time the computer is running)) of the computer after 1 year, after 2 years, after 10 years, after 15 years.

He imagined a graph that would give him the probability of the computer's uptime as a function of its age. Suppose in this graph the probability of uptime remains at 100 percent during the first years and then decreases by 10 percent each year during the middle age of the instrument before dropping off more sharply and finally flattening out in a tail. Would that curve make it any clearer when one should get rid of the device? No, since one would still have to decide on the level of uptime that was acceptable. But in many other ways it should. First, a steady decrease of performance by 10 percent per year up to a certain age is itself important information that might prompt one to make the cut at the point where the curve begins to drop off more sharply. Second, the curve can be used to make further calculations, for example of expected data losses at specific levels of downtime, of subsequent error increases, and of reductions in the probability of finding the result one is looking for. Third, these probabilities in turn provide starting points and baselines for the exploration of additional considerations, such as the expense of a new computer versus the expense of repair costs and the training time involved in the switch. And so on. Thus, unfolding a problem by articulating it in a detailed curve is a machine for generating further unfoldings, for internally articulating the information through redeploying the procedure and adding further loops. One can also say that the ethnomethod of unfolding "unsticks" a stuck decision system by transforming it into a knowledge system (see also Knorr Cetina 1995).

If the object is not the kind whose characteristics one can unfold, then variation is used to achieve a similar effect. This can be illustrated by a typical figure resulting from a trigger study performed in an effort to find a more efficient top trigger algorithm for use in the 1989 collider run (see Figure 3.3). The plot gives a vivid impression of how variation unfolds variables, in this case top trigger rates for different missing momentum cuts as a function of jet transverse energy thresholds (for the details, see Incandela 1989).

The second epistemic strategy I want to look at, *framing,* is to consider objects or pieces of information in the light of other such components, which serve to check, control, extend, or compensate the former. Through framing, different components of an experiment or of the field are related to one another. The relationship may be confrontational (the components may be played one against the other) or complementary (the second object may achieve what the first could not accomplish). Framing is used on all levels of an experiment. For example, detectors are built to verify each other, to act as reference counters in efficiency measurements, to eliminate each other's fake signals, to complete the partial track segments any one of them can produce individually, or to produce track samples to be used as "templates against all other detectors." Besides detectors, different analysis modules (e.g., different fits to data points), different data runs, and whole experiments frame each other. Runs, for example, are constantly produced with some functions switched off so that data produced by other runs may be evaluated, in regard to the

Particle Physics and Negative Knowledge

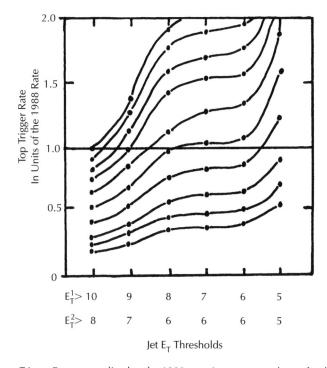

Trigger Rates normalized to the 1988 top trigger rate are shown for different missing P_T cuts as a function of jet E_T thresholds. The E cut for the electromagnetic cluster in the event is 11.5 GeV. (The 1988 top trigger rate was $\approx 7.0\%$ of the combined W^l and Z^0 trigger rates.)

Figure 3.3 Figure resulting from the use of variation in a trigger study. (From J. Incandela, $p\bar{p}$ Note 566, 10 March 1989.)

working of different pieces of the apparatus, the composition and behavior of liminal phenomena such as noise, the underlying event, etc.

One of the most interesting framing strategies is perhaps the institution of "sister experiments"; experiments are set up at the same time in the same laboratory with the purpose of, among other things, comparing each other's results. Typical examples of sister experiments at CERN were UA1 and UA2, the four currently running LEP experiments and the ATLAS and CMS experiments at the LHC. There is more than one reason why sister experiments come about, most importantly perhaps the desire of more physicists to work at a new machine than can comfortably be grouped into a single collaboration. Nonetheless, the way they are organized is similar to other components in the system—as quasi-independent epistemic resources that sustain and control each other. The participants of the sister experiments at CERN often seem to know surprisingly little about the progress of their siblings. There are few occasions for systematic contacts, and participants learn much of what they do know through informal channels. Sister experiments compete in the pursuit of the same or similar goals, but they do not simply replicate each other's results (compare Collins 1975): they work and run in parallel, not at successive points in time, and their design and apparatus differs significantly in crucial respects. UA1, for example, had a magnetic field and a muon detector, whereas UA2 did not. Framing is not based on a principle of similarity in all significant details but on a principle of differences within the limits of similar overall goals. Their partial independence allows sister experiments to be featured as controls. Their differences allow them to compete, to test themselves against each other, and to drift apart in various directions.

Framing also occurs among experiments that succeed each other in time and are located at different places. Its most obvious manifestations are exhibits in experimental papers, which often include comparable distributions from other experiments (see Knorr Cetina 1995). Much like the variations deliberately created to generate bands of uncertainty around possible true values, these distributions create ranges or successive boundaries of experimental values into which the values of new experiments fit. Figure 3.4 gives an example of a multi-experimental display of results. By this framing strategy, physicists convey a more urgent lack of trust of single experiments and measurements than we see in other fields, a disbelief that these experiments can stand on their own as they do elsewhere, supported exclusively by the special linkage they have created between themselves and nature. High energy collider experiments stand first and foremost *in relation to each other,* as these figures imply. The exhibits epitomize a belief in the epistemic relevance of a strategy that joins individual findings through contrast, comparison, and resemblance. The display that includes data from different experiments becomes a display of the state of the field (see also Chapter 7). In a sense, the strategy extends the liminal approach of emphasizing limitations and possible errors and of gaining confidence through this emphasis.

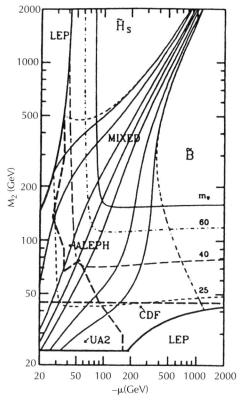

Contours of the LSP mass (short-dashed: 25 GeV, long-dashed: 40 GeV, dot-dashed: 60 GeV, solid: m_W) in the (μ, M_2) plane for tan $\beta=2$. Also shown are the contours (solid) of constant gaugino purity ($N_{11}^2 + N_{12}^2 = p$), with $p = 0.99$ (almost pure gaugino), 0.98, 0.9, 0.5, 0.1, 0.02, and 0.01 (almost pure higgsino), as well as the contours of the almost pure bino $\tilde{B}$ and (anti)symmetric higgsino $\tilde{H}_{A,S}$ (short-dashed), with purity $p = 0.99$, as defined in the text. Regions where $0.01 < N_{11}^2 + N_{12}^2 < 0.99$ are marked as "MIXED." The allowed region is constrained by several experimental data. The results from ALEPH and CDF are preliminary.

Figure 3.4 Published results from one experiment in particle physics (UA2) "framed" by the results of other experiments. (Reprinted from *Physics Letters B*, vol. 262, no. 1, 13 June 1991: Y. Okada, M. Yamaguchi, and T. Yanagida, "Renormalization-Group Analysis on the Higgs Mass in the Softly-Broken Supersymmetric Standard Model," p. 61; copyright 1991, with kind permission from Elsevier Science–NL, Sara Burgerhartstraat 25, 1055 KV Amsterdam, The Netherlands.)

Let me conclude by turning now to what is perhaps a special case of framing—the case where the components are of a very different nature and where the logic of the procedure is based on the conjunction and interaction of these components, or, to use a native concept, on their *convolution.* Perhaps one could say that such intersections between different universes of meaning—between, for example, "Monte Carloed" self-understandings through which theoretical numbers are run and experimental measurements—are a way to push the framing method to its limit, by showing that only the convolution of the different frames can lead to real results. Monte Carlos in general (numerical integration methods for simulating the properties of systems through random walks) play a significant role in the convolution of experimental components, but I cannot examine them here in detail; their manifold uses in HEP experiments require a proper analysis in their own right (for their history, see Galison 1987, 1993; Merz 1998). Suffice it to say that *convolution* is a term used for folding together, in Monte Carlos, mathematical calculations, phenomenological terms describing the "breakup" (fragmentation) of quarks and gluons into jets, simulations of the underlying event, and the modeling of detectors and other components. But it is also a term that describes well the general strategy of mixing together resources and quantities that come from very different origins in an attempt to come to grips with the limitations of specific data or approaches. Structure functions, for example (see Section 3.5), which are often associated with the "theory part" of value calculations, have an experimental portion (data from deep, inelastic lepton nucleon fixed target experiments) and a theoretical portion (the Altarelli-Parisi evolution equations, which make the transition from fixed target to collider experiments), and, as a third component, different fits through which appropriate mathematical functions are fitted to the original data. The fragmentation of quarks and gluons into jets, which is also simulated in these Monte Carlos, has a phenomenological portion—a theoretically motivated but not exactly calculable "model," which is exemplified by the "Field-Feynmann" fragmentation supplemented by a model of soft gluon radiation; and a data component—model parameters like the number of gluons and their angle of radiation are adjusted to calorimeter data until they coincide reasonably well.

Mixtures are also constantly created between data and Monte Carlos. For example, when one cannot play different parts of the detector off against others to measure the tracking efficiency of an algorithm, one can take a real event and "stick in its middle" (superimpose on it) a single Monte Carlo track. The question then asked is whether the algorithm can find the test track that one knows is there. Another example is the analysis of Alpha S briefly described in Section 3.3. Alpha S is determined for a certain momentum transferred between two quarks in an interaction that, in the analysis performed, was set equal to the W mass squared. Through experimentation one could determine a ratio between different W events. The same ratio was generated through Monte Carlos in the above fashion: including the detector model and all the other components that finesse the end result and lead to a determination of systematic errors. Since the ratio is proportional to Alpha S in the Monte Carlo, one ran a great number of these to obtain different values of the ratio as a function of Alpha S. The result was a curve that was then entered in the same plot as the experimental value for the ratio. Where the curve for the expected values of the ratio intersected with the experimental value, the "true" value of Alpha S could be read off the plot.

In the original case, the "convolution" of theoretical functions with detector simulations and other components represents, at least in part, convolutions that are thought to be in the data. All data are seen as mixtures of components—including, besides the signal, the background, the noise, and the underlying event—which are distorted and truncated through detector losses and smearings. "I cannot think of a case where (the data) is not mixed." This is where we come almost full circle, back to the starting point of the meaninglessness of measurement and the presence of antiforces in the experiment. Participants react to these convolutions by matching them with precise determinations of the single components, *and by converting the principle of mixtures, which they find in nature, into an epistemic resource in their own endeavors.* They draw upon the different possibilities of calculating mathematical functions theoretically, of simulating events that are neither easily calculable nor measurable, and of making measurements experimentally; and they bring them together continuously by specifying the results of experiments. They do not shy away from extending data points through theoretical or Monte Carloed predictions, from superimposing one element upon another, or from correcting and revising data through Monte Carloed theories and predictions. The crucial difference this approach has from some other fields is that the *convoluted tangles* thereby created are expedient in creating *experimental outcomes*. They are *not* tests of theories through data, simulations used for purposes other than data processing (as in the planning and design of an experiment), or similar conjunctions of elements before and after the specification of data. Convolutions of experimental data with Monte Carlos and theory precede the framing strategy outlined earlier. But they are also an extension of it, as when they occur in the interplays created between the respective elements. They are a stratagem in generating experimental outcomes in a world that refers back upon itself and seeks recourse in manipulating its own components.

4

Molecular Biology and Blind Variation

4.1 An Object-Oriented Epistemics

In the last chapter, I tried to convey the sense in which the experimental strategies of high energy physics are marked by a loss of the empirical; in this chapter, I want to move on to consider the contrasting case of molecular biology, which, I shall maintain, constitutes itself as a system open to natural and quasi-natural objects. In experimental HEP, experience appears to provide no more than an occasional touchstone that hurls the system back upon itself, and "success" may well depend on how well—and how intricately—the system interacts with itself. Molecular biological practices, on the other hand, in the areas studied (see Section 1.6), appear to rely on maximizing contact with the empirical world. In HEP experiments, natural and quasi-natural objects are admitted to the experiment only rarely, while in molecular biology they are sought out and encountered on a day-to-day basis. Data in experimental high energy physics are firmly embedded in a network of anticipation, simulation, and recalculation, while in molecular biology they stand on their own, subject only to questions of adequacy and interpretation. In HEP experiments, it is not the phenomena themselves which are at issue, but rather their reflection in the light of the internal megamachinery that envelops and tracks down physical occurrences. In the molecular biology laboratories studied, in contrast, the phenomena assert themselves as independent beings and inscribe themselves in scientists' feelings and experiences. In experimental high energy physics epistemic practices are principled on self-analysis of the experiment, internal reconstructions of negative images of the world, and the acquisition of liminal knowledge. In the molecular biology laboratories studied, they are based on interaction with natural objects, processing programs, and the acquisition of experiential knowledge. Experimental high energy physics can be characterized by a negative, self-referential epistemics built around sign systems. In molecular biology laboratories, on the other hand, the epistemic culture is orientated toward positive knowledge built from the manipulation of objects in an experiential regime that continuously turns away from sign processes.

Consider for a moment sign processes in the two sciences. According to a general theory of semiotics, the world is a world of signs. Peirce thought he could identify the common denominator for the logic of the universe, the logic of life, and the logic of language in semiotic relations (Krampen et al. 1987: 182). In physics, this idea made sense; we have seen how experimental work starts from signs of objects and is based upon representational technologies. In molecular biology, too, sign systems play a role. The genetic code, for example, is considered by some semioticians as the most fundamental of all semiotic networks. On an experimental level, much of what is considered "data" has the character of signs—they are technically generated indicators pointing to an underlying reality of molecular processes and events. Despite the presence of such signs at this and other occasions, however, the molecular biology laboratories studied appeared far from being sign-determined environments.

Different cultural systems of behavior, as we know, construe the world differently. If they involve sign processes, as they invariably do, the question is nonetheless on what, figuratively speaking, do they place their bets and stake their money—on signs or not on signs. They may choose to process signs in ways that upgrade their impact and make the most of their potential, or in ways that downgrade their role and minimize interaction with them. In short, they may construct their world in terms of sign processes, or continuously construct it away from such processes. Molecular biology practice, in the laboratories studied, shows the latter tendency. It shows a preference for experiential knowledge acquired through mechanisms that reduce representations and *turn away from* sign-mediated experience.

Three aspects of this preference stand out in observations of experimental work. One is the construction of the evidential domain as a world of small *objects* present in the laboratory and addressed through a pastoral mode of care-taking, on the one hand, and through processing programs that transform objects, on the other. The second aspect is the *"blind" variation–"natural" selection* strategy deployed in molecular biology when problems arise (see also Campbell 1990). Natural and quasi-natural objects are not only present in the lab on a continuous basis, they also provide a selection environment for experimental strategies when procedures do not work. The third aspect that stands out is the enhancement of objects and experience in what one might call an *experiential register*—a register that brings to attention scientists' sensory way of working and their strategies of preserving invisible phenomenal realities and embodied experience. Before examining these characteristics, we will briefly consider the human genome project, to discuss, through the perspective of molecular biologists, its possible influence on the experiential strategies and object-oriented concerns just described.

4.2 The Small-Science Style of Molecular Biology and the Genome Project

Molecular biology will be characterized in the rest of this chapter as a benchwork science conducted in small laboratories. The question this may raise with some readers is whether the small-science style of molecular biology has not been changed by the human genome project. Has the genome project brought molecular biology closer to the big-science ways of working examined in the last chapter? The suggestion here is that it has not, or at least not yet—partly because the genome project is itself far from being a centralized research effort comparable to experimental HEP.

The genome project's goal is the mapping and sequencing of the human genome (see Watson 1990; Kevles and Hood 1992; Hilgartner 1995). In terms of the magnitude of this task, the time involved (projected for 15 years) and the financial investment ($88 million in 1990 in the United States, slated to increase significantly over time), the genome project is molecular biology's first big-science project. Accordingly, genome proponents and enthusiasts sometimes envision that the project will bring about a "paradigm shift" in molecular biology (Gilbert 1992). They foretell a shift from small-scale experimental benchwork to a "theoretical" science that manipulates masses of sequence data rather than biological samples and reagents. They also foresee a redistribution of work from small labs to large "centers" equipped for this kind of processing and for technology development. In response, some critics of the genome project have expressed concern over the implied bureaucratization of research and the "production quota" mentality underlying certain genome concepts (Hilgartner 1990, 1995; compare also Crawford 1991).

Neither the proponents' "vision" nor the critics' fears were quite shared by the molecular biologists studied. To them, the genome project counted as a "politically aggrandized" special case. The knowledgeable members of the laboratories thought the genome project's work not particularly exciting, since knowing the genetic maps would not provide direct answers to any of today's burning questions. Nor did they think the work would yield more than systematically organized data banks. The concrete significance of these data would have to be investigated step by step in regular bench laboratories. The genome initiative itself is, to a significant degree, also conducted in such labs. As Kevles and Hood have pointed out, the genome initiative may be "Big Science" in terms of financing, but institutionally it remains a dispersed international effort. It is not comparable to the large collider experiments studied in this book or to other big-science projects, like the space station. In a recent comparison of such research, the authors (1992: 306ff.) propose that the genome project falls into the category of the "coordinated encouragement of local initiative by pluralist, decentralized efforts." Such efforts may be federally financed out of a concern for biomedical issues, perhaps, but they are not conducted, as HEP experiments are today, in worldwide centralized facilities through large transnational collaborations. In 1991, the U.S. National Institutes of Health funded some 175 different genome projects (!), at just slightly more than the average NIH grant size. These projects were conducted by "small groups" of scientists scattered across the United States in normal-sized labs. NIH also established eight "centers" committed to the development of new technologies and informatics for biology, as well as to large-scale physical mapping. But the size of these centers, in Kevles and Hood's terms, is "modest," with the largest center budget amounting to no more than $4 million in 1991; in addition, the centers fragment into individual research groups. These authors also point out that several widely used technologies in biological research, such as chromatography and electrophoresis, started out big, expensive, and relatively exclusive but, unlike particle accelerators, they soon became "small, cheap, widely obtainable, and dispersed" (1992: 308).

In sum, the genome project is itself largely conducted through multiple, decentralized, small-scale efforts and is still trying to come to terms with the task of coordinating these efforts. In addition, the initiative is considered a means of supplying dispersed molecular biological researchers with tools and technical information and of relieving them of seemingly boring and tedious tasks such as DNA sequencing. Whether the project will alter biological research beyond the access provided to genome maps and the automation of "accepted" procedures is an open question. Any such changes, however, will not happen quickly, since the genome project itself first must develop the appropriate information technology and instrumentation. As yet, the biologists we spoke with did not see the genome project as a spearhead effort for transforming their field on a grand scale into Big Science or into Theoretical Science. As Hilgartner has commented (1995), "it is thus unclear, as the genome project continues to evolve, what the 'Human Genome Initiative' will end up becoming" (see also Cantor 1990).

For the time being, then, much of molecular biology is still organized largely in terms of benchwork laboratories. Some components of these laboratories (for example, procedures for manipulating clones) are part of standardized "packages" (Fujimura 1987, 1996; see also Jordan and Lynch 1992) and have been automated as commercially available products ("kits")—a process already fully in evidence when we first stepped into the labs studied in 1984 (see also Keating, Limoges, and Cambrosio 1999; Cambrosio and Keating 1992). Perhaps these processes will be enhanced through genome technology in the future. At present, however, such packages—whether industry-provided, self-made, or obtained through the exchange network connecting different labs—simply become components of manual work. Along with the data banks available today, they free researchers from routine tasks and allow them to spend their time exploring "more interesting" goals and ever newer techniques. The benchwork style of molecular biology is apparent even in studies that have focused on other aspects of the field (e.g., Fujimura 1996; Jordan and Lynch 1992; Clarke and Casper 1998; Hilgartner and Brandt-Rauf 1999).

4.3 The Laboratory as a Two-Tier Structure

We can now turn to the peculiarities of the benchwork style of doing science, beginning with a characterization of the laboratories studied, of their material culture, and of object-oriented processing. Imagine the layout of a new, well-equipped laboratory, such as the ones studied at the Center for Molecular Biology in Heidelberg and the Max Planck Institute for Bio-Physical Chemistry in Göttingen, Germany. Such facilities include, besides regular, small-sized rooms where up to four scientists work next to one another at the bench, radioisotope laboratories, cell culture labs, "warm" rooms kept above 30 degrees Celsius, "cool" rooms with freezers, "mouse laboratories," centrifuge rooms, photographic labs, microinjection rooms, halls that are important because they too serve to store and treat objects, and glassrooms for cleaning and sterilizing equipment. All of these (sub)laboratories are built for and around material objects and their special requirements. Radioisotopes are used to trace molecules in cells and organisms, and the purpose of the radioisotope lab is to isolate "hot," radioactive materials from other, less dangerous substances and to avoid the contamination of regular work benches with radioactive nucleotides and waste. The warm room, which includes different sorts of shakers, is where petri dishes and flasks, filled with bacteria in liquid media, gently vibrate. Temperature and humidity is regulated to maintain optimal growth conditions for bacteria. In the cell culture laboratory, specialized "hoods" provide for the sterile manipulation of living cells during growth and replication or differentiation. There are cell incubators, special centrifuges, glass and plastic ware for cell culturing, microscopes for monitoring cells, and refrigerators for keeping media and reagents cool and fresh.

Work in these places is keyed to material objects, and it is organized into a two-tier system: object-oriented work on the laboratory level and on the level of experimental activities. To begin with the first, a significant percentage of work with material objects is done to maintain the laboratory as a well-equipped, well-stocked *repository of tools and resources*.[1] These tools and resources are the capital without which a lab could not maintain its place in the field. Bench scientists devote part of their time to reproducing this capital: they prepare plasmids, solutions, nutrients, etc.; they grow cell lines, order chemicals, keep enzymes in stock, establish libraries of DNA and other cellular molecules, raise and manage mouse colonies. The laboratory is a *toolshop* and a *nursery* on this level, a place where different plant and animal materials are maintained, nourished, and prepared for experimental manipulation. Few of the tools in this workshop are technical instruments of great expense and sophistication, but there are a good number of "little" instruments, like spinners, shakers, micropipettes, dryers, microscopes, and radiation counters. The most widely used technical instruments are often centrifuges and self-made gel electrophoresis apparatuses. To make the latter, glass plates are clamped together, set in glass tanks, filled with a separation gel, fitted with "combs" (to create slots into which samples of cellular materials are inserted), and placed under voltage. Many instruments are themselves biological organisms and materials. Examples include the enzymes used to cut DNA into fragments, the plasmids or phages into which DNA is inserted, the bacterial cells in which the plasmids and viruses grow to produce copies of the DNA, and the nucleic acid probes used to localize specific genetic sequences "in situ" in particular types of cells.

The substances and materials prepared and maintained as laboratory objects also provide the *working materials* for various stages of experimental work. This is the second level of activities, distinguished from the first by the massive transformations which it brings to bear on objects. Objects on the level of experimental work are subject to almost any imaginable intrusion and usurpation. They are smashed into fragments, evaporated into gases, dissolved in acids, reduced to extractions, run over columns, mixed with countless other substances, purified, washed, spun round, placed in a centrifuge, inhibited, precipitated, exposed to high voltage, heated, frozen, and reconstituted. Cells are grown on a lawn of bacteria, raised in media, incubated, inoculated, counted, transfected, pipetted, submerged in liquid nitrogen, and frozen away. Animals are raised and fed in cages, infused with solutions, injected with diverse materials, cut open to extract parts and tissues, weighed, cleaned, controlled, superovulated, vasectomized, and mated. They are also subject to being anesthetized, operated on, killed, cut into sections and frozen (see also Lynch 1988a), and their dispensable, "non-hurting" parts, such as tails, are cut off so their genetic makeup may be tested.

Work on this level is sequentially organized in terms of steps and substeps—processing programs summarized as laboratory protocols.[2] Those protocols which have been tried and mastered become part of the laboratory's capital. They are sought after, obtained as favors from other labs, and taken along by scientists who change laboratories. The protocols determine the details of object-oriented processing—which objects to join in chemical or biological reactions, how long to subject them to a treatment, what temperature to use, etc. Protocols specify the many steps, substeps, and sub-substeps of manipulation through which work should proceed. A protocol for the construction of a cDNA library in the possession of an American postdoc who spent part of her time preparing such libraries (authored by Tom St. John, Jon Rosen, and Howard Gershenfeld and issued by the Department of Pathology at the Stanford Medical Center) was 35 typewritten pages long, including several pages listing the materials needed, such as enzymes and primers, substrates and co-factors, chemicals, salts, and solutions, as well as strains of phages and bacteria. Altogether it contained more than a hundred steps, many of which were composed of substeps and sub-substeps.

The many forms of intervention in material objects, and the laboratory protocols summarizing them, illustrate the object-oriented processing taking place in molecular biological laboratories. They should convey a sense of the continuous, daily interactions with material things, of the need to establish close relationships with the materials, and of the experience bench scientists can gain from them. The object-centered interactive quality of molecular biological practice is most apparent, perhaps, when procedures are new to participants and protocols are unavailable or do not work, as is frequently the case. One such procedure in the labs observed was the technique of microinjection, needed to create the transgenic animals used in the late 1980s to investigate the function of genes. Germ cells (blastocysts) are surgically removed from a live mouse that has been stimulated to superovulate. The cells are then injected with genetic materials, to alter the genetic program of the animal, and are then re-implanted into another mouse for embryonic development (compare also Lynch 1988a).

Since mice are living organisms, different individuals react differently to such treatments. An anesthetized mouse may not be completely numb and may start to twitch, thrash, or struggle to escape from under the microscope where the operation is performed. The scientist, turned surgeon, may also find that the flesh into which s/he tries to cut an opening resists the attempt, the organs s/he is trying to identify move and cannot be found in the expected spot, the wound tears and is difficult to stitch together, or the mouse does not recover adequately from the procedure. At one point, we observed a German student, embarking on his doctorate, make his first attempt to learn the procedure. He wanted to remove blastocysts from two mice and reimplant them in a third, without in-between microinjection. The first difficulty was killing the animal. The mouse, whose neck must be broken in a quick tail-up, neck-down movement, kept twitching and escaping from the top of the cage. With the second mouse too, this step took far too long. After both mice were killed the scientist opened the first, took out the intestines, and found that "our mice are too fat." He struggled with the fat for a while and finally found and removed the uterus with two oviducts. He flushed the oviduct with a syringe attached to a hypodermic needle to recover the blastocysts. He searched for the blastocysts under the microscope, but found none. The second mouse evoked the same complaints about fat; in addition, it appeared to be "pregnant too." When the scientist tried to flush the oviducts, the fluid built up inside and blew up the ducts without coming out: "must be stuck together." The scientist then cut off the ends of the oviducts and released the fluid. But when he examined the result for the blastocysts he found none: "perhaps what I saw before was fat." He flushed again and sighed when again he found nothing. He ran out of the room to find the mouse expert, who had, however, gone home by that time (it was 8:45 P.M.). It then occurred to him to take the dish to a microscope in the cell culture lab that had a different phase contrast. Unlucky again, he took the material back to the microinjection room: "perhaps I haven't flushed them out correctly." He started to suck out the fluid with a little capillary tube and found "ahh, now I am lucky, there are two (blastocysts)." He recovered seven blastocysts with this method, at which point he re-examined the first mouse and also found some.

Meanwhile, a third mouse, who was to be reimplanted with the blastocysts, bounced and performed somersaults on the ceiling of her cage. The scientist gave her a shot of anesthetic and then "collected" (sucked up into a capillary tube), transferred, and counted his blastocysts: "didn't I have eight (with the second mouse)?" We, the observers who could do nothing else, had kept close count of the blastocysts and told him "you had seven." The numbed mouse got another shot and was transferred to the operating table. The scientist realized he had forgotten the tampons (used to clean wounds) and made one out of paper towel. Then he cut a hole in the body, dabbed the wound with the tampon, continued the incision and—let the mouse go: "now I forgot the clips (to clip the wound together after reimplantation)!" White-faced and angry with himself, he ran out of the room to find either clips or the key to a downstairs room where surgeries were often performed. He found neither—the mouse expert had taken the key home, as usual: "shouldn't do these things upstairs." "Especially not in the cell culture lab," another doctoral student still working at this hour added. This researcher had seen him use the microscope there and was concerned about contamination. The lack of clips ended this day's practice session. The mouse who could not be stitched together was killed. Reimplantation was to be tried again on another mouse the next day.

Laboratory protocols provide scripts for going about whole courses of events, but the scripts must be negotiated in practice with obdurate materials and living things. They may include a producer's directions in the form of warnings, rationales for particular moves, and preferences (see Figure 4.1), but these too require practical interpretation and enactment (see also Lynch 1985; Pickering 1991, 1995). The point I want to draw attention to is how the various protocols enhance empirical experience by ensuring a continuous stream of interactions with objects.[3]

4.4 "Blind" Variation and Natural Selection

Having to endure varying degrees of failure, for any number of reasons, is generally the rule in experimental work. There are many ways in which

COLLECTING BLASTOCYSTS

Blastocysts can be flushed from the uterus between 3.5 and 4.5 days p.c.

PROCEDURE

1. To remove the uterus at this stage, grasp it with forceps just above the cervix (located behind the bladder) (A) and cut across with fine scissors (B). Pull the uterus upward to stretch the mesometrium and trim this membrane away close to the wall of the uterine horns (C). Then cut the uterus below the junction with the oviduct. The utero-tubal junction acts as a valve, and if the cut is made across the oviduct rather than the uterus, flushing will be very difficult.
2. Place the uterus into M2 and flush both horns with about 0.2 ml of medium using a 25-gauge needle and a 1- or 2-ml syringe (D). This can be done without using a dissecting microscope.

The yield of blastocysts is very low after they have hatched from the zona and have attached to the uterus. The yield can sometimes be increased by leaving the utero-tubal junction intact, blowing up the uterine horns by injecting medium, and then cutting the junction to release the fluid.

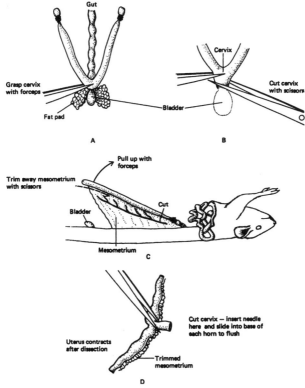

Dissection for flushing embryos from the uterus. The uterus is removed by cutting across the cervix (A and B) and the membrane (mesometrium) holding the uterus to the body wall (C). Be sure to cut the uterus below the junction with the oviduct (C). Place the uterus in a small volume of medium, and flush out each horn with about 0.2 ml of medium (D).

Figure 4.1 Instructions for collecting blastocysts in mice. (From B. Hogan, F. Costantini, and E. Lacy, *Manipulating the Mouse Embryo: A Laboratory Manual* [Cold Spring Harbor, NY: Cold Spring Harbor Laboratory Press, 1986]. Reprinted with permission.)

things "do not work," but the most typical is perhaps that the results are ambiguous and cannot be easily interpreted. This problem has to do with the inscription devices used in molecular biology. Consider an example from attempts to characterize "new" mouse genes, such as the gene called *m31* (later *Hox3.1*) reported in the *EMBO Journal* (vol. 5 (9), pp. 2209–2215) in 1986. The main goal of this work was to characterize the transcription products of the gene, their expression over time, in specific tissues. One of the first steps in identifying these products is to choose a suitable "probe." A probe is a radioactively labeled fragment of single-stranded DNA or cDNA that can be used to pick out and thereby identify complementary fragments of RNA (or DNA), through a process called hybridization; since the DNA is normally double-stranded, it will form double strands with the fragments being investigated, provided they are complementary. In this example the targets were homeobox-carrying genes, however, containing a few genes that are similar, and their transcription products have an extraordinary resemblance. As a consequence, the DNA probes may identify not one particular transcript but a number of similar RNA molecules. These may be similar transcripts derived from the same gene or transcripts from different genes that resemble each other sufficiently. In other words, the results cannot be unequivocally attributed to a specific transcript. In the work observed, an additional signal appeared above the expected signal for the cell line investigated in the autoradiography of the hybridization blot. Interpretation problems were also raised by the fact that the bands obtained were quite weak.

How were these and similar problems resolved? When procedures have become established and are common knowledge, they nonetheless continue to raise problems, but their solutions are seen as self-evident. One example in the labs was the use of restriction nuclease to cut DNA into series of fragments and map the location of the restriction sites. When the resulting pictures deviated from expectations, they did so in self-evident ways. For example, missing or additional signals, as well as "smearing" between signals, were seen as mistakes in the procedure: not enough enzyme, inactive enzyme, too short a reaction time, mixup of enzymes. Bands that were not well separated or occurred at too great a distance from each other indicated that the gel had been run for too short or too long a period of time; empty slots meant omissions in pipetting, black photographs mistakes in film development, and missing marker bands problems with the marker used. "Wrong" patterns of bands were blamed on the usage of the "wrong" DNA fragment or on impurities in the material. Explanations for the problem, in cases such as these, could be determined immediately from the patterns of black and white bands that the picture represented.

The RNA analysis described above was not an established procedure. It posed open problems, and in addressing these problems, in the labs observed, *blind variation* and *natural selection* came to bear. What is the meaning of the analogy? In evolutionary biology, mutations introduce variations in the genetic material that can be passed on to descendant molecules or organisms. Which mutations are beneficial—and hence survive—is determined by natural selection: the differential advantage bestowed on those organisms whose qualities, introduced by variation, are more effective in a given environment. Mutations are "blind" in the sense that they are random errors, not "adjustments" pre-adapted to the environmental conditions which they encounter.

If there is a general strategy molecular biologists adopt in the face of open problems, it is a strategy of blind variation combined with a reliance on natural selection. They vary the procedure that produced the problem, and let something like its fitness—its success in yielding effective results—decide the fate of the experimental reaction. Variation is "blind" in a very precise sense: it is *not* based on the kind of scientific investigation and understanding of the problem that was so popular among high energy physicists. Confronted with a malfunctioning reaction, a problem of interpretation (as in the case of the RNA analysis described above), or a string of methods that do not seem to work, molecular biologists will not embark, as physicists will, on an investigative journey whose sole purpose it is to understand the problem. Instead, they will try several variations in the belief that these will result in workable evidence. Note that in physics understandings and self-convictions are based upon demonstrable data points detailing the crucial aspects of the difficulty. Nothing of the sort is necessary or desired in molecular biology.

In the RNA analysis with which we started, the bands obtained were hardly noticeable, and there was an unexplained additional band above the signal. Both results posed questions of interpretation and thus characterized RNA analysis as a nonestablished method. Scientists discussed and tried out a number of variations, which included:

longer exposure time to increase the strength of the bands

switching from the "Genescreen" filter material to a different filter batch (the filter is used in the hybridization reaction)

changing differentiation times for the F9 cells used (the number of days cells are allowed to differentiate before they are harvested)

the inclusion of embryonic RNA extracted at other time points

the use of RNA extracts from extra-embryonic and embryonic tissues

the use of additional RNA extracts from differentiated and undifferentiated P19 cells

the use of a shortened DNA probe (to reduce the possibility that similar sequences were picked up from other homeotic genes)

From these variations, participants gained results that passed the critics and could be published. They also acquired experience in doing the analysis and thus moved it one step closer to achieving "established" status in the lab. But they did not, in the process, do experiments to investigate why the problems arose or to explain obscure data.

Recall that physicists also turn to variation for certain purposes. But in physics, variation is a strategy employed in the service of learning the effect of a variable, such as the missing transverse momentum, on trigger rates or of different structure functions on the systematic error. It involves studying the impact of one factor upon another in systematic ways, through changing by equal amounts energy levels, mass bins, luminosity ranges, and so on. In molecular biology, on the other hand, variation is blind insofar as understanding the effect of a variable is concerned; and although it is by no means chaotic, it is also not systematic in the physicists' step-by-step, equal-change sense. Moreover, variations rarely involve just one variable, as the above list indicates. Finally, the whole strategy is not, as in physics, one way of unfolding the details of a problem, and in that sense it is not just one method among others. Rather, it is the master strategy of dealing with experimental problems, equivalent to the master strategy in physics of self-analysis and self-understanding.

Let us dwell for a moment on this equivalence. It is important to realize that molecular biology's preference for blind variation and natural selection by no means implies that this method is any less effective than physics' care of the self and negative epistemics. In fact, molecular biology, by all standards, has been very successful in the last 20–30 years, and seems bent on remaining successful in the foreseeable future. Moreover, from the perspective of molecular biologists, it is not at all clear that a strategy like the one adopted by experimental high energy physicists would work. Molecular biologists will argue that their attempt to "understand" a living organism, of which little is known, quickly reaches its limits. Since the machinery used in molecular biology is largely the life machinery of the cell and of organism reproduction, attempts at "self"-understanding the tools and components of the experiment are jeopardized by the same limitations as investigations of the subject matter of molecular biology. Furthermore, they will argue that liminal knowledge, so useful in physics to correct for errors and systematic problems, may be less useful when one is presented with an intervening technology. If an inadequately construed vector (plasmids enlisted to transport and replicate DNA) generates the wrong sequence, the result cannot be subtracted out of the experiment through remedial calculations—the vector has to be remade until it performs. Biochemical reactions, as used in experiments, are not formulated mathematically and, hence, cannot be calculated in the way the reactions in a detector can be computed. Thus, for molecular biology to behave like experimental HEP, many components of its system would have to change in synchrony with other components. In other words, it would involve a change of the whole epistemic culture. The argument is not that this is impossible. It is just that any central component of a system is often sustained by other components—rendered effective by them and works in conjunction with them. Blind variation is a successful strategy in molecular biology, with its vast amount of small objects, its intervening technologies, and its many ways of placing a premium upon empirical reality while de-emphasizing representations.

4.5 The Experiential Register

Blind variation works in combination with empirical selection by success. It is a method of relegating judgments about an experimental strategy to the empirical world; if the results push through the barriers created by obdurate materials, if they work, they can be published. Laying oneself open to selection by success of experimental strategies is one way of enhancing empirical reality in molecular biological work. Other ways include bringing in the body of the scientist as a (black-boxed) information processing tool, rendering natural courses of action present wherever possible, or preserving the scenic qualities of phenomenal events through specific forms of communication. The experiential register sums up these features; I begin with the premium molecular biologists placed on the sensory body as a tool in accomplishing experimental work.

4.5.1 THE BLACK-BOXED BODY OF THE SCIENTIST

According to historians (Kutschmann 1986), the scientist's body is no longer a relevant tool in the conduct of research. While the fact that scientists have a body may be granted to be a precondition for doing experiments (Merleau-Ponty 1962), few believe that this body still plays a role as an instrument of inquiry (for feminist questions about the body, see Martin 1991, 1992a,b; Schiebinger 1993). Two factors aided in the "disembodiment" of science. One is the inclusion, into research, of technical instruments that outperformed, and replaced, sensory bodily functions. The other is the derogatory attitude important scientists developed toward the sensory body. For Galileo, Bacon, and seventeenth-century experimentalists, who promoted the *nuova scienzia,* it was wrong to believe that our senses were the measure of all things. As Kutschmann has shown, Galileo himself "never tired" of denouncing the senses for their ability to deceive and to introduce errors (1986: 156, 168ff.). He demonstrated their need for assistance and recommended the "sublime sense above the ordinary and the natural," the telescope. Galileo's arguments were self-serving—the inclusion of technical instruments and the distrust of the body were not as independent as they seem—but his attitude won out. More and more technical instruments were introduced into the empirical sciences, and we believe today that our senses have severe limitations.

Yet in the laboratories observed, there were several ways in which bodily presence and activities were essential. By the scientist's body I mean the body without the mind. If the mind were included, hardly anyone would deny the presence of the body. The *body,* as I use the term, refers to bodily functions and perhaps the hard wiring of intelligence, but not conscious thinking. What does this body do? Why is it still important? How does it reduce the intermediary role of signs and symbols? The body is and usually functions as one piece. Nonetheless, I want to distinguish for a moment between the acting body, the sensory body, and the experienced body.

The *sensory body* refers to the use of sensory organs as instruments of inquiry. It circumscribes the most apparent involvement of the body in science: the role the promoters of the *nuova scienzia* campaigned against. Sense organs are organs that perceive and observe, listen and hear, and smell and taste. If anything is indeed irrelevant to the conduct of research in molecular biology, it is the sensory body *as a primary research tool.* This qualification is important, given that the senses, especially vision, are crucial as silently presupposed support mechanisms in every other respect. However, the intervening technology of benchwork in molecular biology implies a shift toward the manual or instrumental manipulation of objects and away from the kind of naturalistic *observation* of events that Galileo and others belittled. Molecular biologists do not spend long hours watching real-time objects in their natural environment, as ethologists do. Nor are they required to differentiate noises that emanate from an object, as were the early users of the stethoscope described in Chapter 2. Their work is also not, in a crucial way, based on a sense of smell or taste. All of these senses are involved, however, in secondary ways. As an example, consider vision. Being able to see is, of course, a prerequisite for laboratory work. But there are also endless occasions when seeing becomes instrumental in checking and determining the status of experimental processes. Biochemical reactions, cell differentiations, "plaque" formations (holes in a lawn of bacteria that indicate the presence of phages), material absorption by a filter, gel runs, blots on photographic paper—all are processes that develop over time. Materials need to be *visually inspected* from time to time—for example, by holding a test tube against the light and seeing whether a "pellet" has formed. Inspection requires visual know-how. For example, the size and kind of plaques, whether they appear murky, clear, or speckled, indicates a particular kind of phage.

Furthermore, there is the activity of visually *noticing* what is going on in one's own and other workbenches; an activity without which none of the visual scripts and replays described in the next section would be possible. This noticing results in subconscious memories of situations.

The sensory body can also come into the picture in a holistic way. The best illustration of this comes not from molecular biology but from transsexual research (Hirschauer 1991, 1993). Transsexuals who desire a sex-change operation must, for a period of about a year, see a therapist to be diagnosed as a transsexual. During the encounters, the therapist (in the cases studied, a man) employs his sensory reactions to assess the "real" gender of the transsexual: does the therapist get the "sense" that the person is a man or a woman? Does he "feel" a gender barrier between himself and the patient? Does he "see" the patient as a man or a woman and feel the need to treat him or her accordingly? Does he "experience" the transsexual as a person of a certain gender or does the transsexual remain "sponge-like," without contours? Does he have the "urgent feeling" that with this transsexual, "the penis must go and a vagina be provided"? With transsexual research, the rudimentary vocabulary of "sensing" someone to be of a certain gender illustrates the holistic involvement of our sensory equipment in scientific (and therapeutic) judgments.

In the molecular biology laboratories studied, there was no equivalent vocabulary, but a scientist's sensory skills, in the holistic sense, were continuously required. They were implied when some participants were said to have a "golden touch" or to be "excellent experimentalists." When students were recruited into the laboratory, older members watched for these qualities and selected students accordingly. Conflicts arose when someone, highly recommended by an outside scientist, turned out to be "hopeless in the lab" and "incapable of getting an experiment to run." In one conspicuous case, a French postdoctoral researcher, well versed in the relevant theory, proved incapable of performing a gel run in the orderly fashion needed to obtain results. He would mix up the reaction agents and spill the gel; he could not hold the large glass plates properly and would be unable to put the apparatus together without help; he would soil the workbench and himself with poisonous chemicals and radioactive materials, much to the annoyance of other researchers;

and he could be observed sweating, swearing, and throwing things in the lab in fury and desperation when, once again, he failed to perform a routine but skill-demanding task. He did not improve significantly in two years, despite much help from others, and was finally recommended for a teaching position in his home country. The laboratory leader emerged from this experience nursing a grudge against the famous colleague who had recommended the postdoc.

The last example involves not only the sensory body but also to a significant degree the *acting body*. Sensory performance and action go together, especially when, as in molecular biology, almost all experimental work is *manual work*. The acting body is perhaps the first and most original of all automats. It is an information-processing machinery that learns and works without conscious reflection or codified instructions. The simplest illustration of someone using his or her body as an information-processing tool is a person insisting on meeting a phenomenon face-to-face in order to understand its properties and procedural implications. For example, the best-known heart transplant surgeon in Germany insisted just a few years ago on assisting in the removal of the donor's heart; this required great organizational skill (transportation had to be arranged between university hospitals—often in neighboring countries—including the assistance of helicopters, and so on), and athletic skill was necessary, too (since time was of the essence, some running was involved). Why did he insist? He had to "see and feel" the heart, he said, "to know whether it is really healthy and fits" (Halter 1983). Apparently, neither customary measurements nor his own imagination could supply the relevant information. Nor did he think that an ordinary telephone conversation with the donor's surgeon would solve the problem. Lacking his background and concern, the donor's surgeon might not pick up the relevant clues and might not convey the appropriate impressions. Interestingly, heart bypass surgeons in New England, confronted with greatly varying death rates, have recently taken up visiting other hospitals to observe each other's work.

The important point here is that the person insisting on a face-to-face inspection distrusts his or her mind, in favor of his or her senses, in identifying and processing the relevant information. Many scientists feel it is impossible to try to reason through the problem or to pick up the important clues from oral or written descriptions. In order to know what to think, one has to place oneself in the situation. The body is trusted to pick up and process what the mind cannot anticipate. Those who feel this way respond to the Cartesian notion of the separation between body and mind by giving priority to the body.

In the molecular biology laboratories studied, a similar attitude exists. Given that experimental work is skilled *manual* labor, it requires the involvement of the hands and the senses. But the body is also more than simply what carries out an action. It is called upon as an information-processing machine in research. A rudimentary measurement theory features the body as an epistemological warrant for truth. For example, junior scientists are asked by their advisors to "see (the relevant things) for themselves" and to "do things themselves." But senior scientists too will frequently insist on seeing or doing things themselves rather than delegate tasks to technical assistants. This preference is warranted not only by the belief that doing the procedures oneself will increase the chances that they will work, but also by the idea that only through personal experience does one know the real meaning (the strengths, the weaknesses, the implications) of the results obtained. To have performed the relevant tasks of an inquiry oneself—or at least to have seen them done—is the capital on which trust in the results is based. Results not seen directly or not produced through embodied action cannot be properly evaluated and are prone to misinterpretation. In the following excerpt from a conversation, a molecular biologist who had been with the laboratory for several years complained that the head of the lab blurted out to the world results that he had not witnessed in person:

> () If things are as he thinks they are, then ((laughs)) the experiment may have worked out as poorly as you like (). You can't stop him, right? () He is running, he's dashing all over Europe with the wrong data, right? And nobody trusts (). And this will break his neck at some point (). And that's why I am afraid that this is going to happen to him. Right? *Because he doesn't do the experiments himself.* But I have seen this several times when he ((blurted out)) things which were fishy, where, you know, *where you hadn't been there yourself* and saw how it was.

He was absent and telling these things, . . . then he always calls the U.S., and then the whole world knows! [Emphasis added.]

Complaints, admonitions, advice, atrocity stories, like the above, telling how one could "break one's neck" by announcing a result when the relevant work was not performed or witnessed in person—these are indicators of the role of the body. Apart from this need to "witness," the body is a silent instrument. The measurement theory of the body provides for no systematic description of sensory and bodily behaviors, no written instructions as to the appropriate bodily reactions in specific experimental situations, and no behavioral rules to be followed (beyond the general instruction to do things oneself). The scientist's body as an information-processing tool is a black-boxed instrument. The absence of discourse concerning embodied behavior corresponds to the use of embodied information processing as a *substitute* for conscious reflection and communication. The acting body works best when it is a silent part of the empirical machinery of research.

The body may also be described as a black box when it comes to the experiences it incorporates. As a result of using the sensory body and the acting body there results the *experienced body,* which calls attention to the temporal and biographical dimension of embodied work. Embodied processing leads to a corporeal memory, a bodily archive of manual and instrumental knowledge that is not written down and only clumsily expressed. It remains inscribed in the body of the scientist and tends to be lost when the scientist leaves the laboratory. In the field of artificial intelligence, computer scientists tend to refuse to try and understand another programmer's software products; since the key to these products is embodied in the software's producer, "*un*black-boxing" this knowledge appears more difficult than replacing it with new knowledge. The term we usually apply to the body as a competent information processor in expert settings is *tacit knowledge* (see also Dreyfus and Dreyfus 1986; Collins 1990); but this term is derived from the model of a thinking knower and is applied only to the person's unarticulated knowledge. What needs to be stressed with regard to molecular biology is that scientists act like ensembles of sense and memory organs and manipulation routines onto which intelligence has been inscribed; they tend to treat themselves more like intelligent materials than silent thinking machines (see also Section 9.1).

4.5.2 DECODING SIGNS BY PRESERVING AND "APPRESENTING" PHENOMENA

The body as a silent archive of experience, competence, sensory information processing—all are aspects of enhancing embodied experience in experimental work. All eliminate language, work without codification, and do without signs. Signs, however, cannot be eliminated completely from experimental work. Like any other science, molecular biology draws from the power of signs to represent phenomenal occurrences. Autoradiographs have been described earlier as the most widely used method for representing the ingredients of biochemical reactions. Their black bands are signs of the size of cellular molecules or of their fragments and, indirectly, of experimental outcomes. In most cases of original scientific work, these signs cannot be unproblematically "read" and attached to referents; as indicated before, they must be interpreted and decoded. In this respect, working with signs in molecular biology is not different from working with signs in high energy physics. Differences exist, however, in regard to *how* decoding proceeds. In HEP experiments, signs were encircled by more signs, which were used to interpret the former and to specify their range of variation and effects. In molecular biology, signs are made transparent. One looks through the surface of the image at another kind of reality, which hides within it the key to the appearance of the signs.

Consider an analogy. When mouse number 385—the first transgenic mouse obtained in the laboratory, within which a mutation had been successfully induced by microinjection of foreign DNA—died in the night of November 6, 1987, the two workers involved with this research (one a mouse expert, the other a senior researcher in the lab) decided to perform an autopsy. They turned the mouse on its back, spread it across a piece of cardboard, opened the skin with a pair of scissors, "unclothed" the inside by pulling back the fur with surgical forceps, and dissected several organs. They wanted to see the effects transgenicity had produced on the organs, the spine, and other parts where the mutation was likely to have been expressed. Like normal processes of regulation and deregulation of cell differentiation, the processes triggered by the mouse's transmuted gene could not be observed while it was still active.

Decoding autoradiograph bands and other signals in molecular biology is similar to performing an autopsy. Autoradiographs are like objects on a dissecting table, in that they are, figuratively speaking, "opened up"—they are used to cut through the appearance of signs until the observer arrives at phenomenal reality, not visible from the surface of the image. The dissecting instruments, in this case, are not scissors and surgical forceps but, frequently, the talk scientists produce upon inspecting an autoradiograph. Holding up an autoradiograph against the light to view it invariably attracts the attention of other scientists, and a conversation begins. The participants observed rarely argued in these sign-related conversations. *In dissecting the object, they preferred to point.* By referring to the image, they pointed back to the phenomena and the real-time processes of laboratory work (Amann and Knorr Cetina 1988, 1989; see also Lynch 1988b).

Which processes? The step-by-step procedural actions performed in the laboratory and the phenomenal occurrences in biochemical reactions—both were brought together in a *visual script,* a string of images and scenic descriptions, which preserved and instantiated the embodied reality of experimental work. By and large, every verbal exchange attached to a technical image that represents signs could be fully translated into a visual/experiential script. Like a picture screened in a movie theater, the script seemingly reeled off in the mind's eye of the observer, if the appropriate words or sights were available to trigger the response. How does one know about the existence of such a visual script? First, the embodied reality of experimental events was *directly invoked* in talk, as when a participant would give a scenic description of the experience. Second, when asked to explain what they meant, scientists provided visual renderings (schematic drawings) of the phenomena they envisaged. Third, one can, as an experiment, try to understand the respective conversations without the benefit of a string of images and scenic descriptions. I found it impossible, and, conversely, I found the talk radically clarified when it was translated into a visual script.

Consider the example of researchers decoding autoradiograph signs by revisiting the lab, where they specifically invoked experimental events. In the following segment of an image-decoding conversation, one researcher, at the time a postdoc in the lab and a biochemist by training, relates what he saw in the laboratory to what he noticed on the autoradiograph film of a separation gel that he was inspecting with a doctoral student.

> **J:** ((Points to bands on the film.)) Okay, if *this* is 600 . . . and *this* 400, then 300 would be here. ((C. shakes his head.)) No.
> **C:** Well no, the way the gel ran blue was *here* ((points to the film)), and this is 130.

The author of the film recalled his visual impression of where on the gel the blue marker (a blue horizontal band running across the gel) appeared when he stopped the gel run, a position he pointed out on the film and identified to be "130." There were also *scenic descriptions,* which circumscribe technical occurrences in a vocabulary that preserves the visual/experiential quality of embodied laboratory practice. Scenic descriptions point at concrete details in jointly invokable experiences. In the following exchange, C., who was working at the time on the identification of regulatory elements of mouse genes, indicates the amount of RNA used in a gel run in terms of a visually and experientially salient vocabulary of "dishes" and "spinners," instead of providing measured quantities:

> **J:** Why?/ didn't you determine the UD ((amount of GTC DNA))?
> **C:** Naw, I know exactly how much it was.
> **J:** ((Inaudible.))
> **C:** This is from four dishes, this is from two dishes. My/ now, I am doing the spinners, 25 micrograms . . . not much.

Scenic descriptions may be borrowed from everyday life, for example, by referring to the bands on an autoradiograph as "fat," "strong," "tiny," or "weak." The kind of visual clues that are picked up by scenic descriptions are also built into experimental procedures as signals to be noticed by researchers. The blue marker mentioned before was such a purposefully built-in visual signal.

Preserving the phenomenal reality, by invoking its visual residues, is one way of enhancing experience. Another way is to make the invisible phenomenal world visible through graphic renderings of its hidden action. Molecular biologists looked through autoradiograph bands and similar signs to expose the realm of invisible experimental processes that give rise to such signs. These invisible processes are mainly biochemical reactions induced in test tubes and similar utensils. The issues relevant in this respect are often spatial. For example, they may refer to where in a plasmid the start of a transcription must have occurred for the band on the autoradiograph to show a certain length. They also refer to the mix of products one might obtain in a reaction, contrary perhaps to expectations. In the following example, an autoradiograph film, as usually happens, did not turn out ideal. Among other things, most of the marker bands, used to identify the length of the other bands, were missing. But the main trouble was that many more bands than expected had appeared in other lanes. Much as in the case considered before, it was difficult to determine the identity of these bands. For some bands to be plausibly identified as starts, all others had to be accounted for as something else. As they considered various spots on the film, participants in the discussion envisaged that more and more undesirable products had been part of the reaction mixes poured into the gel slots. In other words, they "filled in the test tube" in which a particular biochemical reaction, "S1-digestion," had taken place before the gel was poured.

Ideally, S1-digestion is a clean-up operation: it "clears" the reaction mixture of all but the desired genetic materials before these materials are made visible through the X-ray film exposed on the electrophoresis gel. Strictly speaking, the S1-nuclease that achieves this feat does not eliminate the DNA and RNA strands it attacks, but only cuts them shorter. It thereby prevents these materials from showing up on the autoradiograph, since the image captures only a certain length of DNA and RNA strands. The possibility remains, however, that some fragments are only "partially digested" (left too long), for example, if not enough S1 was used. Also, the S1-nuclease only attacks single strands. Double-stranded fragments—such as "false starts" (longer or shorter than expected hybrids), double-stranded probes, or a DNA and RNA fragment folded back upon itself—are not digested by S1 and may remain in the mixture. Finally, S1-nuclease can attack correct, double-

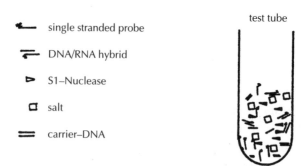

single stranded probe

DNA/RNA hybrid

S1–Nuclease

salt

carrier–DNA

test tube

Figure 4.2 Projected mix of products resulting from S1-digestion.

stranded hybrids if there is a hole in one strand, thereby creating bands that represent the desired start sites but appear to be artifacts, because they are too short. Ideally, the mixture obtained after S1-digestion should have included no more than the products listed in Figure 4.2. After three rounds of image inspection, the test tube finally contained the additional products indicated in Figure 4.3.

"Filling in the test tube" is a process of envisaging the genetic materials and processes behind the trouble spots on an image like an autoradiograph film. Since most of these materials are not visible to the eye, it is a process of glossing over the invisible by employing a language of graphic rendering, also used in the construction of plasmids and genetic recombinants. Ostensibly, participants point again to laboratory occurrences, but they grasp these occurrences by formulating them in a graphic language.

Filling in the test tube, then, is a process that no longer involves direct experience. In the world of molecular and submolecular reactions, signs (a visual language) are needed to stand for the invisible, phenomenal realities. What interests us here is how this reality, through sketches and pictures, is continuously referred to and, to use Schütz's term, *appresented,* how it is rendered present and called upon for assistance in decoding experimental signs. It is this appresentation that qualifies the rendering process as a component of the experiential register. In experimental HEP there are also contexts in which analysts turn to phenomenal, material aspects of technical devices to shed light on the inexplicable

Molecular Biology and Blind Variation

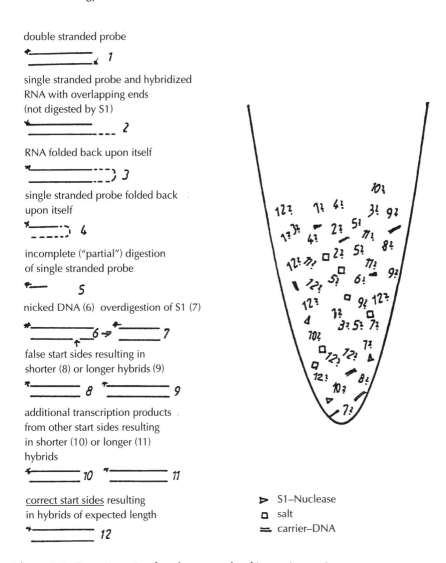

Figure 4.3 Reaction mix after three rounds of image inspection.

"holes" or "spikes" in a data curve—perhaps a wire was broken, the phototube played up, or a crack in the detector gave rise to an unexpected occurrence. These contexts are often for understanding and monitoring instrument performance, however; technical instruments are the *only* materially salient, manually graspable realities in this lab. Furthermore, a variety of additional, sign-based techniques for dealing with problems described in Section 3.6 exist. The signs in this case are not used as a window upon an underlying phenomenal reality that one seeks out as a clue to understanding. Rather, they are data in their own right, data that can be enlisted to solve a problem, used to set it straight, or at least help to determine its systematic error and variation—in the spirit of searching for liminal knowledge.

4.5.3 ENCAPSULATING EXPERIENCE IN STORIES

Visual scripts carry memories of lived or learned experiences. In addition to the experienced body, which silently remembers and performs, they are a kind of memory organ that laboratory practice depends on. There is, in the laboratories studied, another memory organ that preserves experience. This is the narrative culture of the laboratory—more specifically, *stories*. Stories are scenarios of former experiences that participants have had directly or have heard about. They are told and retold, on appropriate occasions, and thus travel through the laboratory. As long as they circulate, they keep the relevant experience alive, turning it into a sort of communal stock of knowledge (see Traweek 1988a, 1992; Gilbert and Mulkay 1984).

Stories are another means of enhancing experience in the laboratories studied, because they preserve the scenic, phenomenal aspects of events. Stories emulate experience. They do not, for example, reduce experience to abstract rules or instructions. Though they are often rudimentary and focus upon essential parts of the events without much regard for suspense or poetic refinement, they keep some part of the experiential context in the picture. They also convey the sense of an original series of events in which anyone might participate and which might happen again in the appropriate circumstances. Consider the following story a member of the laboratory, then still working on his thesis, told about a series of mishaps at his first attempts to pour a gel: on the first attempt the gel cooled down so much that it hardened and could not be poured; next it proved too thin and ran out of the apparatus; when he retried the procedure the gel he poured was so hot that the glass plates burst; then the gel tore in the hands of his supervisor; and, finally, on the fifth attempt, it slipped, after the gel run had been completed, out of his hands and landed in the tank of the electrophoresis apparatus. The story was prompted by someone having trouble pouring a gel:

> **C:** He told me I have to let ((the gel)) cool down. Then it got hard when I tried to pour it ((between the glass plates)).
>
> **F:** Yes.
>
> **C:** Next time I thought, ha, that trick is not going to do you in again!
>
> **F:** ((Laughs.))
>
> **C:** I slapped it on ((poured the gel)) real hot and then it ran out below ((out of the glass plates)). It wasn't tight down there. Okay, (I thought) now you've gone that far, so I boiled it again and poured it directly ((bursts into laughing)). Then the plate burst.
>
> **F:** Ha ha, well this is . . .
>
> **C:** And so it went all the time. Then I got it that far, it was finished. Then I opened ( ) and took away the tape, then I ((laughs again)), then the thing tore with A. ((Laughs.)) And things like that. The worst thing was . . . it took a few days until I had it ((again)), we didn't have a microwave oven, you had to always boil it before ((pouring)).
>
> **F:** Yes, yes . . .
>
> **C:** Then I had it ready, and I ran it ((laughing)). Then it, when I took it apart it was so slippery ((the gel slipped)) into the lower tank of the electrophoresis apparatus. I was lucky there was someone around on a Saturday morning, he helped me to rinse it out, caught it with a glass plate.
>
> **F:** I mean this happens to anybody when they start working in the lab. I could tell you the same story about the agarose gel . . .

Many stories are, like the above, *atrocity* stories. They report undesirable events one has to be prepared to encounter. "I swear," a Canadian postdoc reported, "(the gel) used to set at room temperature in Canada, but here it won't. I made the mistake of picking it up once thinking it was set, and it spilled all over the place." Stories in general, whether they are atrocity stories or not, have lessons to teach about the things that can happen. The precedents reported thereby serve as reference scenarios with which to compare one's own work and that of others. Stories often begin with initiating sequences of the sort "what I once got when I . . .," "what X did . . ." or "what Y found . . ." They may be dissolved in question-answer sequences of the sort "didn't X once do this?" These are followed by the response, "and then what happened?" (compare Bergmann 1993). Some stories that provide strong reference scenarios include parts that have a physical reality, for example, pictures from earlier experiments that are somewhere on file in the laboratory. The picture is invoked together with the story to make a point; for example, a doctoral student working, among other things, on viral regulatory elements uses both story and picture to explain his results:

> **C:** ( ) But the funny thing is, the thing that's really funny is, J. *never* sees the probe up here ((points to a film being discussed)).
> **A:** Sure he does.
> **C:** He tells a different story.
> **A:** C'mon, he's talking ( ). I saw it with my own eyes on his gels.

The passage refers to J.'s film as envisaged by C., as seen by A., and some days later as actually shown by J. in the continuing discussion:

> **J:** This, I've got this, I can show you. I've got something similar ((shows his film)).

The immediate purpose of drawing on such reference scenarios usually is to compare features of one's own results with similar materials. Reference scenarios can provide a resource: a similar problem, an already-worked-out interpretation, or a possible solution arrived at in an analogous case. As precedents enclosed in stories, scenarios are potentially relevant to all domains. They may be recalled when participants look through an image at what happened in the lab, envisage invisible experimental reactions—or plan the future as they consider publishing their results. For example, in image analyses carried out in the context of publication plans, data displays in the published literature act as reference scenarios. Participants recall someone else's data-exhibiting strategy, exemplified in his or her pictures, to substantiate and confirm the editing policy proposed in regard to their own data.

4.6 Blind Variation Reconsidered

The components summed up in terms of an experiential register are of a general relevance to molecular biology work. The sensory, acting body of the scientist is in demand all the time, not called upon for specific purposes only. Similarly, stories and visual scripts are permanent features of all laboratory work. In particular, these experiential resources are also deployed when problems are encountered in experimental work, for example, in connection with the strategy of blind variation. In the practice of molecular biology variation, to recap, is "blind," in the sense that problems are treated by varying components of the experimental strategy until things work out, not by launching an investigation of the cause of the problem. (This approach is in contrast to the quest in high energy physics for self-understanding). Variation in molecular biology, however, is by no means as sightless and undiscerning as the random genetic mutations from which the term *blind variation* is borrowed. For example, the experienced body of the scientist, when it operates, naturally brings its experience to bear on the variations it concocts for selection by success. The retries scientists perform are never just any odd random alterations. Instead, they are based on what a scientist "senses" to be a promising strategy in a problem case, as illustrated below. The narrative culture of the lab, too, contains gems of wisdom about how to come up with more promising results—and participants turn to them when they are beset with problems. If someone else in the laboratory has run into a similar difficulty, he or she is questioned about what steps were taken to improve the situation. Last but not least, visual scripts are an excellent way of explaining a difficulty. The favorite strategy for finding an explanation for experimental results is to look into the biography of a procedure for clues as to what may have gone wrong. Like psychologists and psychoanalysts, who see in the biography of an individual the source of his or her difficulties, molecular biologists look at the biography of their objects and biochemical reactions as a major source of the problems they experience. The visual language, in this case, helps to specify the details of a reaction such that the factors leading to ineffective experimental results can, at least hypothetically, be identified. Talk that recalls these factors, as we have seen, fills in the question marks in test tube reactions.

Thus, the experiential components of this laboratory provide plenty of resources for basing variations not on truly blind trials and errors, but on (embodied) glosses as to what may have happened and what may work out (see also Campbell 1992). The process, however, often sidesteps true clarifications of the problem. First, glosses are not followed up in the sense of being checked and verified experimentally in their own right. They serve as motivations for determining variations of the procedure, not as springboards for attacking a problem at its core. Second, the variations implemented and the glossed explanations, which precede these variations, are often disconnected. Disturbing bands on an autoradiograph film can be dealt with in a variety of ways *not* involving the glossed explanation. Bands can be cut off when editing and pasting up films for publication. This is a perfectly valid strategy *if* one is convinced that the bands are irrelevant noise. They also can be dealt with by varying the exposure time of a film, by taking samples at different points in time, and by choosing a different method of proving the results. Participants choose such strategies in light of the need to produce results within certain time limits—not in response to a need to "understand" the problem. This pragmatic slant can easily be justified by the fact that attacking a problem at its core often is not possible, or is much more troublesome than achieving success by means of semi-blind variation. The impression one gets is that glossed explanations, when they are pursued, serve to convince participants that they know approximately what is going on (glosses are always shrouded in doubts) and, hence, can continue on the same track. The primary mechanism of reaching results, however, is nonrandom, semi-blind variation and selection by success.

5

From Machines to Organisms: Detectors as Behavioral and Social Beings

5.1 Primitive Classifications

For Durkheim and Mauss, primitive classifications were symbolic classifications of a moral or religious nature that were built upon the model of society. Every primitive classification, they said, "implies a hierarchical order for which neither the tangible world nor our mind gives us the model." Instead, these classifications "express . . . the very societies within which they were elaborated" (1963: 8, 66, 82). They derive from social organization, from the forms and structures that divide and integrate social groups. This was Durkheim and Mauss's great thesis, with the singular value, as Needham (1963: xi) pointed out, of directing the social sciences' attention toward the topic of classification.

In this chapter I shall analyze some of the symbolic classifications made by high energy physicists in their talk about their detector, about some of their particles, and about themselves. I will also suggest a rationale for these analogies. Durkheim's explanation of symbolic classifications has proved untenable, and the line of reasoning proposed by Durkheim's followers—for example, by Mary Douglas (1986; see also Lakoff 1987; Wuthnow 1992)—appears problematic in light of modern organizational structures. Douglas argues that institutions are conventions, and conventions need some stabilizing principle, which masks the fact that they are socially contrived arrangements. This stabilizing principle is the connection an institution establishes with "natural categories" through metaphors and analogies. The analogical relation of head to hand can be used to justify such diverse social conventions as the class structure, the inequality of the education system, and the division of labor between manual and intellectual work. However, it is questionable how much purchasing power analogies of this sort have in modern institutions. Does the habit of calling the top level in an organization the "head" and workers the "hands" really buy more legitimacy for a hierarchical structure than other social arrangements do, such as public relations work, returns on investments, or legal principles? Would high energy physics laboratories make massive public relations efforts if they could achieve legitimacy simply by propagating their metaphors and analogies? I think not. Organizational conventions within the education system, for example, are grounded in law, and the legal provisions, in turn, are legitimized by reference to democratic principles, such as equality of opportunity, freedom of choice, and egalitarian forms of social organization. Institutions do borrow analogies from the body and from other areas of natural and social life, but these analogies may be used for different rationales—for example, to express the refiguring of objects and subjects and the relationships between the two categories in local settings.

In experimental physics, as in any other science, the definition of things is accomplished by technical vocabularies. A detector and presumably all of its thousands of parts can be classified or paraphrased into a technical language. Moreover, physicists seem to share enough of this vocabulary to make themselves understood. Yet there exists, in addition to the technical language, imaginative terminological repertoires that reclassify technical distinctions and components. These constitute a *symbolic universe superimposed upon* the technical universe; a repertoire of categories and distinctions from the everyday world that are extended into the scientific world, where they reformulate, elaborate, and at times fill in for technical categories and distinctions. Symbolic classifications of this sort have a *double referent*. On the one hand, they refer to technical categories, distinctions, and practices that could also be expressed, or at least paraphrased, in technical terms. On the other hand, these classifications refer to "natural" and social concepts and kinds. One example hinted at before is the "aging" of a detector. Why apply a biological process such as aging to a technical event? The technical vocabulary should be strong enough to carry the message—the deterioration of the measurement response—to which detector "aging" refers. Why are chunks of experience, perfectly well described in technical terms, symbolically recoded?

I want to suggest that imaginative vocabularies in HEP experiments express the reconfiguration of objects and subjects with which I have associated laboratories. Through symbolic repertoires, it is made apparent how the structure of things is reset in epistemic practice. Symbols describe who, independent of external definitions, is alive or not alive, who are the organisms and who are the machines, who are the agents with powers and dispositions to react, and who are the passive tools and media in an interaction. Symbolic reclassifications make it apparent that there have long been relationships in these settings that include nonhuman participants (e.g., relationships with machines; see also Turkle 1984, 1995; Callon 1986; Appadurai 1986; Latour and Johnson 1988; Serres 1990; Collins and Yearley 1992; Latour 1993; Thévenot 1994; Knorr Cetina 1997) and that define human participation in specifically limited ways. They also make it apparent that the traditional concepts of a person, an actor, or a role are not sufficient to capture the structurings of reality within these experimental arenas. For example, it is not a physicist's role or the role of a machine that is at issue, but the definition of these objects as working components of the setting in relation to other components.

The hidden message, then, is the rearrangement of objects and subjects within the order of the laboratory, the renegotiation of their properties within technical activities, and the relationships of these components. It is a message the technical language does not express very well. In particular, the relational element seems to be missing or interpreted differently in technical vocabularies—the relationship between the parts and the whole, between one object and others, and, most significantly, between objects and subjects.

5.2 Detector Agency and Physiology

To the observer, experimental high energy physics is indubitably a science of big machines. In fact, a HEP experiment looks much more like a technological project than basic science. Advances in high energy physics are often represented in terms of energy regimes, and energy regimes are regimes of machines: colliders and accelerators that provide higher and higher energies, detectors that can deal with ever higher luminosities, and computers that are fast enough to handle huge amounts of information within fractions of a second. It is the technology of colliders and detectors which limits the degree to which physicists can investigate the components of matter, and it is these limitations which they attempt to overcome with every generation of new machines (DiLella 1990). The technology consumes the enormous amount of money experimental high energy physics requires, and the technology necessitates, by its sheer size and complexity, the formation of large collaborations (see also Galison and Hevly 1992; Galison 1987). From the outside, experimental high energy physics is branded, driven, and dominated by machines. Yet, seen from within, some machines turn into organisms, while in other sciences, to anticipate what will be said about molecular biology in Chapter 6, organisms turn into machines (compare Woolgar 1985).

Detectors such as the new ATLAS detector currently built at CERN are as large as buildings several stories high, weigh many tons, and display in a striking way the technological prowess of modern natural science (see Figure 5.1). Yet from within the symbolic code through which the detectors are addressed and talked about by participants, these massive instruments are physiological beings with behavioral states and idiosyncrasies. As indicated in Chapter 3, a detector in HEP (and in areas that use smaller detectors, such as space research; Klein 1994) qualifies as a sort of ultimate seeing device. Pions and photons, as they strike detector materials, initiate movements of particles, which can be registered as signals and, after a cascade of transformations and amplifications, end up as digital response counts. Here the detector functions not unlike the retina; in UA2, participants said the detector "sees" or "doesn't see" certain events, that it was not "looking," "watching," or that it "looked away"; they said that it was "blind," "sensitive," or "insensitive." They continually construed particle detection as analogous to perception. This analogy is also emphasized through the concept of "resolution," an optical term that refers to the degree to which an instrument can still form distinguishable images of objects spaced closely together. A second major behavioral complex attributed to the detector comprises categories such as its "response," its "reaction," and its "acceptance." These are much

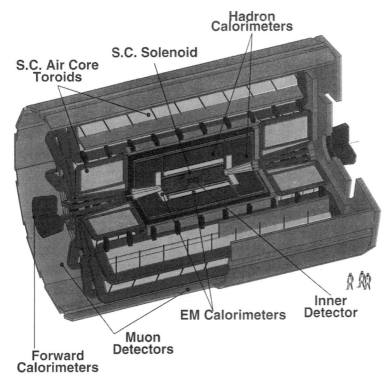

Figure 5.1 The ATLAS detector as depicted in a Letter of Intent (October 1992).

larger concepts that sum up the whole complicated measurement return of the instrument with respect to a signal (Section 3.5). The detector, in this case, is construed as an entity that "interacts" with particles and that particles "interact" with and respond to in certain ways. A further set of categories, more achievement-oriented, portrays the detector somewhat as a competing athlete—as "performing" or not, and as "coping," in its performance, in different environments. Physicists speak of the "performance" of a detector and of performance-enhancing measures. For example, gas-based detectors can be "doped," which means that their performance can be enhanced by adding certain ingredients to the gas. In ATLAS, one question is how the new detector will be able to "cope" with the "hostile" environments in which it will have to perform in the future. The "response," "resolution," "acceptance," and "performance" of a detector refer to characteristics implicated in all stages of detector design and operation.

Added to these action-capabilities of the detector, specifically its capability to see, respond, interact, perform, and also to produce noise, are descriptions of behavioral states and conditions construing the detector as a *physiological* being. The agent appears to be supplemented by a kind of body with its own internal life and problems. Physiology comes into the picture when the detector is seen as continually changing. Detectors, like all of us, are slowly, but relentlessly "aging." In fact, they are aging in such a predictable manner that when for once in UA2 the calorimeter appeared to "get younger," it caused quite a commotion in the experiment, and a thorough investigation of this "problem" followed (Section 3.4). Detector aging can be accelerated by environmental conditions, as by radiation damage. Detectors not only age, but they are also "unstable." They are prone to sudden "jumps" in their behavioral response, which may be environmentally triggered (for example, by temperature changes), and they will, at times, "act up." Because of their aging and instabilities, detectors must be monitored. Monitoring also applies to the physiological states of a detector or parts of a detector, which are mostly described in terms of illness, disease, and death. Detectors and detector parts are said be "alive," "dead," "killed," or "cannibalized." They have a "life expectancy" ("how long do they live?" is a question that may be asked with respect to certain parts), and their life may also be "prolonged." Furthermore, they may have "diseases," be "sick," "ailing," or "congested," suffer from "ion poisoning," or "go crazy." In response to these predicaments and other occurrences, they may "complain" of an illness, which is then "diagnosed" and treated with "antibiotics" and "first aid." "The patient" may then "die" and remain "as dead as ever," or "recuperate" and be "cured" and "healed." Figure 5.2 provides an overview of detector action capabilities and physiological conditions.[1]

5.3 Detectors as Moral and Social Individuals

True human beings are not only equipped with the distinctive characteristic of agency and with a physiology, but they also have moral and

From Machines to Organisms

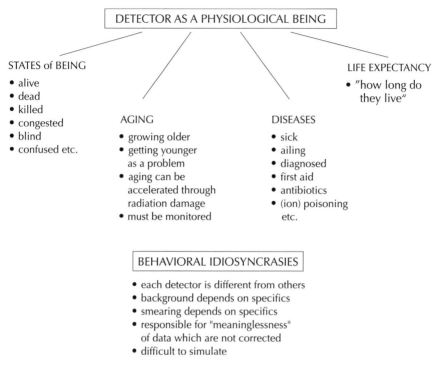

Figure 5.2 Overview of the capabilities and physiological conditions of a detector.

social tendencies. Detectors, which are sometimes likened to human beings, display similar features. First, they are generally construed as strong individuals. Strong individualism means that each detector is, in idiosyncratic ways, "different" from another, as discussed in Section 3.3. As a senior member of UA2 put it:

> There was a time in the 70s where there were more or less standard packages for the analysis, because all the detectors were basically of the same type . . . When you were doing bubble chamber type physics there was really standard analysis packages. In a collider experiment like this each analysis you do must develop all the tools yourself, I mean, you know *it depends on how the detector looks, behaves* [emphasis added].

Thus, with collider experiments, everything depends on the idiosyncracies of the detector—the background it records, the resolution provided, the events accepted, the overall detector response, and, thereby, the measurements. The extreme idiosyncracies of a detector fit into the pattern of analogies from biology. Biological organisms are individuals in the sense that they display great diversity and variation in their physiology and their disposition to react. Idiosyncracies and individualism, however, do not preclude detectors from being considered *social* beings in certain respects. Detectors consist of subdetectors sandwiched around each other and wrapped around the beam pipe. These detectors "cooperate." For example, they provide different segments of particle tracks that are then assembled into one overall track by the pattern recognition program. Detectors also cooperate by correcting for each other's insufficiencies. For example, one can kill all the ghosts in the scintillating fiber detector with a working silicon detector. Detectors cooperate by "consulting" each other, for example, with respect to finding the tracks of particles. If one detector always "consults" another and part of the first detector readout is lost, then the second cannot function either. Detectors in UA2, therefore, performed individually first while consultation was deferred to a second stage. When they are consulted by another detector, detectors will "agree" or "disagree" with each other. Consultation and cooperation implies some sort of communication between detectors; indeed, detectors are said to "communicate" with each other and with other components of the system, with which they may enter a "dialog." For example, the readout chain in UA2 started by a computer "telling" a detector that it was ready to accept an event from it:

> **KK:** How does it work ((the readout-chain))?
> **AP (head of offline operations):** () There is first a computer that *talks* to our electronics, and the electronics *sends signals* down, and the detector *acknowledges* them and sends them back, and then again the computer is *informed*. So you make the closed loop where there is a *dialog* between computer, electronics, detector and computer again [emphasis added].

Finally, detectors can also enter more antagonistic and competitive relationships. For example, they *"check"* each other. In UA2, if one wanted to know how often a detector found a track, one could run the tracking with this detector excluded. As the physicist just quoted above put it in explaining ongoing work on track identification and detector efficiency:

> **AP:** We try to measure ((the efficiency)) on a general basis and you would do that, for example, by taking the JVD out of the tracking, measuring tracks for the SFD in the silicon and then looking at the JVD to see whether it found the track in the same place or not. And similarly you do things, check each detector one against the other by saying all these other detectors saw something which looks like a track going through, so does this guy respond the way you expect? You can say the calorimeter sees something that looks like an electron, does the TRD see it as electrons, and so on.

In UA2, efficiency measurements involved *"playing off"* different detector components one against the other. For example, the preshower of the scintillating fiber detector and the silicon detector were used to measure the former's tracking efficiency, the tracking efficiency and the silicon were used to measure the transition radiation detector's efficiency, two other detectors and the scintillating fiber were involved in the attempt to measure the silicon efficiency, and so on.

Detectors cooperate, communicate, and can be played off against one another, but they are also addressed as *moral* and *morally responsible* beings. Some of the terms mentioned above have evaluative overtones, but detectors and detector parts are also explicitly evaluated as "misbehaving" or "behaving"—as being a "good" detector or a "bad" one. With a "good detector," one can, for example, reduce the background, whereas with a "bad" detector one cannot. Detectors tend not to be "good" or well-behaved at all times, however. They are sometimes said to be "acting up" like a naughty child, to be "confused," or to suffer from similar behavioral faults. A detector, when it behaves (well), "is our friend," as one physicist said. But when it does not behave it is derided and "distrusted." In this sense detectors bear the "responsibility" to perform in certain ways. For example, it may be the "responsibility" of a detector to provide a particle track segment in a certain angle in phi with specific qualities and uncertainties. The vocabulary used to construe detectors as social and moral individuals is illustrated in Figure 5.3.[2]

as a SOCIAL BEING
(Detectors consist of several subdetectors)

- DETECTORS COOPERATE

  e.g. you can kill all the ghosts in
  the scintillating fibre detector with
  the silicon detector

- DETECTORS COMMUNICATE with
  each other and COMMUNICATE
  with other devices

  e.g. with respect to readout chain, there is
  a DIALOGUE between computer,
  electronics, detector and computer again

- DETECTORS MAY CONSULT EACH OTHER

  e.g. in finding the tracks of particles

- DETECTORS CHECK EACH OTHER

  e.g. different subdetectors can be
  played off one against the other in
  measurement of efficiency

as a MORAL BEING

- DETECTORS BEHAVE/MISBEHAVE
  "good"
  "bad"
  "playing up"

- DETECTORS can be TRUSTED
  or are DISTRUSTED

- DETECTORS are RESPONSIBLE
  for certain achievements

Figure 5.3 Detectors as social and moral beings.

5.4 Live Organism or Machine?

Consider once more the structure of the analogies used to describe the detector in UA2. Playing detectors "against" one another, seeing them as "communicating" with other elements in the system, construing them as consulting each other and as cooperating with each other—all are versions of the physicists' tendency to implement individual detectors as components not only capable of but also in need of interaction with each other. In this sense, individual detectors are social beings brought together in groups, where they submit to a specific order and rely on each other. But the detector is also treated as a quasi-biological being with physiological states, a perceptual apparatus, a tendency to fall ill and to need medical attention, and various behavioral capabilities, such as the capacity to perform challenging tasks and to improve. Finally, the detectors have idiosyncrasies and limits, which are expected from biological individuals. The thing to note about these analogies is that they form a relatively coherent cluster. The vocabularies brought together to classify the detector fit together; there are no systematically applied categorizations that break the pattern.

But what is the pattern? To sum it up I want to single out two features that are put on display in the relational vocabulary. The first is that the detector has an internal life of its own: it exhibits an internal dynamic not completely under the experiment's control. In this sense, the detector is like a *complex organism,* whose physiology is ruled by its own laws and which has its own powers, capabilities, and tendencies to react. Recall that the responses of this organism are not self-evident. They must be monitored and measured, so that with sufficient observation, hard work, and familiarity (achieved through a joint biography with the detector), they may be "understood." Moreover, the organism cannot be left on its own. A whole structure of surveillance devices and probes are built around it, and follow all its moves. Thus, the organism remains a kind of being rather than a thing, with essential components functioning like organs to maintain the responses of the whole.

The qualities of a living being that a detector has, like the quality of agency described below, are not, one must emphasize, idle poetic embellishments of technological processes. The internal life of a detector with dynamics of its own is a recurring experience in the experiments. Detectors cannot, for example, be opened up and taken apart at any point in time. Once they have been assembled and "run," their internal life is accessible only indirectly or in small sections, at great costs in time and losses of luminosity during "access periods." But even when they do not run, only certain parts of a detector can be removed and inspected. The internal life of a detector cannot be precisely described, as is illustrated by the following comment by a senior physicist on the appropriate and prevailing attitude toward detector simulations:

> **AN:** () it's quite difficult to simulate a detector like this ((one)).
> **KK:** Because of what? Because it's so ((ununderstandable)).
> **AN:** It's not so much that, well first you have to get the physics right. That's non-trivial in itself. Having generated the correct set of particles, they go through the material almost scattering the material, they pro-

duce other particles which you have to follow. You don't know exactly what material is in there and how it is arranged, e.g. there is a carbon fiber wall in the silicon, then there is an aluminum electron shield and then there is a piece of silicon and then there is a printed circuit and scattered across that are different pieces of electronics. And then there is another aluminum shield and then some carbon fibers and so on, and you can't ((know)) all that in details. So you always end up oversimplifying your MC, to the extent that we see twice as many hits as we expect ((from the simulation)). You might believe the MC for the topology for top events, but all you're understanding is the basic physics. But if you're asking about the details of the charge distribution in the preshower ((a detector part)), then I don't think anybody would seriously believe the simulation.

The second quality of a detector that stands out is its *autonomy* as an agent who interacts with the particles.[3] In this sense, the detector works between the scientists and the objects of interest. It observes these objects and interacts with them, in ways reminiscent not only of biological but of human beings; humans, too, function idiosyncratically, never ideally, and, at certain moments, they get in the way of real progress. In this sense, the detector carries all the emotional ties and ambiguities of a friend who is, at the same time, a business partner, someone with whom one has not only an expressive but also an instrumental relationship. These ambiguities were also expressed by physicists when they told me about their relationship with the detector:

> **KK:** ((What sort of thing is it for you?))
> **WD:** () A detector is a tool, a toy and a friend or whatever, which is used to measure something and the result of our job. So in a way we shouldn't care at all about the detector. But in reality, okay, we live so long with that object, it's like a human being, a detector . . .

Friendship derives from the joint biography physicists share with the detector, and is expressed through emotional attitudes. Unlike particles, detectors are "loved":

> **KK:** How do they compare ((particles and the detector))?
> **WD:** () I think we don't love the W's, but we love our calorimeter, if you may say so, psychologically . . .

On the other hand, it is recognized, somewhat sadly, that the beloved friend has "faults" and "blemishes" which get in the way of its usefulness and the attainment of desired goals. When doing physics analysis, UA2 participants often mentioned or complained that the detector was "not ideal." They complained that "even the best detector" could not distinguish between certain kinds of background and "could not tell you" whether certain jets come from a top or from the initial state in the W production, or that the design of their detector was "not the smartest." This recognition of a detector's limitations ties into the concept of "leaving the detector behind" when it comes to particles and physics analysis.

5.5 Are There Enemies?

The notions of friendship and instrumental usage contrast with the antagonistic way participants depict other components of the experiment, specifically the background (see Section 3.2). Unlike the detector, the background is not a massive material object with a complex internal life. No terms link the background with qualities of a living organism. What agency qualities the background has, as an antagonist, are not based on physiologies. Rather, they derive from the background's relationship to the signal. Recall that the background consists of competing particle decay processes and classes of events that "fake" and "mimic" the signal. When different classes of background are labeled in terms of the processes from which they originate (conversions, overlaps, beam halos, ghosts, etc.), at least some of these categories also suggest something about the origin of the deception. For example, conversions result from particles changing into other particles, overlaps from two particles running close to each other simulating a third; a beam halo is a light effect coming from the wrong kind of particles, which looks like a shower of interesting particles (a jet); and ghosts are projections that fake a real track. The background—undesired events of this sort in inundating quantities—threatens the experiment at its core. If it cannot be held in check, none of the physics data can be interpreted as events of interest.

The background is linked to the detector in a double sense. First, it may be produced through certain processes within the detector as part of the "instrumental" background. Second, a particular class of background events may cause problems when the detector cannot handle it. Detectors are built to deal not only with the signal but also with the background. They are custom-made to allow, recognize, and discriminate against certain classes of events. If, because of a lack of knowledge at the time the detector was designed or because of budgetary constraints, a detector is ill-equipped to deal with a particular background, then the problem persists. The upgraded UA2 detector, for example, had no magnetic field, and hence could not recognize pion-gamma overlaps (which fake electrons) as easily as detectors that do have magnetic fields, in which pions "curl up." Detectors, then, are implicated in the background. Nonetheless, they are not blamed for it. In the words of a physicist as he explained to me his data analysis:

> The background is the enemy, something you are fighting against. And that you don't blame on your detector—that's what you should do actually—you blame the background on itself.

The antagonistic attitude that underlies this conception is well expressed in the preferred way of dealing with the background. One not only "fights against" the background but tries to "*kill*" it:

> () there is this antagonistic attitude, it's something you have to *kill* in some way, there is a whole terminology, you have to *kill* the background.

The antagonistic terms for the background in the experiment included "the horrible case which you didn't want to see"; it was qualified as "ugly," "nasty," "malicious," "bad," "worst," or "dangerous." The most dangerous background was the one even a "perfect" detector is ineffective against—it was "irreducible." For certain particles, one would "get a beating" from the background, or one would have to deal with the background "blowing up" things at low momenta. One was always "buried" and "dominated" by it—the question was only by what sort of background. In return, war was waged against the background. It was "killed," "suppressed," "fought against," "beaten down," "eliminated," "cut," and "rejected."

Killing is the preferred method of dealing with the background in these experiments, and the task may take a variety of approaches—for example, simply killing it, "killing it cleverly," or "living" with it by "controlling" it.[4] Even simple killing usually requires measures of support, such as making sure that one has destroyed the enemy completely. This, of course, means that one has to "study" the background in order to establish its identity and its size. When asked about ways of dealing with the background in the top analysis, one physicist explained:

> You have to be sure that you eliminated it all. You have to calculate how much it should be and how much (). Even when you kill it, you have to know *that* you killed it.

The background, however, cannot always be simply killed. If one has "low statistics" (an inefficient signal) and the signal accounts for no more than a small fraction of the events, if it lies inside an error bar (the distribution of signal and background events have tails that blend into each other, even if the signal and background are reasonably separated), then killing the background usually means that one also eliminates part of the signal. One can afford to eliminate part of the signal only if the statistics are high enough. If they are not, one has to find "cleverer" ways of dealing with the background.

> **KK:** If your statistics are low—
> **AP:** If your efficiency for the signal is too low, you lose (it) if you kill the background. So you have to kill the background cleverly, without killing the signal.

"Killing" a background one way or another has a technical referent. It means using detector information to disentangle the different components contributing to a data curve. Data curves always result from a mixture of processes, of which the majority is usually background (see Section 3.6). "Ideally," the detector can identify these directly: one can "kill the ghosts in the SFD with the silicon," and so on. But if the detector cannot do the killing, then one can use *simulation* as a fall-back strategy, a third front from which to attack the background problem. To simulate a background process, one first has to generate the respective events within the Monte Carlo, then run them through a detector model that recreates the detector response, and then take the resulting raw data through the production and selection chain described in Chapter 3, in order to find out how many events survive and are a measure of one's background. In an interview conducted on background studies in general with the same physicist, this strategy was described as a strategy of last resort:

> **AP:** The other completely independent process is to try and simulate the background process completely from scratch, from physics grounds.
> **KK:** And then you would just predict how many—
> **AP:** Yeah (). Normally we'd use a Monte Carlo analysis, for example to model the calorimeter cuts. () And if it's really a jet faking an electron then () you expect to see bits of energy in the calorimeter around. If it's really an electron coming from the top then you expect it to be (isolated). () Then you can model the isolation in the calorimeter and you can simulate it.

At a later point he added:

> **AP:** If it's a background for which you can do a simulation, you can do a convolution of the distribution for the background and the distribution for the signal and still understand your data, but that makes life very difficult. So when you make a precision measurement it's better to get rid of the background. You can live with the background, but it makes life really tough.

The background, thus, can be lived with if it must, but only at a price. The overall metaphor is one of fighting an antagonist with all means possible.[5]

5.6 Physicists as Symbionts

If the background is an enemy, it is an enemy in relation to someone. Similarly, the detector, as a friend, is a friend in relation to someone who considers it in this capacity. These someones are the physicists, the group of people we have always presupposed as we have discussed classifications. But who and what are the physicists? The traditional answer might be "subjective centers of action." Are not the physicists the ones who do the classifying? Who produce, to a substantive degree, the detector—which they rightly, on occasion, consider their "toy"? Surely, they are the ones who fight the background and perform all the other complicated tasks that make up an experiment? And surely they consider themselves, reflexively, as the personal centers of action that perform their work in a subjectively meaningful way?

This traditional interpretation is not wrong in suggesting who is implicated, as an ontological subject and a subjectivity, in all human constructions. But it is perhaps too limited when it comes to determining the cultural parts human entities play in the reconfigurations of self-other-things with which I have associated laboratories. With a view to these reconfigurations, we can pretend to start from scratch. *Are* there human actors in the laboratory? Assuming that there are, if not human actors, then at least human entities, how are they structured into the ongoing activities of the experiment and what qualities are assigned to them? Who, if not individual human actors, are the epistemic subjects in the laboratory? Some of these questions will be the topic of later chapters, but we can at least ask here, what symbolic classifications are *applied to scientists* rather than to objects? Assuming that we know, as we "knew" that physics is a science of big machines, that human beings "run" these experiments, what qualities do we actually find addressed in these vocabularies, and which ones are ignored or excluded? The problem is that the harvest we gather from the application of symbolic vocabularies to human entities is disappointing. The elaborate imagination that goes into classifying the detector and denouncing the background and that is also apparent in physics theory (see, for example, Holton 1973; Gregory 1988) seems to have dried up. Physicists have little to say—in terms of vivid systematic analogies and metaphors, beyond the use of single terms—about themselves and their colleagues. There is, for example, a relative lack of the physiological subtext that was there for detectors and that associates human beings, in everyday life, with behavioral tendencies, states of the body, etc. Nor is there much of a psychological subtext, through which emotions, biographies, and marital states become a topic of accounts. As one physicist once told me, she had been closely cooperating with other participants for two or three years without ever once being asked whether she was married or not.

Nonetheless, there are two ways of classifying human entities I want to illustrate, since they foreshadow the multiple and partly counteracting registers of organization and self-understanding examined in Chapter 8. The first is so fully in view as to almost escape notice; it is that physicists are categorized and identified in terms of the objects (the machines, particles, and sections of code) on which they work. The second is more hidden but nonetheless pervasive; it counteracts the first tendency of associating human and nonhuman entities. This classification scheme joins physicists together over and above object-oriented classifications with the help of a key human term, *trust*.

Consider the first type of classification. It is partly but not fully predicted by role theory, which suggests that human beings are different programs in different settings. A physicist in an experiment will not be engaged there as a "parent," or a "client," or perhaps as a "donor" of organs, but as someone doing physics. At the same time, role theory assumes the existence of the physicist as a stable unit of action. The symbolic repertoires to be considered, on the other hand, associate individuals with components of the experiment. They join human agents and technical objects in the experiment together, approach the conjunction rather than the individual, and take an interest in the individual *in relation to* these objects (see also Latour 1991).

In the experiments studied, such conjunctions are most apparent in the classification of individuals according to the different subcomponents of a detector. In UA2, physicists were classified as belonging to the "Silicon" group, the "SFD" group, the "TRD," the "JVD" (Jet Vertex Detector), the "Central Calorimeter," the "Endcaps," etc. In addition, another split, related to software and electronics, separated the "online" from the "offline" group: the former was tied to the code and electronics in use while data were taken, the latter to software and data management after run completion. Finally, there were "physics" subgroups distinguished by the kind of *particles* ("electron" group and "jet" group) they investigated. These groups were split further into subgroups concerned with, for example, the top ("top working group") or the W. The latter groups formed late in the experiment and changed over time, depending on the stage of the analysis. They drew upon the same participants as detector groups. Nonetheless, detector groups remained operational as long as the detector was not dismantled.

Note that the groups were related not only to a task but to an object or a set of objects forming a distinctive unit. A transition radiation detector, for example, works very differently from a scintillating fiber detector. In addition, electrons, jets, tops, W's, and Z^0's are equally distinctive entities. As individuals "live with" these objects, they become identified with them and identify with them to the degree that they are always perceived in relation to these objects. Traweek (1988a: 72), in her study of high energy physics communities in Japan and the United States, has observed the way in which detectors supply a system for thinking about various groups' modes of scientific procedure. On a different level, this phenomenon can be observed, for example, when detectors that do not work well reflect on the "disorganized" or "erratic" work style of their groups, and detectors that run smoothly reflect on the "systematic" work habits of theirs. There are many occasions where the torch seems to shine from the object to the human subjects, and vice versa, in circles of mutual attribution—no origin can be reliably identified.

Most important perhaps is the fact that participants constantly seek each other out for the knowledge they have of the objects with which they are classified. There exists, in the experiments, a considerable amount of technical shop talk; much of it reports on technical objects and consultation with "experts" on the objects. Participants speak on behalf of these objects and report their features within the framework of certain procedures. But the objects themselves and the difficulties associated with them also seem to invade participants' minds. Wives of physicists to whom I talked complained that their husbands prefer to stay late at work when they can, that it takes them until Sunday afternoon on weekends to "unwind" and to be able to concentrate on family matters; the wives are given control over house and children, but, they say, with no help. Technical objects live in participants' heads and homes, just as they emerge continually in their talk and consultation. The conjunction of physicists with objects is significant precisely with respect to the pervasive presence of detector components, algorithms, event distributions, and the like in physicists' thinking and talk. Physicists function as symbionts in the experiments, humans that live with technical components in close association and that draw their strength—their identity, expert status, the attention they get from others, their position, and their very raison d'être—from the symbiosis (compare Haraway 1991b; see also Section 7.4).

5.7 Taxonomies of Trust

Seen over time, a high energy physics experiment is, in one sense, a huge exercise in automation. Detector pieces are progressively tested, understood, assembled, and set to work on their own. Programs and utilities are successively integrated into large packages that integrate tasks such as electron identification, pattern recognition, and detector simulation–packages which are then routinely applied to data and Monte Carlo–generated events. Monitoring tasks are implemented by computer programs and need no longer be done by hand. Even a data run, originally a nightmare for the experts in the control room—with alarms sounding, detectors tripping, data acquisition systems overflowing, and countless monitoring tasks continually producing countless complaints—has become a manageable succession of steps. Data runs can now be handled even by newcomers, once all the major "bugs" have been eliminated, safeguards have been implemented, and partial tasks automated. Yet it is important to realize that the result of this exercise is never in one piece, complete, and never like a robot that simply performs all tasks. It is more like a three-dimensional mosaic of working bits and pieces, including human interfaces and human function devices, but it is also a mosaic that remains forever incomplete, precarious, and liable to fall apart in certain corners and segments. The human intermediaries remain firmly entrenched in this mosaic, but they are no more than additional pieces.

The "superorganism" that emerges, "the experiment," cannot profit from the hard-wired division of labor manifest in the insect colonies to which the term is usually applied. An experiment transforms itself "in midflight," one might say, as it proceeds through the stages of detector building, software engineering, and physics analyzing; and as it transforms itself it poses ever new tasks of routinization and automation. It is based on many principles and layers of foundation, which increase rather than decrease the complexity of its thriving and throbbing dynamics. How does one create a superorganism without the benefit of a stable prespecified task, a hard-wired division of labor, and the strict correspondence between lives and work that characterizes ant colonies? How does one, as a human agent fitted into a plurality of objects, stay in control? One response of the physicists in HEP is to build much of the interaction that matters (whose results re-enter the experiment) on *trust* (compare Kohler 1994; Shapin and Schaffer 1985; Shapin 1994).

If physicists are joined with technical objects in conjunctions that penetrate deeply into all communication and interaction, they are also *joined with each other* in an effort collectively to confront and control the experiment. If physicists are, on the one hand, *extensions* of the objects with which they work, they are also, on the other hand, *collaborators* working together in a human endeavor. Collaborations emerge from core groups trusting each other, but participants are also selected by the "money" and "manpower" they can contribute. For example, the more money an experiment can recruit, through clever selection of participating institutes, the better its chances of building an innovative detector. Within collaborations, therefore, "trust" classifies participants not in terms of the money they bring to an experiment but rather in terms of what is known about them: whose work can one build upon, whose results are "believable," and who does one wish to "cooperate with," and, alternatively, who does one wish to avoid?

Trust distinctions do not form a single taxonomy; rather, they underlie and are mixed into several classifications. First, they are used informally to sort people into those "whose results one can believe" and who one wishes to cooperate with, and those one does not. Second, they are superimposed upon formal classifications designating the physicists' professional status. And third, they draw the important distinction between experts and nonexperts. To begin with the informal sorting, consider some attitudes physicists display toward their colleagues. As one CERN fellow put it when I asked how he made distinctions between his colleagues:

> () you get some experience in knowing whether you can believe in the results that a person produces. And very fast. I don't think it takes a very long time in a collaboration to sort out who can you work together with and who can you believe. ()

In the beginning, you don't choose it yourself. () very often you're honored by somebody coming to you and say, couldn't you, wouldn't you come and give a hand, that people really trust you so much. () But when you become a bit older you try to collaborate with people that you trust.

Judgments of the believability of some work are made when physicists "watch" each other present status reports at the frequent internal meetings. In another context I got the following comment, of which variants can frequently be heard also when participants speak among themselves:

I mean, I think you don't have to be a physicist to see who is talking empty talk and who has something to say. () very often it's not the amount, it's not the volume but it's somehow the essence of what's being said with (which) you can distinguish between people.

Physicists distinguish between this kind of professional "trust" they are willing to extend to people and their personal friendship or even official recognition. Even holders of Nobel Prizes (of which CERN has several) may not be trusted:

HJ: I wouldn't trust N.
KK: Now that's for/?
HJ: That's because he wants the honor, he wants that, whether there is anything to be honored about or not. I mean you know he has a long history of mistakes.
KK: Mhm. And he still got the Nobel Prize.
HJ: He still got, CERN got the Nobel Prize there, yes.

Physicists also react rather furiously to people who disappoint their confidence, as this participant working on software and electronics indicated:

If I expect to get something done then it's irritating and it destroys my own work and my happiness in doing the work if I have to after a while go and do it myself or, maybe it's so complicated that I cannot go and do it myself, so it's destructive for my work. It's very important to be sure, that the people you are working with, that you have confidence.

Or consider this response by a senior physicist, talking about what he felt to be important qualities in researchers:

> I think the worst thing which can happen is that people don't realize that they cannot fulfill their task. I mean it's very important that if you take up a responsibility that you, all the time, try to go through it and see can I fulfill it in the time-scale I am given. And the kind of people who are not doing that I think are the most dangerous (). ((If they come and say I can't do it)) then you'll move responsibility from one group to another, but it's deadly when you don't do it.

Mutual dependence, then, with respect to the outcome is related to *trust as a sorting and selection* mechanism on an informal level. But there are also more formal classifications of participants with which classifications of trust are interlocked. Consider the following list of categories of professional and employment status of CERN researchers:

student

postdoc (employed by outside institutes)

fellow (employed by CERN)

outside staff (employed by outside institutes)

CERN staff (employed by CERN)

These classifications combine three dimensions along which people are sorted: their career stage (student, postdoc, senior person), their employment status, signifying whether the physicist is permanently employed or not (staff or nonstaff), and their source of financing—whether he or she is financed by CERN. At each level above the student, considerations of trust become interlocked not only with the career stage but also with the other two dimensions.

In the resulting hierarchy, students tend to draw a blank: since they "vary enormously in their ability," as one older physicist remarked, one needs to discover the distinctions between them in terms of "how much responsibility they can be trusted with and how much checking you have to do." Postdocs, he said, are "usually very good"; they need not be checked, but they still need "suggestions." Since they are not employed by CERN, however, and may not be present at all times, "they can't be jumped on every day," as fellows can. Trust, it seems, is more regularly granted to fellows, who hold the same professional status as postdocs but are at continuous disposal for feedback and contributions to the experiment. The next category in the hierarchy is outside staff members, a category much more ambiguous than the others. Though it includes mainly physicists of a more senior professional status (beyond the postdoc level but not necessarily institute heads, who are often ranked separately), the considerable demands on these physicists (from teaching and administration at their home institutes) may result in a lower ranking on the trust scale than is warranted by their professional status. The CERN staff members I got to know, for reasons of their more or less exclusive involvement in research and their selection, rank high on the professsional trust scale. This is also true for the CERN "spokesmen" of experiments I have met, for example, the spokesmen of UA2 and ATLAS. By contrast, some heads of outside institutes, when they are seen to be mainly preoccupied with "running their institutes" and "getting money," predictably fall short of an equivalent status in terms of technical usefulness. Needless to say, informal reclassifications are often made in response to additional criteria, as with the Nobel Prize–winner who was a "quintessential physicist" and yet not trusted. Nonetheless, reference to status categories is made when researchers account for other individuals' performances, for what they are "trusted with" to work on, and so on.

Finally, "trust" is implicated in another distinction of pervasive importance in the experiment, that between *experts* and *nonexperts*. Experts are those who can be trusted to understand a problem, a data curve, or a detector component, etc. They are the ones to whom, because of this trust, responsibilities are delegated without apparent control. Those in charge of certain detector components were on call for advice and repair services in UA2 at all times during runs, and for monitoring and checking the performance of "their" pieces every day. Other physicists seemed to be content to let them deal with the problems for which they were responsible. Experts were in charge of data run initiation and run control during the early stages of data taking, when things tend to go wrong. Shift schedules at later run periods matched at least one expert with one nonexpert (in UA2, two physicists were placed on main shift at all times).

Interestingly enough, the characteristics of nonexperts were also framed in terms of trust. A consistent comment by physicists was that nonexperts (those entering the field) trust data plots and other results too much. They are too easily deceived by a beautiful-looking peak in the curve, which they believe represents the signal:

> **KK:** What distinguishes ((a newcomer)) from the experts?
>
> **NC:** () They say, marvelous, I've got a beautiful peak there, that's something, that's a signal. But then, when I know the detector, I know that the detector can simulate these kinds of things. And that's something I have to learn slowly, *when* I can *trust* the data and what I see there. () I have to *lose the belief* that what I just wrote to tape and then analyzed, that this is pure physics [emphasis added].

As another physicist put it:

> **AP:** Initially they can't discriminate plots that *are* correct from those that *look* correct. *They believe in what doesn't actually crash* [emphasis added].

Experts, then, are those who have learned to engage with objects in reliable trust relationships and who, therefore, are trusted by colleagues who cannot engage in these relationships directly. Not everyone, by the way, automatically becomes an expert over time. But the point to be noted here is that distinctions of trust unite physicists with objects and, on a second level, separate and unite physicists among themselves. Trust, in the experiment, is a category that feeds upon the capital physicists draw from "living with" these objects. Nonetheless, it is a human category, employed to account for and reflect the factions created between physicists, and to tip the balance of power in favor of the human collaboration.

5.8 Primitive Classifications Reconsidered

Primitive classifications, especially those which form consistent patterns, *accentuate* and *display* the reconfigurations that make up local settings such as laboratories and HEP experiments. When we consider these classifications and distinctions, we look at the same reality as the one described in Chapter 3, but we look at this reality as if through a kaleidoscope that has been rotated—the pattern is different. What springs to life is not the meaning and basic characteristics of an epistemic approach, but objects and their qualities, and agents and their involvements. I have illustrated how the detector is construed not as a mechanical and electronic device but as a physiological organism that is, at the same time, an alter ego, a substitute for humans, a self-created homunculus writ large which, after its creation, is only painfully understood. The background, on the other hand, was construed as an antagonist whose maliciousness is not attributed to sources but to itself. Human agents in the experiments, under systematic pressure to link up in useful ways with physical objects, seemingly let themselves be invaded by objects for whom they function as a host. But they also unite against an object reality by building links between each other and basing these links upon trust.

The classifications and distinctions recorded in this chapter display the essential *flexibility* of these entities, the uncertain character of their boundaries and qualities. What characteristics are assumed by objects and subjects, organisms and machines, appear to depend on the reconfigurations accomplished in stable local settings. Whether they are fashioned as objects, subjects, organisms, or machines depends on these reconfigurations. Primitive classifications exhibit the work accomplished in refashioning original entities into new orders of self-other-things.

This interpretation must be qualified, however, by a recognition of the fact that entities which are simultaneously involved in other contexts, as human beings are, are resistant to reconfigurations that run counter to their makeup in these contexts. For example, qualities of individual agency that are not only granted but required of human beings in many contexts continue to leak into situations in which this characteristic is superseded by others. "Resistant" properties, stabilized in other contexts, may intrude in local situations as problems. For example, participants in HEP experiments do on occasion complain about their lack of *individual* authority, responsibility, and identity, and recruitment problems are often blamed on the phenomenon that students hesitate to commit themselves to a field that offers them no prospect of individual authorship or creation of scientific work. The message to be taken from primitive classifications and distinctions is that they call into question and render problematic the boundaries between the objects and the characteristics of the original beings entering the experiment. The message itself says little about the success or the side effects of the attempted reconfigurations.

6

From Organisms to Machines:
Laboratories as Factories of Transgenics

In Chapter 5 I referred to ontologies of objects and subjects as these are expressed in symbolic vocabularies, but only in the context of experimental high energy physics. Turning again to molecular biology, in this chapter I examine how the live organisms molecular biologists deal with are configured and reconfigured. If the last chapter showed how a technological detector displays itself, in experimental settings, more as a physiological organism than as a machine, this chapter will show how living organisms become, in molecular biology laboratories, similar to (industrial) production systems and production sites—they become molecular machines.

6.1 A Science of Life without Nature?

Molecular biology dates back to the 1940s (Judson 1992), but its prehistory can be traced to a much earlier time. From Foucault's perspective (1973: 125ff., 226f.), it starts with the end of storytelling about plants and animals, and with the beginning of a natural history of these entities. Telling the story of a plant or animal meant listing its organs and parts and identifying the similarities it had with other things. But it also meant describing the powers attributed to a plant or animal, the legends in which it occurred, the insignia formed by it, the cures and potions made from it, and the food prepared from it. The whole formed a web of meanings in which the observable could not be disentangled from the reported, and the documented could not be distinguished from hearsay and legend. With the natural history approach, biology began to focus exlusively on the entities themselves and their visible properties. It described these properties one by one, sorted them into series, and tried to establish the orders of differences and identities between them. From the end of the eighteenth century onward, biologists began to distinguish between visible properties and "important" and "essential" characteristics, which were seen as functions and related to the life and survival of an organism. This made the notion of *life* an important ingredient in the new understanding of biology. Earlier naturalists had seen the living being as an instantiation of a particular classification; now the fact that something could be classified became for biology a property of life.

Molecular biology today is based on a central dogma, which retains the focus on life but at the same time breaks away again from earlier conceptions. The central dogma is that DNA contains the building blocks of life; all information needed to create an organism is coded in the large molecule known as DNA (desoxyribonucleic acid). DNA consists of a linear sequence of four smaller molecules, called bases (A, T, C, and G, short for the nucleotides adenine, thymine, cytosine, and guanine). The sequence of bases in DNA works like a code. The cell copies this code into a "messenger" molecule called RNA (ribonucleic acid). This messenger carries the information out of the nucleus of the cell into its cytoplasm, where the information is decoded and proteins are made. Proteins constitute more than half of the dry mass of a cell, and their synthesis is essential to cell maintenance, growth, and development. "Genes" are sequences of bases in the DNA that specify the structure of a protein. The gene is said to be "expressed" when it makes the protein it codes for (see Alberts et al. 1983: chap. 5).

The central dogma of molecular biology implies that the ordered variety of life, which biology had investigated before, is really an endless variation of the same: permutations of four kinds of molecules, the bases A, T, C, and G. All visible variations of life can be traced back to different configurations of these building blocks of the DNA. In this way, the question the physicist Schrödinger once posed to biology, "What is life?" seems to have found a simple answer: life is the realization and expression of the information contained in the segments of DNA called genes. The individuality and differences of living beings—the units which biologists had classed into their elaborate taxonomies, the parts which they had determined as being responsible for different life functions—have disappeared. All an organism's differences are reformulated as mere variations of the genetic code and its expression. Thus life is no longer a vitalistic force or the breath bestowed by a god upon every single creature. It is suddenly at the disposal of the molecular biologist—provided he or she can decode the plan and decipher the molecular processes underlying the respective variations.

This challenge has not been easily met in the fifty years that have passed since the nature and transmission of genetic information was first worked out. The underlying processes have been shown to be vastly more complex than originally perceived. As a consequence, the hope of understanding the essence of life by understanding the nucleic acids has been toned down. The cell, for example, has proved to be an object of almost "overwhelming complexity" governed by a myriad of well-regulated biochemical steps. The cell's structural elements and how these enable it to grow, divide, and differentiate into specialized tissues remain shrouded in "mysteries." Nonetheless, parts of these mysteries are often pronounced solved (e.g., Beardsley 1991), and molecular biology persists despite the difficulties. For the plants and animals with which the science of life began, this success had far-reaching implications. It meant the disappearance of naturally occurring plants and organisms from the field of molecular biology and their replacement with new entities; and, second, it meant the culturing of these entities in the laboratory.

Mice, flies (Kohler 1994), or frogs, as naturally occurring entities, are external to molecular biology.[1] Like the psychological and physiological person in the physics lab, they are part of the environment rather than part of the system of work. The first mouse the ethnographer Klaus Amann saw in the laboratory was a common household mouse, not an experimental specimen. The next lot of mice, the first "laboratory mice," were delivered in cages from another lab. The technical assistant (TA), who had to get RNA from them by dissecting their organs and dissolving them mechanically in a device not unlike a food processor, did not know how to kill the animals properly—he put them to death by placing them in a −70 degree Celsius freezer. (Mice should be killed "humanely" by placing them on top of the cage and breaking their neck "by applying firm

pressure at the base of the skull and sharply pinching and twisting between thumb and forefinger while at the same time pulling backward on
the tail"; Hogan et al. 1986: 97.) At that point in time (the mid-eighties),
mice had not yet become a common part of experimental work in this
particular lab, and established routines for manipulating them were not
available to lab members. Incorporating mice into the routine required
introducing into molecular biology many of the techniques mammalian
embryology had established in the decades before, including thinking of
the mouse not as an animal but as an experimental device. Classical
mammalian embryology had identified many areas thought to be "ripe
for" molecular studies, including those relevant for human reproduction
(Hogan et al. 1986). To a significant degree, the two sciences were
brought together through special workshops and courses offered at laboratories such as the Cold Spring Harbor Laboratory in the United States
in 1983 and 1984, which had the explicit goal "to help catalyze the
interaction between mammalian embryology and molecular biology"
and which produced widely circulated laboratory manuals.

What did mammalian embryology have to offer molecular biology?
Above all, "laboratory animals," that is, animals workable, manageable,
and reproducible in the lab. The origins of the laboratory mouse apparently lie with Abbie E. C. Lathrop, described as a self-made woman who,
around 1900, established a small mouse farm in Granby, Massachusetts,
to breed mice as pets (Hogan et al. 1986: 2ff.):

> [Her] mice were soon in demand as a source of experimental animals
> for the Bussey Institute and other American laboratories, and she
> gradually expanded her work to include quite sophisticated and well-
> documented breeding programs . . . As source material for the farm,
> Abbie Lathrop used wild mice trapped in Vermont and Michigan, fancy
> mice obtained from various European and American sources, and im-
> ported Japanese "waltzing" mice . . . The Granby mouse farm was to a
> large extent the "melting pot" of the laboratory mouse, and . . . many
> of the old inbred strains can be traced back to the relatively small pool
> of founding mice that Lathrop maintained there.

For example, at least five of the primary strains today may derive from a
single female in Lathrop's group. One of the advantages of old laboratory

mice strains over wild mice and newer strains derived from them is that the former show far fewer genetic variations. These mice strains are inbred (derived from more than twenty generations of brother-to-sister mating), a fact that is said to have revolutionized studies in cancer research, tissue transplantation, and immunology.

The vocabulary that describes inbred strains is suggestive: there are "strict" (brother-to-sister) mating patterns, even when the breeding stock is low because of diseases or accidents, "strict" health monitoring, and "standard" methods for maintaining breeding colonies and testing mice for genetic purity. The hundreds of mouse strains and substrains are labeled in terms of a "standardized" nomenclature that reveals details of their history and characteristics. Finally, recombined inbred strains are given the advantage of "cumulative" data, since new genetic patterns can be compared with stored or published patterns of previous generations. In sum, mice are linked to an effort to *rationalize* studies and to an effort to discipline wild animals for laboratory use. Even the "wild-type mouse" of today, which is used in laboratory research as a control for experiments with genetically or biochemically altered mice, is the result of prior attempts to improve upon its naturally occurring siblings. The "wild type" is the product of laboratories specializing in mouse breeding and not by any means a biologist's catch from the field. The naturally occurring sibling of the wild-type (laboratory) mouse would be unsuitable for laboratory work. Its various diseases alone would "pollute" the experiment; nature as it occurs in the wild is of no use to experimental work.[2]

Besides mice, fruit flies and other species transformed into laboratory animals through strict regimes of breeding and standardization, there are also new types of organisms, living things never considered by natural history, which now have the laboratory as their natural environment. These new pets of molecular biology are bacteria, especially the bacterium *Escherichia coli,* viruses like the monkey virus SV40, and yeasts.[3] With the discovery of plasmids (small circular molecules of double-stranded DNA that occur naturally in both bacteria and yeasts) and of phages (linear DNA molecules occurring as bacterial viruses), multicellular organisms that are complex creatures above the level of their DNA have also disappeared from the purview of molecular biology: plasmids and phages consist almost entirely of DNA. Plasmids and phages have many advantages. The DNA of plasmids, for example, is smaller and simpler than cellular DNA, yet it carries vital genes. Because it is so much smaller, plasmid DNA can easily be separated from the DNA of the host cell and purified. And, as the host cell proliferates, the plasmid replicates independently and produces large quantities of copies of its DNA.

Are these new organisms animals? No, for they are much smaller than any we recognize in everyday life, reduced to genetic essentials, and reproducible to enormous quantities in a short time. They do not carry proper names (even the SV40 virus is simply the fortieth simian virus discovered) and pose no moral difficulties for the scientists and technical assistants who have to process them. Viruses, plasmids, and bacteria do not have to be treated and killed "humanely," as mice do.[4] On the other hand, these organisms too are subject to conditions of life and have to be treated, in some ways, *like* more familiar animals. Their life is drastically reduced and subject to temporal optimization. As long as they live, however, they need attention and care.[5] This also holds for another category of objects, *cell lines,* used in molecular biology. Cell lines can be propagated indefinitely in a laboratory dish. Most cells have a limited life span, related to the life span of the animal or human from which they are derived. Accordingly, they die after a finite number of divisions in culture. Occasionally, however, "variant" cells that are effectively immortal arise in the culture. In addition, tumor cells, which divide indefinitely in situ, can also be used as cell lines. Many cell lines have year-long or perhaps even decade-long biographies; some are older than the lab where they are used. Most younger molecular biologists do not know, for example, that "HeLa" cells are named after a woman by now many years dead, from whom the cancer cells propagated in today's cell line had originally been removed.

Cell lines are used to determine the effects on cell behavior of adding or removing specific molecules, to study the interaction between one cell type and another, and to perform biochemical analysis. However, most plant and animal cells will survive, multiply, and express differentiated properties in a cell tissue culture only under appropriate conditions. Like bacteria, they need to be nursed along in flasks, bottles, and dishes under special environmental conditions. They have to be induced to divide, propagate, and differentiate, but at other times they have to be prevented from propagating and differentiating. Cells must not grow too densely or too sparsely, they must be repeatedly split and removed from the culture dish to form secondary subcultures, and the media supporting their growth have to be changed and refilled periodically. Their environment must be kept absolutely clean, because bacteria, yeasts, and fungi threaten the tender balance of conditions that enables their growth. Cells may "look sick," media may turn "sour" and stop cell growth, and cells may "sit too long" in the same spot or "swim off" when they are supposed to adhere to other cells. Certain cell lines must be regenerated by being reintroduced into an animal and then isolated again. Protocols for cell treatment remind one of the treatment of human bodies in, for example, operating theaters: sterile tools and conditions, mutual protection from contamination of cells and bacteria, as well as of the experimenter. As with bacteria, plasmids, and viruses, however, the care extended to cells is motivated not by moral considerations but by an economy of time and resources. The concern for their well-being is a concern for the work and materials wasted if things go wrong. As one senior researcher who seemed to have a good "feeling for the organism" (Fox Keller 1985) explained when asked to describe his cell culture work:

> **KA:** How do you treat them ((the cells))?
> **MN:** In principle you try to make the cells feel well. You try to avoid contamination with other cells or with bacteria and yeasts, because these can destroy your results. () If you can unthaw ((new)) cells and put them in a culture then you're not that schizophrenic, then you don't say if they ((the cells)) die then everything dies. But if I have only one very important cell culture, for example, if I have these ganglia which are enormously difficult to isolate and perhaps they are from a single mutation which has been sent to you ((from another lab)), then you definitely want to get them to work in culture, and then you develop this schizophrenia.

6.2 Organisms as Production Sites

The disappearance of naturally occurring animals and plants from workbench biology, and their replacement by microorganisms, cell lines, and wild strains of animals redesigned to perform as laboratory types—these are not new developments;[6] for example, microorganisms have been examined in the laboratory at least since the time of Pasteur (e.g., Latour 1988; Geison 1995). Yet their reduction in size, the search for entities consisting of barely more than genes, and the strict regimes of breeding, growing, maintaining and documenting point to a deeper transformation; the change no longer concerns the transition between nature and the laboratory, or between fuzzy holistic practices and strict, standardized routines, but *the transformation of organisms into production sites and into molecular machines.*

First, the warm rooms where cell lines and bacteria are cultured and grown, the rooms in which mice are raised and bred, are *production facilities.* For example, laboratory mice are today bred and put on the scientific market by special laboratories dedicated to producing stable strains that are simple to maintain, robust, free from diseases and that have certain genetic features. Once these mice have been acquired by a research lab, they are again put into isolated facilities in which the conditions for their further breeding and reproduction have been optimized. This is where breeding colonies are created, and where mice are submitted to the preparatory treatments to condition them for their tasks. Well-kept facilities pride themselves on their fastidious record-keeping: they record the date of birth of each mouse, the mating patterns, the size of each new litter, the deaths, and the special features. They also collect aggregate data about potentially interesting variants, the number of the males and females that are sexually mature, of those which may serve as wet nurses, and so on. Well-kept mouse facilities are also continually reorganized; males that have reached the reproductive age are put into separate cages, males and females designated for mating are placed together, litters are separated from parents, and mice that are no longer needed and young mice that are redundant are put to death or transferred to other units. A well-maintained, well-recorded mouse facility is a well-oiled production line. It produces and manages a steady flow of mice of the kind desired in the laboratory.

Second, the mouse, the cell, the bacteria, and the vector have become *production devices* themselves. Consider the use of plasmids, phages, and bacteria in DNA cloning. Cloning is often described as the most powerful DNA technology (see Lewin 1990: chap. 23; Alberts et al. 1983: 187ff.).

It amplifies fragments of DNA by more than a millionfold from even a single original molecule. Once a particular fragment has been cloned, it can be characterized and probed for the presence of particular genes. Finding the genes is necessary, because they represent only a portion of the genome of a typical mammal, and the fragments to be cloned are randomly cut from the DNA molecule.

Cloning is made possible by inserting fragments of DNA from any source into plasmids and phages (bacterial viruses). To construct the hybrid plasmid, its DNA is cleaved or "cut" at appropriate sites by a restriction enzyme, and the two ends of the break are joined to the ends of a fragment from foreign DNA. The result is a regenerated "chimeric" plasmid, which grows in bacterial (or yeast) cells just like the original. As these bacteria divide, the plasmid also replicates and produces an enormous number of copies of the original fragment. At the end of proliferation, the copies of the original DNA fragment are excised from the plasmids with the help of the same restriction enzyme.

Since plasmids (or phages) "carry" the foreign DNA as an inert part of their genome, they are called "vectors." A vector in biology is any organism that is the carrier of, for example, a disease-producing virus. Cloning vectors are production devices: they use the proliferation potential of plasmids in bacteria to produce genetic materials. In other words, biological materials are manipulated so that controlled production will occur. Standardized cloning kits are available from private companies, though most participants in the laboratories studied use their own well-worked-out procedures (see also Fujimura 1987; Jordan and Lynch 1992; Keating, Limoges, and Cambrosio 1999). Though it is still a "hot topic" in the newspapers (in regard to higher animals and humans), cloning as a research procedure is less than exciting for those who perform the work. A molecular biologist who spent a fair amount of time on cloning, with the goal of building constructs (vectors) to be used in microinjections, had this to say about it:

> Cloning is perhaps one level below what one calls exciting in the lab. You sit down, you think about a particular construct, and then you clone it. That's not very different from deciding to dig a hole in the ground, and then to dig it—it's about that exciting.

Cloning has opened up a number of possibilities, which can be summarized as follows:

1. Cloning has made it possible to produce any fragments or combination of fragments of DNA from the most varied "natural" or artificial sources (from DNA synthesis) in any desired quantity, thereby making DNA available for analysis. Until now, large volumes of DNA have been necessary for DNA sequencing.
2. Cloning has opened up the possibility of generating constructs of DNA molecules by design and using them as probes in testing DNA molecules for the presence of a particular sequence. It has also opened up the possibility of inserting them in the genome of organisms as additional genetic information.

Thus, the plasmids and phages working as production systems furnish both "natural" substances (fragments of any naturally occurring genome) and artificially created substances, such as combinations of regulatory DNA elements and coding elements that translate into proteins and "express" genetic information. These are little apparatuses that induce various effects in cells and organisms—by the transfection of cells, by injection into germ cells, and by injection into the blood of organisms for the analysis of cancer genes. They free molecular biologists from confinement to "natural" production sites and their normal products and enable them to produce "designer" molecules—for example, new proteins can be created with the help of in vitro systems of translation. Vector systems not only turn DNA molecules into pure, reproducible substances, but they also turn them, in the vocabulary of the lab, into "building blocks" and "construction elements." These can be put together according to "plan," rearranged at liberty through a procedure called "ligation," cut apart by the restriction enzymes mentioned before, and extended through artificial connecting elements called "linkers." They can be joined together with "elegant," "complicated," "simple," "well-functioning," and "incomplete" pieces and then realized in vitro in test tubes.

The important point about these small production systems is that they are *autonomous units* with which certain substances and materials can be produced in desired quantities and purities. As autonomous units, they are optimized. Optimization has been made into a fine art with, for example, the phage lambda, a linear DNA molecule into which fragments of DNA are inserted as they are into plasmids. The phage lambda has been made into a new molecule: its DNA has been manipulated to produce a shorter genome that lacks nonessential genes. This genome is too short to be packaged into the phage head where progenitor particles are located. Since the phage head has a minimum length requirement for the genomes (as well as a maximum length requirement), a foreign DNA fragment must be inserted into the genome in order to create a phage that can be perpetuated as progenitor particles. This demand, as Lewin (1990: 453) describes it, creates "an automatic selective system" for obtaining phage genomes with the inserted DNA of interest.

Autonomous production units are systems that can be separated from biological functions and from organisms with which they thrive "naturally," for example, from the bacteria in which plasmids and phages proliferate under normal conditions. To be sure, the resulting vector is reincorporated into bacteria, but it now performs a biological task for the human manipulator and not for its own or its host's functions and needs. *Autonomy* refers to this separation of biological functions and the redefinition of these functions within a different setting for human goals. The development of autonomous production units in molecular biology can be compared with industrial development in general—with a logic of production not confined by the application of craft and by individual or household needs. In a sense, cloning is the *steam engine* of molecular biology.[7]

The decomposition of biological organisms into parts that are usable as production devices is a very special kind of process. It is not based on the morphology of organisms, nor even on the elements of their program, the genetic code. It is also not concerned, as physics is, with atoms, particles, or the smallest elements of biological materials. Rather, it concerns interlaced patterns of structural elements and their specific, well-regulated interaction. These patterns are abstract in that they can be created from elements of different origin and be activated to fulfill their capacity in many host materials, under different circumstances. But they are concrete because they involve the interaction and regulation of material substances and their functioning within "natural" organisms, and *not* the interaction of symbols or pure information. Molecular biologists occasionally use the term *molecular machines* to refer to the well-regulated molecular and biochemical processes of genetic expression and cell differentiation. I suggest that this expression can serve as a master analogy for the ontology of objects in the laboratory: the objects that stand out are not used as organisms, they are implemented as *machines*. The autonomous production units into which organisms are decomposed in this way are *molecular machines*. Other materials in the lab may not function on a molecular level, but they are still used and usable as *biological machines*.

6.3 Cellular Machines

The notion of a machine can be extended to include not only the utilization of cells in the laboratory but also the utilization of whole organisms, like mice. Molecular biology is still a science of life in a more holistic sense, in that it demands that results obtained in vitro be replicated wherever possible and relevant in more "natural" systems, as in cells and animals. Molecular biologists are aware of a hierarchy of indirection in their work. They attempt to improve upon the derived character of the processes generated in reaction mixes by moving back to processes generated in the cell, and from there to processes generated in the mouse. What happens in cellular systems, for instance, counts as "direct" evidence when compared with in vitro systems, but when compared with procedures that involve the whole organism, it counts only as indirect evidence.

The picture is complicated by the fact that there are always two uses of cells and organisms, one linked to the activity of these objects as *production systems* and the other to their role as *model systems* representing naturally occurring processes. The complications arise from the phenomenon that although the goals in the two contexts are different, both goals can be pursued at the same time, and the actual involvement of these objects in laboratory work can be quite similar regardless of which goal is being pursued. Consider cell lines. On the one hand, these are used for the production of the cell's own substances, for example, for the production of DNA, RNA, or proteins. On the other hand, cells also serve as models in examining cell differentiation and the regulatory mechanisms that govern the life of the cell. If one wishes to investigate the cell specificity of regulatory DNA components, the vector constructs that include these components cannot be replicated in bacteria, but must be used to transfect the cells of interest. In such cases, foreign DNA, or regulatory factors that intervene in the normal cellular processes, are inserted into cells, where they stimulate effects from which one draws conclusions about cell mechanisms. The resulting effects can be observed under the microscope or made visible through dyes and similar means. They are also made available for further analysis through cell cloning—that is, through the self-generated, identical replication of cells. A clone is a population of cells derived from a single ancestor cell (Alberts et al. 1983: 163ff.) One of cloning's most important uses has been the isolation of cell lines with defects in specific genes. If the gene is defective, the cell is defective in a specific protein; this defect can reveal a good deal about the function of that protein in normal cells.

Cloning increases the uniformity of the ground material and makes it available in great quantities. As with DNA cloning, the end results of cell cloning are products of a production system; they are uniform, purified, analyzable streams of material. These materials, however, are used simultaneously to derive information about "natural" biological processes, in accordance with the character of the production system to serve as a model for these processes. For example, if F9 cells (embryonic stem cells) are used as a model system for processes of cell differentiation, then evidence for a particular cell product or effect is at the same time evidence for certain aspects of the specific kind of differentiation that the cells model. The proliferation of the respective cellular materials is an indicator of the "biological relevance" and effectiveness of the phenomena investigated. But it also means that the production cycle—the biological machine through which cell lines, like vector systems, generate quantities of purified, analyzable substances—is at the same time a machine that simulates the biological machines of "natural" cellular processes.[8]

Compared with the vector systems, the present machine is made of cellular (as opposed to just genetic) materials. A third candidate qualifies as a machine in the molecular biology laboratory: the higher organism, such as the mouse. Despite the disappearance of "natural" animals from biological laboratories and the temporary disappearance of all higher organisms from many molecular biology labs, molecular biologists have always maintained that the results of their investigations in model systems must at some point be reconnected with the processes in "real" plants and animals. "Technical difficulties" make this goal problematic, however. For example, the time and resources needed to work with bacteria and cells is several factors smaller than those needed for animals like mice. Furthermore, techniques for obtaining embryonic tissues in the earliest stages of mouse development were not available until recently, nor were the techniques for unspecific or specific alterations of the genome of the mouse. Microinjection, available for a few years, has changed this, yet a fundamental difficulty remains: compared with plasmids or cell lines, the mouse is enormously *resistant* to technical manipulation. It is impossible to implement certain alterations of its genetic makeup or other relevant changes without, at the same time, killing the animal. Changes in natural cycles of reproduction have deadly consequences, particularly when genes or functions in the initial process of embryonic development are involved. If one attempts such manipulations, one cannot create a functioning production unit.

A second fundamental problem with living animals is establishing a correspondence between technical intervention and visible effect. If the attempt is made to transfer one allele of a mouse gene into a strain carrying a different allele and in the process the resulting mouse is born too small or dies soon after birth, it is by no means clear whether this occurrence is at all related to the attempted genetic manipulation. The problem has to do with the fact that a large number of cellular processes and other interactions within a complex organism are unknown, are unavailable for direct inspection, and cannot be adequately controlled. Moreover, the availability of mouse strains with single defective mutations in their genetic makeup, offering a starting point for controlled, technically generated variations of genes, is small.

Are mice, then, unsuitable production machines for materials and substances that may tell us something about their functional relevance in developmental processes? No, since parts of the mouse can be made to furnish such materials, in particular those parts which undergo the least

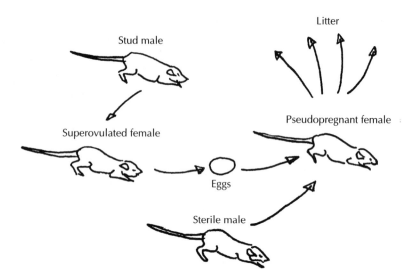

Figure 6.1 Four classes of mice involved in the production of transgenics.

complex developmental processes. These are processes surrounding the fertilized egg, which all current procedures target. The goal is to create "transgenic" mice through the deliberate manipulation of egg cells, with the help of techniques of microinjection and recombination. For this purpose, animals are turned into hosts, or *containers,* for manipulated genetic materials produced from the ground materials (eggs and sperm) of other animals. Fertilized eggs are removed from "donor" females that have been superovulated and placed individually with stud males. The eggs are genetically manipulated and then reintroduced into (other) "recipient" females that have been turned pseudopregnant by mating them, in natural estrus, with vasectomized or naturally sterile males. The very best recipients, manuals say, are females who have already successfully reared a litter ("experienced mothers"). An excess of pseudopregnant "plugs" (females mated) is needed, since attempts to transfer embryos to pseudopregnant females often fail. Thus, backup options need to be available. Eggs successfully developed to term in recipients result in litters of potentially transgenic mice. These are screened for the presence of the injected gene by a method called Southern hybridization to DNA extracted from the tail of the animal. Figure 6.1 offers a diagram of the cycle of egg donors, studs, embryo recipients, and sterile males required in this production process.

This production process should be maintained, as the manuals advise, at "peak efficiency." The individual mouse donates its body for this process, or rather parts of its reproductive system. It has been transformed into a machine at the weakest spot of its wholeness as an organism, at the site of sexual reproduction. The involvement of four different classes of mice, each one optimized differently for their tasks (superovulated, waited on until they have produced a litter, vasectomized, raised specifically as stud males), indicates that these animals are used as *individual (re)production machines,* which are joined together to create a *factory* of transgenic mice.

6.4 Industrial Production versus Natural (Re)production

Genetics is generally associated with the "genetic code" (Watson and Crick 1953; Kevles and Hood 1992; Fox Keller 1992), conceived as a sequence of information that governs the development and growth of an organism. If the above systems are correctly characterized as molecular machines, however, another aspect of the DNA that constitutes this code becomes relevant. DNA is one of the most complex molecules known. Nonetheless, via a series of steps implied in the above description, DNA and other genetic materials have been turned into isolated *substances* that can be cut into fragments, analyzed, reorganized, and used as the ground materials for further production processes. The notion of a "substance" refers to the physical matter of which a thing consists. This physical matter must have several qualities: uniformity, purity, and mass existence.

First, the substances produced by biological machines are *mass produced.* The goal in these production chains is never to produce single animals, individual cells, or DNA molecules. To be sure, the volume of materials needed for analysis and manipulation has been continually reduced over time, as a consequence of more precise measurement techniques. Nonetheless, the end results are never single molecules or organisms, even if the first animal with a new transgenic property is always a celebrated event. Rather, the results are measurable or countable quantities of *identical elements* that are used in the aggregate. A single transgenic mouse is part of such an aggregate, since it becomes practically and theoretically relevant only if it produces an adequate number of offspring. Thus, the goal is to produce masses of materials with the help of stable procedures that can regenerate these masses. This goal is analogous to that of *industrial mass production.*

Second, the substances produced are *uniform.* If the products are to be uniform, heterogeneity has to be reduced in a number of respects: in the production units, in tools and instruments, in scientists' skills, in the recurrent cycles of production and purification, in the materials entering the cycles, in analysis procedures. For example, only a restricted number of *kinds* of production units—a few strains of bacteria, a few cell lines, one species of animal, and only a few strains of this species—are used in a lab. Production units that yield stable and uniform materials are an important capital of the lab. They can also be patented; a notorious example is the onco-mouse, a genetically manipulated mouse with a special propensity to develop cancer, which has been patented in the United States and in Europe (see also Fujimura 1996). Stable production systems need stable, reliable tools, such as centrifuges, pipettes, electrophoresis apparatuses, shakers, and mixers; they also require stable skills on the part of those who handle laboratory objects. Furthermore, production processes must be controlled to yield identical results, to reduce or control inherent variations in biological materials. In these respects, too, there exists no difference in principle between industrial processes of production and the ones installed in laboratories.

Finally, a third aspect of the products of biological machines is that they require *purification* from pollutants and contaminants that threaten their uniformity. A special feature of biological machines is that they are sensitive to all kinds of contaminations. Keeping things uniform assures the identity of production processes and products. But keeping things uniform requires keeping things clean.

The organisms used most frequently in molecular biology are also those which in other contexts are considered the most pernicious, agents that must be fought rigorously. Bacteria and viruses are the main causes of many illnesses, and fruit flies and mice are equally unwelcome parasites in our food. In molecular biology, these "animals" are pampered, bred, and stimulated to high performances; but they are also themselves at risk from other "animals"—bacteria and viruses from competing bacteria and viruses; cell cultures from yeasts and fungi; caged animals from infectious diseases. On one occasion in the lab the transgenic mice obtained from a litter were small and died early. Somewhat later, other nontransgenic mice showed the same symptoms. Extensive examination of the whole mouse colony was requested immediately. The tests showed, however, that the germs and pathogens found were the harmless kind present in almost any breeding facility, and not responsible for the strange behavior of the mice.

Extreme precautions with regard to hygiene and sterility are part and parcel of all laboratory work. Chemicals are always characterized in terms of their specific purity, and this purity has to be maintained through storage conditions and care during processing. Technical devices, flasks, tips of pipettes, test tubes are sterilized and placed in autoclaves. Substances are stored so as to prevent chemicals and environmental agents from degrading or otherwise affecting them. Processes of purification and sterilization also involve nitrogen tanks for cells and cleaning cycles for the glassware.

With production processes carried out by biological machines, there is not only the danger of external contaminants but also the danger of contamination from within the process itself—from unknown, potentially present contaminants or from those which are known but unavoidable. For example, in vitro tests of the expression of certain DNA constructs can produce more than the desired products, as a result of contamination by the cell extracts used. Equally, cell manipulations can lead to additional effects, which pollute or change the results.

6.5 Biological Machines Reconsidered

Purified, uniform, mass-produced substances are the product of the biological machines that shape and constitute molecular biology. What is the nature of these machines? Can we summarize their most important features? One underlying characteristic is the new notion of life as essentially the reproduction of genetic materials, and of organisms as the carriers of this reproduction. In the words of a textbook introduction to molecular biology:

> The main purpose of an organism's existence is (of course) to perpetu-
> ate its genetic material, and the properties of the cellular structures by
> which this is achieved are the crux of heredity. (Lewin 1990: v)

This notion of life as a self-reproducing machine motivates and legiti-mates the use of organisms as production systems in the lab. The new techniques are also based on the experience that parts can be isolated from organisms (e.g., viruses and plasmids can be isolated from bacteria, eggs and germ cells can be isolated from mice, DNA can be subdivided into fragments), just as they can be detached from machines. These parts can be mended and tampered with and then rejoined with original or similar materials to resume the work of production. Machines are de-composable, physiologies are not. Machines can also be regulated by cause-effect relationships of a rather mechanical kind—contributing fac-tors can be specified, the conditions under which cascading effects arise can be indicated, and interactions between components can be known and simulated. The regulation processes assumed to rule intracellular life and cellular differentiation are quasi-mechanical processes of this sort, even though some of these processes involve feedback loops and self-sta-bilizing mechanisms. Finally, machines and their manipulation pose no moral problems, higher organisms do.

There is a self-reflexive twist in molecular biology's use of biological machines, which is interesting to consider. On one level, molecular biol-ogy sees life as self-reproducing biological machines. On a second level, it reproduces some of these machines in the laboratory in, as one might say, slow motion, yet while rebuilding them it optimizes some of their parts and substitutes its own goals for those of the original. The point of this rebuilding is to get to know the original machines by bringing their power and production potential to bear upon themselves, i.e., by using their products to reflect and thereby clarify the original machines. Finally, on a third level, the machines that are rebuilt in the lab are, at the same time, simulations (model systems) of real-time processes recreated not in order to produce substances that may be used to reflect the working of the original machine, but in order to represent these processes directly.

Reflexive uses of machines can be made part of and can overlay simulative uses, which makes it difficult to disentangle the different deployments of machines.

The machine metaphor is sustained to some degree by molecular biology's self-conceptualization of its most powerful techniques. These techniques are called "genetic engineering," which suggests that molecular biology considers itself in some sense more a branch of technology than the sciences of botany and zoology, where it started. This self-definition has been embraced and propagated by those who see the techniques of the new bioscience—including recombinant DNA methods, embryo transfer, plant cell and protoplast culture, plant regeneration and somatic hybridization—as implying a "third technological revolution" (Buttel et al. 1985). The engineering metaphor, however, exclusively emphasizes the constructionist aspects of laboratory techniques like DNA cloning, with hopes for wider applicability in agriculture and the health sciences. It tells us little about the ontological makeup, in the laboratory, of organisms as production units, of their installment within cycles of reproduction in factories of transgenics, or of the notion of a "substance" as pure, uniform, mass-produced material of restricted origin. Furthermore, the original hopes have since been toned down, the technological impact declared "substitutionist" at best: it seems likely today that existing products will merely be replaced by biotechnologically engineered products without profound implications for productivity and the international division of labor (Buttel 1989; Otero 1991; Busch et al. 1991).

Finally, there is, as in high energy physics, a play upon boundaries (for the notion of boundary-work, see Gieryn 1983). The boundaries of interest are those between organisms and machines and between life and nonlife. Molecular biology teaches us, first, that the character of objects as "animals" or "organisms" in everyday conceptions does not make them immune to reconfigurations as machines in other settings. Second, it also tells us that machines, if they are carved out of live materials, require special attention, since these machines may die. In a laboratory full of live machines, the possibility of death needs to be kept in mind and worked around (but, of course, death is also worked *with*—for example, death is continually dealt to the mice who have completed their production services). Finally, molecular biology tells us that with the use of higher organisms, such as mice, as machines some moral issues continually reoccur and give rise to conflicts and difficulties (see also Campbell 1975; Lukes 1989). These issues may materialize in the form of participants' self-reproaches when animals are mistreated because of neglect or insufficient preparation. Moral considerations also underlie some analysts' refusal to work with animals, and the general "dislike," in one of the labs observed, for animal work. Nonetheless, molecular biology bases its success on the fusion of two ancient categories, life and machines, which, in the history of biology, have long been separated (compare also Porush 1985; Turkle 1984, 1995; Haraway 1991a). Its success is grounded on the exploitation of the *mechanical infrastructures of life* and the *re-entry* of these infrastructures into research—as machines that can be used to mass-produce certain materials and, through these materials, can be used to clarify the infrastructures themselves.[9]

7

HEP Experiments as Post-Traditional Communitarian Structures

In the preceding chapters I have discussed several aspects of the epistemic machineries in high energy physics and molecular biology: their empirical policies and strategies, the symbolic reorganization of entities in laboratories, the understanding of tools and resources used to approach these entities. So far, however, I have said little about organizational practices and about other social dimensions of the areas studied. These topics will be the focus of the next three chapters, two of which (this chapter and the next) will be devoted to high energy physics—a small indication, perhaps, of the social complexity of the large-scale "megaexperiments" of HEP. The way I have set up this section is first to address some of the mechanisms through which these experiments establish themselves as collective and communitarian structures; I will focus on the erasure of the individual as an epistemic subject and on the experiments' object-oriented management (their management by content rather than by bureaucratic or hierarchical means). In Chapter 8 I will discuss social registers, beyond the collective and communitarian one, at work in the HEP community; in particular, I will look at how individual scientists and institutes remain in the picture through confidence pathways, gossip circles, and the strategic and interest-ridden activities of the birth stage of new experiments.

7.1 Large Collaborations: A Brief History

The major sociological question HEP experiments pose today derives from their size: how is it possible to conduct an experiment with 100

(UA2), let alone 2,000 (ATLAS), participants over the course of twenty years? What organizational policies are needed to keep 200 physics institutes—located all over the world and representing virtually all major languages, national scientific systems, and cultures—focused on a common goal? It is surely surprising that experiments of this size work at all; and they work, by scientific standards, very successfully. For a sociologist it is even more surprising that the ones observed work in nonbureaucratic ways, without overbearing formal organization, without hard-set internal rules, and without the management problems apparent in industrial organizations of comparable size. There is no denying the sociological interest of the eruption of structures in contemporary science that are at once global and seemingly communitarian in nature and that represent possible alternatives to the small-scale conduct of expertise on the one hand and to other global structures (e.g., markets, multinational corporations) on the other.

Before we get into the details of these structures, we should briefly consider their historical roots (the social history of large, long-term collaborations is just beginning to be explored; see Hevly 1992: 358; Krige and Pestre 1986; Pestre and Krige 1992). We should also ask how the question of their organization has traditionally been posed. HEP experiments, of course, have not always been so large. They jumped in size in the last ten years for reasons having to do with the size of the detectors needed to explore the current energy regimes, and also because physics institutes from outside Europe are seeking access to the only setup able to do so: the Large Hadron Collider (LHC). At the time the Superconducting Supercollider was canceled in 1993, ATLAS included approximately 100 institutes and 1,000 physicists. It grew in size and "weight" by 46 percent in the summer of 1994 alone, when 35 new institutes (the majority from the U.S.) were approved during the June collaboration meeting, and 11 more institutes (10 from Japan) were added in the September meeting—and it continued to increase to 160 institutes by March 1997. The ATLAS experiment will be 15–20 times as large as the upgraded UA2 experiment was at the end of the 1980s. Before the 1980s, changes in scale were not quite as pronounced. Even UA2 was, in its earlier stages, rather similar in size to the giant bubble chamber "Gargamelle," constructed at CERN between 1965 and 1969. In the 1970s this detector produced results and involved collaborations of more than 50 physicists (e.g., Hasert et al. 1973). Particle detectors had already jumped in size once, following the invention of the bubble chamber by Donald Glaser in 1952 (Galison 1987: 139). The bubble chamber preceded today's electronic detectors as the "workhorse" of physics for the best part of 30 years. It started out tiny (Glaser's first bubble chamber was a small glass phial 2 cm in diameter), but was scaled up immediately at the Lawrence Berkeley Laboratory in Berkeley, California, by Luis Alvarez and his team (see Close et al. 1987: 114 ff., 119).

The earliest forerunners of today's large experimental collaborations before the bubble chamber were presumably not experimental teams, but the groups that built particle accelerators. Accelerators were invented in the early 1930s, when E. O. Lawrence designed the first "cyclotron," a circular "whirling device" that accelerated protons to 80 KeV. Lawrence's cyclotrons grew in rapid succession from the "11 inch" machine (11 inches in diameter; the machine was the first to reach 1 MeV) in 1932 to the "60 inch" in 1939, and the groups that built the cyclotron grew accordingly. Lawrence is generally credited with creating, during that time, "Big Science" in particle physics—research on an industrial scale involving unprecedented budgets and the collaboration of scientists, engineers, and technicians in a concentrated task force (Heilbron and Seidel 1989). Seidel (1992: 28) reports that this work force was boosted significantly by free-labor contributions—doctoral students and postdocs on extramural fellowships, and victims of the Great Depression unable to find jobs but willing to participate in the development of the cyclotron to carve out an acceptable career in physics. Accordingly, "at least three unpaid graduate students, two unpaid post-docs, one professor on sabbatical leave, and three holders of extramural fellowships" worked in the Lawrence Berkeley Laboratory at any one time, in addition to a staff of approximately 60 members (of which nearly 60 percent were funded by the state or by external funds), in the period 1938–1940.

Seidel (1992: 38) and Galison et al. (1992: 46) argue that modern big science did not originate with World War II, as frequently claimed, but evolved more gradually from the prewar period. The Radiation Laboratory in Berkeley had already developed models for large-scale research organization in connection with cyclotron construction before the war, and another line of large-scale research arose from an alliance of industry and universities (Stanford, Caltech, and Berkeley) formed to solve the problems of providing hydroelectric power to California in the 1920s (a venture in which Lawrence was also involved, see Galison 1992: 3). Besides physics, the German chemical industry also provided early models for large-scale research (Seidel 1992: 38). Heilbron (1992: 45) even suggests that if we take "squads of disciplined teams using instruments so expensive that they appear as line items in national budgets" as the mark of big science, Tycho Brahe's observatory, begun in 1576, qualified as an example. According to Heilbron, Tycho had a dozen assistants, many of them medical students, along with other observers, mechanics, and calculators. He had them collect great quantities of data, from which his "computing division" derived parameters of planetary motion. His main building was a palace surrounded by walls, five meters high, that housed a great brass mural quadrant, a chemical laboratory, and living quarters and a games room for the assistants. He also ran a branch observatory to ensure discovery of systematic errors. The Danish king financed this "empire," and cheap labor from the surrounding inhabitants took care of the construction, tended his garden, and raised his crops. The second example of early big science described by Heilbron is the Society of Jesus, which in the seventeenth and eighteenth centuries maintained seminars and collections in which members could work. The Jesuits also possessed a network of scientific collaborators with whom they conducted extensive correspondence for the benefit of training students and scientists. Most members of the Paris Academy of Science and the leading mathematicians of France, Italy, and southern Germany in this period were Jesuit-trained. Other examples of international collaborations before the twentieth century cited by Daston (1993) were the expeditions to observe the transits of Venus in 1761 and 1769 (Woolf 1959) and, later, geophysical measurement projects and the standardization of electrical units (Schaffer 1992; Smith and Wise 1989).

Clearly, if these projects are all "Big Science," they are not big science of the same type. A network of independent correspondents is something other than the system of supervisors and crews that Seidel (1992) identified with the machine-building effort at the Radiation Laboratory in Berkeley. Authors such as Galison (1992: 2) and Hevly (1992: 355ff.) emphasized the diversity of projects often classed together as big science, and Kevles and Hood (1992: 306 ff.) correctly criticized attempts to see efforts such as the Human Genome Project, the United States Geological Survey, and the Superconducting Supercollider as all of one category or kind (see also Section 4.2). Nonetheless, most sources mentioned assert that the move toward bigger science implied more hierarchy and control. According to Heilbron, Tycho Brahe ruled over his staff with a feudal authority; he designed the instruments, the buildings, the way of life, the observation protocols. Seidel also describes the machine-building organization at Berkeley in terms of an increasingly formal hierarchy: a hierarchy of components including committee leaders, assistant directors, crew chiefs, supervisors, and a directing committee that appeared in effect to be headed by Lawrence (who is described as having presided on a sort of "throne" when the committee met; 1992: 22, 38f.). Hevly, too, mentions hierarchy and the "more complex management structures" brought into play when scientific efforts become concentrated in centralized institutions (1992: 357). Must we assume that large-scale research, however diverse in other regards, always becomes more industrialized, more hierarchical, more organized in terms of division of labor and control?

In my view, the hallmark of the HEP experiments I saw is not that they organize a work force of employees in industry-like ways but that they bring about truly collective forms of working: they entice participants into some form of successful cooperation. It needs to be emphasized that the present experiments are composed not of individual scientists but of legally and financially independent physics "institutes." These are mainly university departments but also government-financed research facilities, such as the Rutherford Appleton Laboratory in the United Kingdom, the Instituto Nazionale di Fisica Nucleare (INFN) in Italy, the Lawrence Berkeley Laboratory in the United States, or the MPI Munich in Germany. ATLAS can even boast, since September 1994, the participation of KEK, the national high energy physics laboratory of Japan. Such institutes cannot be controlled and directed as contractually bound workers may be. Institutes bring to the experiments the manpower and financial resources they need: for each of the two LHC experiments, in the order of several hundred million Swiss francs. They draw these financial resources from their national financing organizations over and above the standing financial contributions CERN gets from its European member states for maintaining its accelerator and computing facilities and services. The financial and legal independence of institutes, especially the fact that they finance most of the physicists working on the experiment, means that experiments not only "approve" institutes that apply to participate, but institutes also choose experiments, sometimes with the help of internal reviews of the possible choices.

Clearly, CERN and the physics institutes need one another simply to continue to do experimental HEP. Moreover, CERN and these institutes are interlinked in numerous ways; for example, the CERN management and ECFA, the European Committee on Future Accelerators, try to influence countries to support physics institutes in their participation in an experiment, and a country's physics institutes may rally for political support to influence decisions made in CERN member countries with regard to the building of a new collider. Nonetheless, the financial and legal independence of physics institutes means that experiments think of themselves as "collaborations" of autonomous units coming together "freely" and on a relatively "equal" basis to reach an "understanding" about what they will contribute to the common goal (since the LEP experiments, there exists a document of understanding). Against this background, these experiments can be seen as seeking cooperative formats for working that cannot simply be subsumed under the rubric of an "industrialization of research."

The industrial model is inappropriate for another reason: it is a "human impossibility" effectively to control technical decision making in such big and complex undertakings. In the words of one of the two spokespersons of ATLAS in 1992, "it is simply asking too much from the spokespersons if you charge them basically to do all this job and come up with extremely good and extremely motivated decisions which require a lot of work and a lot of inside/() understanding. () This goes beyond human capacity." Although some experiments feature outstanding leaders during some of their careers (UA1 was noted for its leader, as is the currently running L3 experiment at CERN), equally many do not, and the leaders who stand out appear to have not only unifying but also divisive effects (see Taubes 1986).

From the standpoint of seeing these experiments as efforts to pull together worldwide resources in a necessary partnership centering on a detector (rather than as particular scientists' local projects that have grown in size), it is only a small step to envision them as incidences of *post-traditional communitarian structures*—as structural forms attempting to implement collective ways of working that downgrade the individual as an epistemic subject and that emphasize instead such communitarian mechanisms as collective ownership and "free" circulation of work. I choose the term *post-traditional* to suggest that the communal life-form of the HEP experiments observed is based neither on altruism nor on commonality, characteristics that are traditionally associated with community (see the recent discussions of communitarianism versus liberalism, Taylor 1989a,b; Barber 1989; Mansbridge 1990; and see Tönnies 1957). Although physicists in a collaboration are united by some common background knowledge and the task of designing, building, and analyzing the detector and its outcomes, they are also divided by the failure to fully understand each other's work, by being at cross-purposes with respect to how to build the instrument (see Chapter 8), and by concrete dissatisfactions with collaborators, with the shortcomings of the instrument, with "how things are run," and so on (see also Campbell 1958). It should also be noted that, given the global composition of collaborations, participants do not even share a common language, culture or national background. If one can characterize these experiments as communities, then they are "communities without unity" (Corlett 1989).

In the following, I shall illustrate the communitarian mechanisms implemented in these experiments; I will discuss the decoupling of the work from the scientist and its sharing in a collaboration, the shifting of authorship to the experiment, the featuring of individual scientists as representatives of the whole, and the emotional attitude that results from individuals' awareness of their collective responsibility. In Section 7.3, I illustrate the idea of management by content by showing how it is based on proximity with objects and on distributed cognition. Sections 7.4 and 7.5 extend this explanation by focusing on formats based on the combination of communitarian practices and management by content: I discuss the voluntaristic self-organization, the form of leadership, the group structure, and the time formats of HEP experiments.

7.2 The Erasure of the Individual as an Epistemic Subject[1]

In many scientific fields, work, publication conventions and career opportunities are centered on the individual scientist; scientists, their research, and their publications (or other products) form a sort of cluster, which is further stabilized and extended through other components focused upon individuals, such as research financing and scientific positions (compare Buss 1987; Beck 1992). In the HEP experiments observed, work, publication, and to some degree research financing are dissociated from this compound; they are taken over by collectives, which now stand in the center of the cluster. To illustrate this it is best to begin with an example; we can simply consider once more the calculation of the strong force-coupling constant, Alpha S, explained in Section 3.3. The work was performed by a doctoral student as thesis work and submitted and accepted at his home university; the student became directly involved in the rest of the experiment only after he had completed his dissertation and acquired a job as a fellow at CERN. When the time came to publish a paper from the dissertation, this scientist, no longer a student, prepared the draft, revised the manuscript according to suggestions for improvements from the collaboration, and got all the exhibits ready for publication. The paper, however, was not published under his name but under the names, in alphabetical order, of all members of the collaboration. In many fields, doctoral dissertations are contextualized in resulting publications through the addition of the names of advisors who provided direction and ideas. In this case, however, a scientist's achievement was dwarfed by the collective author "The UA2 Collaboration."

Consider, for a moment, authorship itself and its handling in other areas. Foucault defines authors as those figures to whom the production of a text, a book, or a work (including a discourse or line of research) can be legitimately attributed (1984: 103). This kind of authorship defines scientists. It is used in evaluating scientific work, has given rise to the Science Citation Index, and informs our image of science and many sciences' practices (see also Mullins et al. 1977; Holton 1978; Edge 1979;

Small 1985; Leydesdorff and Amsterdamska 1990; Hicks and Potter 1991; Leydesdorff 1993). In the molecular biology laboratories studied, participants monitored their own and their fellow scientists' authorships, laboratory leaders planned and cultivated journal and publisher contacts and thought in terms of publications even at the very beginning of an idea, postdocs structured their research in terms of authorship possibilities, and most participants also defined their social relations through opportunities to publish—they never got so angry and involved as when they were embroiled in authorship quarrels. Though papers in molecular biology are increasingly authored by two, three, or four people, individual responsibilities and accomplishments remain clearly demarcated by authorship conventions: the first-named author contributed the most in terms of performing the actual inquiry, the ones in the middle have provided specific ingredients, and the last-named author is the laboratory leader who supplies the resources, guides the direction of research, and contributes ideas. This rule, which is widespread, does not erase but maintains the distinction between authors, and it can be seen as an attempt to sustain the individual as an epistemic subject (as the entity through which knowledge is procured) in the face of increasing incentives to collaborate.

In experimental high energy physics, such attempts are no longer made. Individuating authorship conventions have disappeared; papers reporting experimental results will have all members of the collaboration listed on the first page(s) of the paper (with the LEP experiments at CERN, this amounts to two or three printed pages listing several hundred names). The names are in alphabetical order; no clues as to who originated the research or performed large chunks of it can be derived from the list. There is no special authorship position for the spokesman of an experiment or for important contributors. The work for which Carlo Rubbia at CERN received the Nobel Prize in 1984 is referenced as UA1 Collaboration, G. Arnison et al. (1983a,b).[2]

Naming, then, has shifted to the experiment, and so has epistemic agency—the capacity to produce knowledge. The point is that no single individual or small group of individuals can, by themselves, produce the kind of results these experiments are after—for example, vector bosons or the long "elusive" top quark or the Higgs mechanism. It is this impossibility which the authorship conventions of experimental HEP exhibit. They signify that the individual has been turned into an element of a much larger unit that functions as a collective epistemic subject. The work which resulted in the Alpha S publication, though it seemed individually accomplished, also rested on this collective. It used data from a unique and complicated instrument that had required a whole collaboration to build and run. In addition, such analyses are often of direct interest to others in the experiment who can use the results in further calculations. In a sense, individually achieved results must first be returned to the experiment from which they derive before going to the community at large, and the return is made visible through collective publications. Third, experiments, not just individual physicists, have a need to prove their worth through the production of results. Large collider experiments of the kind studied are legitimated by having center-of-mass energies higher than those of previous experiments. As a consequence, they are expected to contribute to the picture of physics as a whole by providing not only new results in their areas of research, but also recalculations of existing constants and measurements derived from higher energies. The individual scientist is fitted into the picture as a contributor to the task the experiment is charged with. It is the work of the experiment which travels through the community under the experiment's name, not scientists together with their work.

The preeminence of the collaboration is also illustrated at scientific conferences. Except for the meetings of national physical societies, all conferences in the field (such as the meetings in La Thuile and Moriond, the p-$\bar{\text{p}}$ workshop or the Lepton-Photon conference) feature only talks on particular experiments (e.g., "New results from UA2"), or summaries of several experiments and of the status of a field. They do not provide slots for reports on individual work. Scientists who give experimental talks stand for the experiment whose results they present and represent, reporting on materials worked out by many others. An example is a presentation prepared on the "hot" topic of the calculation of "the limit on the top." The talk was prepared in UA2 by a physicist who assembled the various contributions, which was then reviewed by the collaboration and rehearsed in special meetings. This talk was delivered at a number of conferences and other events by several different physicists. Whether a physicist was selected to present a talk did not necessarily depend on whether he or she had worked on a topic (though this could be a consideration), but, for example, whether the person had had any other opportunities to present a paper, or whether, at a given time, he or she needed "exposure" at important conferences with a view to securing a job, or whether the conference was held in the person's home country (which is important with regard to careers), etc. Students toward the end of their dissertation and postdocs were especially eager for these opportunities, and they were frequently selected. The following announcement on conferences was made by the spokesman of UA2 during one of the last collaboration meetings. The passages in italic indicate that experiments and not individuals are invited to give talks, and that "taking turns" is one criterion for choosing speakers to represent the experiment:[3]

> Okay, now let's discuss conferences (). We announced last time this Aspen meeting where *they wanted a talk on direct photons in UA2*. Well, F. has finally agreed that she would go. Okay, for the next year we have a few more, and in fact, what I've done, *I have to remind you people who have given talks in the past four years, '87, '88, '89, and '90*. This is the list of speakers so that you can yourself establish priorities in choosing speakers for the next time. () There is an SSC Symposium in Madison, Wisconsin, at the end of February where *we are asked to provide a speaker (for) new results from UA2* and the talk would be 45 minutes long. That looks interesting. The next in time is La Thuile, is the 3rd to 9th of March . . .

When an individual's achievements are always contributions to, and can be judged by, the success of an experiment, the welfare of the whole is on every individual's mind. Also kept in mind is the interdependence of various detector and analysis components, and the associated dependence of physicists upon each other's work. It is this interdependence which creates a form of *emotional involvement* that, in addition to authorship provisions and representational formats, strengthens and sustains the communal life form. Participants indicated this involvement through anxieties. They talked about what gave them headaches, what bothered them about an issue, what lurked as a potential problem in the back of their mind, and what caused nightmares. A physicist in charge of online operations in UA2 described it this way:

> **KK:** Can you give me specific examples of these?
>
> **LM:** ((Gives examples of problems; then continues)). In fact one of the *nightmares* that people like me have, well at the beginning you have the *nightmare* of being able to take data efficiently and of good quality. Then you have the *nightmare* that, when you analyze the data, that it's really correct. And that all goes around the data-taking if you want to be able to read the tape that you've written etc. But even now you have the *nightmare* that maybe that particular operation which could not be grossly wrong otherwise you would have found (the mistake) immediately, it could be a bit wrong with a small bug. And then you would influence the quality of the analysis because you lose 10 percent of the events. Because in 10 percent of the cases you were setting a flag in the wrong way. () So if that operation was not done properly then your data are in serious trouble. So that tells you that the interest you can develop in being involved in these things is by no means a secondary one. [Emphasis added.]

Pronounced worries of this kind are brought up by people who are no longer acting for themselves but as links in a chain of operations. The fears may be experienced negatively by individuals, but they also goad people to act responsibly and cooperatively.[4] They prompt the participants to think in terms of large connections and spur them to perform "at higher pitch." Physicists in UA2 often appeared to be consumed with their tasks virtually day and night, including weekdays and weekends. The expert just quoted, for example, had a computer terminal installed in his bedroom so he could answer questions and solve problems encountered at any time during a run. In the language Matza once used to describe marijuana users (1969: 130ff), these experts appeared *engrossed* in their project, *entranced* by the thing they were doing; they created the impression that they forgot themselves and their immediate environment. The drug, of course, is not marijuana, but the experiment; it is work that weighs more because it is embedded in and interlinked with the work of others.

To conclude this section, I want to emphasize that what needs to be appreciated is the effect practices of collective authorship, representation, and responsibility—the reverse of individualizing practices (see Chapter

9)—have in contemporary sciences. The erasure of the individual epistemic subject in HEP experiments unleashes something that is urgently needed in this area, cooperation. In fields that insist on individuation, like molecular biology, cooperation is always tenuous; it requires trust and continual negotiations and renegotiations of interest and contribution, which are tedious to maintain even in small, two-person groups. Authorship, project assignment, grant allocation, and other patterns in these fields are a formidable *individuating force,* one that takes advantage of the ontology of discrete individuals in everyday life (e.g., Beck 1992) to locate the will to knowledge in persons (who extend themselves through non-authorial technicians, research assistants, and other helpers). Whatever its benefits, this force hinders the synergy effects that may result from cooperation. In experimental high energy physics, the barriers that make cooperation such a precarious achievement are removed. Practices like the ones found in HEP research result in the redefinition of the physicists as true "members" and "participants"—as elements in a larger unit.

7.3 Management by Content

So far I have located the theme of this chapter, the organization of HEP experiments, in communitarian practices that emphasize the group level. In Section 7.4 I will return to this level by providing a glimpse of the actual participatory structures of the experiments. Here I want to make it clear that HEP experiments also involve object-centered—and not only group-centered—formats of organization. I want to maintain that these experiments' seemingly "natural" ways of working, their relative lack of cumbersome structures of organization, derive from this object orientation. In other words, the success and feasibility of HEP experiments not only has to do with their communitarian practices but also with the fact that they extend these practices into, and combine them with, object-centered management or management by content.

The idea of management by content can be captured by two principles: it is management that maintains participants' proximity to objects or to the substance of scientific work; and management that substitutes, where possible, object-oriented structures for social authority structures. Our concept of complex organizations has been significantly enlarged and transformed in recent years by authors who emphasize the role of cultural beliefs and symbols in shaping organizational structures (Meyer and Rowan 1991; DiMaggio and Powell 1991) and who point out changes in organizational policy illustrated by flexible work arrangements, vertical disintegration, slimming and fattening of organizational hierarchies, and (inter)organizational networks and relations (e.g., Drucker 1988; Perrow 1991; Lipietz 1992). Nonetheless, the concept of organization essentially remains a concept of the coordination of human groups. Where knowledge is concerned, it tends to assume away the rich processes and relationships between experts, organizational formats, and the object world through the simple presupposition of the technical competence of knowledge workers. The notion of management by content aims at bringing into focus these relationships. While the ways in which object-centeredness is enacted in organizational settings is open-ended, the term itself points to "mixed" systems of care and attention developing around epistemic entities in which organizational governance crucially works through the manipulation of problem content rather than solely through people and structures.[5]

The first level of management by content in HEP experiments relates to where in the organization decisions are made. In Section 5.6, I briefly described how physicists are categorized and identified in terms of the objects on which they work. Physicists are technical objects' caretakers and, frequently, their makers; they are also their spokespersons, accountants, lobbyists, and investors. They know "their" technical objects with whom they share part of their life and their biography (Seidel once wrote of the "lust for machinery" in early accelerator labs, 1992: 33). But this link between persons and objects creates a situation where objects cannot be decided or acted upon without "their" physicists. In organizational terms, vertical lines of command between people that exist in other settings are replaced, in the experiments studied, by horizontal links between scientists, or groups of scientists, and objects. Experiments are built from such horizontal circuits, where the bulk of the competence circulates. They work "naturally" if tasks are not divided by the *similarity* of the behaviors performed but in terms of the *proximity of the objects* toward which they are directed. In molecular biology laboratories, with their individuating policies, this proximity is always given. But in large-scale collaborative research, tasks could also be broken into sets according to industrial forms of division of labor that maximize control and the speed of task performance. This scenario is often envisaged by commentators on big science projects (Section 4.2) and appears to be implemented at least in some—for example, in those genome project centers that specialize in large-scale mapping and sequencing (see Kevles and Hood 1992: 300ff.; Seidel 1992: 30). In the HEP experiments studied, however, there is astonishingly little division of labor along these lines. Instead, these experiments rely on circuits of information and work flow in which participants develop common story lines with "naturally" separated objects (subdetectors, specific particles, codes, etc.). Information need not be gathered and processed by a centralized control hierarchy that decides what is to be done and issues commands to individuals who then perform the task. Instead, the information resides, and remains, in the immediate environment of technical objects, where it is transported by the scientists engaged with these objects.

Now, a second level of management by content. The technical objects from which we started "require," beyond the action of larger collectives, a new medium where they can be "grasped" and configured as complex wholes. This new medium is discourse. Discourse runs through HEP experiments; it provides the experiment with a massive spectacle of object features, of their story lines and technical dramas, which are held by and spill from computer displays and printouts, transparencies, internal notes, "documents," and together with all these, talk. Through discourse, the proximity with physical objects is extended beyond the individual subject's object relationship to working groups and larger sets of experimental participants, and eventually to "all" participants. Discourse channels individual knowledge into the experiment, providing it with a sort of *distributed cognition* or a stream of (collective) *self-knowledge,* which flows from the astonishingly intricate webs of communication pathways (see also Coulter 1979; Brown 1987). The HEP experiments studied were and are marked by a constant humming of the experiment with itself, about itself. If these experiments do not need cumbersome organizational structures, it is not only because of the object circuits with which they replace lines of command. It is also because in addition to these circuits they create a discourse within which the features, reactions, and requirements of technical objects are continually exhibited and expressed, and in which everyone can, in principle, assess and follow technical needs and co-shape the strategies adopted.

The presence of a discourse suggests the presence of discourse occasions, of localities and time slots suited for "distributing cognition." Numerous created and proliferated discourse spaces exist in the experiments studied. Almost any situation, it seems, in which a participant finds him- or herself in the presence of another generates technical talk, including jogging in the vineyards and fields surrounding CERN or a bus ride to town. Many informal occasions revolve around "the cafeteria"—actually three restaurants in different locations where physicists have "coffee breaks," lunch, drinks, and dinner (in the main cafeteria from early morning until past midnight). More opportunities occur around apparatus and equipment, for example, the testbeam area, the "pit" (the hole in the ground in which the detector intersects the beam from the collider), and smaller testlabs. There are also the *virtual face-to-face* occasions created on computer terminals (of which several were installed in every office) for talk with colleagues who may be located two doors down the hall or halfway around the globe. The experiments studied were and are mapped along a fine *grid of discourse spaces* created by such *intersections between participants*. This grid was and is today perhaps the most important vehicle of experimental coordination and integration.

This is particularly apparent if we now look at the more formally arranged discourse occasions. They are provided, over time in ATLAS, by an exploding number of "meetings," for example, R&D (research and development) group meetings, working group meetings, detector meetings (divided according to subdetectors), panel meetings, institute meetings, steering group meetings, collaboration meetings, technical board meetings, editorial board meetings, referee meetings, accelerator meetings, fixed committee meetings (which allocate and coordinate infrastructural resources), special (sometimes week-long!) workshops dedicated to detector complexes, submeetings of some of the former, and the very important "meetings after the meeting" (the informal exchanges that occur after scheduled events). In fact, the group structure of experiments is exemplified by a meeting structure, illustrated during collaboration weeks. During these weeks, full days of working group or detector group and subgroup meetings held simultaneously are followed by detector-related steering group and institute meetings (if such are implemented for subdetectors), and these in turn are followed by a full day of plenary meetings and concluded with a collaboration board meeting at the end.

The sequential and temporal structure of these meeting schedules is not without significance. As indicated, institute meetings placed at the end of several days of working group meetings and the plenary allow the earlier meetings to inform the institute meeting. The same succession of meetings existed in UA2, and it exists in ATLAS on the level of detector or R&D collaborations. The sequential order suggests a passing of knowledge and technical decisions from the expert group where the responsibility lies to wider and wider circles that take note of these details and play them back—through discussions, questions, and comments. Several rounds of this feed-forward and feedback result in the major technical decisions that are made by institute meetings (e.g., choices between competing detector technologies) after months of discussion. These rounds of discussion include panel feedback and panel recommendations, which are also channeled through working group meetings, submeetings, and plenary meetings.

What happens at the meetings? A number of things, of course, but prominent among them is a sort of narrating and accounting encapsulated in a particular genre of communication (see also Hymes 1964; Goffman 1981; Luckmann 1986; Boden 1994), the *status report*. Status reports comprise the vast majority of talks given at meetings. They demonstrate a high degree of uniformity, which results from the fact that participants themselves have practical knowledge of these forms and use them in accordance with their knowledge. The status report is a summary of what a group or a person, drawing upon others, has been doing and has experienced in dealings with equipment, data sets, physics calculations, and the like. It is a summarized history of physicists meeting the object, whose exact reactions and characteristics it details on transparencies. The following excerpt from a status report given in an ATLAS plenary meeting by the spokesperson of the muon working group gives an example:

() And let me remind you that for the last meeting it was reported that there were two processes, namely the decay of the search for a new particle like the Z', there is a sensitivity up to a mass something like 4 GeV, even (with the old efficiency) until you get a resolution of something like 10 percent. Then there was another (process) the Higgs search into muons and into other electrons, it has been shown by many authors that a resolution of something of the order of 10 percent is always sufficient to dig out the signal. So we are looking for other processes to justify a very high resolution, like, for example, () the search for light Higgs where maybe a good mass resolution could help. However, the plot he showed yesterday showed here ((pointing at plot)) the mass range between 100 and 200 GeV, and this is the tail of the Z zero peak, and you see here with infinite good resolution the points here how their light Higgs would look like, and if you have a (?) resolution like for example 10 percent you sit down here, so if you go for a 1 percent you're somewhere in the middle, so it looks also here, this is two orders of magnitude, that the sensitivity for this process is very small, so it's very unlikely that a good mass resolution helps you here, because the signal to background rate is just too bad.

Status reports unfold all relevant wrinkles of a problem ("and this is the tail of the Z zero peak, and you see here with infinite good resolution . . ."), display the continuity of research ("And let me remind you that for the last meeting it was reported that there were two processes . . ."), and display the embeddedness of meetings by making reference to preceding submeetings ("However, the plot he showed yesterday showed here the mass range between 100 and 200 GeV . . ."). Reports stitch meetings together, and through meetings they do the same for groups. Eventually, as they are selectively repeated not only in series of meetings but also in informal talk, they stitch together the collaboration itself.

Informal talk, too, contains reports, though they may be more fragmented, interactively elicited, and less reliant on the paraphernalia of meeting presentations. The following is an example of an interactively assembled and expanded status report from a UA2 collaboration meeting:

> GM: Uh, lemme first talk about the Image Intensifiers, and go back one month behind, when we installed the power supply which has been . . . the distribution of the HT, and we found out that they didn't work.

And that, uh, we had to decide then to rebuild them . . . Now several things have been done in between, but to continue on the Image Intensifier, one of the chains, chain number 6, was found to be a CCD killer, so there was one chain where there was no signal, and one which was killing CCDs. Now when the first CCD happened to be killed, since we had never had any CCD which died, and there was no evidence of anything being wrong, we put another CD, which was killed within one hour. So then we decided there must be something really wrong, and we didn't have very much clue right away . . .

LB: Could you perhaps say why you are so sure that it is a bad contact inside, because you have tried all the other possibilities, and by exclusion, or

GM: ( )

LB: You took the chain and you brought it down to the experiment and you connected it to the cables?

GM: ( )

XX: You mentioned you observed (a) smaller spike, can you tell them to be or not to be crossed?

GM: ( )

CB: GM, you can also say that the noise is small and random in time, and this other effect is bigger, at a more or less regular period. So it's obviously something completely different. It wasn't just ordinary noise.

In UA2, a setting brimming with reports was the "counting room" of the experiment, a control room from which data taking was monitored during runs. On prime occasions, participants continually entered and exited this room—these were physicists beginning and leaving their shift, detector experts on shift with their subdetectors in other rooms who checked things with the main shift or came for a chat, online experts who had been called because of problems or who wanted to see how things were going, spokespersons taking care of "their" part of the apparatus, looking in on the progress of things, or simply "being there," visitors from other experiments or other labs, and we, the ethnographers. An almost continuous reporting developed among these participants, each visitor informing new ones about what had happened and what was going on, with the physicists on shift and at work in the room occasionally taking over the conversation. Such reports dissolved in question-answer sequences, as in the following example recorded during a UA2 run in 1988:

> **LB ((after coming back to control room)):** So what did the coordinator say?
>
> **KH:** They say they will keep this fill until in the morning. They would prefer to dump it at 3 at night, but are not sure they can be as effective then.
>
> **LB:** And what happens in the morning?
>
> **KH:** ((Shrugs shoulders.)) I don't know.
>
> **LB:** Because then I will come in the morning and get this timing person. They refuse to admit that their unit is not working, but it is not working! ((LB puts jacket on and leaves.))

The stories articulated in formal and informal reports provide the experiments with a sort of consciousness: an uninterrupted hum of *self-knowledge* in which all efforts are anchored and from which new lines of work follow. The communitarian structure of experiments may rule out the individual epistemic subject as a procurer of knowledge. But it does not rule out all traits of subjectivity; in particular, it does not rule out self-knowledge as a form of (partly material) cognition distributed among participants about the states of experimental components. Discourse propels private experience and specific analyses into public attention and creates a continually summarized "state of affairs"; of the "shapes" detector parts and physics analysis are in, of contours of resistances, of work assignments waiting to be taken care of, etc. The HEP experiments studied, in continually integrating over themselves (to put it in mathematical terms), continually assemble the collaboration into a community reflexively bound together through self-knowledge. The medium that brings this assemblage about is the conversation a collaboration holds with itself. This conversation, I maintain, replaces the individual epistemic subject, which is so prominent in other fields. It construes, and accounts for, a new kind of epistemic subject, a procurer of knowledge that is collective and dispersed. No individual knows it all, but within the experiment's conversation with itself, knowledge is produced. For those who still remember Durkheim (1933: chap. 3), the conversation produces a version of his much-rebuffed "conscience collective"; not growing, however, from social likeness or common sentiment, but from the reflexive integration of objects and subjects in discourse spaces and forms of talk.[6]

7.4 The Intersection of Management by Content and Communitarianism

Collective consciousness distinguishes itself from individual consciousness in that it is public: the discourse which runs through an experiment provides for the extended "publicity" of technical objects and activities and, as a consequence, for everyone having the possibility to know and assess for themselves what needs to be done. A collective consciousness, like an individual consciousness, is also a moral force. This, I think, is what leads us directly to the marked self-organization of the experiments observed, a form of voluntarism where management by content (through distributed cognition and decisions residing with the experts) intersects with the communitarian attitude of individuals taking responsibility for the whole. Self-organization can be illustrated by physicists "coming forward" and aligning themselves with tasks that need to be accomplished. In the following excerpt from a plenary meeting in 1990, the spokesman first called attention to "high-priority studies" and then reacted to the suggestion to create formal working groups:

> Well, the question is whether to make really formal, a formal working group or I was more thinking of trying, and that would be really the duty of the conveners, I guess, to figure out which are the people in their groups which have showed a particular interest in some topics and at least communicate and hopefully find somebody willing to somehow coordinate a bit the work of these people, maybe that would be the easiest concrete way. Yes?

The "gentle" approach—"hopefully" finding volunteers ("somebody willing") that have a "particular interest in some topics" and "at least communicate" this interest—can be witnessed whenever new tasks require attention. While self-organization is also the morally preferred way of organizing things, it is not "morale" per se that is its origin, but the discourse that expresses necessities and interdependencies and allows for groups "freely" (with a little nudging on the part of conveners and spokespersons) to respond to demands. Self-organization, in turn, keeps social relations liquid (and presupposes their liquidity): there is the fluidity of everyone's readiness to become drawn into temporary engagements with others in voluntaristic collaborations, a fluidity aided by the breakup of forces of individuation and the holistic competence of individuals trained in object circuits.

Management by content, based on distributed cognition and joined with communitarian mechanisms, is also reflected in the form of leadership of the experiments studied. Graphically speaking, leaders were not the "top" of an experiment, nor its "spearhead" pointing forward, but were centrally placed within it. Above all, they were *centrally located in the conversation conducted within the collaboration*. First, leaders, as I suggested before, were featured as *spokespersons* and representatives of the experiment and its parts. They spoke for the experiment when such action was required, and they were the ones who were addressed by the CERN management, by conference organizers, etc. At the same time, their status was much like that of a "secretary general"—a position for which discourse is also central. A secretary general is someone who gathers information and relays it—someone who functions as an intellectual administrator, who "handles," knows, passes on matters, and can be contacted about them. In the experiments observed, the secretary general also tended to be an "administrative" administrator: in UA2 this meant, for example, that leaders also handled the travel and position applications. Third, the leaders in UA2 and ATLAS, and the leaders of three LEP experiments I spoke to, always wanted to be, and have been to the end of UA2, true *participants*: they took care, with co-workers, of parts of the equipment and their functioning; they were present not only at meetings that concerned them as leaders but also at relevant technical meetings; and they worked closely with some postdocs and younger collaborators. The following is an example of a conversation in the UA2 control room on a Sunday afternoon during the second UA2 run. Two leaders interact (LdL and PJ) over the phone after a problem with endcap cell 9 has tripped an alarm:

> **LdL:** Okay, this is the trip. ((Runs off to reset button; comes back, saying "Brrrr"; looks at log book. Telephone rings.))

CG: Luigi, this is Peter.

LdL: ((Reports endcap problem to Peter; consultation over phone for 5 minutes; LdL walks back and forth with receiver in hands and then hangs up.)) So, Peter says not to do that because he wants to do it himself.

Lu: That's what I expected ((laughs)) ((Everybody laughs, LdL looks straight.))

LdL: So, he says switch off the cell, and he will come and do it himself. I will put the register (in place).

Lu and Da: ((Laughing.))

Pi: ((Comes in to say that she is going home.))

LdL (to Pi): I wanted to change the card but Peter said to switch off the cell because he wanted to do it himself. So I did it. ((Message appears on screen.)) But now LINSUR protests that the channel is now off. ((Interacts with terminal to get LINSUR to not complain any longer; formulates what he is doing.)) . . . and we start the survey or operation, and we see if it yells ((looks at message screen)) and it does not, so we made it!

The second half of this conversation illustrates the reporting system discussed in the last section. Some of the leaders' technical involvement, illustrated in the conversation, continues even now with the much larger ATLAS experiment. In UA2 and ATLAS, leaders often spent more hours with the experiment than other participants. They monitored closely crucial parts and processes, and, not quite irrelevant in international collaborations, they spoke several languages. This brand of leadership by participation sets good examples, but it also maintains centrality in the discourse. There is no difference, in this respect, between what is required of leaders as discourse centers at the top of the experiment and leaders on the level of working group conveners. However, there are differences, in physicists' terminology, in "personality" and "competence," which leads to categorizations of "better" or "worse" leaders. These categorizations allow some persons to stand out, or try to stand outside the format.

Finally, the group structure of the experiments studied is itself an indication of their communitarian organization but also strongly corresponds to the notion of management by content. By and large, participants in HEP experiments sort themselves into "groups"; collaborations are not subdivided into departments, divisions, units, or other fixed organizational substructures. The groups were foreshadowed when we discussed meetings; different meetings in these experiments tend to correspond to different kinds of groups. The group structure is noteworthy for four reasons: first, it preserves and "represents" (natural) divisions among technical and physical objects wherever possible (see also Section 5.6); second, coordinating levels also tend to be instituted as groups—for example, as panels and steering groups or technical and editorial boards; third, almost all groups on all levels are working groups, meaning they not only coordinate or review but maintain the proximity with objects and create knowledge; and fourth, groups are created according to orthogonal principles that counteract one another.[7]

To quickly run through some examples, the centerpiece of the group structure of ATLAS in its birth stage was the "working groups," which included calorimeter, inner detector, muon, trigger/data acquisition, offline, and physics working groups. Working groups evolve into more specialized units that implement a particular subdetector or other part of the experiment once the designs have been frozen. The experiment UA2, when we joined in 1987, had such "detector groups" occupied with installing, testing, and calibrating a particular subdetector, and with monitoring its performance and tending its problems after it went under beam. When data taking began, additional "analysis" groups were formed around specific particles and events (such as the top analysis group). In ATLAS, working groups generated an ever-increasing number of subgroups studying certain entities or problems with respect to the technical proposal (submitted in December 1994) and later milestones. Working groups drew on other technology-oriented groups created at CERN, the R&D groups, which were financed by CERN and participating institutes outside the framework of a particular experiment with a view to developing (detector) technologies. R&D groups offer institutes from different countries the possibility of getting access to CERN resources (facilities, beamtime, money, etc.) without (immediately) committing themselves to a particular experiment, and they offer CERN and funding agencies in countries the opportunity of gaining some control (through a CERN approval process) over the research and the use of the resources.[8]

R&D groups, detector groups, and working groups constitute the central working units focused upon technical objects. But groups also emerge in the same flexible way on other levels. Important examples are the creation of steering committees and review panels for the detector working groups when it became apparent that these groups, confronted with complex technological options, had difficulties in arriving at an "optimization" of these options. Review panels in particular were constituted as a response to conflicts over which technology to choose in the bigger subdetector complexes by certain dates. Review panels illustrate what one might call the principle of "orthogonal groups"—groups that are created to counteract the dynamics and power structures that develop in the group toward which they are directed. The steering groups implemented in some working groups in ATLAS can also be seen as orthogonal groups. Not only were they proposed as coordinating teams that enlarged the coordinating capacities of conveners, but, at least in some detector areas, they were set up to counteract the power acquired by R&D groups within working groups. R&D groups are technological interest groups with strong investments in the technology they are exploring and developing. Steering groups counteract the influence of a financially strong R&D group by including within their ranks representatives of institutes and technologies not part of R&D groups.

Consider now one group formed according to principles of social authority rather than proximity with objects, the institute meeting or collaboration board. The group consists of one representative per physics institute participating in the experiment. It holds the decision-making power of the experiment, according to the rule one-institute, one-vote, on matters such as the ultimate detector design, which technology to choose when several options are available, whom to accept as a member of the experiment, financial matters, the naming of the experiment, and so on (the list is open-ended). In UA2 it was called the "institute meeting"; some R&D groups and subdetector groups (which in ATLAS are sometimes larger than UA2) also hold institute meetings. Institute meetings reflect the phenomenon that a substantial portion of the manpower and money needed for these experiments comes from independent physics institutes and laboratories. In the early stages of ATLAS and throughout our presence in UA2, there existed, besides the detector and other working groups and the spokespersons, only the institute meeting as a separate hierarchical level.

Institute boards are not challenged because they are seen as "democratic," according to the one-institute, one-vote rule, and because they are also seen more as control groups than as decision-steering bodies. Institute decisions are heavily prepared, usually not taken until long delays in problematic cases have allowed "the reasonable thing" to emerge, and they are always placed at the very end of collaboration meetings so that the institute representatives can participate in all relevant discussion, partake in an emergent consensus, and listen to "the mood of the collaboration." The idea that institute meetings exercise "control" may suggest that the controllers are external agents who come to CERN for the purpose of a board meeting. In practice, however, institute representatives participate in other meetings, and they are often not institute heads but other institute members who work in the experiment and have been asked by their home base to act as representatives. Accordingly, institute representatives may vary across different meetings, and "only half" of the participating institutes may be represented at any one time. Thus institute meetings do not break the communitarian order. In the proposal for a general organization of ATLAS, the "real power" was said to reside in the plenary meeting of all collaboration members.

It might be noted that the attempt to create another group, one that seemed to adhere to principles of social authority rather than to be based on the proximity with objects, failed miserably in the experiment. This was the "parity commission," a group proposed before the merger between EAGLE and ASCOT from which ATLAS developed. This group was to look into the conditions of the merger and make sure that the interests of both experiments were maintained and brought together. The parity commission was widely seen not as a safeguard but a threat to what I called the "communitarian collaboration." It was interpreted as a move toward a decision-making "aristocracy" and, hence, not tolerated; it never took up its work. In the words of the coordinator of one working group who objected to it: "It was clear that () when they were proposing ((it they)) imagined it as a steering committee, based at CERN, with (up to) ten members that would make, you know they come in and decide things () I spoke to them privately and it was clear that's the way they saw it (). And I objected (against) that violently."

To conclude this section, I want to reiterate a few points to bring into focus again the communitarian policies of these experiments and what I have called "management by content." The first point is that the main organizing format of these experiments are groups that focus on technological objects; where "coordination," "steering" or decision or result preparation is needed, it is also implemented in the form of groups (called panels, technical, editorial, or executive boards, steering groups). Conveners and spokespersons are sometimes also paired and always operate by "consulting" with other members of the collaboration, thus emulating the group structure. The group organization can also be found in the immediate environment relevant to experiments: in the R&D groups and committees that coordinate and review experimental needs and proposals. The group structure is flexible; many groups are oriented to special tasks and exist only for a limited period of time. And the group structure maintains and extends the communitarian policies that tone down the individual as the rightful and primary epistemic subject.

Second, it needs to be appreciated that virtually all groups with the exception of the collaboration board are "working" groups in the sense of groups that "study" and "work out" technical questions. This holds not only for all primary task groups, but also for the review panels, boards, and committees. For example, the very important LHC committee that evaluates experimental proposals interacted with ATLAS over a period of six months, after the Letter of Intent was submitted (a technical proposal of approximately 100 pages), with the referees "sitting down and digesting" virtually each number and figure in the proposal. During that time, members of the LHCC sent the collaboration lists of queries, asked for additional information, set "milestones" and timescales for further analyses, which the designs needed to satisfy for decisions to be made, requested new "documents" (study results) working out such matters as a possible staging of the experiment, and thereby produced knowledge. The review panels created inside ATLAS were involved not only in reading proposals but also in creating knowledge; for example, by "sitting down for hours and hours" to unfold a problem, by collecting information from outside sources, or by redoing calculations. The phenomenon that virtually all groups are working groups in different senses maintains the proximity with objects on all levels, which is also displayed in the structuring of group divisions in terms of preexisting divisions between natural and technical objects. This (working) proximity with objects also characterizes "coordinators" or spokespersons. For example, the coordinators constituting the executive board in ATLAS are group organizers (for the detector groups, for instance), but they are also involved in the implementation of their own apparatus and software component. Management by content in these experiments entails participatory leadership formats, which are at the same time sustained and demanded by communitarian orientations.

Finally, I want to reiterate that I have described the strategies of "community craft" of the HEP experiments observed not in terms of unity and commonality but in terms of counteracting and supplementary tactics. These were tactics that counteract processes of individuation through the participatory formats of collective authorship, through the "free" circulation of work and services between individuals and groups, through physicists feeling responsible for the working of the experiment, and through individuals acting as representatives of the whole. They were also tactics of counteracting and dissipating *social* power accumulated by individuals or groups. With leaders who have such power by virtue of their status, counteracting occurred through their aforementioned participation in technical tasks, and also through their taking a central role in the technical conversation experiments hold with themselves, in the circuits of distributed cognition. With the group structure, the power-counteracting tactics were exemplified in the principle of orthogonal groups: groups whose composition was based on a new dimension, which allowed them to balance or confront interest and investments in earlier groups.

7.5 Communitarian Time: Genealogical, Scheduled

It remains for me in this chapter to add a word about genealogical time in HEP experiments, and about the temporal device of the schedule. Both time formats are related to the communitarian order and also reflect management by content. Experiments—collaborations—have a certain extension in time. The time frame now is perhaps twenty years. To recall: ATLAS began as a concrete experimental effort called "Future UA2" from approximately 1989 onward and is scheduled to start data taking in 2005, thereafter to run and perform analysis for several years. Native descriptions distinguish stages in these experiments, for example the "birth" stage, and they refer to experiments of the same period as "generations." Generations involve "sister" experiments that are set up and approved at about the same time and that "milk," as one might say (physicists don't use the term), the same collider (see also Section 3.6). The largest number of sister experiments I have seen is four. These are the four LEP experiments currently running at CERN. Before them there were two large collider experiments moving in parallel, UA1 and UA2. Two sister experiments are scheduled and approved with regard to the LHC (ATLAS and CMS), and a similar number was scheduled for the SSC before it was canceled.

Experiments come in generations, but participants think beyond them. The communitarian ontology involves temporal orientations toward the "life" (time) of an experiment and simultaneously toward future generations, especially the one succeeding a currently planned, constructed, or running experiment. The notion of genealogical time can perhaps capture this double orientation. Participants not only think beyond the lifetime of their current experiment, they also organize activities that point beyond it and involve themselves in these activities. Such activities, just a trickle at first, nonetheless begin long before serious planning is pursued. In fact, preparatory work for the *next* experiment may begin *at* or *before* a current experiment is deigned ready to go ahead (before a detector is planned out, for example).

This expansive approach to the future can be illustrated by Carlo Rubbia's opening talk at the 1990 ECFA workshop in Aachen. The Aachen meeting summarized the activity of working groups in the ten months before the workshop. Its proceedings were described as being the "most important scientific basis for the decision on the LHC program." In the last part of his talk, Rubbia, Nobel laureate and at the time director of CERN, summarized the activities with respect to CLIC, a e^+e^- linear collider in the R&D stage at a time when the collaborations for its precursor at CERN, the LHC, had only just begun to form.

Rubbia believed CLIC might be operational in 2010 (Rubbia 1990: 19f.):

> In this part I will widen the discussion to possible alternatives to the LHC, such as e^+e^- linear colliders. There is no doubt that for many decades to come progress in particle physics will be crucially dependent on progress in instrumentation and in particular in accelerator technologies. It is therefore appropriate to investigate the future possibilities of even higher energy e^+e^- colliders such as CLIC, mnemonically the "Cern LInear Collider."
>
> The physics potential of such an accelerator operating in the TeV or multi TeV range is considerable. However a cautious optimism prevails concerning the feasibility of such a machine. Clearly we are not yet ready to design and build such "monsters," *but R&D is being vigorously pursued at CERN and elsewhere.* In this respect, wave-field ideas are apparently being replaced by more conservative approaches. An important milestone is the 50 MW generator operated at a 2 cm wavelength in Novosibirsk. Notice that, typically, one needs a power of 150 MW to achieve fields of 100 MeV/m. A final focus experimentation is ready to be started next year at SLAC. Intense workshop activities are being sponsored by ECFA, ICFA, etc.
>
> My present expectation is that by the year 2000 we should be ready to start a large-scale facility of that type, likely to be operational by, say, 2010. In this respect, this prospective machine appears to be the logical next step *but after the presently planned LHC and SSC.* [Emphasis added.]

Thus genealogical time stands in relation to the communitarian ontology of HEP experiments in that it matches collective mechanisms with long-term thinking, instilling in participants the orientation toward future generations. The time periods themselves are strongly determined by the perceived needs of objects—for example, the time it takes to design and test the necessary technology and to install detectors. On the other hand, the actual time it will take to complete the LHC and ATLAS and CMS is also influenced by national budgets and the payment installments to which participating countries commit themselves. Before the cancellation of the SSC, the schedule for completion appeared to be moved forward as much as possible with a view to the potential of producing data earlier than the competing collider. After the cancellation, the schedule for completion moved further into the future.

This brings up schedules in HEP experiments, which I interpret as another device that substitutes "neutral," object-oriented mechanisms for social authority mechanisms. Through schedules participants become less committed to collaborations than they become focused—driven to produce certain results by certain times, and focused on fitting particular activities into particular time slots. Innumerable schedules populate high energy physics experiments: schedules for declaring one's "interest" and "intent" in conducting an experiment and for reviewers to respond to such declarations; schedules for experiments to incorporate revisions into final proposals and for external committees to approve the proposals; schedules for institutes, experiments, and the laboratory to arrange for financial commitments; schedules for various excavations, constructions, and installations; schedules for completing and testing various detector parts, for access to the beam, to "test-beam" and to (radioactive) sources used for measurements; schedules for the occupation of certain buildings and "areas"; schedules for lowering equipment components into cavities or for moving assembled detectors behind (lead) walls; schedules for runs, test runs, cosmic runs, and anything else related to data acquisition; schedules for access to a detector under beam to inspect and heal its problems; schedules for numerous participant and "expert" shifts at various occasions; schedules for calibrations, simulations, and innumerable calculations; and, of course, across all of these schedules, schedules for meetings.

Everyone can imagine such schedules. Thus, the illustration given in the following is not a typical shift or meeting schedule, but references to dates and schedules in a review panel report from 1993. The report began:

> One of the tasks requested from the collaboration by the panel was: "Which of the three options for the () shall become the baseline design of the ATLAS (subdetector)?" (Recommendation to the plenary meeting *no later than in November 1993.*)
>
> Due to the *schedule of beam tests,* the panel had requested to postpone the recommendation to the *end of the year 1993.* The three groups

made a lot of effort in order to present to the panel as much information as possible. But some important points remain to be better understood (temperature effects, alignment corrections, toolings for mass production . . .).

Following the enquiries of the spokesmen, the different groups involved in the (subdetector) community agreed to merge, after decision by the ATLAS Collaboration Board, on one common design.

The panel decided that a *small delay* was not useful, the choice being between a *"recommendation now" as scheduled or "in 6 months or a year from today."* A clear request from the (detector) community, based on the need to unify behind one single project, and to go forward with the design of the (detector) layout, was for *"recommendation now"*. [Emphasis added.]

The times referenced in this excerpt were: the schedule for a plenary meeting, the schedule for beam tests, the end of the year, the delay (of original schedules) due to "some important points remaining to be better understood," the recommendation "now" and the recommendation "in 6 months or a year from today." The whole introductory section of the report can be read as an argument about schedules, their keeping, their delay, and the rejection of a substantial extension.

Time manifest in schedules is, in a sense, the counterpart of discourse. Objects (and subjects) become fluid, detailed, disassembled in discourse, but also composed and configured as a consequence of it. Discourse—the conversation an experiment holds with itself (and with reviewers and the like) in public—is the workbench of a sign-processing experiment, the activity through which much of the construction work is not only exhibited, but done. Schedules, on the other hand, pace construction work. The public summing up of an experiment, by the experiment itself, unfolds objects creating a form of collective cognition. Schedules *pace, phrase,* and *slate* the work, allocating turns within which certain points must be made or else the points, and the turns, may be lost. For someone to hold their turn in the collective conversation, other activities (a study, a check, a calculation, an assembly task, a panel recommendation) must be performed on time and the results exhibited in status reports. Unlike a production schedule for a film, schedules in high energy physics experiments are not in any individual's hands. Schedules originate from dispersed and diverse sources, among which object requirements and the expertise of the researchers whom they regulate play a central role. Schedules lock experimental activities firmly into deadlines and time slots, but my point is not that schedules work by exerting, always and everywhere, a hold on things—even though, on the whole, schedules seem much more often maintained in high energy physics than not. My point is that schedules, which are also publicly displayed and discussed in meetings, are a strong coordinating force, one which again forgoes principles of social authority in favor of principles formulated in terms of the content of the work.

8

The Multiple Ordering Frameworks
of HEP Collaborations

In the last chapter, I looked at the HEP experiments as a particular package of communitarian formats and object-centered managing practices. In this chapter, I want to complicate the picture somewhat by arguing that we should see these experiments as comprising several packages, or "orders," simultaneously. The previous description accounted for only one layer of order (the communitarian one), which exists in a cluster or "texture" made up of several layers edging against and folding into one another, and at times clashing against one another. For large stretches of experimental time, the communitarian order appeared to be the dominant one as a practical accomplishment and as a normative choice. Nonetheless, other orderings made their presence felt, in particular one (the actorial order) that brings back individuals, interest groups, and the actorial registers of other domains.

The communitarian formats discussed in Section 7.2 pushed the individual as the main and rightful knowledge-creating unit to the sidelines. But physicists also participate in other social contexts in which they are sustained as individuals and in which they become linked with other agents and epistemic objects—and these contexts run on different logics, ones that stand in contrast if not in contradiction to the communitarian regime. When physicists enter these experiments, they act as locality- and ontology-breaking creatures as they step from one regime of being into others. And when they switch, they carry the residues of their other frameworks with them. In HEP experiments, this means that the order of "components" (of individual physicists and groups) leaks into the communitarian order; it commands attention by the collaboration and influences the conditions under which it operates.[1]

In what follows, I will first discuss the birth drama of HEP experiments. As an experiment comes together, the communitarian superordering of formerly more individualistic contexts must first be established, and resistance to the transition is most apparent at this time. In the rest of the chapter, I illustrate how the actorial order manifests itself in later experimental stages, concluding with some pointers to additional ordering frameworks.

8.1 The Birth Drama of an Experiment

The conflicts I announced are played out in the stage of HEP experiments that participants call "the birth of a new collaboration." They refer to this stage, appropriately, in genealogical terms—the birth stage is the beginning of a new experiment and part of the emergence of a new generation of instruments suitable for new (higher) energy regimes. They also appropriately refer to the human element—the birth stage brings together groups of different origin with different technological investments. Some new experiments are formed when core members of an old collaboration stick together to become the core members of the new one. In the past institutes and physicists continued to work around one another over successive generations of experiments (experiments were shorter then), but the increasing size of experiments alone forces each generation of experiments to seek many new members—to forge a coalition with institutes and physicists outside the seeding experiment. The technology is always "new," not in the sense of involving revolutionary new concepts but in the sense of having to be built from scratch. Experiments establish themselves during a period of configuration and incorporation: when the technology is chosen in light of the physics to be explored, the groups that will participate in a collaboration are selected.

Much of the script in the unfolding technical drama of an experiment is written during the birth stage, in which individual physicists and single groups play an important role. The conflicts are fueled by the close coupling that exists between physicists and technological objects. While physicists who join a running experiment seemingly go along easily with much of the new communitarian framework, they do not easily accept the breakup of their former object circuits, which this framework occasionally demands—and which in fact is necessary for creating a working instrument that functions as a whole. Those longer in the field stake their reputation and worth on the biography they have created with particular knowledge objects; they have "interests" and investments in it. They publicly place their bets on certain technologies, and these bets are observed by the grant agencies financing the investments, by students who act them out, and by, in a sense, the whole field. Lost bets entail setbacks—social, political, financial, emotional, and psychological. Status may be temporarily diminished and political clout dampened, grant agencies may become more hesitant, and identities, which are formed from object relationships (see also Section 5.6), may unravel. All participants agree to share the work, but they want *their* work to be shared.

The same may be said of institutes and R&D groups, which also specialize in certain technologies or other knowledge developments. Groups have investments in the technology they have worked with in the past; experiments need the groups (their manpower and the money they bring), but they must choose between technological options. Groups have the option of joining different experimental proposals forming at about the same time with respect to a new collider, but they also do not want "to miss the boat" (arrive too late to be of interest to an experiment), and they want to be part of a leading experiment with "successful" proposals. There are also other considerations. In forming collaborations, physicists may wish to go with the groups with which they have worked with in the past, but they must not alienate new groups, whom they need in order to build ever larger detectors. Groups have loyalties to their old collaborations, but may wish to choose the time of collaboration-forming to switch to another experiment, which is risky because they may have to enter "cliques" among participants who have known each other longer and who can use mutual communication and knowledge as power against new participants. In this situation personal offenses are always just around the corner, political costs and uncertainty are enormous (e.g., offending a group can mean offending the country from which it comes, making the wrong move may mean risking experimental approval), strategizing is rampant, friendships are broken, and coalitions are formed and re-formed. Actors emerge from the communitarian life form as individuals who are outspoken in this game, or outstanding in this practice.

Before an experiment like ATLAS settles into a technological track, the game is played by institutes and individuals: no community is yet in place. The detector, the centering object, is still a set of *dividing possibilities*. It offers not one but many identities to an incipient experiment, among which choices must be made. Most major choices are technological in nature. In physics goals appear largely fixed—they are the residue from former experiments, the particles not caught, the measurements not finessed, and the physics mechanisms not reached with a former energy range. The detector technology, however—the choice and combination of subdetectors, along with it the choice of triggers, data acquisition procedure, simulation programs, analysis software, and so on—is not fixed. Major decisions at the beginning of ATLAS concerned these choices. Behind the choices stood individuals and groups or institutes who had developed a history with certain technologies and pushed for their use. The major cleavages in ATLAS derived from competing technological choices. In 1992 I asked a convener of a working group, and a long-term member of CERN, whether the groups behind "his" detector technology would remain in the experiment if the technology was not chosen:

> I would hope so. Sure. I think these detectors are so big and require so much work that many groups will have the same problem. Many groups who now work on a particular technology will not find their technology in the final detector. This is one of the big unpleasant problems we will have to face in the coming years and years. But there is no way out ((of the fact)) that many technologies will have to be (sifted?) out and only a few retained.

Birth in high energy physics is, significantly, a strategic maneuver through a paradoxical situation: one needs to move from competing detector designs to a common design by sifting technologies while, at the same time, *not* sifting out the groups and physicists to which the technologies are attached. Basically, all willing groups and physicists are needed to carry out a convincing experiment—needed for the money they bring but also, of course, for their manpower, competence, and political support. But not all technologies make a good detector, and some cannot even be combined. In the following passage, the convener of another ATLAS working group recalls for me how he raised this issue at the very beginning of collaboration forming:

> And I remember when we started up with EAGLE I discussed it with (). I said one of the things we have to find a way (for) is that we can come to choices between options. And it's not only in ((this subdetector)), that is in general, without scaring people off. We should try to keep the people, convince them that () we have good arguments, both ((in regard to)) physics and technology, that one should choose this option. What I find is important that, if an option is chosen, that everybody can defend this at home, to his home institute, to his funding agencies, saying "the technology which has been chosen was not our technology. ((But)) we think that after all the discussion that we had that what the collaboration has chosen is the best. And we want to put all our effort behind that."

8.2 Delaying the Choice, or Contests of Unfolding

The paradox of which technology to choose can only be overcome by breaking up object circuits, by dislodging groups and individuals from their attachment to technological objects. In this section, I want to make an excursion into ATLAS, to show how old coalitions were dislodged and the emerging communitarian order was slowly put into place. The answer was found in a combination of temporal and unfolding strategies, embedded within a particular approach to collaboration forming. Consider first a native characterization of this approach by a physicist who compared ATLAS's approach with the one taken in ASCOT, the experiment that had merged with EAGLE to form ATLAS and that was said to have had difficulties finding enough groups to do the R&D:

> They ((ASCOT)) decided they had this unique group () It was going to do the design and then they thought because they () have a clever design then the R&D would follow, people would join them and say, yes we build this. We ((ATLAS)) took the opposite (approach) of forming a coalition of R&D projects and taking many options with it, open to

everybody. And then you suffer a process of going down to very few options which is going to be very hard. *But of course you've locked people in.* It (was the?) smart thing to do, because (when) you take that approach, you make everybody feel wanted and when the time comes for hard choices they are already committed. [Emphasis added.]

The "wide openness" toward everybody was continually stressed during early collaboration meetings, a policy that brought the experiment its impressive initial size (84 institutes were already listed in the Letter of Intent). But it also gave the experiment the "painful" problem of making technological choices without losing groups. This is where a particular temporal policy became important, a policy that drew on the unfolding strategy described in Section 3.6. Participants were "locked in" through a policy of *not* deciding between technological options rather than by deciding. Decisions to eliminate a technological option were seemingly endlessly delayed, so much so that muttered complaints about this indecisiveness could be heard from many sides. During that time (which lasted in some cases until 1996 and beyond), the space created by decision delays was filled with technical work. Laboriously, the problem was heaved from the political arena, where groups compete, into the technical arena.

The advantage attributed to decision delays in regard to technological choices typically invoked an interpretative pattern that one might call, following Gilbert and Mulkay (1984: 90 ff.), the "truth will out" device. Technologies that are "better" would display their quality in the long run, if more time was available to study and test their properties—with sufficient understanding, the better choices would become obvious even to those whose technical options would be ruled out. The process through which decisions were nudged into obviousness was that of *unfolding* the object. In the example given of the unfolding strategy in Section 3.6, the decision was between keeping an older main online computer or replacing it before the next data run. That decision had been translated into the need for a curve that unfolded the deterioration of such devices over time. In such a curve, the uptime per year of age can be fed into calculations of expected data losses for specific particle signatures, expected error increases and efficiency decreases, etc., thus adding further unfoldings. With detectors rather than computers, many more rounds of unfolding can be imagined. During the birth stage of ATLAS, participants went through seemingly endless rounds of simulations and measurements of detector (component) performance with regard to technical characteristics and physics goals.[2]

Unfolding *unlocks* a "stuck" (decision) system through the reflexive reapplication of the unfolding procedures. It is an attempt to turn the nature of technical objects and the process of their interaction with other technical objects and with an environment inside out, an indefinite business. In ATLAS, several things were felt to be accomplished during the delay. On the one hand, one captured and "appresented," to choose a term from Schütz, the future: during the early stages of the experiment much effort went into the simulation of processes and behaviors expected to occur in the possible instrumental environments. As the participants spent time getting to know objects which did not yet exist or existed only in (test) fragments, the future was explored, mapped, measured and calculated, and, as fully as possible, anticipated. On the other hand, the delay challenged object circuits by confronting groups with alternatives and feedback from other groups, and it made it possible, in the long run, to break open these circuits. In the end, some technologies displayed themselves as preferable to all participants, or at least to a majority: the majority of those who had no intrinsic stake in the technology and/or of those who won. Finally, during the long period of time during which no decision was taken, groups did seem to become firmly lodged in ATLAS. The hope that they would become identified with it and find it difficult to leave even if their technology was not chosen materialized. Groups always have the option to concede that the winning technology emerged objectively from a *contest of unfolding,* as a fact of nature, rather than from social arbitrariness or political power. This, too, may seduce losing groups into collaborating with the winners.

The unfolding procedure works equally well for objects and for the social groups associated with these objects—they, too, become unfolded, their properties extracted and displayed, and their competence, knowledgeability, speed, and resources pulled into the limelight—before an audience of watchers to whom they continually present their progress in meetings. The following complaint made about an institute that was considered not to have shown the feasibility of its approach, illustrates this process:

> **AC:** ((Comments on "premature" state of technology.)) Too much faith has been put into these detectors in my view.
>
> **KK:** And when you said it's a political issue you (said that) because they are pushed now despite of that?
>
> **AC:** Sure, it's well I think ((institute)) are pushing them as if they are fully developed detectors and they are going to fall flat on their faces if they are not careful. Or ATLAS is going to fall flat on its face. And I think it's very unfortunate that they are pushing. At such a level they should be much more open-minded. And () having maximum R&D effort.

Groups were not measured directly—for example, their budgets were not disclosed in meetings through data points—but they were nonetheless assessed, through the quality of the results they presented, the speed with which progress was made, the prototypes they built, and the test measurements they performed. The group's properties were discussed in gossip pathways as much as the properties of the technology itself. A winning technology implies that there is also a group that has prevailed throughout these assessments—a group possibly considered more competent, more trustworthy, more powerful, more an asset to the whole. However, the winning group also may have been better "supported" and better positioned to pass such assessments. The two sides are inextricably entangled.

Consider once more the outcome of a process of unfolding: a particular technology wins. Does it mean that the technology is inherently better, and that the labor of unfolding has brought its superiority to light? It may, but it also may mean something else: that the group favoring the losing technology did not find much support, that its home base was weak, that it did not have a big laboratory, like Saclay or a Max Planck Institute, as its backing, or that funding agencies at home or CERN did not finance lavishly enough its R&D proposals. It may mean that not enough physicists knew the technology well enough to be willing to take the risk and join the effort, that these physicists had already committed themselves earlier to other efforts, that the time for developing the technology was cut short by the speed of competing experiments and competing colliders, and so on. In ATLAS, one advantage attributed to winning groups was that they had had a "head start." In one case, a physicist listed all the problems one technology (still) had and then added:

> And I suspect that reflects the fact that they haven't done anything like an (in depth?) study. So there is a continuous fight now where the ((technology X)) people who were just starting their R&D obviously don't want to just concede to the ((technology Y)) guys. But the ((technology Y)) guys having two years head start (and) actually have the answers. So that's politically rather nasty at the moment.

Some of the factors can be manipulated to the advantage or disadvantage of a group by others—and the suspicion that manipulation was involved made some losing groups ask, embittered, why they had not been given more support by CERN or other sources. However, manipulation is not, to my knowledge, easily or frequently accomplished from inside an experiment. The collaboration does not want such manipulations; in one widely discussed case, in which it was felt that a manipulation had been tried at a plenary meeting, the attempt failed and the failure was widely applauded. As one commentator put it, referring to the physicist who was said to have made the attempt, "he was strongly called (back) by all the people in the collaboration. Such a political choice was not acceptable to anybody." Collaboration members could also be seen to deride and oppose those groups and physicists from whom they expected similar behavior, given the gossip record. Many technical "compromises" were also seen to be simply "imposed" by budgetary constraints, which one attempted to manipulate in one's favor through the policy of "wide openness" toward contributing groups. In this light, the insistence on unfolding and delays of decision were an attempt *to ship political decisions out*—beyond the boundaries of things for which an incipient experiment carries responsibility. It was also an attempt to push to the sidelines an interest-ridden, actorial order that runs on such "political" principles. In sum, if unfolded decisions appear "objective" it is not because they flow, exclusively and thoroughly, from the inherent potential of a scientific object. It is rather because one has tried to place their nonobjective components (the parts not flowing from the object) beyond a boundary, the boundary separating an incipient experiment from the effect of activities and conditions beyond (compare Restivo 1992; Daston 1992; Megill 1994).

Unfolding seals over the "politics" associated with collaboration forming. It does not eliminate strategic activities on the part of interested groups or individuals, but it mutes them, waits them out, attacks them from the rear through object-centered data. In fact, it is not at all obvious that the most strategic actors in this early phase of collaboration forming are the most successful, or even that much can be gained from what participants themselves denounce as "politics." One sees notorious political actors being tamed into the communitarian life form, and even learning to cooperate with it. The theoretical point of interest is that the script of the machine to be built and the results to be gained from it is written not only by some actors winning out, but by different sets of order and practices playing against each other. In my account of the experiments observed, the communitarian order wins out once the goals and means are set, when the technology has been "frozen," the stakes have been aligned, and what remains to be done is to implement the chosen options (a nontrivial matter). However, the more individual and interest-centered stratum also remains in place, as an organizational level whose stronghold is outside experiments, in home countries, institutes, and the private lives of physicists.[3]

8.3 Confidence Pathways and Gossip Circles

I now want to illustrate how HEP collaborations are ordered at the actorial level—besides, under, and beyond the communitarian level. I should first reiterate, however, that I see these levels as existing simultaneously and as having their roots in different contexts, which sustain them. Sociological conceptions of micro-macro relations often see the macro (societies, organizations) as somehow subsuming the micro entities (individuals), or they start with micro units and see the macro as the aggregation of these units (see Alexander et al. 1987; Giesen 1987). A preferable picture might draw on geological analogies, however, and depict orders as different strata (or perhaps even plates) with specific moorings and with outside edges that may overlay with others in local settings. These strata can be seen to relate as one environment does to another (see also Luhmann 1984, 1990), meaning they are not simply derivative of or reducible to one another. For example, physicists, with their biographical constitution and career paths (e.g. Mayer 1985; Meyer 1986), remain independent of HEP experiments in many ways and may at any time resort to this independence.

To consider individuals as part of a "layer" or "stratum" (I also used the term *package*) implies that one considers them in relation to some mechanism of alignment keeping the layer together. The mechanisms I will consider are trust and (technical) gossip. I will also briefly mention individual track requirements, which put physicists into similar situations and which "bind" experiments to dealing with these situations in systematic ways. Trust, as indicated in Section 5.7, functions (and is understood to function) as a sort of selection mechanism that brings some individuals together and keeps them connected in *confidence pathways*. Confidence pathways create a form of organization that cuts across technology groups, institutes, and experiments, linking individuals who say they have learned, through experience, to appreciate each other's opinion, work, assistance, or style of thinking. Confidence pathways develop between participants who have common histories in experiments in which they have participated. Confidence pathways that emerge in one collaboration bind groups of physicists together, creating networks or "trust cohorts" that outlast collaborations. We can understand the individual physicists and technological groups who weathered the "sifting" process of collaboration forming as trust cohorts (but not all relevant individuals and groups are part of such cohorts). Consider how one physicist, who had been in ATLAS from the beginning and, like others, had helped organize support for the experiment in his home country, explained how groups come to join experiments:

> **KK:** What are all the different reasons why groups or people join a collaboration like EAGLE? () Or is there one main (way)?
>
> **TA:** Yeah, I think one main reason is that the next scientific goal to pursue becomes ((an issue)) already when one is on one's way on the preceding one. And while one is working on the one at the moment, one has people around (oneself). And of course, while one is thinking about the next scientific goal, one talks to the people around (oneself). And

that gives a certain connection, *and it becomes natural to herd with those of the people around (oneself) that one likes to work with.* To go to the next (experiment). That's, well, an evident I think a big part is just due to that. [Emphasis added.]

Trust accounts for the phenomenon that core members of UA2 now find themselves together in ATLAS, and core members of UA1 in ATLAS's sister experiment CMS. In a certain sense, UA2 evolved into ATLAS and UA1 into CMS. On the other hand, there are also now in ATLAS substantial numbers of members of other experiments (e.g., of UA2's sister experiment at CERN, UA1). This brings into focus the phenomenon that confidence pathways extend beyond experiments, creating networks of individual connections distinct from experimental organization.

Before illustrating this further, I want to include in the discussion the second mechanism that binds individuals together, the evaluative, personal discourse of *(technical) gossip*. To a significant degree, individual linkages are established and maintained by this form of communication, which matches, on the personal level, the status reports that were instrumental in establishing the communitarian collaboration (see Section 7.3). Gossip is a kind of mangle through which all significant events and entities within an experiment and in its relevant surroundings are put. Technical gossip mixes report, commentary, and assessment regarding technical objects and regarding the relevant behavior of persons. It often involves evaluative assessments of physicists' work, intentions, and competence, but it may also refer to groups or whole experiments (significant "theys"). Technical gossip reproduces a personalized ontology in that it cuts across and transcends the boundaries of an experiment and of experimental groups: friends and colleagues from other experiments, from other divisions in the lab, from other labs, from institutes, and in fact any relevant professional (and others) can be senders or recipients. *Gossip circles* overlap confidence pathways, but they appear more extended in their reach.

To give an example of such an evaluative discourse in relation to collaboration forming, we can consider what participants call the "organizational philosophies" of the large collider experiments at CERN. Organizational philosophies function importantly in participants' discourse, where they are referred to, elaborated on, and weighed, to be either rejected or accepted. To put it differently, they function as ritual displays of the habitus of collaborations, and as signifiers of their "character" and "quality" (see also Meyer and Rowan 1991). In the following example, a physicist assesses a third experiment while explaining that he was involved, beyond ATLAS, in a second experiment for the sake of students:

> **BD:** () it's very hard to be involved in both ((experiments)). And in particular I would much rather being involved in something like (?). But there I have political problems with ((names third experiment)).
>
> **KK:** The ((name of experiment)) problem being the usual one people have with it, is it just a reputation (this experiment has) or is it really/
>
> **BD:** Well, I just refuse to work in that environment and I have no plans under any conditions to get caught up in such a dictatorship.
>
> **KK:** Is it really as bad? I mean presumably you have some more direct experience with it, is it just a reputation or is it really/
>
> **BD:** No it's more than reputation, but some people (can swallow) that kind of situation that (other) people cannot. () You see what we're sort of having a fight here, but the fight (is) basically well motivated and you can argue about extremes on either side, but when the final thing is done it will have been extremely capacitive, it will have been a bit of a hard fight, but somehow something will emerge (). In some of these other experiments we are not allowed/ you don't have a fight, you just have a decision by somebody who is not even competent.

Organizational philosophies function like a code within a genealogical sequence of experiments, a set of symbols for a style that attracts or dissuades and, thus, pre-sorts participants into future groupings. As indicated, the break-up of an old and the formation of a new collaboration is the opportunity for realignments, the point at which members can be choosy with respect to the experiment they join. It is also the point at which actorial configurations based on confidence pathways and gossip circles take over as the structures that co-determine the composition and shape of a newly forming collaboration. In other words, actorial configurations cutting across experimental organizations are the layer from which collaborations are renewed and extended beyond the boundaries of a previous collaboration.

I want to discuss now (technical) gossip more directly and also to illustrate the role it plays in grouping individuals together and dividing them up within a collaboration. Bergmann (1993) describes gossip as a genre of communication (see also Hymes 1964; Luckmann 1986). Gossip communication in everyday life has certain relational characteristics (it features A gossiping to B about C) and a sequential structure (there may be an opening sequence, then the gossip, then a closing sequence). It is situationally embedded (there is gossip within purely sociable interactions and within work), and the subject of gossip is established and managed in specific ways (for example, the persons who become the subject of gossip are initially named). There exist a number of policies of information presentation (for example, the information is presented as worthy of communication, as believable, and passively acquired), and the gossipers often appear to indulge in the joy of speculating and are interested in generalization (Bergmann 1993: 71 ff.). Bergmann also characterizes gossip as being about a third *person* and his or her *private affairs*.

The experiments studied contain many variants of gossip in which these features can be identified, as illustrated earlier in quotes from interviews. When gossip becomes "technical," however the last two features mentioned in Bergmann's characterization are transformed. First, technical gossip always includes a fourth character to which the gossip refers or about which it has certain implication—it includes a slot for a knowledge object that is central to the gossip. Technical gossip makes reference to subdetectors, electronics, triggers, wires, analysis segments, algorithms, simulation programs, and so on, about which a comment or an evaluation is offered, usually together with a comment about and an evaluation of the persons and groups in charge of this object. Second, with this sort of gossip in the experiments studied, it is unclear in what sense the information conveyed can still be considered "private." If knowledge objects (together with third persons) are the subjects of technical gossip, these objects usually concern everyone in the experiment in their consequences.

Consider the following segment of a conversation, in which I participated, on the topic of how much sleep one needs in Geneva and the effect of the mistral winds.

B: C. *thinks* he may have an explanation for the broken wire. *Enfin* ((so)) he *thinks*.

H: So?

B: ((Reports explanation.))

H: ((Feels explanation is fortuitous. Continues by sarcastic remark on C.'s lab's electronics and wonders how often C is at CERN.)) You know the () electronics produced noise from 1981 to 1985. ((Pause.)) I have not seen C. in a long time. Where is he?

B: I saw him in the pit this morning, he may be asleep now. But he is here. Next week he will have to go to () for 4 days because of () work, but he is here. In fact I don't know about last week . . .

This passage contains a report (see Section 7.3), its assessment, the suggestion of a connection between earlier problems and the present ones, the suggestion that these may be connected to a physicist's absence from CERN, an inquiry about the current whereabouts of this physicist, and a response to this inquiry. It contains speculation, revelation, and evaluation—less in regard to a third person's private matters, but in regard to this person's behavior and the behavior of technical objects of concern to "everyone." Similar evaluative and speculative passages also appear in interviews with physicists. Consider the following exchange with a member of an R&D group:

KK: The () group still has a strong, as you said an overrepresentation of the () in the () group, so/

AC: Yeah, well, that's fine provided it stops being political instead of being technical. ((Pause.)) It's not (a) complaint about the ((groups)) per se, it's just that they have to follow up on it now. They haven't in the past but they have to change now.

KK: Was it lack of money or what/?

AC: I don't know. I don't really know. ()

KK: Did you have the same problem in the () group?

AC: We had a lot of problems. Well, this is my personal opinion, () I found the ((groups)) very difficult.()

KK: Is the reason some, some strong people like A? What is the reason?

AC: I think A. is one of the best of them. You can say A. is very strong in technical matters . . . What happened in () was that the ()

groups insisted on the major responsibility. And there was almost no financial commitment. And with one or two exceptions, the technical results led to, have led to and continue to lead to, very substantial delays. And especially in what regards the ((technical component)).

The following comments are by another physicist, who offered his opinion during an exchange about detector problems at the time:

> **KK:** () The difficulties are unforeseen or unexpected?
>
> **AP:** They seem to be breaking too many wires and that could be a quality control problem. It seems like it were not but it could just be bad luck. I've always/ ((laughs)) I shouldn't go on tape, but okay, () I've always felt that they're a little slapdash. J.'s style, for example, he doesn't have some of their problems, simply because he is so incredibly careful in checking and cross-checking everything. Whereas they are a lot more anarchistic. The () is a very delicate object, so if you are a little slapdash, you get away with it 90 percent of the time, but then you can have problems. It's also (?), it's quite difficult in use (?) and they are not that large a group to do such a thing. It's not easy. I am really ((laughs)) not qualified to touch (), I know very little about it, but just the atmosphere, my impression is they may be a little bit too easy-going sometimes in it.

Physicists often noted in passages like the above that their words could be understood as gossipy or were personal opinion, or they asked not to be quoted. They sometimes neutralized their comments by indicating positive aspects of the activities they were criticizing, by adding remarks about their own shortcomings or the difficulty of a task. In other words, they indicated they were aware that the disclosures could be seen as morally reprehensible. In real-time conversations among the physicists witnessed, one feature of technical gossip seemed to be the quick arrival of a stopping point at which participants were unwilling to go further. Participants indulged in technical gossip, but they did not go all the way. In UA2, they appeared to pull back (not always, not everyone—pulling back is not refraining) from using gossip to manipulate decisions.

The formal characteristics of technical gossip in real-time conversations cannot be documented and analyzed further, since no recordings of them were made. For the present purpose, however, it is sufficient to point out that (technical) gossip of the kind illustrated here appeared to be the personalized and evaluative equivalent of the omnipresent discursive report discussed earlier. It appeared to be one way of integrating a vast and illimitable sea of technical complexity—of navigating and calculating the whole without losing the spice of personal associations—while at the same time creating, testing, and reinforcing (technical) confidence connections among those who gossiped together. The most noticeable difference between technical gossip of the sort illustrated and "idle" gossip in social situations is perhaps that technical gossip sometimes brought out a dimension of deep-felt concern and anger toward problems that groups and individual physicists created for other groups and physicists, or for the whole experiment. Thus technical gossip not only connected those who regularly had these exchanges, providing the medium for the configuration of those actorial structures that I called cohorts of trust, but it also provided the medium—the workbench—for a type of moral-economic and emotional accounting of individuals' and groups' contributions to the experiment. When the "scandals" addressed in technical gossip were nonworking technical components and/or failures of appropriate contribution on the part of participants, this gossip could be seen to hold the moral memory of a collaboration.

To conclude this section, I want to mention that other aspects having to do with physicists as individuals bear on experiments. For example, physicists have individual career needs that must be met: doctoral students working in the experiment need dissertation topics that frequently must include "real physics data," postdocs want "exposure" at relevant conferences, fellows and postdocs need help in searches for permanent or intermediary positions, etc. Toward these requirements the culture of the care of the self illustrated in Chapter 3 is simply extended to the care of physicists. Spokespersons and coordinators take on some responsibility for knowing what a younger physicist's track requirements are and, if possible, for accommodating these requirements. They may also help physicists whose funds are running out by employing them at CERN, or by securing employment for them through other institutes. Some physicists can be seen moving through several institutes (position-wise) in a period of a few years while continuing to work for the experiment, perhaps on the same topic. The responsibility for providing appropriate dissertation topics is often taken on by the (university) institutes themselves, which may maintain involvement in more than one experiment (of which one is running and supplies physics data) for that purpose. In the words of an ATLAS member and university professor at Geneva, "I believe that you cannot have a pure R&D activity in university () I must have a physics activity (). What we are trying to do which I think is a good thing () we are trying to give hardware experience for two years on ((names R&D group)) or on ATLAS if you like. Software and analysis and physics experience on CDF ((Fermilab experiment in the U.S.)) and just train the students that way for the Ph.D." More generally, the pastoral attitude could be seen at work in the preference for principles of self-organization—for accommodating individual desires by letting participants select their own work activities while simultaneously making clear what the experiments' needs were (see Section 7.4).[4]

The actorial layer also becomes apparent in attributions of style and personality, a feature leading us back again to confidence pathways. Attributions may be triggered by conflicts and difficulties, as when two spokespersons of a R&D group, in a group meeting, surprised everyone by starting to yell at each other—a clash that was subsequently attributed, in the stories that resulted from the experience, to their "incompatible personalities." Personality types, of course, are a silent presence, continually assumed by participants to exist and to play into other attributions, such as "styles" of thinking and working. Through these, participants sort their collaborators into those whose styles are compatible with their own and those whose styles are not (see also Hacking 1992c). Styles of thinking and working often divide—the English and the French, the members of certain institutes with whom one has difficulties and the rest, etc. They are sometimes traced back to a physicist's putative national upbringing and training. In the following quote from an interview, a highly regarded postdoctoral researcher, also at the time working on UA2, offered the following classification of his physicist colleagues:

KK: () How do you distinguish between/ ((individuals))
DW: Some, some people I know well approach problems in very systematic step-by-step ways, and others I expect to be a little more, more erratic, not, not necessarily/ probably both arriving at the same

answer at the end, but those two types of people I would have different expectations of, in working with them or presenting something, (?). And the other thing is a tendency to interpret things conservatively or liberally, some people were, get very excited about small fluctuations, and other people will, will always take a very calm approach/ And some people are very quick, in thinking on their feet and can see through things very quickly, and other people much more slowly. Although, again, the final answer arrived at by the two people (may be the same). () I mean I know some people I can, would be able to answer things quickly and probably be right and, pick up things very quickly and, I mean it's useful to discuss things with them. And other people will have to go away and think about it (?) and probably come up with uh, perhaps a more reliable answer.

The next excerpt illustrates how styles of working and interpretation can lead to conflicts over the speed of publication, an argument that for a time divided two physicists in a UA2 analysis group:

> **BP:** () there has been a fair amount of ((disagreement)) in the () group because of myself and D. disagree on the general interpretation a lot of the time . . . Well it's not just him, I mean the () group work as a team. And they believe it's bad science to rush things I mean/ and to some extent I agree with them but they always have the luxury of checking absolutely everything, and I (?) we've been running this experiment now for ten years, and we're still debating what the best jet algorithm is, and I find that a bit silly. I mean there are some things we do and which may not be most optimal or the best, but we know that they're good enough, and if I was in charge I would stop all the things which are nonessential in order to push the analysis as fast as possible, and that's not being done. Of course that will cost me, I may end up in the end with a slightly worse limit, but my feeling is that it would be only slightly worse, and I don't see any reason to delay over a month or two for a 1 GeV difference which may not even materialize. ((Etc.))

8.4 Other Ordering Frameworks

The last quote indicates again the point I started out with in describing the conflicts at the birth of a collaboration: that layers or levels of organization and framing not only fold into one another, they also create fault lines with one another. How many balls are being juggled in a local setting? How many strata clash, slide, and fold into one another? In this section of the chapter, I want to consider briefly the physics institutes and the laboratory, CERN, from the viewpoint of the fault lines they create. First, institutes. Not all physics institutes are alike; their structure, organizational procedures, financing vary from country to country. Nonetheless, most institutes work with students and teach, a business which provides resources and constraints. All have connections with firms in their home countries, with research funding agencies, and with policy-making bodies. All feature, in addition, internal processes—all juggle internal environments of their own. The institutes in their home countries are a stronghold for the experiment in ways explained in Section 7.1; they are its bulwark and its outposts in an alien territory from which it is often far removed. On the other hand, this local existence of the component institutes also creates fault lines, lines along which institutes and experiments drift apart, along which differences (in interpretation, interest, commitment) arise, along which alignments remain precarious, and along which institutes, included in and incorporated as experiments, nonetheless edge against the latter—as institutes. One problem area arises in relation to the time and attention institutes devote to their home activities. Teaching and all that goes along with it, university "politics," recruitment, service, and national committees—all drain time and attention away from the experiment, and they drain more time and attention away the higher the status of the physicist involved. National laboratories without teaching responsibilities do not quite conform to this pattern, and they may even permanently place some physicists on their payroll at CERN. But in general, participants estimate that at most half of the physicists listed under the name of an institute as a collaborator are actually "active."

A second fault line has to do with the physical "distance" of institutes from CERN, a distance which translates, despite e-mail, into perceived information lags and deficits. With a centrally located experiment (at CERN), a centrally placed detector, central test beam areas (the beam is always at CERN) and computer facilities, much of the immediate activity is also centrally located. Meetings serve to share the decisions, but institute collaborators not continually at CERN nonetheless feel left behind, as if they were chasing after something that is always two steps ahead. In principle, almost everything is accessible to everyone at all times—but in practice, information circulates through local discourse at the center, which one must be physically plugged into, many participants feel, to be up to date. In the attack against the parity commission mentioned in Section 7.4, one problem voiced by the physicist quoted was that outside institutes lose sight of, and lose influence upon, decisions made at the center:

> () And I objected (against) that violently, especially as an outside collaborator, because clearly you get out of view immediately. You have to work quite hard to stay in it as it is if you are flying in from the UK, and imagine (how) much more this is like (that) for the Russians or/, but we need all these guys, we need these guys for their resources and their manpower. And we need them for the analysis and for everything. We want them to be part of the collaboration. So if you set up one of these little (decision committees?) that runs the show and you find decisions are made in your absence by the commission and they get upheld by the institute meeting because an institute (meeting?) will uphold anything. So I was speaking against the parity commission to preserve as much as possible, the freedom of action in the outside groups. And that's why of course the ((country)) institutes were quite keen to support me, ((etc.)).

Other fault lines with institutes can easily be imagined. I want at least to mention the laboratory (CERN) where experiments are located and with which they must seek some alignment. As indicated in Chapter 2, laboratories and experiments relate to each other in the case studied rather like moieties in native tribes between which contacts are restricted. They find themselves in the same physical place, but the place is divided into disjunctive compartments. From the point of view of experiments, the laboratory is a facility that provides everything—from means of transportation to living quarters to nearly round-the-clock nourishment to other life necessities (buyable at a co-op). It provides a bank, post office, travel agency, and newsstands. It also supplies offices, libraries, computer facilities, jobs, research monies, experimental areas, and above all the particle beam for experiments. The lab is a total institution where one can work *and live* for quite some time without ever needing to leave. As a life-support system, the lab poses few problems—just a few unavoidable frictions exemplified by the dislike that results from eating cafeteria food (which is actually quite good; CERN is in the French part of Switzerland) for too long. It is comfortable, convenient, polite, and it offers sports and cultural activities (there are regular art exhibitions and music performances by the staff).

As a system of experimental support the laboratory functions well too. CERN as a laboratory runs rather differently from experiments—for example, it is much more structured—but the order(s) under which it operates are well tuned to experimental needs. As an experimental support system the laboratory includes its own research and development branches, above all those linked to accelerator technology. The CERN accelerator division builds, upgrades, and runs the "machines" (colliders) that produce particle beams for experiments. The most severe intrusions into experimental work I have seen were linked to the working of the machine. If the machine, because of technical difficulties, does not provide the energy and luminosity required and promised, experiments can do little. If the beam is "lost" because of sudden problems, experiments shut down data taking. If the level of radiation rises in detectors due to a machine problem, the equipment may be irreversibly damaged. The most significant "interference" between lab and experiment derives from the beam—a fact that is not surprising since particle collisions are, literally, where machine and detector intersect, the point where the separate configurations of laboratory and experiment merge.

Accelerator physics and the configurations within which particle beams circulate and clash form a different epistemic culture. Equally, the laboratory as a "facility" and "structure" is a story of its own, which I cannot cover in this book. Suffice it to say that they further complicate the picture of the experiment as, at the same time, a communitarian order of its own and as an interference space, a space into which several other orders and ontologies trespass. Like environments, the trespassing orders provide resources for each other in a mutualistic arrangement that must be carefully kept in a mutualistic state. Like geological strata, they fold into each other and create fault lines along which negotiated alignments occasionally erupt and break.

8.5 Reconfiguration Reconsidered

Two points are worth repeating. The first is the persistence, perseverance, and obdurateness of constructs such as the individual or the institute in arrangements that transcend them, such as the HEP experiment as a post-traditional communitarian structure. With respect to this structure, its birth is their time—the time during which institutes and individuals, or their combination in technology-oriented groups, dominate. But even after their time, these entities make their presence felt, create their own structures (gossip circles and confidence pathways), and occasionally create turbulence. The level of individual physicists and groups would also seem to spring into action when the whole breaks, or when it never fully comes into being (the case ought to occur when machines or detectors cannot be made to work). In such cases, one would assume the birth-stage picture to prevail, and the experiment to be struck by the Sisyphean task of continually refitting a large but incoherent enterprise that continually falls apart. The advantage of institutes and individuals over the communitarian life form derives from their outside mooring, their firm lodging in independent regimes.

Now the second point. In order to create a high energy physics experiment one needs to accomplish, and deal with, a series of disjunctures: a physicist's work must be disjoined from his or her authorship, groups must be disjoined from their technological investments and accomplishments, institutes must be disjoined from former experiments and other tasks, and experiments must be kept apart from the laboratory in which they are located. During the birth of an experiment this work of separation, through which the experiment becomes constituted as a distinctive and powerful structure in its own right, is carried out. It is not just the work of rearranging groups and technologies and resources, or of reshuffling networks. It is the work of rearranging the social order, of *breaking components out* of other ontologies and of configuring, with them, a new structural form. The repackaging of efforts accomplished during the birth of a new experiment is also the repackaging of social composition and the creation of a new form of life. In the cases described, the winning communitarian order sealed over the more interactional, more individual-centered social orderings carried over from its component elements. It subdued the social energy that actor- and interaction-based ontologies seem to need and to sustain, at least as it appears today in much of social life.[5]

KK: In your opinion, once you have a (frozen) detector design, will this stop, this political level of activity?

AC: I think it's going to be a couple of years.

KK: But will it stop at some point or will it just move to another level?

AC: When all the big decisions are made I think it will stop. At some point people just got to say stop.

KK: And that's also your experience?

AC: Yeah.

KK: Because I mean UA2 was like that, but I've only seen UA2, and you've seen ((more experiments))/

AC: Well you saw one of the best possible collaborations I think.

9

The Dual Organization of Molecular Biology Laboratories

Now for the social machinery of molecular biology laboratories. I will explain the approach to social organization in the labs studied by picking my way through two central themes: one, these laboratories are structurally set up in individuated units, focused upon single researchers; two, the laboratory itself also constitutes such a unit, though this one is focused on the laboratory leader. The switch to the laboratory level brings with it a rather substantial switch in perspective, orientation, and activity. I will first consider the individuated units as small, lifeworldly arrangements involving object relations, project allocation, and symbolization. In Section 9.2, I discuss how becoming a full-fledged scientific person, for the participants studied, entails becoming a laboratory leader. Section 9.3 presents the dual organization of laboratories in terms of a laboratory level and a single unit level, taking into account the perspective and policies that pertain to the laboratory level. In the rest of the chapter, problems of cooperation and interconnection posed in this field are compared with the problems encountered in physics and discussed in light of the territorial organization of molecular biology itself.

9.1 Laboratories Structured as Individuated Units

HEP experiments, one will recall, face the problem of integrating individual researchers and institutes into communitarian collaborations. The problem derives at least in part from the experiment's reliance on a central machine, whose assemblage, operation, and representation in measurements necessitates human coordination. In molecular biology, there are no such apparatuses. Hence there is also, on this level, no question of coordination. This is perhaps molecular biology's first most important difference from experimental high energy physics: in the molecular biology laboratory, the person remains the epistemic subject. Moreover, the individual scientist in the laboratories studied is not just an author of knowledge and a component of the setting, but also its integrating element—for example, if anything integrates a molecular biology laboratory, it is the laboratory leader. The laboratory, experimentation, procedures, and objects obtain their identity through individuals. The individual scientist is their intermediary—their organizing principle in the flesh, to whom all things revert.

To illustrate this notion fully we need to consider the role of the leader, to whom I will turn shortly. Here I can simply begin by listing some of the elements that sustain the scientific person. The first thing to note is that work is portioned in the laboratories studied through assigning each scientist his or her "own" projects. These personal projects are what laboratories fragment into—they are the experimental activities scientists pursue as their main goals, the tasks they seek to obtain and exhibit as projects "for themselves." When laboratory leaders describe a laboratory's work, they run through the list of current projects. Everyone in small laboratories has a map of each individual's main assignments in their head—one follows the ups and downs of fellow researchers from a distance, exchanges complaints about them, and listens to reports of their progress in weekly seminars.

Around the projects, and the persons, other components are assembled. Together, they create small lifeworlds comprising, besides a scientist, materials, instruments, bench space, and help from technicians or students who may perform part of the work. Postdocs and senior molecular biologists may also seek contributions by other scientists from inside or outside the laboratory to speed up their research—in ways which preserve their primary status as epistemic subjects. The authorship conventions indicated in Section 7.2 uphold this status.

The small lifeworlds can be illustrated further by looking at them from the point of view of skills, unpacked here as relationships with objects. Skills have been mainly discussed in recent years within the context of debates surrounding artificial intelligence, where they have served as a counterexample to the idea that computers can reproduce human knowledge (Dreyfus and Dreyfus 1986). The defining characteristic of this notion of skills is that skills are tacit (Polanyi 1958; see also Biagioli 1995)—which implies, for example, that they cannot be easily described in terms of the complete sets of rules required for modeling expert knowledge with artificial intelligence programs (but see Churchland 1992). This notion of skills has been criticized by Collins (1990: 81 f.) for failing to differentiate between different kinds of expertise and for not taking into account the social collectivities through which skills become legitimate displays of expertise. The present argument is related to this objection but also points in a different direction.

In the terminology introduced earlier (see Section 7.3), what underlies skills are object-centered relationships that come to life within small contextual arrangements such as the ones mentioned before. These relationships and their attending requirements create a primordial setting for the instantiation of individual expertise. They are, in some ways, the laboratory in a nutshell, the smallest space where its reconfigurations can be observed in process. The objectual relationships themselves involve a series of alignments that place scientists on a par with natural materials through a learned and designed process of mutual adaptation.

What this means in molecular biology has been illustrated to some degree in Chapter 4. Here we can look at a different example, to bring out the alignments and rearrangements involved. Consider how a surgeon in an operating theater becomes adapted to the body he or she is operating on, as described by Hirschauer (1991, 1993): before they enter the operating theater, surgeons strip to their underwear, disinfect their hands, step into a dressing room and put on sterile clothing, perform five stages of cleaning their forearms, hands, and fingernails with various substances, and open the door to the operating theater with their elbows while holding their arms stiffly away from their bodies and nonsterile things. In the operating theater, nurses have to help them put on their operating coats and slip on their gloves. Sleeves and gloves must not be adjusted before both gloves are on. The gear, complete with green paper aprons, produces a muffled body. From then on the surgeon can only be identified by his or her eyes, a skill one needs to learn. For all their expertise, however, surgeons in the operating theater are helpless—to carry out routine functions of human agents. Their mobility is reduced, for example, by lead x-ray aprons, or by the fact that they are hemmed in by equipment at the operating table—they are tied to the patient's body, next to which they stand "rooted to the spot, only occasionally switching their standing legs." If surgeons need to move, "jumpers," special assistants for tasks requiring mobility, may have to release them from these positions. Surgeons depend on nurses to act as "messengers," for example, for taking phone calls. They also depend on them for various manipulations on their own bodies: for swabbing sweat off their forehead, for feeding them glucose when their circulation threatens to collapse, for dabbing spots of blood from their masks, for adjusting eyeglasses, and even for relieving itches.

Through aseptic discipline and other means, the surgeon is turned into an operating instrument adapted to an open patient-body, but no longer adapted to him/herself—as an everyday person. An observer overlooking the scene sees mainly several pairs of hands, which, while assisting each other, move on top of and inside an open blue cloth covering a "patient"—a person also radically transformed by, among other things, the "controlled poisoning" of anesthetics. The many hands, the patient's body and its connections to tubes and life support machines and instruments that monitor and display vital reactions, the surgeon's own muffled body, whose functions may be taken over by nurses and other assistants—all these are objects that replace the persons we might know from everyday life. Functions have been separated and redistributed, symmetry relations changed, contexts replaced, and the system reconfigured. When molecular biologists handle laboratory materials and animals, the reconfigurations are less dramatically focused under the spotlights of an operating table, but they manifest themselves nonetheless in structurally similar ways. Considered over time, they constitute what we commonly describe as skills and expertise.

The alignments just described work through the body of the scientist, but they also involve a drastically rearranged environment, a new life-world in which new agents interact and move. When we ascribe skills to a person (for example, when we say of someone that he or she is a good surgeon), the person acts as a symbol—a stand-in for the common life-world with objects, which, in the laboratory as in the operating theater, is continually recreated. In the new lifeworlds configured in molecular bio-logical laboratories, scientists are an element. But when they leave these lifeworlds, they become their symbols and carriers.

What sustains scientific personhood in molecular biology, then, is project allocation, authorship conventions, and the creation of lifeworld arrangements in the laboratory that enhance individuals' competence toward "their" material objects. At the same time, however, personhood is sustained by the fact that objectual relationships are not enacted, as in high energy physics, largely in a symbolic medium (in language and mathematics). Rather, they are enacted through situationally recreated, embodied relationships such as those exemplified by surgical procedures. The primordial units described are the life carriers of "techniques"; tech-niques in molecular biology and similar sciences travel not just through laboratory protocols, but through "packages" of arrangements that in-corporate scientists and material objects and that need to be recreated in local contexts. These packages, tied as they are to a scientist's body, nonetheless need the other aspects of the arrangements (illustrated by the reconfigurations of an operating theater) for which a scientist stands only symbolically. Hence the difficulties often described by individual molecu-lar biologists when they change settings and try to reproduce previous work; when, for example, they move from the United States to Europe, where their embodied competence suddenly is not enough.

So far I have illustrated molecular biology laboratories in terms of small, lifeworldly arrangements focused upon single scientists and objec-tual relationships. Before adding another dimension, let us pause for a moment and compare this situation with that of high energy physics. To be sure, high energy physicists too, when they physically build a detector, function similarly to molecular biologists. They learn how to deal with physical objects in embodied ways. However, these objects continually *slip away* from individual scientists as they are incorporated into larger units. Moreover, these larger units, as they grow, change features—they become new objects in their own right and they *cannot be understood* from the construction of their components. The new understanding is purchased, as indicated, through elaborate studies and conducted through measurements and calculations. More than before, the machine in completion becomes a physiological being interacted with through language. It becomes a text—an unending stream of numbers specifying its various states and performances, a set of controls and codes, and a series of displays on screens. Not much is made of embodied skills in high energy physics once the instruments become collective and discursive. Just the opposite: physicists are required to change their skills with the object and to become, finally, "physicists": calculators of signs rather than engineers and mechanical workers. Finally, as the objects become more and more collective, as one moves from detector parts to whole detectors comprising many subdetectors (and from particles to particle distributions), symbolic accreditation of work also moves to collectives—to "the experiment" and "the collaboration." In fact, authorship moves to a collective arrangement long before the detector becomes a collective object—as the instrument grows on paper in "expressions of interest," "letters of intent," and experimental proposals.

9.2 Becoming a Laboratory Leader

Molecular biologists not only remain epistemic subjects within life-worldly arrangements, they also pass through career stages, from the incipient scientist at the student level to the full-fledged scientific person. The last stage on the track, beyond the postdoc and intermediary senior positions in laboratories, is that of a laboratory leader. The transition is sharp: before one becomes a laboratory leader, one is an element in an arrangement. After the transition has been made, the laboratory is one's own arrangement. "Owning one's own lab" is what most researchers who wish to remain in academic settings desire. Only the laboratory, it seems, completes the scientific person.

The transition to a laboratory leader is interesting in many ways. Its most important facet, perhaps, is that it involves leaving behind the relationship with objects and replacing it with an orientation toward society—more precisely toward those elements in a social field that are relevant to laboratories. The fledgling laboratory leader becomes a player in another game—that of the scientific field and its territorial structure. He or she needs to be recognized not by objects but by other scientists—as a name, a location, a set of topics, and as someone to be reckoned with. "At the moment we are widely recognized internationally as molecular embryologists," the leader of the well-established laboratory in Göttingen could say. But when laboratories are initially set up, becoming a player in the field involves first defining the territory in which the laboratory works. The leader in the "still young" laboratory in Heidelberg, and the new leader in a third laboratory observed, a Max Planck facility that worked on molecular mechanisms in skeleton development, tended to spend much time staking out this territory, by telling external persons what the laboratory is after. These formulations also have the effect of displaying to others within the lab "where one is at" and how one can format what one does. Publications do not do the same work for an incipient laboratory leader. They come too late and tend to be recognized only after one has made a name. Explaining, summarizing, and defining the work of the laboratory to external researchers, on the other hand, builds networks. It builds the personal relationships on which one must draw to obtain, from others in the field, materials one cannot make oneself or the attention one needs to be recognized in publications.

The tactic of summarizing the work of the laboratory appears similar to the discursive strategy of high energy physics. But it is different. In the beginning stage, high energy physics experiments need to incorporate themselves—to sift out options, to hold physicists and institutes, to create a functioning whole without imposing a central decision-making structure, and to measure and install an experimental future. Through discourse, summarizing is pursued in the service of the creation of a communitarian collaboration. In molecular biology, summarizing does not integrate. The laboratory remains as fragmented as ever in terms of individual projects. It never changes its ontology; what changes is the configuration of the field, in which a new unit tries to find a niche. Summarizing is performed with a view to where this niche could be, how one might extend it, and how the peons one needs to conquer can be acquired and put to use. In high energy physics, the leader of an experiment is a "spokesman" for the collaboration. In molecular biology, having a laboratory creates the leader, and the leader speaks for the impact he or she wishes to make on the field.

One of the most important functions of the leader, besides building relationships, is to relay information from his or her laboratory to the outside and vice versa. In the laboratories studied, it was the leader's prerogative to present the lab's results at meetings and in other labs, and to identify and bring back information about new research techniques and findings. The leaders held a near monopoly over interacting with the field. As described by one of the few senior researchers in one lab to have a permanent position:

> J: The problem is we only have access to information that is internationally published. But then it is too old, I already know it. These things are usually one to two years old. This means you need information still worked on in other labs, the newest ((things)) they don't want to publish yet. *Only the leader has access to these,* because he is the one who goes to meetings and gets to know things where we don't go. And if you don't have this ((information)) you cannot plan, because what you plan has perhaps already been refuted—the thing you want to do. Or perhaps it cannot be done for some reasons which you don't know but others know about it. For these problems you have to search for information, you need information, and ((this information)) is all dependent on ((the leader)).
>
> KA: Is this his main role?
>
> J: Yes. To bring information. Technically, with respect to what one can do with this information ((postdocs count too)). Not all, of course. They are differently talented. [Emphasis added.]

Note that the leader's near monopoly over "information" was upheld in relation to highest-level researchers, who were not small laboratory leaders—despite the fact that they supervised students and published with them. Becoming a laboratory leader requires leaving other laboratories and setting up shop for oneself.

Leaders in this and other labs do not usually continue to do much bench work. Besides going to meetings, they write grant proposals, act as reviewers for the field, write parts of papers, organize and relay information, materials, and researchers by phone, and talk to researchers in the lab (see also Latour 1987). Leaders have severed their close coupling with objects in favor of aligning behind them a laboratory-world that needs to be financed, motivated, situated, reproduced, and intellectually nourished from outside, through regular infusions of information. To be sure, leaders maintain, or should maintain, close ties with the work in the laboratory. If they do not, their appearance as last-named author on every publication becomes problematic, and challenged by laboratory workers. Researchers continually observe and evaluate the extent and quality of a leader's involvement. Between the researchers' perspectives and the interest of the leader, a balance must be struck, a balance that tends to be continually renegotiated. Many conflicts in the laboratories observed arose from a leader's actions "in the service of the lab" that were not, at the same time, in the service of the individuals whom they affected. The previous senior researcher pointed this out as follows:

> If I make a cDNA bank, people in the lab do not profit as much as the big people. For example, yesterday there was a letter from Australia, they wanted a Krüppel 2 probe. At the end of the letter they said we are going to organize a meeting, we want to invite ((the leader)), we have a nice tennis court . . . So I make the Krüppel probe, and of course, afterwards, he is invited—they ((leaders)) profit on another level. Then they have a different motivation to give away a ((probe, or)) a cDNA bank. We don't have this motivation.

In the molecular biology laboratories studied, the boundaries between the outside and the inside are strong and crossed regularly only by the leader, who draws his strength from these boundary crossings. Is it possible to imagine a laboratory without a leader, in which everybody crossed the boundaries? Hardly. Such a lab, participants assumed, would fall apart, fragmenting into its component scientist-object units. The units by themselves are units without facilities, without mutual laboratory services, and without someone to take on the task of finding money and cultivating social relations.

9.3 The Two Levels of the Laboratory

Having moved from individuated units centering on researchers in the laboratories to laboratory leaders, we are now in a position to consider both levels and their consequences for the organization of laboratories. The most striking feature of the laboratories observed is their dual organization in terms of the two levels. On the level of scientists, the laboratory fragments into projects associated with individual researchers. From the perspective of the laboratory leader, scientists are seen in terms of how they stock a repertoire of carefully selected technical expertise, which, supplemented by stores of materials—of cell lines, mice strains, bacteriophages, restriction enzymes, and so on—constitutes the lab. For scientists, the laboratory is a setting they pass through—a setting from which they can gain a reputation and in which they complete a stage in their career, limited, for most of them, to two to four years. For the laboratory leader, what matters is an appropriate distribution of career stages, a requirement manifest in a leader's recruitment and personnel selection strategies. With scientists, competition in the laboratory is a mostly disagreeable phenomenon that prevents them from fully sharing individual knowledge and results. On the laboratory level, competition is seen in the context of a conscious policy of risk-taking with a view to maximizing chances of success, a continuation of the strategy of "blind" variation (see Chapter 4). On a personal level, scientists in the laboratory frequently interact with one another through joking relationships that exhibit tension. Against this background there may also be attempts on the part of the leader to keep people "happy" and to promote, between them, "good" social relations.

To consider the dual structure of laboratories in more detail, we can start with the assemblage of the laboratory as a repertoire of expertise. The leader of one of the laboratories studied pursued, as he said, a global, long-term strategy. This strategy involved shifting weight between topics, foreseeing the direction in which important work would go, and being ready to incorporate new lines of research. Thematically, he divided laboratory work in terms of genes—work on homeobox genes, paired box genes, fingergenes, "and a small (branch of) enhancer and in vitro" work. The laboratory had originally carried out much work on enhancers, but then switched "slowly" to other techniques and models. As the lab broadened its focus, several kinds of experts had to be assembled—molecular biologists, embryologists, "mouse people," protein chemists, and, at some point, neurologists:

((Other labs pursue the same strategy)) in principle but there are hardly any, I would claim, who, ((like we)) through the structure of MPG, have been able to assemble the different kinds of expertise. There are ((labs)) which are in the mouse business, or certain aspects of mouse development, but they have a weak molecular biology. I mean, the breadth with which we attack the problem, we isolate whole batteries of genes and try to insert these batteries into embryology, I think I can say that nobody has this breadth.

When asked whether protein chemistry had not been missing in the lab, the leader replied that

protein chemistry is very desirable in all this, and we were lucky, we found someone now. I see him more as a visitor, S. S. had a little problem with his supervisor who just now retired, he doesn't have enough for a Ph.D. in Denmark, he wants to do it in Denmark, so I made an effort to get him the money.

Because chemists were hard to find at the time, students pursuing their Ph.D. in other countries were accepted to beef up the expertise of the laboratory.

But the laboratory, seen from above, is not only a repertoire of expertise, it is also a stock of other resources. Each researcher in the lab carries a load of service functions to help maintain the lab as a facility. The dual organization of the laboratory—the scientific persons and their individual projects, versus the laboratory as a whole—divides individual scientists' functions into two kinds. This division can lead to authorship quarrels, as when someone doing mainly service work loses the right to a first-ranked authorship position. The following account of such a situation, by a senior researcher who had long worked on transgenic animals, illustrates these problems:

B: () Then there was this competence quarrel, who should be first, second, third author. And actually some time ago there had been a decision that I should be first ranked on this paper. This is now overthrown, ((the laboratory leader)) doesn't do it, now someone else gets to be ((first author)). And then I said I am not going to continue like that . . . And then everybody said, you need your own project, because they hadn't seen these transgenic works as my own project, only as service ((to the lab)).

KK: (?) which you had to provide as a service for others.

B: Yes, and then I said, okay, then I am going to work on my own topic, and you people do your transgenic work yourself! Okay, now we agreed that I am probably going to get a second TA. He will be trained and then he will do the transgenic service work. And I work with () on my stuff.

The division of individual work into two streams, one for the laboratory, will come up again later. It can be linked to another difference of perspective between the laboratory leader and the lab's scientists. For researchers, the periods of time they spend in laboratories are part of their career track. Many students make their first contacts with other laboratories while they are acquiring laboratory course credits, which they are sometimes asked to seek outside their university. Later opportunities include master's work, dissertation work, and postdoctoral studies; at the time of this research, two consecutive "postdocs" (periods of approximately two years) in the same or different labs were often necessary before a scientist could hope to get an assistant professorship or a more permanent research position.

For the laboratory leader, these patterns give rise to concerns about the distribution of scientists at certain career levels and about the continuity of technical know-how. When a laboratory is mostly staffed by short-term researchers, the leader needs to ensure this continuity amid the ever-changing wave of students and postdocs:

((From experience)) I decided to take about 50 percent doctoral students/diplomas and postdocs respectively. And if you look around, this is what we have, a 1:1 relationship. Within the 50 percent postdocs I have to make sure that there is continuity. They are only here for a limited period of time, between two and four years. This means if some expert comes here as a postdoc, does good work, and one wants to establish this kind of work in the lab it is only possible if the methodical know-how remains in the lab. We do this through the permanent positions. I have two molecular biologists in these positions, one guy who footprints with in vitro techniques, the fancy kind of protein reactions, and we have a mouse man. I tried to concentrate permanent positions on fields in which they safeguard the continuity of research—so that the loss of a postdoc doesn't mean a break in the continuation of our work.

The strategies chosen to promote the continuity of research also depend on the availability of students and scientists working in similar areas. If students and scientists are not readily available, as happened during our study, opening up permanent positions is one way to "nail" expertise. In the United States, many molecular biology laboratories are "pure" postdoc labs, with few if any students. In the Boston area, for example, one of the central regions for molecular biology, even if the best postdoc leaves a laboratory, the technique "stays put." "There will always be a next" postdoc who can do the work. Notice, in this reasoning, that the emphasis is placed not on "knowledge" or "theory" but on technique, and note also the close association between the latter and individual scientists. It is because of this association that laboratory leaders need to worry when scientists leave the lab. Since departures are the norm, they devise counter-strategies.

The leader's options included, in the cases considered, "training up" students to work in the lab, a process that started with the M.Sc. (or "diploma") thesis. After a six-week observation period during which students worked "next to" a researcher, the possibility of doing an M.Sc. in the lab was either offered or declined. The offers were made only after the laboratory leader had consulted with the supervisor and determined the strengths and weaknesses of a student. The theses often led to laboratory-based Ph.D. dissertations, after which researchers were expected to leave. Postdocs were hired from the outside—usually after a postdoc approached the lab, had been interviewed, and provided letters of recommendation. During our study, there were two American postdocs (and one M.Sc. student) in the lab. The leader believed that Americans prefer staying in the States, to be nearer to their job market. But if they failed to find a postdoc position in a "good" lab in the States, they preferred, he thought, "good" labs (like the ones studied) in Europe to weaker ones in the States. Germans, on the other hand, generally go to the States for their postdocs.

Postdoc selection was also based on the notion that one needed to acquire "techniques." One of the problems the laboratory leader had "to fight" was, in his view, that postdocs who applied were "not up to" the same level of competence as the ones trained in the lab:

> . . . when I look at the applications one of the problems I have to fight
> with is that many people who apply are, with respect to their training,

not on the same level as the ones who just finished their Ph.D. here. And those are, of course, out. One has to get people who are *well versed in a number of techniques* . . . [Emphasis added.]

The problem was mentioned again when the leader spoke about when to switch or end research lines:

this switch we only made it slowly, we kept enhancers, originally for production, *then for technology,* only now it ends. (Now) we work on homeostuff, if you wish, in '82 ((when)) I came, then it started with these models of differentiation . . . [Emphasis added.]

The selection and training of researchers in light of career stages are important matters in the construction of the laboratory as a repertoire of techniques. On one level, a molecular biology laboratory is a *bank of technical expertise.* From a bank one can draw resources when the need arises (as when new topics need to be addressed), as long as one makes enough deposits to balance the account. Banking on expertise, and distributing it as needed, reinforces a policy of risk-taking—and further distributional considerations.

A third difference in perspective between the laboratory and the scientists concerns chances of success. Individuals are concerned with finding and pursuing lines of research that will pay off. The laboratory leader is concerned with assembling a number of lines of research of which *some* pay off. In a molecular biology laboratory, little is fully controlled. Lines of inquiry are continually set back because of unexplained problems, procedures that used to work in the past suddenly stop working, and approaches that looked promising lead nowhere. Most of these difficulties cannot easily be explained, and, in participants' reckoning of how to use one's time, they are not worth trying to explain.

Control is also limited with regard to the scientists in the laboratory. A postdoc recommended by a famous colleague may turn out to be inept and clumsy in the lab, unable to achieve results as effectively as any good student might have. Another postdoc who expertly produced, say, cDNA within the surroundings of her lab in the U.S. may suddenly lose her golden touch, or at least her luck. A third may be considered slow—complaints may maintain that he has not done this or that procedure yet, something a collaborator would have tried long ago. Not only the research, but also the researchers, for their own reasons and in their own ways, may be getting nowhere.

What does a laboratory leader do in this situation? The fact that many things are not in their control did not lead, in the cases considered, to a feeling of defeat. It led to a conscious strategy of variation and risk-taking: there is no guarantee that any one line of research—or any single researcher—will work satisfactorily, but in a competently staffed and run laboratory, some lines do lead somewhere, and some researchers bring results. The leader saw the laboratory as a distribution of lines of research, each of which carried varying risks and varying chances of failure and success. To maximize the chances that some lines would work, the leader distributed risks over a variety of topics. Readers will recognize in this policy a similarity to the strategy of "blind" variation and selection by success (see Chapter 4). Unlike physicists, molecular biologists do not attempt to map, measure, and monitor their fate by calculating and simulating experimental outcomes. Rather, they place their bets on "natural" selection, on trying things and seeing whether the environment and the objects they handle in the laboratory cooperate—whether they select the strategy. Second, a laboratory leader knows that "blind" trial-and-error policies and risk-taking benefit the lab (given the perceived lack of control), but they do not necessarily benefit individual scientists. Given such laboratory policies, some participants end up *not* producing interesting results, having to switch research topics, taking too much time, or all of these. Given this situation, the laboratory leader shifted the highest risks to the career group that was most unencumbered—to doctoral students. Doctoral students, in this view, were better risk-takers for many reasons. Compared with postdocs and senior researchers, they are (still) under less pressure to publish quickly, copiously, and in good journals. For postdocs and senior researchers, the time during which they can, through good publications, purchase a more permanent and interesting position is running out, but for doctoral students it is just beginning. Also, doctoral students were considered to be more willing to take risks—out of a sheer lack of knowledge about the kinds of trouble they would encounter, and perhaps out of greater confidence in a laboratory leader who tends to be enthusiastic about risky research. The more risky the research, if it works out, the greater the profits for the lab—risky research entails using new methods and approaches that may turn a field around:

> () in all our publications in the best journals the first author, with one exception, is a doctoral student. () I think I cannot convince our senior researchers to take on a risky project. They too much want a sure bet (). They are not ready to take the risks which one has to take, that are frequently necessary to work on a project which brings a lot of profit. Take A. ((a doctoral student)). I don't require students to do a specific project. ((Rather)), I use all the enthusiasm and persuasion I can muster to convince them that this project is it. Others in the lab advised A. not do to what he is doing now. But if he should be successful, this kind of thing will revolutionize mouse-molecular genetics in the next ten years, no doubt about it. () The criterion of the quality of a good lab is its total output. And the total output of a good lab is greater than that of a normal or worse lab. We've got this anyway, but then on this level you have these peaks which stand out, and these are, with few exceptions, ((by)) doctoral students.

Doctoral students are more suited for risky projects, because even if the results are few and nonrevolutionary, a dissertation may often be wrested from them. Laboratory leaders try to ensure that students complete their Ph.D.s, but they may not be able to do much for an unsuccessful postdoc, for whom only publications count. A leader can, for example, rank an unlucky postdoc first on a paper on which he or she would normally have been placed only as a second author, in order to keep the person motivated. But these tactics create conflicts, which a "good" laboratory needs to avoid.

Avoiding conflicts is not easy in molecular biology, even if one discounts "normal" authorship quarrels. Researchers appreciate the care extended to them, but they still look at risk and success distributions differently from the laboratory leader. Difficulties in molecular biology do not reflect the whole experiment, as in high energy physics; they reflect the individual researcher. When research is organized in terms of individually attributed projects, research failures are individual failures. Since even a low-risk project usually means numerous difficulties and periods of frustration at any given point in time, some researchers in a lab always fear that they are failing. In addition, a laboratory leader's attention to and "enthusiasm" over lines of work also comes back to individuals. If the distribution is unequal, some researchers feel left out or that they are not taken seriously. These things cause divisions among the researchers, and by doing so they recapture and sustain the more primordial division of the lab into individuals through project allocation.

In a sense, gender also added to the tensions and asymmetries in molecular biology. This contrasts with experimental high energy physics, where the duality of gender appeared to be widely replaced by what one might call mono-gender. Mono-gender is the stylistic rendering of everyone as a physicist, regardless of their gender in everyday life. The mono-gendered physicist looks more like a male than a female (see Traweek 1988a for an elaborate description; and Traweek 1995). Females, too, drive home that they are, above all, physicists, not women. There are exceptions; at CERN, Italian physicists, male and female, appeared not to succumb to the full degree to physicists' code of appearance: for example, they were well dressed, and the dress habits of the females differed from those of males. In the molecular biology labs observed, the duality of gender also appeared to be maintained and to play a role in everyday interactions. The style of appearance for both sexes was informal, but distinctive. Moreover, gender surfaced in many other ways, for example, in mild flirtations and the forming of "relationships" between participants—a phenomenon "felt" more directly in small labs (see also Simmel 1923). Gender added to asymmetries in the expected sense of an unequal distribution across positions: most technical assistants in the molecular biology laboratories studied were female, while laboratory leaders were male (among doctoral students and postdocs these distributions are more equal—for example, the "best" postdoc in the laboratory in Göttingen, while she was there, was female).

As for personal interactions, the tensions which divide molecular biologists (gender included) find their way into *joking relationships,* which Radcliffe-Brown (1952) once described as relations of permitted disrespect developing between people between whom there is both social conjunction and social disjunction. Molecular biologists find themselves socially joined in a laboratory in many ways—not only through their formal association with it, but also through the services required of them in maintaining the lab as a facility; not only through the topical connections of their work, but also through the concrete help they give each other in exchanges of materials and services. Finally, they find themselves joined through the laboratory leader, who considers them to be components in an arrangement that makes sense only as a whole, as a laboratory. Yet to an even greater extent, they find themselves divided by the divergence of their interests, by competition, by their "luck" in obtaining results, by the selective attention of the laboratory leader, and by gender. Joking relationships ease the frictions arising from these disjunctions; they help in maintaining satisfactory relationships between people for whom association, even friendliness, is always accompanied by tension and the possibility of hostility (see also Bradney 1957).

Joking relationships are confined to teasing and being teased, and to telling funny stories relevant to the subject of conversation (one example of such a story was given in Chapter 4; but most informal occasions when joking occurred could not be recorded). The laboratory leader also teases and jokes, and is teased and joked about. However, the laboratory leader also deploys other means. Given that the laboratory is close to his heart, his involvement in easing tensions and "keeping participants happy" is strong. "Being a psychiatrist" was once described to us by the laboratory leader as the main function of a leader. Above all, this leader used a "social engineering" approach to keep the motivation high and researchers satisfied. Strategies included a "happy hour" in the laboratory on Friday afternoons; the leader's "going for a beer" with whichever researchers wanted to come when he had time in the evening, his joining in in tennis and other games organized for laboratory members in the summer and in squash in the winter; and the scheduling of retreats for laboratory scientists in a castle obtained for this purpose from the Max Planck society. Researchers knew, and sometimes regretted, that an ulterior motive was behind these gestures:

> You realize that all this is really out of necessity. I still remember, I was part of the lab when it was founded (). This was at the time much more from the heart, it was heartfelt, he ((the laboratory leader)) still had time, because he was not that famous. Then he could still chat with us, and have coffee, beer, etc. Now it's an obligation. He has to do it. He

looks at his calendar, "Ah tonight is still open. How about tonight?" Tonight is of course bad for us ().

9.4 The "Impossibility" of Cooperation in Molecular Biology

In concluding this chapter, we should consider once more cooperation in molecular biology, and compare the situation with that of high energy physics. The important point is that the things that unite individual units in molecular biology tend also to be the things that divide—that create tension, conflicts, resistance, and feelings of exploitation. The native conception of cooperation between researchers and laboratories is that it comes about as a "service" being rendered. Several kinds of service renderings between researchers can be distinguished. First, products obtained by one researcher are often needed also by others in the lab. Products whose preparation requires new skills and training are particularly valuable. When someone in the laboratory has learned to produce a result in effective ways while researchers elsewhere have difficulties with it, this result is a candidate for "sharing." In high energy physics, everything everybody does is shared—participants use each other's results continually, and they combine them in common products and goals. In molecular biology, *some* products benefit others, and researchers look out for these and try to take advantage of them. But when they do, conflicts ensue. The following comment by an American postdoc in the lab provides an example:

((The protein extracts P. makes)) are important, useful for everybody. And they go to P. and want the extracts (). Nobody likes to do them. It is too much work. That's the problem, most people want to profit without doing anything for it, they don't want to use their own time, they want to use P's. With cDNA, that's another partial service, one person does it, the others just take it over without paying anything for it, cDNA. And this guy invested two months or three months, or perhaps even six months.

Asked whether the provider of the service would not be named on the paper, the postdoc answered:

That's a problem. You don't know that. No . . . You are a member of a lab, that's a service you provided, you have to give it to everybody. You can't say anything against this argument.

Cooperation between laboratory members may also come about through the exchange of information. Again, this may lead to conflicts, with the complaints in this case directed against fellow researchers:

> () in Stanford or Berkeley, it's the same, the first thing you have to do is to develop sharp elbows, 'cause it's just quite aggressive. And here, it's not so aggressive, but still there is a certain competition, and it's—more a protective thing. It's almost paranoid, it's like trying to hide things that you're doing all the time in case someone else does it, in case someone else does it better or faster. () I find it really refreshing to deal with P. because, he, and S. is the same, they talk about things that they're doing without calculating what they're gonna say. () You can just talk about what you're doing, the problems, the new ideas that you have, throw it out and say, what do you think of this. And without being afraid that the other person is gonna do it . . .

Service, in this sense, means including others in one's work, giving advice, and listening to them without taking over their ideas. The third kind of perceived service is the training of students. This, too, creates resentments, as one of the four senior researchers in a supervising position, J., states:

> I have to give students a lot of attention, to keep them busy and to talk to them, they make technical mistakes, all kinds of ((mistakes)). ((Meanwhile my own)) topic doesn't go anywhere, I cannot publish, it's slowly getting uninteresting and too old, and therefore I want to change things, I want to take only postdocs, no students. One wants to publish a lot. Success, only success counts. You could say we are not a welfare organization. We are not here to help people, or to train students, but to make a career here. ()

Cooperation within laboratories based on the sharing of materials, work, and information is extended through cooperation between laboratories. Other laboratories also want to "share" what some laboratories do well, and some people consider these accomplishments a service to the field. As indicated before, sharing of this kind usually also gives something in return—to the laboratory leader. Other laboratories in the field must be prepared to render similar services when the need arises. Providing services to other labs may be resented by researchers who must do the work, but they are not resented by the leader, who, through them, works in a different setting, that of the field.

Turn now to the more general question. What do we conclude from a situation where every attempt at interconnection—every activity that implies the existence of a larger unit, which must be "served" across and beyond individual units—creates resistance and negotiations? Service rendering in molecular biology appears to be construed within a *logic of exchange:* one expects something in return for the service. Since the equivalence between various types of services is always problematic, there are bound to be conflicts. Recall that in high energy physics, conjunctions between participants were continually sought after and built upon. High energy physics had erased the individual epistemic subject, working instead through collective frameworks built on communitarian principles rather than on a logic of exchange. In the molecular biology laboratories studied, the opposite scenario dominated daily work. Researchers, structurally set up in individuated units, could survive, everyone thought, only as individuated units. These beliefs, and these structures, run counter to a rising need for cooperation. The need for cooperation in molecular biology derives from the complexities of the research and from competition in the field, which accelerates the pace of research. Researchers in the labs increasingly perceived the synergism that is possible when researchers share materials, learn from each other through talk and training, and collaborate as an advantage—an advantage in dealing with difficult objects, in keeping up with ever new techniques, and in managing to survive and outperform the competition. Nonetheless, few scientists actively pursued the strategy of cooperation that is illustrated in the following comment by a senior molecular biologist:

> **H:** () Actually I have great fun cooperating with others, both inside the lab and outside.
>
> **KK:** You have got several ((participants)) involved in your research, as I noticed: O., B., H., G.,—soon the whole laboratory will be working for you!
>
> **H:** ((Explains involvement.)) Well, then now I asked M. because () these Northern blots, T. ((M.'s technical assistant) does them best in the laboratory and instead of losing a lot of time trying this while I could be doing other things I said if you give me the result, I give you the RNA

and the probe and T. should do all the hybridizations, and when this will be published you are on the publication. None of these things is a lot of work for them, and I, I didn't care even three years ago how many ((authors)) are on the publication, as long as I am first. I mean, because it is my project.

Several facets of the "cooperation problem" in molecular biology can be distinguished. One is the problem of having to function as part of a laboratory while one's career is affected by the requirements and evaluations of the larger field of molecular biology. If a researcher cannot get on with his or her career on the basis of "contributions" to research that is not his or her exclusive product, such contributions are, on the whole, unwelcome burdens. In high energy physics, the needs of individuals to develop careers were accommodated by other means—for example, individuals held claim to some of the quality of the experiment to which they contributed, their presentations at meetings added to their reputations, and they were evaluated, in part, by letters of recommendation by recognized physicists from the experiment in which they participated, and so on. The second facet is that laboratories, the larger units created at least in part through service activities from individual participants, tend to become individuated again through the laboratory leader: they are known under the leader's name, become familiar through the leader's travels, and are approached by calling the leader. They are, in a word, *embodied by the leader.* "At the meetings," the laboratory leader quoted earlier said, "(my) most important function is to represent the laboratory." The conflicts between the level of research in the laboratory and the standing of the laboratory itself are, perhaps mainly, conflicts between two categories of persons. In high energy physics, leaders tend to be dwarfed by the size and complexity of experiments. They may be recognized as speakers, but no leader seems to have the "size" to embody an experiment of dozens and now hundreds of physics institutes spread around the world in which the competence, the manpower, and substantial parts of the money reside. In molecular biology, embodiment is possible, and it brings power to the leader.

There is a third facet of the problem. Individuation of the leader appears to be built, at least in part, on the invisibility of the supporting cast, which becomes larger as individuals change categories. Throughout a career in molecular biology, a person's transition between (career) stages is also a transition between classes of support. When a researcher becomes a laboratory leader, his or her support of perhaps one technical assistant and one or two master's students is replaced by a supporting cast that consists of the laboratory itself. The tension voiced by researchers with regard to their use as "service" providers for the lab (and for each other) has to do with their invisibility in these roles. They associate their resentment against rendering favors to the field with the fact that visibility accrues, mainly, to the leader. Similarly, their reluctance to render services to one another arises from the phenomenon that providing a service may not bring them visibility. Recognition may be denied because such services are part of a researcher's task as a "member" of a lab and need not be specifically credited; because scientists prefer to publish with as few contributors named as possible; because someone decides that the service was "minor"; because the first author needs high exposure and the contributor "does not need the exposure that much at this point in time"; or it may be denied without argument, as when papers are sent off while a contributor is absent with his or her name omitted. Visibility in high energy physics experiments, despite their enormous size, is not focused on persons. Instead, it accrues to the experiment as a whole, which is named and indicated in exhibits, and to the collaboration as a collective whose individual members are alphabetically listed in reports and publications. In molecular biology, on the other hand, successful projects seemingly take the embodied individual as their prototype—as a sort of *moral entity* assumed to have performed all tasks by him/herself, and as a *symbolic* entity that, by standing for many things one does not need or want to know, reduces the complexity of the situation.

On a more theoretical level, the dual organization of molecular biology laboratories should not be seen in terms of the struggle between ontological modes—the individual versus the collective—which experimental high energy physics exhibits. Instead, it should be seen as one piece: as an individuating ontology extended into all levels of organization and occurrences. In molecular biology, career stages and levels of organization collapse—they are conflated in the scientific person.

Boundaries are defined by the projects into which the domain fragments—on the one hand the laboratories and their leaders in the scientific
field, and on the other the micro-environments centered on individual
researchers in each single laboratory. The ensuing struggles bear the mark
of a territorial conflict among units officialized as scientific persons competing for resources and success (compare Geertz 1993). The units that
make up this topology are constantly in flux: laboratories are continually
emerging and evolving, and scientists change from one career stage to
another (see also Geison 1981, 1993). There is a temporal aspect to the
territorial topologies, which points back to categorizations of scientific
persons. But the main point is that the scientific person stands as a symbol
for and moral carrier of expanding and contracting arrangements that
both coexist and compete with one another.

Contrast the territorial topology of molecular biology with experimental high energy physics. The feature most notable in the latter is that
territorial arrangements pertain mainly to the components of collaborations (to physics institutes). Given that these need to collaborate with a
small number of large laboratories in Europe and the United States,
institutes do not "stand" or "run" against one another as molecular
biology labs do. Consider for a moment the relationship between the
large laboratories, CERN in Geneva, Fermilab near Chicago, and for a
while the SSC in Texas, of which the first two worked, within the last
decade, with comparable machines on similar topics. There were overlapping segments of time during which they stood in direct competition with
each other (e.g., Fermilab's CDF experiment and UA2/UA1 from 1988
onward in the search for the top quark), but these laboratories also
contend for slots on a time axis when they can have the field for themselves. During these periods they are the only ones to run at a given
energy and to measure a physics mechanism or particle in this energy
range. This striving for a time monopoly (however short in terms of the
overall length of such experiments) could also be observed when the
building of the SSC was still being negotiated in the U.S. Congress before
October 1993, and the budget for building the LHC at CERN had not yet
been approved. The CERN machine was designed for a lower energy
range, but compensated by higher luminosity. Above all, by using the
existing LEP tunnel and facilities, it was designed to be built *faster* (and

more cheaply) than the SSC, which was to be built from scratch. It is important to note that budgetary and other political considerations in the United States and Europe (or problems with building the machine and detectors) may at any point defeat such strategies and lead to the delay or even "scrapping" of such plans, as they did with the SSC. Nonetheless, what the big laboratories strive for is sole occupancy of a temporal terrain for at least a few years, which is equivalent for them to "having a shot" by themselves at an important discovery, and perhaps at the Nobel Prize.

In high energy physics, then, the tension of molecular biology is projected upon a temporal axis: competition is transformed into competition for time monopolies. Needless to say, the transformation of a state-like territorial topology into a temporal topology has many consequences, some worked out earlier in the book, some, like the implications of temporal monopolies for the notion of consensus formation, described elsewhere (Knorr Cetina 1995). It suffices to repeat that molecular biology, which displays its own versions of temporality, favors the proven if conflict-prone spatial arrangements when it comes to relations between units—scientists and laboratories. Experimental high energy physics, on the other hand, significantly involves in the building of its collective universes temporal devices. As illustrated by the unfolding device and the schedule discussed in Chapter 7, it plays with and to some degree transcends more common social forms by substituting for them temporal schemes. Among these lies the pursuit of temporal monopolies in place of the territorial regimes of molecular biology.

10

Toward an Understanding of Knowledge Societies: A Dialogue

READER: At the beginning of the book you claimed that epistemic cultures are the cultures of knowledge societies. Then you went about illustrating these cultures. Suppose now I buy this idea of a knowledge society, and I actually believe that it captures something useful about the transmutations of today's world. What have I learned from your analysis that helps me understand these transmutations? Why should I believe that the esoteric behavior of some physicists in their underground areas at CERN has anything at all to do with the large questions confronting society? Society rearranges itself, many former states of affairs are drawing to a close, as references to current transitions as post-capitalist, post-traditional, post-modern and so forth indicate, and we are confronting a new era about which we know nothing.

KARIN KNORR CETINA: These rearrangements, or "transmutations" to use your terminology, surely are not all of one kind. I don't believe what we have before us is a single process, but a complex mixture of processes, many of which presumably started out long ago. Only some, I think, are directly bound up with knowledge, and even these may act in contradictory ways. Processes of change produce eddies of confusion, and conflicting evidence pointing in different directions. However—

R: A knowledge society, then, is a can of worms giving us mainly problems and contradictions? I can surely identify with the can-of-worms notion of knowledge—

KK: However, I was going to say, this only repeats that epistemic cultures are not the whole story; there are certain things one can learn from them with respect to your "larger question," but obviously they will not shed light upon everything you may be interested in. Perhaps we should stick with your odd notion of transmutation. I claim that some of the structural forms one finds in epistemic cultures will become or have already become of wider relevance in a knowledge society. For example, the laboratory is such a structural form, and practices of management by content are associated with it. Other structural forms are, on a micro-level, object-centered (rather than person-centered) relationships, which I claim characterize knowledge societies perhaps more than person-centered relationships, since they also characterize expert settings (see also Knorr Cetina 1997).

R: Wait! Let's stick with the laboratory, since you discuss this several times in the text. Why would you bring up laboratories as a structural form if we already have the notion of the modern organization and a well-developed literature on organizational behavior?

KK: I certainly do not wish to contest our notion of organization. I am just saying we should look at the sort of organization most experimental sciences thrive in, consider the features of these organizations, and wonder whether the idea of a knowledge society would not require the modern organization to become more like a laboratory (see also Drucker 1988). What distinguishes the notion of a lab from that of an organization is that the former brings into view the substance of the work—the object world toward which laboratory work is directed—whereas "organizations" tend to be seen as frameworks of coordination for human groups.

R: The organizational literature has long recognized that experts need specific frameworks of coordination; for example, they need flat organizational structures (e.g., Kornhauser 1963).

KK: I think that organizational analysts have tried to some degree to answer the question of what the presence of object worlds means in expert settings with respect to human coordination. But I also believe we need to go further than they have gone. For example, HEP experiments maintain the proximity with objects on a collective level through their discourse and meeting formats. They create a sort of distributed cognition, which then also functions as a management mechanism: through this discourse, work becomes coordinated and self-organization is made possible. These experiments also substitute temporal, object-oriented mechanisms for social authority mechanisms of management (for example, the unfolding strategy). I tried to capture all this by the term *object-centered management* or *management by content*—by which I mean coordination achieved through procedures of the sort that the unfolding procedure illustrates, and management that maintains the proximity with objects and lets itself be structured by them.

R: I am not at all sure that what you can learn from scientific laboratories can be generalized to other kinds of organization. What would management by content mean, for example, in a bank?

KK: We actually studied some banks, on the notion that arguments for the knowledge society must prove themselves outside science. Frank Mars, who studied company analysts (see also Smith 1981) in two banks in Germany, found that one bank displayed the strategy, the other did not. For example, you could virtually determine whether there was object-centered management from the spatial arrangements of the offices and desks. Where management was object-oriented, analysts' desks were arranged in a circle in a large office, with those analysts whose firms or branches had some connections sitting next to each other (for example, the German auto industry is involved in the electrical industry and the latter in transportation areas). Filing cabinets were moved outside the circle. The idea was that analysts who related to one another because their objects were related should be able to observe and overhear what other analysts were doing, and talk to them. In the second bank, analysts worked in separate offices sequentially arranged along floors in ways which seemed to correspond to seniority and to hierarchical principles: for example, the person with the greatest seniority had the largest office, offices of leaders were located next to one another but separated from the rest of the staff, etc. The first bank also moved during the observation period to integrate knowledge of foreign countries with analysts' knowledge of particular branches: it reasoned that since more and more firms were dealing with global markets and global competition, analyses also had to become global. Also, the bank saw itself as a player in a global competition for global clients. Its internationally oriented clientele expected internationally comparative analyses. The second bank, during this period, moved in the opposite direction. In sum, ordering patterns in the first bank were motivated by the content of the work; they attempted to reflect as far as possible the ontology of the object worlds with which the analysts dealt and the changes this world experienced, and spatial arrangements were designed to allow for and enhance distributed collective knowledge. I think this is a version of the object-centered management found in HEP experiments and an attempt to turn the respective parts of the organization into something more like a laboratory (see Mars 1998).

R: Max Weber is famous for the list of criteria he produced specifying "the pure type" of a rational bureaucratic organization (1947: 333 f.). Can you give us a list of practices that turn a setting into a laboratory-like organization?

KK: A variety of practices can realize a lab and the respective object orientation; the list is open-ended. At this point we don't even know sufficiently how scientific laboratories work. For example, other characteristics of laboratories may also be relevant to understanding knowledge societies, such as the phenomenon of labs within labs. In HEP, experiments themselves are a sort of laboratory—a point underscored when participants say that the birth of a new experiment is the period when they create their lab. Another lab, a lab in the lab in the lab, is the numerical world of simulations. The experiment (the detector and the expected outcome) is simulated almost continuously while it is simultaneously designed and built, and even while it runs. In molecular biology, the most interesting lab in the lab is what participants call "model systems"—cell lines or animals particularly suited for the study of certain processes and effects. For example, a particular slime mold serves as a model system for the study of cell communication during cell differentiation, the mouse is a model system for the study of mammalian development, and for the mouse there is, in turn, the model system of the in vitro differentiation of F9 cells. And the list goes on. What this boils down to, I think, is the creation of alternate object worlds within which one can reapply laboratory principles and continue substantive work. One creates, and works with, a proliferation of object levels that stand in relation to one another, not with a proliferation of levels of social authority through hierarchy or other means. This sort of structure is a sort of unfolding applied to object worlds and to some degree to reality levels rather than to the objects themselves.

R: Are you suggesting that this also characterizes knowledge societies?

KK: It might, might it not? The point is that the alternate worlds of working don't reduce to one level, they do not swallow each other up; you have a form of expansion or supplementation that unsticks whole systems by taking detours into other systems, which one creates and uses. Since knowledge society arguments are always interested in productivity, perhaps stepping into other systems is a way of boosting or assuring productivity where knowledge is concerned? Of course, the levels also increase the complexity of the whole.

R: We know from differentiation theory that we live in complex societies, and what this means. If you want to suggest that institutions in knowledge societies in general "expand" through the invention of new ontologies and the exploration of new forms of order, aren't you again overgeneralizing? You are looking at one particularly dynamic forefront science that has had to come to grips in the last decades with issues that may be challenging but may also be rather specific: with runaway technological necessities and explosions of size and cost, with the creation of "global" world laboratories and experiments, with multicultural participants, and with the organization of cooperation. Not to mention the fact that this science has surrendered the empirical world of things to sign processes and processes of simulation.

KK: Perhaps these processes emulate some others in society. We are certainly confronted with globalization and runaway technologies and issues of multicultural cooperation in many areas. I also use the notion of complexity somewhat differently, to refer to the creation of second- and third-order structures that in some way reflect or interact with and presuppose the original level, creating complex tangles. For example, the HEP experiment as a laboratory presupposes the CERN as a lab—it could not be conceived as a lab, be built like one or even function at all, if CERN did not exist. Similarly, the communitarian ontology of HEP experiments presupposes and draws upon individual physicists and institutes—it could not exist without them. The machine ontology that likens the detector to a physiology assumes the existence of the detector as a technical instrument. Simulations assume an empirical world in many ways—as the world to be modeled, as a test case for the validity of the results, or as the world in which the results of the simulation are implemented (as they are, for example, in a detector). Nonetheless, at the same time these second- and third-order structures depart from the original ones, they institute new principles and entities and follow their own logic—they open up new worlds.

R: Aren't we just talking about the social differentiation of modern societies? Or a micro-social version of social differentiation?

KK: Differentiation theory is based on a functional argument; it maintains that modern societies are divided into parallel subsystems (such as the scientific or the legal system) according to function. Depending on the theorist, the systems may be conceived as more or less autonomous—but they are not seen as structural or symbolic orders emanating from local configurations. Complexity, in differentiation theory, results from societies dividing up unified social functions into numerous special functions. In contrast, the complexity I mean results from the interference and blending of locally configured and anchored orderings that are based on different construction principles and yet draw upon and reflect one another. If you wished, you could look at this from within the framework of reflexive modernization theory (Beck et al. 1994) and consider it as a particular kind of institutional reflexivity—one referring to registers of practices and their relationship, not to actors and their interpretations.

R: It is unclear to me how your ideas about a knowledge society relate to the notion of epistemic cultures. You said that epistemic cultures are the cultures of knowledge societies. But I sense a contradiction there, and I want to come back to your notion of culture.

KK: On one level, the notion of epistemic cultures simply refers to the different practices of creating and warranting knowledge in different domains. It can also be applied to other sciences (e.g., Müller 1994), to discussions of scientific objectivity (Gieryn 1994), or to expert cultures outside science. I introduced the notion to bring out differences in epistemic procedure in HEP and molecular biology. These were the differences between the liminal approach to truth in physics and "blind" variation in molecular biology, or the difference between physics' way of locating data at the intersection between signs, simulations, and theory and molecular biology's experiential conception of measurement, or the difference between communitarian mechanisms in one case and individuation in the other.

R: Then culture is simply a particular take on an ensemble of practices and preferences, a take that brings out their characteristics in relation to other such ensembles?

KK: Some notion of culture of this sort can serve as a starting point for empirical inquiry. It is shared by many anthropologists, and is probably too useful ever to give up. But culture also highlights the symbolic aspects of modes of life, and I am also using the notion in that second sense. This sense is also much to be preferred to our sociological notion of culture, which either refers to the area of values and norms—the Parsonian definition of culture—or to cultural products such as art, literature, movies, and the like (see also Robertson 1988). Jeffrey Alexander called much of sociological thought after Parsons pre-symbolic in this respect (1988). I think he is right.

R: You did not mention Durkheim, who established symbolic processes independent of their interactional base, opening a channel to a more interesting notion of culture. You also leave out Weber, who paved the way for the interpretative approach to culture, which now dominates in anthropology. Sociology, too, has rediscovered these possibilities.

KK: It has changed. Sociology of culture now harbors a conglomerate of interests old and new—or old and very old, the latter closer to Durkheim and Weber (see Swidler 1986; Lamont 1992; Peterson 1993; DiMaggio 1994; Dobbin 1994; Crane 1994). This new conglomerate is very fertile, but if the knowledge society argument is right, epistemic cultures need to have more attention—and with it the symbolic makeup of scientific-instrumental reason, of our Western "rationality." There is still the tendency in sociology to draw a sharp distinction between symbolic, "cultural" beliefs and orientations, on the one hand, and technical activities, demands for efficiency, etc., on the other. For example, the influential "New Institutionalism" locates institutional myth, ritual, and ceremonial rules in the formal structure of organizations (DiMaggio and Powell 1991: 13), criticizing their functional explanation. At the same time, some authors point out that the "logic of efficiency" embodied in technical activities conflicts with these cultural elements (Meyer and Rowan 1991: 55). This sets apart organizational culture from organizational task performance and work requirements.

R: It seems to me that our whole understanding of modernity hinges on this. The most prominent perspectives in sociology, from Marx and Weber to Habermas, looked at the development of modern institutions as a major transformative trend toward greater commodification, rationalization, and technicization. Detraditionalization theory today is concerned with the loss of meanings carried by traditions that have disappeared, to some degree at least, due to the expansion of instrumental action, though it replaces this with the idea of invented traditions (e.g., Heelas et al. 1996). Habermas (1981) links rationalization to the takeover of the lifeworld by technical systems, and to the marginalization of traditional knowledge, personal forms of communication, substantive experience, and so on—they have been replaced by formal procedure and cognitive-reflexive steering mechanisms. Do you want to deny the trend toward technicization and rationalization? How broad a claim can you make?

KK: I am not denying rationalization, but the disenchantment of the world and the thesis of the loss of meanings in and through science and technology. I also reject the notion that there is a sharp distinction between technical (instrumental, productive, rational) activities and symbolic processes. It is the exclusionary definition of the two which poses the problem. The thesis that there is a loss of meanings rests on the equation of the content of particular belief systems or modes of operation—which have disappeared or changed—with "meaning," "substance," and the lifeworld in general.

R: How can a set of drab instrumental tasks possibly be turned into, to use Geertz's (1973, chaps. 1 and 5) expression, "imaginative works"?

KK: Geertz may mean something else by imaginative works, but let me try to answer your question. On the one hand, physicists "enchant," you might say, their technical work by resorting to analogies and metaphors in understanding and classifying what they do and how they relate to their objects (Chapter 5). On the other hand, they pursue their goals and construe their tasks in a medium of images, indicators, echoes, and projections of referent objects rather than of substrates of them (Chapter 3). The empirical, in high energy physics, has been transposed into a reality of technical symbols whose referent objects themselves are unreal or "phantasmic"—these referent objects have always already disappeared, decayed, and been transformed into other objects. The signs are phantasmic too: they are continually suspected of being mere appearances and semblances—shams produced by objects mimicking other objects, the ones one is really interested in. Physics operates within and processes this artifactual reality, it moves within a medium of simulations and material "fictions" according to its own designations. Yet from this operation in a medium of the unreal, truth effects can be derived (through an alternate epistemology), technologies can be put into effect, and universes can be "understood."

R: If you put so much emphasis on this, aren't you separating the notion of culture from the hermeneutic tradition, where culture is associated with interpretation?

KK: Interpretation cannot be excised from cultural analysis, or any other sociological analysis. I am continually using participants' interpretations and understandings of their situation, and I am obviously also offering my own interpretations. However, hermeneuticists usually approach interpretation more ambitiously, as the uncovering of the deeper meaning and masked messages of social events; a business seen as analogous to the decoding of textual materials (Dreyfus and Rabinow 1982: 124). This approach seems to me too close to our understanding of a text as a literarily interesting but somewhat gratuitous narration and of drama as the complementary plays being staged from the experiences of social life—and too far from the symbolic *and* instrumental notions of signs, of information, and of simulation.

R: You are not suggesting, are you, that the cultural, in your second sense, should be defined in terms of the unreal?

KK: The notion of culture, because of its link with the symbolic, can help in shining the analytic torch on the very real role of the unreal, the nonempirical, the simulated, the reconstructed, and the technologically imagined in knowledge processes. You can use the notion of epistemic cultures to bring into focus differences in the epistemic and social machineries between expert settings, but you can also apply the notion of the epistemically cultural to knowledge societies in general—attempting to highlight with this idea the specific symbolic makeup and the fictional inroads into a knowledge society (as compared, for example, with industrial society).

R: What about human beings? Are the communitarian superorganisms you described not a prime candidate for a fiction?

KK: As with the other cases, they are both fictional and real. A re-classification of a detector as a physiological being is clearly fictional; it is a metaphoric classification by native standards. At the same time, it is an expression of the very real ways of handling the instrument, of the kind of responses one gets from it, of the sort of relationship one has with it when the instrument is completed and running, of the type of thing *not* expressed by the technical vocabulary, which is *also* present. HEP experiments, as communitarian collaborations, are fictional in the sense that they are "contradicted" by the forms of order centered on the individual subjects. But they are very real in the sense of the integrated functioning of these experiments, without which HEP could not produce results. This functioning, in turn, is purchased by the transition from interactional mechanisms to discourse and temporal devices as the medium of sociality—by, if you wish, the implementation of semio-temporal mechanisms in place of social authority devices.

R: Your sense of the epistemically symbolic still baffles me. On the one hand, you seem to refer to the imagination and "enchantment" that experts like physicists bestow on their machinery and their experience through symbolic classifications of that experience. On the other hand, you seem to link it to such aspects of their behavior as technically installed signaling, imaging, and "echoing" systems with maximum indirectness, and the many kinds of artifacts and ambiguities this involves. If I understand you correctly, here you are saying that this level of a symbolic-fictional medium is where much of our reality business is conducted, and this medium has certain characteristics that move it far away from purely instrumental understandings of expert work. On a third level, you seem to suggest that the coexistence of levels of whatever orders (for example, of orders of social organization) between which accents of reality can shift and from which contradictions arise gives rise to fiction and simulation effects, and these also add to the symbolic makeup of technological and knowledge worlds.

KK: Indeed, I think all three levels—and probably more—are important and illustrate symbolic-cultural dimensions of knowledge societies. I suppose one could bring them all together by emphasizing that all levels involve alternate reality designs: for example, symbolic classifications, too, confront "technological" things with an understanding of how these things feature in human experience; the medium of signs and appearances in which work is conducted is such an alternate design, compared with the "really real" (as Geertz once called it); and, of course, a similar situation obtains with respect to the various levels of communitarian and other orders exemplified in HEP experiments. The fictional arises when the real begins to shimmy. And the real begins to shimmy with the ambiguities, the contradictions, and multiple references introduced into a system through alternate reality designs, which include technological "enchantments." The fictional has something to do with the "as if," as Vaihinger once put it (1924); today we would see the "as if" in scientists' ability to create and work within technologically imagined worlds (see also Wimsatt 1987). But the fictional has even more to do today with the "and also"—it arises from multiple structural perspectives and levels. A notion of epistemic cultures might include fiction effects of the latter sort, and this might be relevant to knowledge societies if, as I think they do, multiple references increase in such societies for reasons having to do with the unfoldings described earlier. I would not want to link the notion of knowledge societies to an increase of truth and unambiguous solutions, but rather to its opposite.

R: You seem to have a deliberate policy of using central notions in more than one way! But I will ask you another question. You suggest that we consider the fictional as an effect of the existence of more than one reality—of multiple references and domains that supplement each other—and that we include this idea in our notion of knowledge society culture. Yet in science, an everyday notion of fiction as untruth or fabrication prevails.

KK: There are many situations in expert work where the distinction between "reality" and "fiction" becomes epistemically relevant, as Lynch (1985) has shown. For example, in molecular biology the difference between what happens in a model system and in the referent system may be highlighted. At the same time the referent system may itself be considered fictional in relation to a third component, and so on. How the distinction between truth and artifact is used in different areas, and how the real becomes a local continuum in cases such as the former, is a topic in the analysis of epistemic cultures. But this shouldn't prevent us from associating fiction effects with the expansion of object worlds and levels, and from suggesting that since such levels play an increasing role in knowledge settings, for that reason alone (there might be other reasons), a knowledge society might show more and not fewer fiction effects—and problems—as part of its cultural makeup than, say, an industrial society. But these are speculations. And this is not, after all, a book about knowledge societies . . .

R: Then let me venture a last question: can one generalize the things you say about HEP and molecular biology to other expert cultures?

KK: Perhaps I should rather tell you how I would use the results—not by generalizing them, but by using the patterns I illustrate as templates against which to explore the distinctive features of other expert domains, and as pointers to possible dimensions in other areas. For example, the liminal epistemology explored in Chapter 3 includes features such as the switch from an emphasis on observing the world to the care of the self, meaning to procedures of self-understanding, self-observation, and self-description. It illustrates specific ways of developing and exploiting liminal phenomena—knowledge of the limitations of knowledge. And it illustrates the working of ethnomethods such as unfolding, framing, and convoluting. These notions can be used as sensitizing concepts in any other study of epistemic cultures to determine how these cultures are configured, what similarities might exist, and how to account for them.

R: I am not sure whether you have broadened my ideas of culture, or confused me. Nonetheless, I want to ask you about another idea I had some difficulty with, your notion of ontology and of multileveled analysis. Why the need to introduce a quasi-philosophical concept? A concept philosophers—philosophers of science, in particular—have by and large rejected?

KK: I am not the only one to address ontological questions; such questions are present in attempts to conceptualize individuals (e.g., Beck 1992; Taylor 1989a), organizations and corporate actors (Perrow 1991; Coleman 1990), intellectuals (Turner 1992), and communities (Rosenblum 1989). In science studies, ontological questions have been raised, for example, by Haraway's post-modernist sensitivity for the ubiquity (and invisibility) in our society of "cyborgs"—hybrids between cybernetic machines and organisms (1991b). For philosophers, ontology has implied an investigation into the most general nature of things—into their "necessary" structure. From this view, logical principles may be principles of being as well as principle of inference. It is this idea—the view that things have an immutable essence from which, for example, the rules of logic derive—that has been rejected (e.g., Nagel 1956: chap. 4). For me, ontology is something quite different. It refers to a potentially empirical investigation into the kinds of entities, the forms of being, or the structures of existence in an area. It is an interest that prompts one to look at the way the empirical universe happens to be configured into entities and properties. By not fixing an ontology from the start—by not committing oneself to the thought that the modern world is populated by rational actors, as in rational choice approaches, or by liberal actors, as in political theory, or by systems, as in systems theory—one can see the configuration of several ontologies side by side and investigate their relationship.

R: Consider the worldwide reconfigurations now affecting microelectronics and the semiconductor industry as it merges with the telecommunications industry and as traditional forms of monopolistic control over technological norms and standards are eroding. Would you say a different ontology emerges from these reconfigurations? Is it not just a matter of rearranging existing entities like the pieces in a game—some units gaining power and increasing in size?

KK: Empirically it could be. But from the present perspective one does not assume that it necessarily is. Possible rearrangements might mean that the situation turns from a network regime to an exchange pattern, or from entities constituted as actors to units constituted as communications, or that a different combination of such patterns emerges. The interesting case, from the present point of view, is not when the same actors realign themselves but when the conjunction of patterns changes. The unification of Europe, for example, will presumably lead to formations not previously in existence—ones that contain Europe as a set of commissions and norm-setting agencies, which include joint venture conglomerates and so on. These entities are not simply nation-state institutions rearranged, and they involve new kinds of statecraft (see Bach 1992).

R: Are you saying that domains need not be ontologically homogeneous?

KK: Right. Presumably, few are homogeneous. In high energy physics, we had, as one ontology, the communitarian collaboration (Chapter 7), whose means of existence was, significantly, discourse; but we also had individual subjects, physics institutes, and technology groups as partly incorporated, political actors (Chapter 8). Molecular biology struggles with the ontology of "live" animals that penetrates into the internal reconfiguration of these animals as production instruments in "factories" of transgenics. If I dwell on this point, it is because the presence of different ontologies imposes a more encompassing question on the analyst. This is the question of the arrangement and relationship of different local ontologies and registers among each other.

R: I remain more puzzled by the case of molecular biology. You said few domains are homogeneous with respect to the entities they feature. But in your discussion of molecular biology's social side (Chapter 9), this is precisely what you seemed to suggest—an ontology of individual scientists continuous with the ontology of biographical individuals in everyday life, no more.

KK: But also no less! The interesting thing about molecular biology is its nested games of individuation. In the laboratories studied, the scientific person is continually enhanced; success and failure focus upon the person, the person is the embodiment of competence, and so forth. On another level, this relevance is also indicated by the functioning of the leader as a symbol of the lab, as the lab's information interface, as its "provider," and as the one who plays the games of the field with the lab. The reliance, in molecular biology, on the body enhances scientific persons. Borrowing results may mean borrowing the molecular biologist who can produce the results.

R: Not a struggle between forms of order, then, but between individuals fighting for scientific personhood first in the laboratory and then, as laboratory leaders, in the field?

KK: Well—there are at least three elements to consider: the practice of exchange; the individual ontology—the phenomenon that the system reverts back to individual scientists and their interaction at so many points; and the homology between orderings on the level of the laboratory and on the level of the laboratory leader. Exchange interconnects—scientists in the lab, laboratory scientists with the lab leader, and scientists/laboratories in the field. Participants in the lab render services to each other in exchange for other services and co-authorships. Equally, the leader is often approached with requests for services by other labs, which he or she gladly renders, knowing that return favors will be forthcoming and might be needed. Some such exchange relationship also ties the lab leader to participants. The leader co-authors most papers from work done by lab members, from which he or she gains visibility and reputation. But the leader, in turn, pays for this by providing direction, research money, and his or her network of relations in the field, on which participants depend. Exchange is the response to the problem of cooperation in molecular biology. It is the cultural solution to the problems of sharp competition in the field and of research steeped in uncertainties. Participants realize the need for cooperation, yet their response is not physics' post-romantic communitarianism, but rather a system that maintains the individual scientist.

R: Such a system should work well enough; all economies rest on exchange, don't they?

KK: The obvious problem is that the prices for the services in this exchange system are not fixed, and payment is in kind—there is no neutral medium, money, through which goods could be paid for immediately and in "objective" ways, decoupled from personal relationships and subject only to the laws of some market. Services rendered constantly raise the question whether they warrant a thank-you note in a resulting paper or co-authorship. Useful products or skills may be held back, even among laboratory colleagues, because their exchange value is not clear, and because one fears becoming disadvantaged by giving them away. Differences of opinion about value and returns are part of participants' everyday fare. Also, irrespective of whether the deals go smoothly or lead to conflicts, the exchange system sustains the individual epistemic subject. These are two sides of the same coin.

R: It would mean, wouldn't it, that there are no temporal aspects connected to epistemic subjects in this system?

KK: HEP experiments produce strategic actors, both individual and collective (R&D groups), during their birth stage. In molecular biology, individual epistemic subjects, with their object relations and perhaps their technical assistants, appear enhanced at all times, but the radius of their activities is limited before they become laboratory leaders.

R: Are there no strong scientists in HEP? No outstanding leaders of experiments who are prominent at all times? Aren't you underrating the scientist in HEP?

KK: Of course, there are some outstanding leaders. The fact that no leader can really run an experiment any longer does not preclude them from cutting more or less striking figures on the level of personality, responsibility, communication, and the like, or from having good ideas. On the other hand, strong leaders may be a source of conflict in HEP—for example, when they are scientists who aggressively further their own interests, or who do not play by perceived communitarian rules. Cooperation in HEP is not built on exchange relationships between individual epistemic and strategic actors, who pursue their own goals with their own scientific projects and who purchase the assistance they need by giving away some of their results and authorship rights.

R: Let us return to molecular biology. You had a third element, the homologous construction of the domain?

KK: The order within the laboratory and the order of the laboratory are structurally similar in that they both feature, and revolve around, scientific persons. Phrased differently, what matters is the positioning of these persons in relation to each other. If there is a struggle, it is between scientists in these positions. The position of a laboratory leader carries with it investments, tasks, and a perspective that differs from that of laboratory scientists—these differences inform exchange relations. Of course, one can consider the ontology of laboratories attached to scientists (lab leaders) and the interactions of these units in a scientific field—and compare this with the ontology of participants in the laboratory. But this is not a transition between a communitarian and an individual structure, or between temporal, reflexive practices and interactional ones. In my rendering, it is the same type of structure all along—involving scientific persons, small lifeworlds (laboratories or arrangements with objects within labs), and exchange practices. HEP experiments, on the other hand, do not have homologous relations between levels; they have superordering relations.

R: Alternate object worlds, post-romantic communitarianism, reconfiguration, homologous or superordering constructions, perhaps even ontology—these concepts may be interesting to discuss, but they have one great flaw. I can see how culture might involve expansions into alternate object worlds and forms of order that are both fictitious and real—fictitious in regard to an original referent domain, but real in expressing and setting new references. I can see how reconfigurations play a role, as when individual scientists and institutes become folded into and enveloped by a communitarian process while maintaining their independent existence. I can even see how it might be useful to look at the social ontology of a domain—at its entities and structures of being, depending on how much weight these entities and structures carry in accounting for what goes on. But what does all this have to do with epistemology—with how these sciences know what they know? Aren't you just looking at these domains as any odd sociologist interested in modern institutions would? Where is the sociology of knowledge in these arguments?

KK: Yes, from a sociology of knowledge point of view this book is politically incorrect! Epistemic cultures and sociology of knowledge questions are two separate issues. Some parts of this book can be read without keeping sociology of knowledge questions in mind. But there are also other parts. And sometimes taking a detour brings you to unexpected places—for example, back to epistemic questions! In Chapter 3, I describe the liminal epistemology of experimental HEP—its non-Baconian way of locating measurement at the intersection between theory, simulation, and actual measured events. This idea of measurement already incorporates and makes use of the symbolic expansion of empirical physical reality—it exploits it, not only for the purpose of theorizing about reality or of simulating it, but for the purpose of constituting the empirical itself—of constituting *data*. Symbolic expansions of the world are a more common phenomenon, they are not limited to science. But the recursive implementation of this phenomenon into the constitution of the empirical world through science is epistemically relevant. It shows, on the one hand, how general developments in modern societies flow into science and technology. But it also shows how our notion of data and the empirical changes, and how the physical world construed by science incorporates the social and the symbolic in ways other than through actor interpretation and negotiation.

R: Can't you give me an example of what a sociologist of knowledge interested in the central issues of the field, for example in consensus formation, might learn from the study of epistemic cultures?

KK: I am convinced that there is an interesting connection between the social ontology of HEP experiments and consensus formation (see also Knorr Cetina 1995)—another case where I found myself facing epistemic issues after a detour into the "purely" social universe. We can start with the claim that consensus formation need not happen through a process of contestation over propositional or sentential claims among relevant scientists; the latter is only one variant among others. If this is correct, the locus of consensus formation can shift, for example, from the end of a series of experiments to their beginning, and from explicit opinion formation over results to the implicit incorporation of selected results into new efforts. In my opinion, this is what happens in HEP experiments. There you have distinctive generations of experiments that are at least partly self-financed, semi-independent, and organized around technologies—the kind of thing one might call mobile corporations. For entities like these, their beginning or "birth" stage becomes increasingly important for questions of consensus formation. The most important selections seem to be made at the birth of new collaborations, where choices become incorporated into equipment design and data generation. The communitarian ontology brings with it a shift in the locus of consensus formation. But it also brings with it the phenomenon that the scientific results of these mega-experiments, provided they can be made to work, cannot be ignored or neglected. Even if the results are negative, if the top quark or the Higgs mechanism is not found, the "limit" analyses and precision measurements they do put forward are normally published and incorporated into further research and particle searches. Thus, much of the traditional process of consensus formation is transferred inside these experiments. It is worked out when the switches are set to provide the kinds of results that can be technologically produced by a detector—when the detector is designed, when the simulations of physics analyses performed, and when the groups to conduct the experiment are selected.

R: The interesting question, of course, is *how* these selections come about. Surely not without negotiations?

KK: Certainly not. But negotiations carry only part of the weight. The more important ethnomethod of consensus formation is a scientist's constant summarizing of an experiment's state of affairs and of that of the field, the uninterrupted hum of self-knowledge this creates in which all efforts are anchored and from which new lines of work follow. HEP collaborations continually assemble the whole by summing up states of technologies, the behavior of equipment, the progress of measurement, and so on. This tactic is combined with a second, the "unfolding" and articulation of technical objects described in Section 8.2—of their properties, behavior, performance, and connections. The story of communitarianism and the story of consensus formation are linked through these tactics of procedure. Summarizing and unfolding play down individual social actors and seal over their conflicts and competition, thus creating the collective form of consciousness and cooperation. But these procedures also continually forge and distill selections from a diversity of experimental efforts and from the field. When the selections are hardwired into detector technology, production programs, and so on, they set the stage for a whole generation of results and for their acceptance and use.

R: The birth stage of an experiment is an arena of settlement and convergence?

KK: Indeed. We have to ask ourselves what the relevant *arenas of convergence* are in different areas. My point is that these arenas and predominant methods of consensus formation depend on the ontology, the structure of entities in a domain.

R: I am not convinced yet. Wouldn't this mean that controversies ought to disappear in experimental HEP? Yet I still remember the last controversy over experimental results, which arose just a few years ago in connection with the sister experiment of the one you studied (UA1). Carlo Rubbia, after he shared the Nobel Prize for the discovery of the W and Z^0 vector bosons, announced additional discoveries in this experiment, which he then retracted because the results were so controversial. This shouldn't have happened according to your logic, should it?

KK: When an experiment spawns actors, as it occasionally does, or when it fragments (when the equipment and collaboration cannot be made to work), other variants of consensus formation should occur. Rubbia is often credited to be an individual actor ("a personality," "a man," "a character," "a genius," "a politician," etc.). Besides, I am not proposing a new unitarian account of consensus formation, but rather opening up our existing model by suggesting variation in the ways agreement, conformity, or stability are reached. One variant is the model of genealogical change, which seems to be operating specifically in experimental HEP. The main point is that there is an interdependence between ontology and means of consensus formation, an assumption I still want to maintain!

R: We, in any case, may not reach a consensus on this point.

KK: According to my model, we shouldn't.

Notes

References

Index

Notes

1 INTRODUCTION

1. See for example Collins (1975, 1985); Knorr (1977); Latour and Woolgar (1979); Knorr Cetina (1981); Zenzen and Restivo (1982); Lynch (1985); Pinch (1986); Traweek (1988a). See also other studies written in the tradition of the new sociology of knowledge or stimulated by it. These include work on the history of experimentation (e.g., Pickering 1984; Shapin and Schaffer 1985; Gooding 1989; Gooding et al. 1989), on the history of statistics (MacKenzie 1981), the computer and brain research (Suchman 1987; Star 1989; Heintz 1993), studies of mathematics (Livingston 1986; Restivo 1983), studies of applied questions and of technology from a constructionist perspective (Wynne 1982; Pinch and Bijker 1984; Bijker et al. 1989; MacKenzie 1990; Henderson 1991, 1993; Law 1991; Latour 1991; Rip 1995; Wise 1993; Rammert et al. 1998), recent anthropological investigations of science, beginning with Traweek's important study (1988a) cited above (Martin 1991; Hess and Layne 1992; Krieger 1992; Downey 1992, 1998; Forsythe 1992; Rabinow 1996), and work that extends the notion of a laboratory to other areas (e.g., Krohn and Weyer 1994; Miller and O'Leary 1994). See also studies related to the present approach, but focusing on everyday life, such as Lave (1988) or Lenoir (1992), and studies of science as process (Hull 1988; Campbell 1990, 1992). For examples of historical controversy studies related to the above approaches, see Rudwick (1985) and Shapin (1979). The philosophers/historians who influenced these discussions are Kuhn (1962) and Feyerabend (1975). For reviews and critiques of constructionist studies, see Gieryn (1982), Hagendijk (1990), Herrnstein Smith (1991, 1998), Cole (1992), Winner (1993), and, most comprehensively, Sismondo (1993, 1996). For an excellent general review of the sociology of science, see Zuckerman (1988).

2. See for example Bloor (1976); Barnes (1977); Barnes and Shapin (1979);

Mulkay (1979); MacKenzie (1981); Restivo (1983, 1992); Pickering (1984); Bloor (1987); Latour (1988).

3. For a brief review of this trend and its implications, see Nagel (1956: 230ff).

4. Among the latest challengers are Habermas (1970), Geertz (1973), Giddens (1974), and Soeffner (1992).

5. For an interesting attempt to develop a "perspectival realism," see Giere (1999).

6. Analysts have often tied any epistemic disunity acknowledged between disciplines to their level of "advancement" or "maturity." See Kuhn's distinction between the natural sciences and the humanities in terms of the amount of consensus they display (1970), or the "finalization" theory of Boehme, Daele, and Krohn (1973).

7. Some early beginnings of "sustained international collaborations" are described by Daston (1993). For the growth of large-scale research in this century, see Galison and Hevly (1992). For the contemporary history of high energy physics as interpreted from a recent sociology of knowledge perspective, see Pickering (1984) and the different interpretation of Galison (1987). For an account that is particularly pertinent to the history of the experiments studied in this book, see Sutton (1984) and Watkins (1986). A more controversial, "journalistic" rendering is given by Taubes (1986). See also Martin et al. (1987) on the quantitative assessment of CERN research.

8. See for example Knorr Cetina (1997, 1998).

9. For examples of book-length studies of this sort, see Latour and Woolgar (1979), Knorr Cetina (1981), and Lynch (1985). For a particularly relevant formulation of practice in terms of agency that is oriented to historical science, see Pickering (1995).

10. Several recent volumes on practice theory discuss similar conceptions of practice. See for example Lynch (1993); Turner (1994); Rouse (1996); and Schatzki (1996).

11. For discussions of this notion of culture, see Shweder and LeVine (1984) and Wuthnow (1984). See also the interesting proposals by Swidler (1986), Zelizer (1988), DiMaggio (1994), Dobbin (1994), Lamont (1992), Mukerji (1997), Alexander (1998).

12. See for example Shapin and Schaffer (1985), Traweek (1988a), Knorr Cetina (1991), Pickering (1992), Daston (1993), and Daston and Galison (1993).

13. For a different analysis of how boundaries matter in science and technology, see Gieryn (1983).

14. These ideas are worked out in more detail in Knorr Cetina (1994).

15. As Penrose (1993) puts it in a helpful, commonsense description of the phenomenon (which is rather complicated to derive, as it involves the decomposition of fermions into right- and left-handed components, isospin rotations, and so on; see Meyers 1990: 193ff.): if there were an exact

symmetry between these particles, the masses of all of them would have to be the same. See also Sutton (1984); Close et al. (1987); Jenni (1989).

16. In the early 1990s Fermilab had the highest-energy accelerator in the world. On April 22, 1994, CDF researchers mailed a 150-page manuscript describing the search for the top to *Physical Review,* claiming that it had good evidence but not yet a discovery. For the firm establishment of the top quark, more data would be needed, which they hoped would be obtained by the completion of the collider's run or from the collider's $230 million upgrade by 1998 or 1999.

17. The building and termination of the SSC, and the political and economic decisions surrounding it, are fascinating stories in their own right. Some of the details can be gleaned from the statement issued by the U.S. Secretary of Energy, Hazel R. O'Leary, upon the House's decision on October 21, 1993: "The decision by Congress to terminate this project is a devastating blow to basic research and to the technological and economic benefits that always flow from that research. The SSC was expected to be the flagship of the world's high energy physics program, but Congress has now decided that the SSC will not be completed. The House made this decision based on the need to reduce the federal deficit, yet the outcome will be the loss of an important, long-term investment for the Nation in fundamental sciences. I deeply regret the House decision, but we see no prospect of reversing it. Accordingly, we have begun the process of an orderly termination of this project." See also McDonald (1992).

18. See UA1 Collaboration (Arnison et al. 1983a,b) and UA2 Collaboration (Bagnaia et al. 1983, 1984).

19. Textbooks on ethnography (e.g., Spradley 1979) have long recommended occasional withdrawals for the purpose of analysis and to avoid going native. In the present case, the strategy took on a different quality because of the frequency and timing of visits to the field.

2 WHAT IS A LABORATORY?

1. **READER:** Before we go further in this book, I want to say that I am not completely satisfied with what you told us about the field, especially about high energy physics. You present its technical complexity and size but not its diversity and fragmentation, the many perspectives of different physicists it must include! I hope you are not going to present us with a view "from nowhere" (Nagel 1986; see also Clifford 1986; Marcus 1986).

   KARIN KNORR CETINA: I am not sure how you come into the picture, but I agree it is interesting to get to know the people and their views in a strange place (see for example Dumont 1978). On the other hand, this book is not about physi*cists* or molecular biolo*gists.* It is about our rethinking of what goes on in modern scientific laboratories where knowledge is made. Besides, HEP collaborations understand and display themselves as cooperative research efforts. Cooperativity is what the field has seemingly opted for since the 1940s (see Heilbron 1992), and cooperative research is coupled with an emphasis on collective and consensual problem definitions and solutions. There are also frequent reminders in the field that it is the *machine* that creates the particles and events that physicists investigate; in the terms of Roy Schwitters, the director of the SSC until its cancellation, the machine even creates the discoveries! Frankly, I don't wish to personalize a field whose "art" consists in merging and associating its components. This is what appears to me interesting and surprising in experimental HEP.

R: But surely these physicists do not all speak with one voice! Surely there are conflicts, differences of opinion, and so on (e.g., Mulkay 1985).

KK: Indeed. Many of the striking and interesting differences are linked to structural features of the HEP situation—for example, to the unavoidable competition over which technologies will be used to build into a detector. The birth of new collaborations seemingly brings out a particular social register that runs counter to the communitarian register on which HEP collaborations build—that of strategic actors who attempt to optimize their utilities. But this, in my view, deserves separate treatment (see Chapter 8). Then there are differences which the natives attribute to some scientists still learning and knowing less about a subject than others. For example, I sometimes got "explanations" which other scientists then "put right" when I repeated them or checked them. The natives themselves recognize differences in "styles of thinking" and align themselves with one another along these differences (compare Geison 1981, 1993). Then there is the vast area of optional uses of terms and strategies (what one scientist may call a "nightmare" the other may call just a "worry") and of the "tricks" scientists come up with to solve a problem.

R: Then why aren't these last differences in the text?

KK: Isn't what we are doing here part of the text? But to seriously engage your question, I need to reiterate that physicists also represent their empirical practice as collective and shared. Why ignore these self-representations as collective, the attempt to speak with one voice in crucial matters of procedure? Besides, the social organization of HEP militates against fragmentation and dispersion. Participants are forced constantly to consult with each other and to coordinate what they do, to share and circulate among themselves numbers, transparencies, analyses, programs, instructions, and data sets, and they make their procedures equivalent through on-the-job training and the need to produce results *jointly*. Every physicist brings to the experiment "common" background knowledge. But in addition, physicists are stitched together as they finesse, adopt, and extend skills and procedures in the details of problem-oriented work. Beyond subtle differences in how to define some experimental quantity abstractly (see the notes to Chapter 3), everyone learns how to calculate it in practice so that the calculation can pass as competent in a collective of 100 or 1,500 participants. What I do is attempt to spell out some parameters of this acquired competence. It's a bit of an attempt to run the empirical machinery of a field before our eyes while paying some attention to maintenance work, but none to how the machinery was invented, or how construing a particular scientific claim might require one to make strategic use of it. To some degree, this approach is a "parametrization" of HEP's experimental policies—it focuses on the parameters of physical inquiry that stand out for a social scientist, in relation to another field, molecular biology.

R: Reading their procedures in this way does not preclude you from specifying the context and circumstances of your reading.

KK: What would it really change if I told you, as Malinowski relates in his diaries, about my occasional illnesses at CERN? About the admiration I have for the deep knowledge many participants hold? About the annoying tendency of physicists to be so preoccupied with their work that they don't notice you when they pass you—something I have to get used to afresh every time I go there. Perhaps you would like to know that I love this field and have been fascinated by it from the start—as a scientific enterprise seemingly like no other, a dynamic center of modernity, and a scenario for possible futures.

R: No confessions, please! Many anthropologists would concur with Bourdieu's criticism of "narcissistic ethnography" (1993)—they actually rejected this attitude much earlier (e.g., Marcus and Fischer 1986; see also Woolgar and Ashmore 1988; Ashmore 1989). But that doesn't lessen the demand I am making for concrete particularities, and what Donna Haraway calls "situated knowledge" (1988). One thing that interests me in your last remark is your relationship with physics and how that might be related to your relationship with your own discipline. It seems to have been at least an ambiguous, love-annoyance relationship.

KK: The HEP field has the drawing power of the Sirens, but also at times the charms of an insect repellent. It is so warped that unraveling some of its aspects is like blowing into one of those rolled-up paper whistles that children play with: you can make them extend and unravel, but they roll up again immediately afterward. HEP indeed constantly raised for me the question of sociology as the Other—of *our* laboratory compared with that of physics, *our* epistemic procedures, *our* trigger in data taking, *our* use of theory, *our* background and signal. This was the real existential question between us—not the persons, but the disciplines. A collection of epistemes meets, through an observer, a collection of other epistemes. The strangeness, the struggle, the recognition of difference, and the question of how to evaluate an alternate world—it all relates to this meeting of disciplines, and my being in the middle of it. I suppose that as an analysis of "strange" epistemic cultures, the book is also a bit of a commentary on sociology. The other question between us relates to the field, especially HEP, being a "hot" one: a field in which politically sensitive conflicts over the ultimate detector design are still burning as I write this, in which the participants involved in these struggles are conducting an experiment that will begin taking data only in the year 2005, in which gossip still hurts and it makes a difference who says what in speech or writing (see Chapter 8). It is not by chance that historians usually have access to confidential documents only a decade or more after they were written, as was the case at CERN (see the history of CERN by Krige and Pestre 1986; Pestre and Krige 1992).

R: Critics might suggest that you could have taken a stance as a member of a certain race, class, gender, etc. Feminists in particular (e.g., Hartsock 1983; Fox Keller 1985; Rose 1986; Smith 1987; Haraway 1988, 1989; Harding 1990, 1991; Traweek 1988b) might say that embedding your results in a specific standpoint might have strengthened your position and given you a privileged perspective on certain aspects of the field, for example, on its gender relations. Such a perspective would have allowed *you* to determine the meeting ground with physics.

KK: In my case the standpoints that imposed themselves were those of different disciplines. I must admit that I found the confrontation between disciplines richer than a confrontation between gender standpoints.

R: Is it going to be all your account of epistemic cultures or the natives'? Your construction or theirs?

KK: I hope mine, not theirs—at least as far as the emphasis, the structure, the selections, and social interpretations go. You wouldn't want a molecular biologist analyzing molecular biology for you if you are interested in that field from a social science perspective. You would first have to turn the molecular biologist into a sociologist or anthropologist so that he or she would see not just the genetic, chemical, organic, bacteriological, physiological, enzymatic, neurological, and even veterinary questions, but ours. When I am in the field my concerns are not, for example, how to increase the success rate in my microinjection procedure or how to get this vector to work, but what these concerns and these procedures tell me about how this science works. In that sense one needs to distance oneself continually from a field's intentionalities and concerns, while simultaneously knowing its intentionalities and concerns. I am afraid the construction must remain ours, unless we want to start asking biological questions . . . Besides, scientists have strong voices themselves, they talk back forcefully when they don't agree with an account (e.g., Weinberg 1992). In fact, it is not clear at all whether these natives need protection from observing analysts or whether the researcher, as an analyst, needs protection from them.

R: Others (e.g., Geertz 1988; Haraway 1991a; see also Brown 1987; Lash 1988; Herrnstein Smith 1997) are more interested in what a text (including their own text, and yours) systematically conceals and excludes.

KK: Certainly. But many microsociologists (Goffman, for example) exposed a lot of these suppressions, such as the ones which trouble our notions of the self or of institutions. Earlier studies in the sociology of science have exposed what much of sociology, philosophy, and history of science had excluded from their view in regard to science—the hidden work of knowledge making. You could look at this book as an attempt to reveal some of the fragmentations and articulations within the quietly assumed unity and monadic totality of what we call "science" . . .

R: For you, the concealed and excluded has everything to do with the field, but perhaps not enough with rhetorical operations. As to your fragmentations within the assumed unity of the sciences, how far are you prepared to go?

KK: What interests me is not to "disappear" things in the post-modernist fashion—the material, the subject, truth, even texts—but to pursue to some degree their settled and unsettled version, the text and its expansions, if you wish, and the relation between the two (see Johnson 1990). In this chapter, I first offer an account of laboratories as reconfigurations of "self-other-things." But I am also at least gesturing at how laboratories change from stage props to constitutive setting to "facility"—to being eclipsed by experiments in high energy physics. This, of course, is not the end of the story. One could pay attention to the further articulation of laboratories *in* laboratories, to their migration into and replication in elements of scientific work, such as model systems and simulations (see also Chapter 10). One could write a whole book on the different articulations of laboratories. In a chapter, however, there must be an end.

R: There are other chapters.

KK: The next two chapters are limited to the articulation of the empirical in the two sciences studied; fragmentation is limited to the differences between the two fields. Being empirical toward a domain is sometimes exhausting; I am afraid I will have to leave it to others to further extend my formulations. For example, someone might go *into* one of the large genome project centers (see Section 4.2) and expand on the account of molecular biological research in this book by studying these large-scale projects from within—something that has not been done till now. In Chapters 5 and 6, I present some expansions myself—the physicists' symbolic expansion of technical instruments into something else, and molecular biologists' expansion of live animals into machines. In the later chapters I try again some combination—I try to exhibit the articulation, in each science, of a basic form of order, but also the infiltration, in each field, of these forms of order by additional orderings that supplement, contradict, or in some sense dissipate the other. You see I am not very consistent in my strategies.

R: We all can learn! Though it might be harder for the type of unashamed empiricist you seem to be. Perhaps I shall do some further deconstructions in these footnotes.

KK: Right on! Like the bathroom, Anthony Grafton says in a historical paper on the footnote—given at the Princeton Davis Center colloquium in 1993, a paper now part of a book (Grafton 1997)—like the bathroom, the footnote enables us to deal with ugly tasks in private. Like the bathroom, it is tucked genteelly away. I shall accept your obstinate meddling, especially if we agree that the text persuades, while the footnote has only secondary significance!

R: Actually, Grafton says, the footnote is like an engineer's diagram of a splendid building. It reveals the occasionally primitive structures, the unavoidable weak points, and the hidden stresses that an elevation of the facade conceals . . .

3   PARTICLE PHYSICS AND NEGATIVE KNOWLEDGE

1. **PHYSICIST:** In the spirit of our discussion of the footnotes (which are actually endnotes!) at the beginning of Chapter 2, let me get back into the picture. I shall be the physicist who read your chapter and suggested improvements, which, as I can see, you mostly included. However, some sloppiness in your language remains. A hadron collider, for example, does not produce large inelastic cross-sections because . . .

KARIN KNORR CETINA: Wait one moment. If we are going to bring in some context to the statements I make in the text we might as well be precise. Several physicists read this particular chapter, and many more listened at various places to talks I gave about HEP. Will you be the "generalized other" or any particular one of them? I am sure that those of my readers seasoned in recent discussions of ethnography would like to know.

P: We are not just bringing in context, we are going to reveal some of the occasionally primitive structures, the unavoidable weak points and the hidden stresses that your text conceals, just as Grafton says, if only by way of a few examples. As to who I am, you know me very well. I am a member of UA2 and now of ATLAS, you transcribed my comments, I taught you a few things about physics analysis, and now I shall simply stand for others. I am specific, but my name is of no relevance.

KK: Your evasiveness gives me the opportunity to take the literary freedom of editing and summarizing your comments, and of joining them with a few other comments. Go ahead!

P: You are also selecting them, as the reader should know. I began by saying that there is some sloppiness in your language. A hadron collider does not "produce" large inelastic cross-sections because the large inelastic cross-section is just the probability for a given type of event, which is nothing produced by an accelerator. It is just that as a *consequence* of this large inelastic cross-section the accelerator produces a large number of events of this type. The cross-section is a physical fact.

KK: But I am quite sure I took this wording from a physicist.

P: The cross-section is a physical quantity like mass or charge. The low energy events are more common because the cross-section is many orders of magnitude larger than the cross-section of high energy events, but the accelerator produces events, not cross-sections. Sometimes physicists speak a bit carelessly about these things in conversations.

KK: I think this sort of formulation can also be found in technical writings, though I would have to go back to the literature to show you where.

P: It's like saying the collider produces the big Z mass which of course it doesn't. The Z mass is what it is.

KK: Right. Mhm.

2. P: There is an intermediary step missed here. The fact that the transverse momentum of the W is important is because we are not really measuring the W mass itself. The smearing here comes in because we measure a correlated quantity, not the transverse momentum on the W.

KK: But is this possibility not implied, since I talk here only about the uncertainty which surrounds the measurement of certain physics processes and quantities?

P: It's almost there. I admit this is a very detailed comment. You say the transverse momentum distribution is seen to smear the mass measurement of the W because it is not well known, but if we really measured the mass it would not matter at all. It is not only the fact that the W mass is not well known that makes this smearing. It is also the fact that we measure the mass in an indirect way. The relation between what we measure and the quantity we are trying to establish gets blurred because of that. It's a very detailed comment.

KK: I can at least put a footnote there to point this out.

3. P: This is a point I am coming back to from our private conversation, because I think it is important, and because you haven't done anything about it in the text! You say in several places, and this is one, that we "choose" an approach or some strategy, as a cultural preference, part of our culture. Here you say we choose to be obsessed with understanding ourselves, and later you say we are obsessed with (systematic) errors. I, however, don't think we have a choice.

KK: You think you haven't the choice?

P: I think we have to act the way we act. The reason we must be interested in self-understanding is because there is only one experiment like ours. If there was only one thermometer in the world, we would have to spend a lot of time trying to find out how it works. Some people once spent a lot of time trying to find out how these thermometers work and then they put a scale on them. If there were thousands of experiments like ours, someone would have found out how we work and would give us just a book saying "if you are getting this measurement in the detector, the following thing has happened inside." But we have to learn from scratch how everything works. So I don't really think these strategies are part of our culture. I think they are necessary.

KK: I find it interesting that you compare your experiment with a thermometer, with an instrument. Isn't it much more than an instrument? Also, you seem to think that because something is cultural it is irrational. Whereas I believe cultural preferences usually have good reasons, but the reasons are local. I argue from a comparative point of view. What I have in mind, for example, are disciplines like the social sciences which, like you, deal with aggregate phenomena, yet their concern with self-understanding is rudimentary compared to yours. Our error potential is at least as great. There are the uncertainties of measurement (Cicourel 1964), the smearing of distributions, there are underlying events—we often measure more than one event simultaneously with our data—we have plenty of fake signals, and great uncertainties surrounding our theories. We have lots of reasons to deal with our measurement process. I was not implying that you should be doing something different, but rather that I know a number of disciplines which, given the problems they face, should have a more developed concern with their "self" than they do. Epistemic strategies do not seem to simply flow from objective constellations of problems. The necessity you feel becomes a contingency when you see that other disciplines, confronted with similar problems, develop different strategies.

P: But you say here it is us who choose a different road, whereas I say we do not have a choice. If you use apparatus which is unique, you have to do things in the way we do. You can measure the temperature of the water in your bathtub or you can measure the temperature outside, once you have a thermometer you don't need to recalibrate it every time you measure something.

KK: Our measurement instruments, for example, our questionnaires, are usually unique too. So are the designs molecular biologists use in their experimental activities—there are very few attempts at exact replications of experiments, as we know (e.g., Collins 1975; Mulkay 1985). Moreover, the positive use and mobilization of errors and uncertainties in your case is not just relevant with respect to calibration; you also deploy the strategy when you deal with different theories, it is just one component of the shift toward the study of liminal phenomena which you do not deny. When one talks about cultures one usually has in mind a whole system of procedures which somehow hang together and sustain each other. Given the framework of the system, every single strategy appears necessary. But the whole is a specific development and articulation of strategies.

THEORETICAL PHYSICIST: I would like to jump in on this and support my fellow physicist, albeit from the point of view of a theorist. The calibration example does strike me as illuminating. What came to my mind when I heard you talk about the need of these experiments to understand their detector are scales. Suppose I want to know my weight. To know my weight I need an instrument—some way to measure what I am after, plus the exact knowledge how this instrument reacts. What, if I put five pounds on it, it will indicate, its errors and efficiency, and the systematic error I make by using this instrument rather than another. What more is an experiment in HEP? Is it not just the testing of scales for measuring something that comes from theory? The weight, the thing we are really interested in, are the theoretical predictions. Experiments are, in the last analysis, preparing and calibrating the equipment.

KK (to TP): Frankly, I am not surprised by your comment. It corresponds to an understanding I have come across over and over again by theorists—the understanding that the intellectually important ingredient is physics theory, while the experiment is just what we imagine happens on the scales (or thermometer) level, writ larger. What interests me about this understanding is how it renders HEP experiments invisible despite their size and complexity, and despite authors, such as Galison, Traweek, and Sutton (and perhaps even Pickering from the theory side), who bring them to our attention.

READER: You forget, if you allow me to come back just briefly from the notes in Chapter 2, you forget the role our disciplines, philosophy and history (but also sociology), have played in promoting this understanding, by paying attention almost exclusively to physics theory. You also forget that physics is a segmented universe in which fundamental theorists and experimentalists live, work and think detached from each other, without knowing much about each other. Theoretical physicists often simply do not know what goes on in experiments. You also forget that studies such as the above are only appearing in the last ten years.

PWA (second theoretical physicist): The question by the theorist should be answered, nonetheless. Perhaps I may point out what I, as another theorist (however, a theorist working at Bell Labs!), wrote more than twenty years ago in an article in *Science* (Anderson 1972: 393), namely that the main fallacy in the above kind of thinking is that the reductionist hypothesis on which it is based does not by any means imply a "constructionist" one.

KK: The reductionist hypothesis supposes that once theoretical predictions have been made there is nothing left but "device engineering"?

PWA: Sometimes. What I said was that "the ability to reduce everything to simple fundamental laws does not imply the ability to start from those laws and reconstruct the universe. And the more the elementary particle physicists tell us about the nature of the fundamental laws, the less relevance they seem to have to the very real problems of the rest of science." I was not talking about experimental HEP then. But it seems to me now that it is a case in point within particle physics. Experimental HEP is a constructionist project. It needs to reconstruct conditions that existed at the beginning of the universe, and design and develop the equipment to do so. It needs to create an operation in which fundamental particles, like the top quark, and qualities of particles *not* predicted by theory, like the Higgs mass, may reveal themselves—and this is an operation no less complex, time-consuming and energy-expending (and only somewhat less costly) than perhaps the military invasion of a foreign state, or a space exploration. It needs to exactly predict the environment in which this operation takes place and its own future states in order to conduct the research. In short, it operates at an entirely new level of complexity at which new properties appear, understanding of new behaviors is required, and research that is as fundamental in its nature as any other is needed. None of this can be done by a simple extrapolation of the standard model.

KK: In my terminology, we are in a different but equally fundamental epistemic culture. Whose existence is concealed by the emphatic articulation of physics theory—and the celebration of individual physicists—in the more popular press and the academic literature. For example, as Galison said in the preface to his book on *How* (physics) *Experiments End* (1987: ix), "despite the slogan that science advances through experiments, virtually the entire literature of the history of science concerns theory."

P: You are, of course, right about the annoying neglect and misconstruction of our project. But I reiterate, you are wrong in calling what we do cultural. To go back to the text, look at Section 3.5.

4. **P:** Here you go again. And also later on when you talk about variation. The point is that there is only one experiment like ours. The more you know about how your detector reacts, the better you can tell what happens, and that is always true. There is nothing magical about our use of errors or variation. You have to subject a tool to variations such that you understand it. It is not a cultural preference. These other sciences you were thinking of use tools that exist in large numbers and have been calibrated . . .

KK: Actually, one attempts to standardize them, as I said earlier (3.3)—think of the standardized questionnaires in sociology—but standardization is not calibration. Standardization just means trying to use the same stimulus or the same procedure. In molecular biology, one also at-

tempts to use standard procedures, the procedures fixed in laboratory protocols. The point of the laboratory work is to get the procedure to work—to
use it in a way which brings the desired results. The point is not to understand exactly why or how it works, in particular what systematic and
statistical errors, uncertainties, efficiencies, and response functions exist in
all composing steps. A protocol is like a recipe, you use it without necessarily
caring about the chemical, biological, thermodynamical and other processes
which make it work.

P: I have been thinking a lot about biology, trying to understand how
they work and why we are different. One of the reasons is that when we look
at matter at the quantum-mechanical level, we get probabilities. For example, you don't know if you produce an electron pair, and because of the
width of the Z particle, the mass of that electron pair is going to be 91 GeV
plus minus 2.5 GeV. There is no unique number you can get on this. But if
you take two hydrogen atoms and one oxygen atom they always make one
water molecule. Chemistry at that level is not probabilistic, it is completely
predictable. I believe it's the same in molecular biology. If they have a certain
enzyme that cuts at a given sequence, it always cuts at that sequence and
nowhere else. And if they run their inverse chain reaction, they always
produce a particular molecule.

KK: Molecular biology may not be probabilistic in the same describable
sense, but many reactions seem to be contingent. It is not feasible or condu-
cive to the goals to isolate each factor and deal with it separately. You have
to think in processes and systems. If you deal with a vector, for example,
however simple it may be, you deal with a changing biological system and
not with an elementary, undifferentiated point-like entity. The results of
biological reactions are usually unclear and need interpretation.

P: I think problems arise from the messy initial state. They don't come
from their apparatus. It's just that at this time molecular biologists may not
know what they have in their bottle before say some enzyme. But the enzyme
does not have to be investigated, it always does the same thing. In science, we
always do the same thing . . .

KK: Each science always thinks the other has more control. Molecular
biologists often make comments about physicists in this spirit. They will also
say that any attempt to investigate their procedures in your way is far too
time-consuming and probably doomed to failure in a situation in which they
know little about their systems, and all investigations are subject to the same
uncertainty as the one that gives rise to the investigation (see Section 4.4).
They optimize the system in some holistic way.

P: We cannot do that. We couldn't optimize without knowing. I don't
know enough about their work to explain why there is a difference. But it is
clear to me that *we* cannot do our work in any other way. If we did not use

these methods, we would not generate any results. They can obviously do without this obsession with errors, for example. While we could not possibly. There is no cultural choice for us in this.

   KK: In a cultural analysis, one explains, in Churchland's sense of explanation (1992: 198), by recognizing a pattern. You may well have set up your problem in a way which demands certain kinds of treatment. But your problem definition is itself part of the pattern, isn't it?

5. **P:** Well, the terms *acceptance* and *efficiency* flow a bit into each other. If you want to differentiate them I would rather say that *acceptance* usually refers to geometrical terms, for example, to pseudo-rapidity cuts or transverse momentum cuts. Whereas *efficiency* refers to the less clear cuts we make, like the electron quality cuts. The pseudo-rapidity is a very clear cut. Either the particle is inside or outside this cut. This defines your acceptance in a very clear way. The same holds for the transverse momentum cut. Either it is above 20 GeV or below 20 GeV. Whereas for efficiencies you almost always have a sliding scale where at some point 50 percent of your events pass the cut and at some point 90 percent. So you get the types of efficiency *curves* you know. The definition you give here is probably a better definition of the efficiency than of the acceptance. But you could in some instances define acceptance that way as well.

   KK: Aren't there two notions of acceptance? The overall acceptance and the geometrical acceptance?

   P: The geometrical acceptance is an efficiency, if you like. Here I think it is rather common that we talk about it in terms of acceptance when it is geometrical—or kinematical. If you look at the very basics, you would probably define both notions (efficiency and acceptance) in the same way which is this way. But . . .

   KK: It did pose a lot of problems trying to work out from documents, comments and interviews what you mean, and how to separate the two notions. It did not seem very clear!

   P: Perhaps you clarified things too much. They do slide into each other.

6. **P:** Here you actually quoted me in the text, thank you very much!

7. **P:** There is actually an important difference between errors and uncertainties. We have uncertainties when we need some input from theory and that input is not well defined. For example, you may have a range of possible (theoretical) inputs and this range of inputs propagates through your analysis and gives a range of possible answers—and this is not really an error, it is an uncertainty. But if you make systematic errors in your measurement, it is just you—you, yourself have an error in your measurement which you do not quite control. *That* is an error. However, in your example it is true if you say here that these systematic errors are also called uncertainties, because we are sloppy when we talk about these things.

KK: So uncertainties refer to an additional distinction you make?

P: We usually lump uncertainties together with systematic errors because traditionally the statistical and systematic errors separate the ones which would be improved by better statistics from the ones which would not. That is why the uncertainties end up with the systematic error, but in reality there are more categories than just the two.

8. **P:** If you come from the theoretical side and generate top quarks (through Monte Carlo generators) then the mass of the top quark reflects the number of events you would produce. But that is not what we measure. We measure that there are zero top quarks and then we lead that back to a mass limit. The limit we set is the limit on the number of events.

9. **P:** The limits we produce also affect theory quite a lot.

KK: In what sense?

P: Take LEP, for example. LEP set the number of neutrinos to three. That immediately rules out everything which has more than three neutrinos. Every theorist who has been working on more than three neutrinos can stop doing so and do something else.

KK: You are confident that such limits are not contested by theorists?

P: They need our input. Experimental results overrule theoretical assumptions.

KK: In fact, some theorists regularly attend experimental meetings. Someone (an experimentalist!) once told me they flock to them like vultures looking for prey. The prey was supposedly experimental results which indicate to theorists ways to go and channels to avoid, they provide empirical parameters which enter calculations and above all food—food for new theoretical work. Not surpisingly, with the cancellation of the SSC in Texas it has been theorists who cried out because of the scarcity of input, the "lack of food" if you want to stay in the metaphor, they anticipate if only one collider, CERN, will produce "prey" in the future (Horgan 1994).

R: If you allow me to jump in once more, are you suggesting a reversal of the theory-experiment relation we usually assume, where the theory makes the predictions and the experiment tests them?

KK: Not just a reversal, but a variety of different relations. Among them the one where the theorist needs experiments to continue in interesting and intelligent ways. Or the one, mentioned in Chapter 1, where the theorist (a phenomenologist) is thought of as a kind of calculation machine for experimental needs. But this is not a matter for this chapter . . .

4 MOLECULAR BIOLOGY AND BLIND VARIATION

1. **KLAUS AMANN:** Since we collaborated on this chapter, I want to come in as your co-worker and add a few things. When you talk about the laboratory

as a repository of tools and resources, I talk about a "laboratope" (Amann 1994). This emphasizes the existence, in the lab, of a version of what biologists call a biotope [a functioning ecosystem]. Only it is a biotope system that is artificially created.

KARIN KNORR CETINA: These notes seem to develop into a scheme for everybody to jump in and provide their own picture! But you are more than welcome. I like your notion of a laboratope. It gives appropriate weight to several aspects of the lab's object culture: the caring and growing activities that exist in the laboratory with respect to source materials and the total artificiality of the laboratory compared with natural settings, with biotopes. It suggests that substances and organisms exist in the lab within their own interdependent system of life-sustaining mechanisms.

KA: Or life-suspending mechanisms.

KK: Indeed. Perhaps we should give more weight to the laboratope as a morgue. There is this whole infrastructure of refrigerators, freezers, storage rooms, there is the liquid nitrogen, the stoppage procedures that prevent decay . . . If one wanted to distinguish a laboratope from a biotope at least three features of laboratopes would have to be mentioned: the fact that its inhabitants often exist in arrested states within preservation and conservation systems; the reconfiguration aspect, the fact that the inhabitants are transformed variants of natural objects in various processing stages; and the constrained growth and reproduction of some elements, like cells or mice. All three aspects limit life. Preservation suspends it, reconfiguration reduces life, insofar as it continues at all, to a lower level (the level of cells, viruses, bacteria), and growth and reproduction are usually ended by sharp stoppage points and are interfaced between preservation and processing stages. The laboratope rests on suspending, reversing, and selectively infiltrating biotope processes.

KA: You make the laboratope into a molecular horror cabinet. I rather want to emphasize the live aspects of laboratopes. Laboratopes are production systems for biological materials, only they run on different, "scientifically elaborated" principles, and they create new, reconfigured creatures. But these laboratories are nonetheless growing systems, highly sensitive, highly artificial life factories, if you wish.

2. KA: Laboratory protocols are also distinctive characteristics of fields such as the present. I suppose there are no procedural protocols of the type found in molecular biology and other biochemical sciences in HEP—recipes that have an autonomous existence of their own, that are treasured, traded, and in some sense the units from which knowledge emerges. If one stresses the omnipresence of substances and organisms "living" and reproducing in laboratopes in molecular biology, one also has to emphasize the existence of these other "objects," the codified practices embodied in protocols.

DS (a biologist): Remember, we once had a long discussion about this, when I was doing the FPLC purification of the protein that I had produced.

KK: A friend from the lab—you are most welcome at this point. I suppose you will set things straight about objects and procedures in no time.

DS: You asked about protocols. We not only work with protocols, we think in terms of them. When I am doing the protocol, pipetting say, I don't really think about the objects I am dealing with. When it's a routine, there is, for me, no differentiation between the bacteria that I am using there, and the DNA that I'll extract and the enzyme that I am placing on to cut the DNA. "A thing to do" is more a protocol than dealing with DNA, it is more in the procedure than in the material.

KA: That means "500 micrometers," "this tube labeled this way," "incubate 5 minutes" and so on.

DS: It also has to do with the time, "I have 10 minutes so I can do that" or "I have to do that and it takes me a whole day"—that's the main thinking.

KK: What about your protein?

DS: Well, the protein, because it has previously been a problem, the protein is a bit more moody. I think about it, I get more visual, I treat it differently, in one word, I pay more attention to it, it's more precious. I don't handle it routinely yet.

KK: How do you visualize it?

DS: I see the protein in a certain size in front of me. I visualize why it is precipitating, then I visualize the solution and I visualize the falling out and the refolding process. I also visualize the protein denaturing, stretched out and then coming together, and I visualize how it is being shot into the solution and what it is going through when it starts to fold. With the expression, I visualize the bacteria when they grow in a more anthropomorphic way, why are they happy? I try to visualize them shaking around, I visualize aerobic effects, the shaking, how much they tumble around and what could have an effect.

KK: That suggests, doesn't it, that when the objects come into the picture they do so with their specific qualities, *undergoing* the procedures you apply to them?

DS: Or experiencing the things they do to each other within the procedure.

3. **KA:** When we began to discuss objects in the context of laboratory protocols they seemed more like patients than agents. They seemed like someone to whom things happen, and who shows certain movements and symptoms as a consequence. But, in the last few paragraphs, objects appear more powerful in their obdurateness and resistance. Isn't there a contradiction? Should one not say more about this resistance? Much of the new sociology of scientific practice has been adamant about the existence of a material world, yet has been reluctant to say more about it other than claiming its "resistance."

KK: There are such attempts as Pickering's (1991, 1995) to conceive at least the consequences of this resistance in terms of "accommodations." Pickering analyzes Morpurgo's search for quarks and sees a radically contingent process which he calls the "mangle" of practice. Morpurgo, in his search, runs up against obstacles which prevent him from attaining his goals ("resistance"), to which he reacts by revisions of his strategies ("accommodations").

KA: In my opinion, this just reiterates that the material world is there and creates problems for the analyst. Pickering develops a characterization of practice, not of resistances. I am asking that we stop talking about "resistance" per se and begin to analyze the phenomenon.

KK: But you can analyze resistance in terms of the epistemic strategies different fields use in response to it. For example, you can analyze it in terms of molecular biologists' variational strategy (Section 4.4), as compared to the many strategies of self-understanding in HEP, or to HEP's focus upon liminal phenomena (Section 3.5). These strategies show that the response to resistances is structured, is built into a field's epistemic culture.

KA: You talk too much about the response to resistances. There ought to be still more to say about the resistances themselves. For example, how are they conceived of, what types are distinguished in molecular biology?

KK: Your guess is as good as mine, but I can make a start. First, some scientific work not only anticipates difficulties by structuring them into its procedures, but it articulates them. I suppose we can see at least some scientific activity as an attempt to bring forth resistances, or to clarify where they are, and not just as an attempt to eliminate them. Second, resistances seem to always appear in specific ways in scientific practice, as specific kinds of resistances or as suspected kinds. They have a context. They may have names. There are terminologies which refer to them even if no attempt is made to understand the nature of the difficulty. Some of theoretical physics' resistances, for example, are referred to as the "hardness" of calculations.

KA: In molecular biology, I think we need to distinguish between several instances of resistances. For example, there are the difficulties having to do with the "vague its" (a term taken over from ethnomethodology) that appear on autoradiograph pictures—the bands which are perpetually unclear and need to be interpreted. Second, there are the instances when the things in themselves become a problem, when one refers to their obstinacy and stubbornness. The latter gives rise to the former, but they also arise separately in the lab. Then there are the procedures which resist—they have, in D.'s terms, "contours of resistance."

KK: D. said once that things are *"eigensinnig"*—they have their own proper will and intention. She should have something to say on this, if she thinks about her protein.

DS: It is a very *eigensinnig* adult. I mean there are strict rules about what it will do.

KK: Is it like a person? Someone you interact with?

DS: No, not necessarily a person. It takes on aspects of some personality, which I feel, depending on if it has been uncooperative or not. If it's cooperative then it becomes a friend for a while, then I am happy and write exclamation marks in my book. But later it becomes material again, it goes back to being in a material state. When it stops doing what I want, then I see a personal enemy and think about the problems.

KA: It becomes antagonistic?

DS: Not antagonistic. It's stubborn about what you can do with it, it doesn't bend just because you want it to. You have to discover what it wants; it's not going to come and do what you want. In that way, I mean *eigensinnig*, but not antagonistic in the sense that it will purposefully do something to make you have negative results.

KK: And procedures, are they like that too?

DS: Yeah, procedures somehow have a shape. When I first start with them they somehow have a shape, I can't really explain it. And then as they become part of the routine they lose that. It's something about how you visualize what you think you have to do, how you first learn about it, and whom you first talked to about it. The procedure somehow forms an entity, but after you have accustomed yourself to it, it's routine, it's part of you, and then it loses this sense.

KK: By shape, do you mean contours of resistance?

DS: I mean shape, but it's more, yeah, contours of resistance, of the problems of learning how you should do it.

KK: "Contours of resistance," "*eigensinnig*," "vague its"—perhaps the notion "enigma" should also be brought into the picture. Problems often mysteriously, cryptically, and ununderstandably crop up with procedures that have worked in the past, but suddenly stop working. Resistances in HEP, because they lead to an attempt at understanding, are not paraphrased as enigmas. Instead, they are paraphrased as problems, troubles, worries, diseases—we shall get to some of this in the next chapter. In molecular biology, resistances also seem to be enmeshed in temporal reasoning. Difficulties are said to stop you in your tracks—to make you lose time, to force you to back up and to start again. Resistances imply a temporal backlash for the individual scientist who cannot go on as intended. In physics, the whole research business is immersed in a sea of problems. But the problems do not stop you, they make you go ahead.

DS: Perhaps I will have the last say on molecular biology. Part of the difficulty with our problems is that they separate you from your work. When at a standstill, when you feel you are going nowhere, the trouble is that you get in some sort of psychological state where you separate yourself from the work, for instance, you pipette although you don't believe any more in the results. Once you get into this pattern of disbelief in what is happening it doesn't work and will never work. You have to take a vacation, or develop a certain amount of anger, or greed, and say I am going to make this work! Once you start believing in it, it will work.

KK: Right. You are saying that one has to include in resistances not only the ones associated with laboratory objects, with signs, and with procedures, but also one's own, for example, resistances deriving from a lack of trust and belief. There are, of course, also other problems associated with the social world, the "contours of resistance" provided by grant agencies, resistances from reviewers on papers, the troubles a laboratory leader has with the researchers in the lab. If we ever write a paper on resistances, we will have to choose a symmetric approach. And not to forget the resistances we forgot until now, the problems associated with technical instruments and machines.

KA: It seems like one would have to write a book, not a paper!

5   FROM MACHINES TO ORGANISMS

1. KLAUS AMANN: To continue our conversation from the last chapter, I wonder whether these classifications can simply be read as classifications of resistances.

KARIN KNORR CETINA: They have much to do with the detector's functioning. And its dysfunctional states and parts. In an operational detector, resistances are dysfunctions.

KA: But why do they need to be expressed as diseases? Why not in more antagonistic terms, for example, as enemy activity? I am thinking of the way D. talked about her protein turning into a personal enemy when it was uncooperative.

KK: The disease terminology refers to the underlying pattern of the detector as some sort of organism. A collective organism, to be sure, but an organism nonetheless—which you need, on which you depend, which acts for you as a sensory and interacting *body* that "accepts" and "copes" with the particles you cannot deal with yourself. Moreover, this substitute body you build yourself. You wouldn't normally consider your body as an enemy.

KA: You are becoming more and more metaphoric yourself! I agree that the disease terminology fits the overall picture or better still it helps paint it. But how much does it really tell us about the kinds of resistances in experimental HEP?

KK: Not enough perhaps, but it does tell us a few things. It suggests, for example, that the problem to which it refers ought to be approached in the same way in which a doctor approaches a patient—with care, and in a healing manner, since you have a physiology in front of you, the parts hang together with other parts. It also suggests that it is life you are dealing with—and that the ultimate resistance of life is death. Some parts may already be dead, or on the verge of dying, and you may kill some more through incompetent meddling. It suggests that you cannot do anything against the ultimate resistance of death—except sometimes you may replace the part that is dead, if you can get to it and if you have spare parts. But the best strategy may be to prevent death. It suggests, therefore, that a complicated physiology like that of a detector needs constant attention—the kind of preventive and curative monitoring which takes place (see Section 3.4). It suggests that detectors and detector parts are decaying—they are getting older—and as they get older, they catch age-related diseases. It suggests quite a bit, for example, that resistances in this case are something plastic, a continuum of malfunctions increasing over time which cause one to never reach a point of absolute health, and of which one tries very hard to avoid the other endpoint, death. Complete absence of resistances on the part of essential components, like whole subdetectors, is as unlikely as their death is undesirable. It suggests that health is a combination of states in which the resistances are minor, limited to nonessential subcomponents, and "can be lived with," as physicists would say.

KA: You can stop now. We don't want to turn this conversation into a shadow paper on resistances, do we? But I am beginning to wonder how much of what you said has to do with the fact that we are not dealing with objects, but with machines.

KK: It has a lot to do with the distinctive features of the entity one is dealing with, with the specificity of a particular domain. This ought to become clearer when we look at another kind of entity, for example, at the background (Section 5.5).

2. AC (an artist-philosopher): I wanted to jump in on your conversation earlier, but you two are absorbed with your resistances. I wanted to bring in a term which seems to be present continuously in your discussion, yet you never mention it—a term that almost jumps into your face right from the beginning of the chapter. The term is *anthropomorphization*. Aren't these physicists simply anthropomorphizing machines? I have collected lots of examples of anthropomorphizations from all kinds of contexts. It is a predictable and familiar phenomenon. Even the critics of your book will probably not argue with it, but they may also find this chapter less interesting—because it is less surprising—than some of the others.

KK: I wish I could conduct my conversations with just one opponent per chapter! But you do indeed bring up a notion that has been hurled at me every time I talk about these classifications. Anthropomorphizations, just anthropomorphizations! As if this term would explain anything! You may indeed wish to describe the phenomenon that the detector vocabulary is modeled upon our conception of human beings and their interaction as an anthropomorphization. But I wanted to point out the systematic patterns in these "anthropomorphizations," and offer an interpretation that differs from the accounts Douglas and others have given.

AC: I anthropomorphize my car, for example. When it doesn't start, I say the battery is sick. The disease vocabulary is everywhere!

KK: I want to distinguish between the occasional metaphor for each and everything, and classifications. Classifications are more systematic. They are built from a number of terms which are consistent with each other. The detector vocabulary, for example, is built from at least four terminological clusters which hang together; the sensory performance, disease/physiology, and social and moral clusters. Physicists don't always employ such classifications. One of their backgrounds is called a "snake" because of the shape in which it appears on event displays. But as far as I can see, none of the other background classifications draw upon shape. Shape may characterize this one case of beam halo, but it doesn't characterize the whole bedeviled phenomenon of background. Shape does not suggest anything about the ontology of the domain, though it may suggest something about a single background in one particular context, the context of event displays.

AC: Why couldn't a car be treated like a detector? I don't see the difference between my car as a machine and your detector machine.

KK: Indeed, any complex entity that is like a detector, with which we live like physicists live with a detector, might produce this or a similar kind of vocabulary. I am not suggesting that the detector classification is unique. What I am suggesting is that it expresses the particular "nature" of an entitity and the nature of the relationship between you, the user, and the entity. It expresses the reconfigured order of a particular context which the technical vocabulary cannot express.

3. AC: Sherry Turkle (1984) described anthropomorphizations of computers under the apt title of the computer as our "Second Self." Just a while ago you explained that detectors, with all their "senses" and "reactions," are our substitutes. We model these machines after us. And us upon them. Anthropomorphizations may be seen as alter egos.

KK: Detectors don't simulate our minds, or our mind's capacity, as computers and artificial intelligence supposedly do. We have to be much more precise. There are very different kinds of machines. And they shouldn't all be referred to with the same metaphoric classifications. Even if all classifications were modeled upon human existence, there should be systematic differences between them depending on the nature of the machine. Otherwise, my thesis would indeed be proved wrong.

AC: There should be such differences, but are there?

KK: I can only go by the evidence I have. There are systematic differences between the categorizations applied to detectors and those applied to the background, as you can see for yourself (Section 5.5). Or between those applied to the detector and those that pertain to the code, the computer programs which physicists constantly write and use. Or, in addition, between detector classifications and the categorizations of human beings.

AC: Not only in the context of HEP experiments, I hope.

KK: Correct.

4. AC: This vocabulary of a war-against-the-background which you referred me to might have a different interpretation. Since I live not far from Clifford Geertz let me put it as he might—if he was interested in your classifications. I think he would offer the view he suggested in the Balinese cockfight (1973: 443)—he might say these classifications are cultural figures that "catch up" themes close to the heart of our society and some of its subcategories of members—themes like illness/disease, death, aging, performance, and so on. The themes which are encoded in machine ontologies. But also the themes of enmity, danger, and struggle—the ones which are more present with the background. He would say that the classifications provide, to the physicists, a metaphor of themselves, but that they have no other reality or function. In terms more like Goffman's, the categorizations would be a dramatization of physicists' concerns and experiences. Anthropomorphization is a way to make drab technical tasks meaningful—by projecting upon them the very real human dramas and anxieties that physicists experience in their life.

KK: Actually, I am not confident at all that Geertz would endorse this view. But let me give you mine. Your account doesn't explain the systematic differences between categorizations. If you were right, dramatizations through categorizations should be random—anything goes for any domain, as long as the metaphors capture and project human concerns and experience. The killing vocabulary might be unloaded upon detectors, and the physiological one on the background. But clearly that wouldn't work at all. The background has no physiology, and the last thing we should do to a detector is kill it. Your explanation is also vague. Can you imagine a classification that does not somehow touch upon human existence and human concerns? Mary Douglas's suggestion was much more specific. She referred to analogies to the body. She would say that the analogy from physiology confers natural status on the crystallized social relations represented in a machine. The analogy builds strength for a physical instrument that does not in itself have legitimacy, consumes huge amounts of money and manpower, and would be, without the analogy from life, an amoral, asocial, nonnatural being.

KA: Persuasive, but not convincing. You are again focused on the detector, whereas we were already talking about the background. There is not much of an analogy from the body in the background, not much that confers natural status to it, unless you want to see the killing metaphors as evidence for the biological status of the background. Does talking about "bugs" in a computer code naturalize the code and thereby make it more legitimate? I think you already challenged this line of thinking. The reference to anthropomorphization does indeed not explain anything. All it says is that we attribute human form or personality to something. I do find your suggestion that these metaphors express local ontologies and subject-object relationships, the kind of thing that cannot be expressed by technical vocabularies, more convincing. But you do not explain why local ontologies and local subject-object relationships *need* to be expressed.

5. **KA:** I wish to go back to the question of resistances. The background vocabulary also makes strong references to resistances—it basically refers to the kinds of problems backgrounds pose. Are all classifications in this chapter, at the same time, categorizations of resistances? It seems to me that even what you say about physicists includes this component.

KK: I suppose not only the vocabularies in this chapter, but almost all I encountered—in as far as they include a number of terms and distinctions—have this aspect. You could rewrite this chapter, or simply read it as a chapter about different kinds of difficulties. But then this is not surprising. You could rewrite these particular collider experiments as a chapter on beating down the background, for example.

KA: Let me ask then whether, with the background, we have finally reached the object level, the real object world that interferes with the project of an experiment and fights back before it surrenders to its quest?

KK: Well, not quite. First, the background is made by the collider and experiment, just like everything else that flies through a detector as a particle. Second, the background, in as far as it is physics and not instrument- (machine-, beam-, detector-) related, is, as you heard, "last year's" or the "last ten year's" physics (Section 3.2). You identify and eliminate it only through knowing this physics. The background does not simply stop you in your tracks, as an unrecognized and unidentified entity. It is produced and (almost) simultaneously recognized and eliminated through triggers, thresholds and cuts—through a whole machinery of anticipation, identification, and calculation. It does not seem to exist outside this machinery. Here we are back again to the self-enclosed universe of experimental HEP.

KA: If all resistances in experimental HEP are instrument- or knowledge-related, where does this leave our attempt to place more emphasis on the material world? Is there no way around an understanding of resistances as cultural figures?

KK: Perhaps we should pose this question to a realist?

6   FROM ORGANISMS TO MACHINES

1. **R-H (a philosopher):** As the biologist that I once was, I read this chapter with interest, but also with mixed feelings. What worries me most is your tendency not to take seriously nature as the object of natural science and the special character this lends to science. From a biological point of view you come uncomfortably close to a creationist conception of science and of living nature!

   KARIN KNORR CETINA: This is the first time I have been compared to a creationist! I might agree with your worries about "nature" being taken seriously if you put nature under quotes and if you don't draw any quick conclusions about the special character it lends to science. After all, many professions, for example, farmers and landscapers and forest rangers, deal with living "nature" in a more direct sense than science.

   R-H: But you seem to deny its relevance. Here, for example, you claim that mice, flies, or frogs, as naturally occurring entities, are external to modern biology. But molecular biology, as a central part of modern biology, uses living organisms in general as its central object. The basic mechanisms of genetics occur generally in the living world. Of course, the organisms that are most fruitfully investigated in the laboratory are carefully chosen for that purpose and often modified to be even more suitable, but that does not mean that laboratory work/research is not motivated by a wish to understand the outside world.

   KK: You will grant us that we are not talking about motivations here, but about procedures, practices, and transformations. Take transformations. Laboratory sciences would not have a problem of "translating back" their results into naturally occurring processes if there were no transformations. Mostly, however, they don't translate these processes back into nature, they translate them into technology, pharmaceutical products, medical treatments, agricultural strategies, and the like. Results prove themselves in human practice, not in nature as it may exist independently of us.

2. **R-H:** Your notion that nature as it occurs in the wild is of no use in experimental work is a provocation! I would say that quite to the contrary "wild" nature is a constant source of new experimental objects. It is because of this constant traffic and the correspondence of the laboratory organisms with the natural ones that experimental laboratory science is generally interesting and valid.

   KLAUS AMANN: I find your notion of a "traffic" completely compatible with what we say. What interests me in this chapter are the rearrangements which occur at the endpoint of the travel. It seems to me that the whole idea of a laboratory becomes ununderstandable, if you assume that nature just continues to exist in the lab as it did outside. Besides, the notion of a "laboratope" would be redundant. Perhaps if your suggestion of a correspondence does not mean identity, we might start talking.

3. **R-H:** What bothers me is your apparent belief in the externality of nature. Bacteria and even viruses are also part of nature and objects of natural history!

   KK: The point in this paragraph is about the replacement of traditional plants and animals by new ones. I am beginning to suspect that we have very different notions of nature.

4. **R-H:** If bacteria have no claim for humane treatment in the laboratory, it is not because they are artificial creations from the lab. The same applies to bacteria in nature.

   KK: Completely correct. In fact, I would go even further to say that the outside existence of creatures like bacteria, or mice (or, for that sake, human beings; see Chapter 8) determines moral aspects of their treatment in the laboratory. For example, in the case of animals, it determines "humane" killing or sacrificing procedures.

5. **R-H:** Bacteria and viruses are simple organisms when they live outside the laboratory. Their life is not drastically reduced as a result of coming into the lab, it is always in a reduced state.

   KA: But there are manipulations, interferences, and limitations to which they are submitted in the lab. And a biochemical reaction is not a simulation of natural processes. Again, you seem to be put off by the suggested non-identity of "nature" inside and outside the lab.

6. **R-H:** And again you write of the disappearance of naturally occurring animals and plants as a break with earlier practices of biology. There certainly are changes in the practice of biology, but do you really want to claim this much?

   KK: Aren't we just having a disagreement about what we mean by "nature"? We don't use the term to refer to those naturally occurring processes which are not interfered with by human existence. Nor do we use it as a synonym for "reality as it really is," which is what I suspect you mean by nature. Actually, this book is not about nature.

   R-H: But for me, as a natural scientist, nature is there all the time. Concealed by your writing, but crying out from underneath it!

   KK: We are not natural scientists, though. For us, the interesting thing is how specific differences between "nature" and the laboratory are created and managed in scientific work, and what role these differences play in shaping this work. "Nature" in the way you seem to understand it is not a sociological term.

KA: In fact, we can only study "nature" as a cultural resource, for example, in the way in which Gooday (1991) studied Victorian naturalists' claims to the "naturalness" of certain forms of research over others. For example, we can look at how "nature" is construed as an independent reality behind various appearances in the lab in arguments and displays. Or we can look at how participants distinguish between degrees of "naturalness" as they differentiate between in vitro and in vivo procedures, between the lab mouse and the "wild" mouse, and so on.

7. R-H: It would help if you also addressed the differences between production systems in scientific experiments and in industrial production. It would help not to mix things up and to lose sight of interesting characteristics of science. An analogy is based on differences, as well as similarities.

KA: Are there interesting differences with respect to this logic of production and the engines which drive it? Surely some of the more obvious differences are that production in industry often means mass production of goods sellable on a market, and it means assembly lines, optimization, division of labor, and the like. But, if you look more closely, the differences are not so straightforward. The market and consumption aspect may be missing, but the advantages of cloning, for example, rest on the possibility of mass production of DNA fragments. Molecular biology exploits the distinct division of labor which lies in the separability of biological functions. It optimizes processes, and so on. With respect to this logic of production, analogous principles can be found at work in industrial production and in molecular biology. Moreover, these principles seem to have given molecular biology an uplift.

8. R-H: The term *simulation* strikes me as a misleading expression in this context. The laboratory organisms can better be considered as parts of nature taken into the laboratory to be more efficiently studied. They are nature rather than a means of simulating nature. *Simulation* is a term used to express a fundamental difference with the "real" thing.

KK: You ignore the reflexive double build of these production cycles, and once again, the labor and accomplishment (the constructive work) that goes into creating production systems in the lab. Perhaps all we can do at this point is to agree to disagree.

9. R-H: I agree to disagree, as you suggested before, but I do wish to make one comment on your last pages. In my view, you are saddling molecular biology with a more simplistic reductionist attitude than is necessary. Isolating it from traditional biology is part of an unrealistic picture of what biology is. But it does to some extent present a trend presently developing. Presenting this trend as a fact, a more or less inevitable result of the logic of science, may contribute to unwanted and detrimental developments of the scientific enterprise.

KK: I am flattered to hear that you think we may have such an impact on scientific development! But why do you imagine the development is unwanted?

R-H: Most of the new sociology of science lacks a political dimension. Its followers do not address the interaction between science and politics. But with the new environmental problems becoming central political issues, this side of science will most likely come into focus in the not too distant future.

KA: And with the environmental issues, biology rather than molecular biology will again rise to political attention? This may be so. But, I imagine, there will be two distinct, if somewhat interlaced, developments.

R-H: From a political point of view the crucial question is how malleable is science—and nature. But this is not only a challenge to recent sociologists of science. More traditional philosophers and sociologists of science are also much at a loss to provide an answer to this question. They still more or less hide behind the idea of value-free science. I find the parallels between the development of social studies of science and the philosophy of science more striking than the differences. Take Rorty (e.g., 1991), Hacking (1983), Fine (1986), Rouse (1987, 1996). The tendency to cut nature off and to avoid a political dimension is a common trait.

KK: The tendency "to cut nature off," as you say, corresponds perhaps to the tendency of some sciences to become more "constructive"—more of a laboratory than a field science, more technological, and more oriented toward the making and remaking of the world than toward the exploration of original worlds. Perhaps modern science has a tendency to leave nature "as it is" behind and substitute for it—or construct from it—new patterns and possibilities. Molecular biology is such a constructive science (think of genetic engineering!). So is experimental high energy physics. Its "nature" is mostly particles and processes which, today on earth, don't exist. Perhaps the success of constructionism in recent studies of science has to do with the fact that it captures this "cut off" from nature in the sciences. As to a better alignment between science studies and politics many call for it, and some, including presumably yourself, work toward it (e.g., Chubin 1992; Fuller 1988, 1992; Longino 1990; Jasanoff 1990; Restivo 1988, 1992; Wynne 1982, 1987; Cozzens and Gieryn 1990; Nelkin and Lindee 1995). We shall see . . .

7 HEP EXPERIMENTS AS POST-TRADITIONAL COMMUNITARIAN STRUCTURES

1. **SOCIOLOGIST:** With the title you gave to this chapter and the communitarian vocabulary you use, you are almost bound to raise some sociological eyebrows. Communitarianism? How can megaexperiments like the ones now in HEP escape the basic rules of normal social life? As a sociologist, I am a

believer in power and inequality. I shall watch your argument closely, but I shall warn you that I am not likely to be convinced by the likes of the concepts advanced so far.

KARIN KNORR CETINA: You shall have your power and inequality later. Let me at least begin by mapping out a way of life that includes more than that. After all, these additional mechanisms beyond power and inequality in the sense of social stratification would be the interesting ones for a sociologist, wouldn't they? The ones which are not completely familiar and expected!

S: That depends on the mechanisms and whether they are effective. I suppose political scientists would give you a more charitable reading—after all they have been quite interested in communitarianism recently. In fact, they have long been interested in it; political philosophers of the social contract were the ones that depicted a world where all individual interests are perfectly equated and realized through a common definition of the common good. An idealized world—but I fear yours may still be akin to it. You denounced commonality as a ground for communitarianism—that is already a step in the right direction.

KK: It's a step recommended by William Corlett in the book I cited and whose slogan I borrowed: *Community without Unity* (1992). If you can get past the subtitle of Corlett's book ("A Politics of Derridian Extravagances"), you will find that he makes the sensible argument that we don't need to assume unity in a community, followed by the less exciting proposal that we can somehow form communities through gift-giving.

S: But now you announce the erasure of the individual subject—and that is more likely to be a step in the wrong direction. But, we shall see!

2. **S:** Let me start with a simple question. If authorship no longer confers distinction, are there other mechanisms which do? How do departments make hiring decisions if they cannot go by authorship as a basis for differentiating candidates? Or do these physicists never face career changes and career needs?

KK: They do, and this is sometimes posed as a dilemma. On the other hand, there are many means of evaluating an individual indpependent of his or her authorship. Some distinction is already conferred on individuals through their membership of certain experiments. HEP experiments are the central entities and "events" in this field; they are watched by everybody from their very beginning, continually evaluated informally, and they are also listed in field directories. If you check the name of a physicist, the first answer you get is which experiments he or she was a member of. Second, letters of recommendation are important, and they may spell out what a scientist has contributed to an experiment. Third, scientists who present papers at conferences are looked over and watched for how they handle the talk and the questions raised, regardless of the fact that they do not present their personal work. Fourth, experiments today gather up much of the field within themselves. When the two LHC experiments start running in 2005, they will divide among them a large portion of all relevant physics departments and institutes. The members and heads of these departments and institutes have ample opportunity to meet and observe candidates, since these candidates are likely to be members of their own or a sister experiment. Finally, there are the gossip and confidence pathways (see Chapter 8), which hold the moral memory of experiments—the evaluative knowledge about who performed what and with what degree of success.

S: This introduces an element of differentiation into your community!

KK: A "community without unity" is not undifferentiated! The communitarian practices of HEP experiments are a far cry from the romantic ideals of community you may have in mind.

3. **S:** You argued that high energy physics work travels through the field not by the names of the people who conducted the work, but by the names of the experiments and the equipment. You also say that physicists at conferences act as representatives of experiments and equipment. But aren't you leaving out completely one sort of event that counteracts these tendencies, the talks given by individual researchers when they are invited to give seminars in specific laboratories? Aren't these the contexts in which individuals make claims for solving this problem or that, and in which gossip analyzes who is really responsible for this or that contribution? I assume that individual subjectivity and claims to fame are omnipresent here. These small seminars only for the invited may be particularly important in the diffusion of attribution and reputation because it is a small and tightly bound field.

KK: The point of this chapter is to work out mechanisms that unleash cooperation and leave the individual behind as an epistemic subject—as the procurer of the kind of knowledge that these experiments are after. But these mechanisms do not eliminate biographical regimes, individual career needs, forces of individuation that drive them, or individual personhood in other contexts. If they did, they would probably rest upon coercion or upon the kind of self-effacing identification with a leader that we imagine exists in religious sects. The physics mechanisms seem to me to be successful because they introduce a bifurcation—between the person as a member and contributor and the person as an individual. The social order is split in two, if you wish. It redoubles itself and draws advantages from this reduplication. Your small "invited" seminars have to be seen in the context of individual careers. Especially since they are often related to career moves—someone is invited to give a seminar because he or she may be considered in a search process, or because he or she wants to advertise his or her availability on the market.

4. **S:** You seem to be suggesting that individuals' emotions also surrender to these experiments—that they are taken over and made use of, to enhance an individual's contribution to the whole. Do experiments thrive on exploiting negative emotions, individuals' fears and anxieties?

    KK: Physicists' emotions are certainly affected, but they are not, as far as I can tell, consciously manipulated. I see the anxieties as reactions to a pressure that derives from the knowledge of mutual interdependence. Threats or acts of applying (group) pressure are hardly needed in this situation.

5. **S:** You switch from a community imagery to a management imagery. I like the departure from the former, since I seriously doubt whether the classic notion of community is appropriately used to describe the huge HEP assemblages of the order of 2,000 scientists and technicians. After all, community as a concept was developed in contrast to "society," suggesting in the former a personal intimacy, moral commitment, and continuity in time that only metaphorically describes people linked via a detector. What I am not sure of is whether I like or even understand your notion of object-centered management or management by content.

    KK: Wait. I did not describe a collaboration as a community, certainly not in the sense you just mentioned. I was talking about communitarian mechanisms. Perhaps the notion of object-centered management is a way to prevent readers from having the community associations you have.

    S: But isn't this simply the old Weberian idea that technical competence is a basis for bureaucratic efficiency?

    KK: Weber indeed stated that bureaucracy is "essentially control by means of knowledge" (1947: 335, 337). Yet as Parsons pointed out upon the translation of Weber's work into English (1947: 59), technical competence and the legal competence Weber emphasized in bureaucracy call for different kinds of organization, a problem Weber ignored by lumping the two together and never really following up on the technical side. Also, the idea of competence locates all there is to say about the object-world in the person. What interests me is, for example, how the object-world is allowed to structure organizing formats, how it is represented and preserved in these formats, and how object-oriented schemes replace group-oriented schemes or social authority schemes of managing. Hierarchical means of control as in bureaucratic organizations would be an example of the latter.

    S: With the idea of object-centered management, you rhetorically play on nature rather than society?

    KK: I think HEP plays on naturalizing mechanisms as opposed to using the classical social structural ones. And I try to pinpoint this by the idea of object-centered management.

6. **S:** First, you are bombarding us with communitarianism, and now you throw Durkheim's collective consciousness at us! Isn't it a bit much?

KK: I am trying to work with a series of images simultaneously. To build a sense of these experiments by coming at them from several angles.

S: I strongly prefer the concepts of discourse and self-knowledge. One can indeed ground in them some notion of collective cognition. I also like the idea that these experiments hold a collective conversation with themselves. These notions seem to me to be the most concrete; they capture what I imagine could actually happen.

KK: They are most concrete. Self-knowledge is not a metaphor in this context, nor is discourse, nor for that matter collective consciousness. It simply suggests that there is a level of collective awareness of the state and requirements of the various components of the experiment that is actively created and maintained through sequentially ordered meetings and other forms of summarizing and distributing information.

7. **S:** Aren't these experiments also corporate actors? You keep telling us about their internal makeup, but aren't they also acting toward the outside?

KK: It seems to me that these experiments—unlike perhaps industrial corporations—are not notable for their "agency"—for behaving as if they were individual actors. What would be the field of activities in which this agency could act itself out? For industrial firms, competing firms, suppliers and buyers provide an external environment in which the firms make their moves as units. They are also legal units subject to corporate law, commodities on a take-over market, and so on. Firms have an intraorganizational environment, but they are also part of a field of extraorganizational activities in which they are attributed unit status, and in which they legally and economically act as units. Experiments, on the other hand, have few occasions to act like corporate actors—they have few if any competitors at any given time, there is no longer a "free" market on which their products sell, and they are not commodities themselves or entities of legal status. What they have are complex internal processing structures, dispersed and yet integrated circuits of effort, will, initiative, and knowledge. For the corporate actor concept to make any sense, you need a field of activities for collective units.

S: What happens if such experiments interact with each other? Could institutes not be seen as corporate actors?

KK: Experiments rarely do interact with each other as units. For example, now after the cancellation of the SSC, the SSC experiments are not joining CERN's ATLAS experiment, small groups and institutes join. Interaction, when it occurs, is often simply on the level of personal confidence and gossip pathways (see Chapter 8). Perhaps we should also see this interaction as the partial meshing of two discourse and processing webs, the enfolding of one circuit into the other. Institutes, on the other hand, can often be narrowed down to something like "institute heads" and "their" groups. I imagine them somewhat like laboratories with their lab leaders in molecular biology

(Chapter 9), but there are significant differences between what "institutes" mean in different countries! Experiments tend to activate and draw upon members of institutes for the work to be done rather than upon leaders. And this work is the displayable, accountable input in and part of the above discourse and processing circuits. Again there is the intermeshing of webs, the enfolding of one circuit into the other, rather than the interaction of two independent actors.

8. **S:** Your description of these collaborations reminds me of the work by two sociologists, Faulkner and Anderson (1987), who have written about Hollywood film-making. Is a HEP experiment not like the "collective" that comes together to make a big studio movie? A particular assemblage of people who come together *just* for *that* project, then they go off and reshuffle themselves into subsequent temporary projects?

   KK: I have gotten a number of suggestions of possible comparison cases. Space shuttles were one case, the Human Genome project another, cross-cultural engineering ventures such as the Anglo-French channel tunnel a third, and fusion reactors a fourth. Given their size, cost, and duration, HEP experiments are at this point surely a somewhat specific development in contemporary science. But there is no reason to believe that the ordering mechanisms they implement are in any way unique. As to Hollywood film-making, I have my doubts whether it would be found, by the same method of study, to display mechanisms similar to those in HEP—time and money involved are still orders of magnitude below that of HEP, the producers and directors presumably hold all the power, self-knowledge of the whole cast may be reduced to gossip, and so on. But, can I not entice you or someone else to look into these cases?

8 THE MULTIPLE ORDERING FRAMEWORKS OF HEP COLLABORATIONS

1. **SOCIOLOGIST:** Is what you are telling us here not invalidating the thesis of the vanishing individual epistemic subject? How can subjects come back if they don't exist? I am quite confused by this curious twist in your argument. Are you trying to eat your cake and have it too?

   KARIN KNORR CETINA: I surely am. More importantly, I think physicists do. The trick lies in the division they introduce and make use of: a time period during which individual interests and strategic action are the rule (the birth stage of an experiment); and a time period in which the world has been divided up and the remaining struggles are no longer fueled by the same interests as the ones before. But also by a split between the local environment and the nonlocal one, or between individuals as biographical entities with careers, interests, investments and individuals (or institutes) as members of experiments. Perhaps if you follow me through to the next section . . .

2. **S:** I was pleased to hear that you finally brought in some of the divisions between members of experiments. The conflicts, the interests, the investments, and the real subjects. But with your unfolding device, you again shift back to the implicit notion that the dynamic of the superorganism, your experiment, is essentially organized via a consensual culture.

   KK: No. The losers in these contests of unfolding almost invariably disagree with the decision to eliminate their technology. But the decisions are naturalized in as far as this is possible, this is the important point. They are placed beyond the boundary of open denouncement and rebellion. I saw only one case of such a rebellion.

   S: In some sense one could of course easily understand why the permanent need to collaborate creates a consensual culture. However, as in any group, it is much more likely that some get to impose their agenda more often than others. As in many academic departments, if consensus spontaneously emerges, it is because meta-power is being exercised, for example, because the agenda and the solutions have been defined through informal interaction before the meeting. Isn't it only after the fact that decisions are reconstructed as "obvious" and "reasonable?" I am tempted to believe that consensus does not "naturally" emerge from meetings.

   KK: Perhaps you forget that there is no central power in these experiments. CERN contributes much of the financing of the infrastructure, but CERN is dependent on the member states from which the institutes come. The institutes carry much of the financing of new detectors, some much more than others. But the experiments I saw do not give the institutes voting power commensurate to their financial contribution, or to their size and manpower—the rule in the institute meetings remains one vote per institute. Certainly one does not want to alienate an important institute, for example a national lab. But then there are alternatives. Others can build detector parts if some institute declines. The threat (or the announced fear) that some institutes and perhaps a whole country may withdraw from participation—I have seen it made once—does not sit well with the rest of the collaboration; such threats may backfire. Institutes are as dependent on the possibility of participating in an interesting experiment as the experiment is on them. It's a delicate balance of power in which everything constantly shifts, but it is a balance of power.

3. **S:** High energy physicists obviously live in an extremely dense world in which colliders are scarce resources. I would suggest that this scarcity does not erase subjectivity but enforces distinct forms of impression management. These forms allow physicists to pursue their ambitions while at the same time making it possible for them to coexist with others whether they lose or win, since all actors are unconditionally attached to the same breast, to the same detector and collider. Isn't it because physicists need access to the same

infrastructure that they are forced to maintain and manage a civilized presentation of self? Doesn't this impression management give *you* the impression of naturally emerging decisions?

KK: I tend to agree with Goffman that public occasions always sustain some impression management. But if you work your way into a culture the question is whether impression management is a cultural vehicle of some importance, something that allows you to identify a whole pattern. It is there where I disagree. The unfolding contests don't seem to me to have just the effect of maintaining a civilized appearance. Who would be fooled by it? Physicists know very well what is at stake for them and for others in these experiments. But they also seem to tell us (through their procedures) that they know full well that they can't build a detector with impression management alone, and that no group in the experiment can juggle the game well enough such as to be independent of the cooperation of others.

S: This eliminates power?

KK: It asks for a different conception of power—not for the traditional sociological notion, according to which power rests with a ruler, or with a power elite, but for a notion of power like Foucault's (e.g., 1982). Power is distributed, it doesn't reside in single individuals but in procedures, and it includes an element of care. This form of power—which I locate within the superorganism structure—does not eliminate the power strategies of strategic actors who dominate at the birth stage of an experiment.

4. **S:** I still didn't learn how it is decided that anyone gets the Nobel Prize in these experiments!

KK: Physicists in these experiments consider the Nobel Prize a relict from the past. I would see it as a relict from a scheme that once dominated in the sciences, and still does in a significant number of them, but that has been superseded in experimental HEP. Some scientists in these experiments, I am sure, also play with the idea of a Nobel Prize for themselves. But most wonder what the Nobel committee will actually *do* if the top quark is confirmed to have been found by CDF at Fermilab, or the Higgs mechanism is discovered by the ATLAS or CMS experiment at CERN. These discoveries could warrant the prize. Will the committee award it to a spokesperson, or perhaps change its rules and award it to the whole experiment, or will it consider these discoveries, because of their collective nature, as outside its range of responsibility? Certainly most physicists you ask will tell you that an individual award in these cases is unwarranted today.

S: But then is it just chance that the Nobel Prize doesn't go to a graduate student?

KK: None of the mechanisms that we associate with individuals in science are ruled out, except that you find some superseded by others (see Section 7.2). In addition, individuals creditable for outstanding contributions may continue to emerge in these experiments. But the experiments, this is my strongest thesis, do not depend on them for finding the top quark or the Higgs! What they do depend on are these other mechanisms, which allow them to perform a close to 2,000 experts and several hundred million Swiss franc task successfully and on time. If I am not emphasizing the old individual-centered differentiation structures it is because I have nothing new to add to them. They exist, and make a difference in individual careers, but they do not explain the functioning of these collaborations.

5. **S:** I wish to share with you one final consideration—you point out that physicists can choose to be members of beehives and that they may step from one form of ordering to the other. Biking during the weekend, watching TV with their families, or even voting, after having completed their workday. What puzzles me is that, even assuming that the elite culture of scientists in Switzerland is radically different from the one of their American counterparts that I know, which is unlikely given the international nature of elite scientific circles, you seem to presume that researchers can step out of the intensely competitive and individualistic culture that prevails in the upper-middle-class world to which they belong, and that they can develop new selves and lose their Promethean claims as soon as they cross the steps of CERN or Fermilab.

KK: I am glad to hear that I may soon be able to go back to the text! I find these exchanges enthralling, but also quite exhausting. Perhaps we should continue them in the final chapter, where you can raise some of the more encompassing questions.

S: Thank you for letting me do that! I suppose by inviting me into the text what you wish to avoid is writing any more notes? In any case, I shall switch the turn back to some generalized reader, since I am somewhat exhausted too. To have to constantly invent new objections—what, by the way, is your answer to my last one?

KK: I shall pass it on to the real readers who will criticize my book!

References

Ackerknecht, E. H. 1968. *Medicine at the Paris Hospitals, 1794–1848*. Baltimore: Johns Hopkins University Press.

Åkesson, T., et al. 1990. "Search for Top Quark Production at the CERN $\bar{p}p$ Collider." *Zeitschrift für Physik C—Particles and Fields*, 16: 179–189.

Alberts, B., D. Bray, J. Lewis, M. Raff, K. Roberts, and J. D. Watson. 1983. *Molecular Biology of the Cell*. New York and London: Garland.

Alexander, J. 1988. "Introduction: Durkheimian Sociology and Cultural Studies Today." In *Durkheimian Sociology: Cultural Studies*. Cambridge: Cambridge University Press.

——— 1992. "Some Remarks on 'Agency' in Recent Sociological Theory." *Perspectives*, 15(1): 1–4.

——— 1998. "The Computer as Sacred and Profane." In Ph. Smith (ed.), *The New American Cultural Sociology*. Cambridge: Cambridge University Press.

Alexander, J., B. Giesen, R. Münch, and N. Smelser (eds.). 1987. *The Micro-Macro Link*. Berkeley: University of California Press.

Alitti, J., et al. 1990. "A Precise Determination of the W and Z Masses at the CERN $\bar{p}p$ Collider." *Physics Letters B*, 241(1): 150–164.

Amann, K. 1990. "Natürliche Expertise und künstliche Intelligenz: eine mikrosoziologische Untersuchung von Naturwissenschaftlern." Ph.D. diss. University of Bielefeld.

——— 1994. "Menschen, Mäuse und Fliegen. Eine wissenssoziologische Analyse der Transformation von Organismen in epistemische Objekte." *Zeitschrift für Soziologie*, 23(1): 22–40.

Amann, K., and K. Knorr Cetina. 1988. "The Fixation of (Visual) Evidence." *Human Studies*, 11: 133–169.

——— 1989. "Thinking through Talk: An Ethnographic Study of a Molecular

Biology Laboratory." In R. A. Jones, L. Hargens, and A. Pickering (eds.), *Knowledge and Society: Studies in the Sociology of Science Past and Present,* vol. 8: 3–26. Greenwich, CT: JAI Press.

Anderson, P. W. 1972. "More Is Different: Broken Symmetry and the Nature of the Hierarchical Structure of Science." *Science,* 177(4047): 393–396.

Appadurai, A. 1986. *The Social Life of Things: Commodities in Cultural Perspective.* Cambridge: Cambridge University Press.

Arnison, G., et al. 1983a. "Experimental Observation of Isolated Large Transverse Energy Electrons with Associated Missing Energy at $\sqrt{}=540$ GeV." *Physics Letters,* B122: 103.

——— et al. 1983b. "Experimental Observation of Lepton Pairs of Invariant Mass around $95 \text{GeV}/c^2$ at the CERN SPS Collider." *Physics Letters,* B126: 398.

Ashmore, M. 1989. *The Reflexive Thesis.* Chicago: University of Chicago Press.

Bach, M. 1992. "Eine leise Revolution durch Verwaltungsverfahren." *Zeitschrift für Soziologie,* 21(1): 16–30.

Bagnaia, P., et al. 1983. "Evidence for $Z^0 \to e^+e^-$ at the CERN $\bar{p}p$ Collider." *Physics Letters,* B129: 130.

——— et al. 1984. "Observation of Electrons Produced in Association with Hard Jets and Large Missing Transverse Momentum in $p\bar{p}$ Collisions at $\sqrt{s}=540$ GeV." *Physics Letters,* B139: 105.

Banner, M., et al. 1983. "Observation of Single Isolated Electrons of High Transverse Momentum in Events with Missing Transverse Energy at the CERN $\bar{p}p$ Collider." *Physics Letters,* B122: 476.

Barber, B. 1962. "Resistance by Scientists to Scientific Discovery." In B. Barber and W. Hirsch (eds.), *Sociology of Science.* New York: The Free Press.

——— 1989. "Liberal Democracy and the Ghost of Consent." In N. L. Rosenblum (ed.), *Liberalism and the Moral Life,* pp. 54–68. Cambridge, MA: Harvard University Press.

Barger, V. D., and R. J. N. Phillips. 1987. *Collider Physics.* Redwood City, CA: Addison-Wesley.

Barnes, B. 1977. *Interests and the Growth of Knowledge.* London: Routledge and Kegan Paul.

Barnes, B., and S. Shapin. 1979. *Natural Order: Historical Studies of Scientific Culture.* Beverly Hills: Sage.

Beardsley, T. 1991. "Smart Genes." *Scientific American,* August 1991: 72–81.

Beck, U. 1992. *Risk Society: Towards a New Modernity.* London: Sage.

Beck, U., A. Giddens, and S. Lash. 1994. *Reflexive Modernization.* Stanford. Stanford University Press.

Bell, D. 1973. *The Coming of Post-Industrial Society: A Venture in Social Forecasting.* New York: Basic Books.

References

Beniger, J. R. 1986. *The Control Revolution.* Cambridge, MA: Harvard University Press.

Berger, P., B. Berger, and H. Kellner. 1974. *The Homeless Mind: Modernization and Consciousness.* New York: Vintage Books.

Bergmann, J. 1993. *Discreet Indiscretions.* New York: Aldine de Gruyter.

Biagioli, M. 1995. "Tacit Knowledge, Courtliness, and the Scientist's Body." In S. L. Foster (ed.) *Choreographing History,* pp. 69–81. Bloomington: Indiana University Press.

Bijker, W. E., T. P. Hughes, and T. Pinch (eds.). 1989. *The Social Construction of Technological Systems: New Directions in the Sociology and History of Technology.* Cambridge, MA: MIT Press.

Bloor, D. 1976. *Knowledge and Social Imagery.* London: Routledge and Kegan Paul.

——— 1987. "The Living Foundations of Mathematics." *Social Studies of Science,* 17: 337–358.

Boden, D. 1994. *The Business of Talk: Organization in Action.* Cambridge: Polity Press.

Boehme, G., W. van den Daele, and W. Krohn. 1973. "Die Finalisierung der Wissenschaft." *Zeitschrift für Soziologie,* 2: 128–144.

Bourdieu, P. 1993. "Narzißtische Reflexivität und wissenschaftliche Reflexivität." In E. Berg and M. Fuchs (eds.), *Kultur, soziale Praxis, Text.* Frankfurt am Main: Suhrkamp.

Bradney, P. 1957. "The Joking Relationship in Industry." *Human Relations,* 10: 179–187.

Brown, R. H. 1987. *Society as Text.* Chicago: University of Chicago Press.

Busch, L., W. B. Lacy, J. Burkhardt, and L. R. Lacy. 1991. *Plants, Power and Profit—Social, Economic and Ethical Consequences of the New Biotechnologies.* Cambridge, MA: Basil Blackwell.

Buss, L. 1987. *The Evolution of Individuality.* Princeton: Princeton University Press.

Buttel, F. 1989. "How Epoch Making Are High Technologies? The Case of Biotechnology." *Sociological Forum,* 4: 247–260.

Buttel, F., M. Kenney and J. Kloppenburg. 1985. "From Green Revolution to Biorevolution: Some Observations on the Changing Technological Bases of Economic Transformation in the Third World." *Economic Development and Culture Change,* 34: 31–51.

Callon, M. 1986. "Some Elements of a Sociology of Translation: Domestication of the Scallops and the Fishermen of St. Brieuc Bay." In J. Law (ed.), *Power, Action and Belief: A New Sociology of Knowledge?* London: pp. 196–233. Routledge and Kegan Paul.

Cambrosio, A., and P. Keating. 1992. "A Matter of FACS: Constituting Novel Entities in Immunology." *Medical Anthropology Quarterly,* 6: 362–384.

Campbell, D. T. 1958. "Common Fate, Similarity, and Other Indices of the Status of Aggregates of Persons as Social Entities." *Behavioral Science*, 3(1): 15–25.

——— 1975. "On the Conflicts between Biological and Social Evolution and between Psychology and Moral Tradition." *American Psychologist*, 30(12): 1103–1126.

——— 1990. "Levels of Organization, Downward Causation, and the Selection-Theory Approach to Evolutionary Epistemology." In G. Greenberg and E. Tobach (eds.), *Theories of the Evolution of Knowing*. Hillsdale: Lawrence Erlbaum.

——— 1992. "Distinguishing between Pattern-in-Perception Due to the Knowing Mechanisms and Pattern Plausibly Attributable to the Referent." In M. E. Carvallo (ed.), *Nature, Cognition, and System*. Dordrecht: Kluwer.

Cantor, C.-R. 1990. "Orchestrating the Human Genome Project." *Science*, 248 (4951): 49–51.

Chubin, D. E. 1992. "The Elusive Second 'S' in 'STS': Who's Zoomin' Who?" *Technoscience* (4S Newsletter), Fall 1992: 12–13.

Churchland, P. M. 1992. *A Neurocomputational Perspective: The Nature of Mind and the Structure of Science*. Cambridge, MA: MIT Press.

Cicourel, A. 1964. *Method and Measurement in Sociology*. New York: Free Press.

——— 1968. *The Social Organization of Juvenile Justice*. New York: Wiley.

——— 1974. *Theory and Method in a Study of Argentine Fertility*. New York: Wiley.

Clarke, A., and M. J. Casper. 1998. "Making the Pap Smear into the 'Right Tool' for the Job: Cervical Cancer Screening, 1940–1995." *Social Studies of Science*, 28(2): 255–290.

Clifford, J. 1986. "Introduction: Partial Truths." In J. Clifford and G. E. Marcus (eds.), *Writing Culture: The Poetics and Politics of Ethnography*. Berkeley and Los Angeles: University of California Press.

Clifford, J., and G. E. Marcus (eds.). 1986. *Writing Culture: The Poetics and Politics of Ethnography*. Berkeley and Los Angeles: University of California Press.

Close, F., M. Marten, and C. Sutton. 1987. *The Particle Explosion*. Oxford: Oxford University Press.

Cole, J., and S. Cole. 1973. *Social Stratification in Science*. Chicago: University of Chicago Press.

Cole, S. 1970. "Professional Standing and the Reception of Scientific Discoveries." *American Journal of Sociology*, 76: 286–306.

——— 1992. *Making Science*. Cambridge, MA: Harvard University Press.

Coleman, J. S. 1990. *Foundations of Social Theory*. Cambridge, MA: Harvard University Press.

References

Collins, H. M. 1975. "The Seven Sexes: A Study in the Sociology of a Phenomenon, or the Replication of Experiments in Physics." *Sociology,* 9: 205–224.

——— 1981. *Knowledge and Controversy: Studies in Modern Natural Science.* Special issue of Social Studies of Science, 11: 1–158.

——— 1985. *Changing Order: Replication and Induction in Scientific Practice.* London: Sage.

——— 1990. *Artificial Experts: Social Knowledge and Intelligent Machines.* Cambridge, MA: MIT Press.

Collins, H. M., and S. Yearley. 1992. "Epistemological Chicken." In A. Pickering (ed.), *Science as Practice and Culture.* Chicago: University of Chicago Press.

Corlett, W. 1989. *Community without Unity.* Durham and London: Duke University Press.

Coulter, J. 1979. *The Social Construction of Mind: Studies in Ethnomethodology and Linguistic Philosophy.* London: Macmillan.

Cozzens, S., and T. Gieryn (eds.). 1990. *Theories of Science in Society.* Bloomington: Indiana University Press.

Crane, D. (ed.). 1994. *Sociology of Culture: Emerging Theoretical Perspectives.* Oxford: Basil Blackwell.

Crawford, R. 1991. "A Culture Clash over Big Science." *Science,* 253(5016): 128–130.

Daston, L. 1992. "Objectivity and the Escape from Perspective." *Social Studies of Science,* 22: 597–618.

——— 1993. "The Moralized Objectivities of Nineteenth-Century Science." Paper presented at the Davis Center Seminar, Princeton University, May.

Daston, L., and P. Galison. 1993. "The Image of Objectivity." *Representations,* 40: 81–128.

Dennett, D. 1987. *The Intentional Stance.* Cambridge, MA: MIT Press.

DiLella, L. 1990. "Hadron Colliders: Past, Present and Future." *CERN-PPE Note,* 90–160.

DiMaggio, P. 1994. "Culture and Economy." In N. J. Smelser and R. Swedberg (eds.), *The Handbook of Economic Sociology.* Princeton: Princeton University Press.

DiMaggio, P., and W. Powell (eds.). 1991. *The New Institutionalism in Organizational Analysis.* Chicago: University of Chicago Press.

Dobbin, F. 1994. "Cultural Models of Organization: The Social Construction of Rational Organizing Principles." In D. Crane (ed.), *Sociology of Culture: Emerging Theoretical Perspectives.* Oxford: Basil Blackwell.

Douglas, M. 1986. *How Institutions Think.* Syracuse: Syracuse University Press.

Downey, G. L. 1992. "CAD/CAM Saves the Nation? Toward an Anthropology of Technology." *Knowledge and Society: The Anthropology of Science and Technology,* 9: 143–168.

———— 1998. *The Machine in Me: An Anthropologist Sits Among Computer Engineers*. New York: Routledge.

Dreyfus, H. L., and S. E. Dreyfus. 1986. *Mind over Machine: The Power of Human Intuition and Expertise in the Era of the Computer*. Oxford: Blackwell.

Dreyfus, H. L., and P. Rabinow. 1982. *Michel Foucault: Beyond Structuralism and Hermeneutics*. Chicago: University of Chicago Press.

Drucker, P. F. 1988. "The Coming of the New Organization." *Harvard Business Review,* January–February: 45–53.

———— 1993. *Post-Capitalist Society*. New York: Harper Collins.

Dumont, J.-P. 1978. *The Headman and I*. Prospect Heights: Waveland Press.

Dupré, J. 1993. *The Disorder of Things*. Cambridge, MA: Harvard University Press.

Durkheim, E. 1933. *The Division of Labor in Society*. Glencoe, IL: Free Press.

Durkheim, E., and M. Mauss. 1963. *Primitive Classifications,* Trans. R. Needham. Chicago: University of Chicago Press.

Edge, D. 1979. "Quantitative Measures of Communication in Science: A Critical Review." *History of Science*, 8: 102–134.

Edge, D., and M. Mulkay. 1976. *Astronomy Transformed: The Emergence of Radio Astronomy in Britain*. New York: Wiley.

Faulkner, R. F., and A. B. Anderson. 1987. "Short-Term Projects and Emergent Careers: Evidence from Hollywood." *American Journal of Sociology*, 92: 879–909.

Feyerabend, P. 1975. *Against Method*. London: New Left Books.

Fine, A. 1986. *The Shaky Game*. Chicago: University of Chicago Press.

Forsythe, D. E. 1992. "Blaming the User in Medical Informatics: The Cultural Nature of Scientific Practice." *Knowledge and Society: The Anthropology of Science and Technology*, 9: 95–111.

Foucault, M. 1973. *The Order of Things: An Archaeology of the Human Sciences*. New York: Vintage Books.

———— 1980. "Questions on Geography." In C. Gordon (ed.), *Power/Knowledge: Selected Interviews and Other Writings, 1972–1977*, pp. 63–77. Brighton, Sussex: Harvester Press.

———— 1984. "What is an Author?"In P. Rabinow (ed.), *Foucault Reader*. New York: Pantheon Books.

———— 1986. *The Care of the Self. Vol. 3: The History of Sexuality*. Toronto: Random House.

Fox Keller, E. 1985. *Reflections on Gender and Science*. New Haven: Yale University Press.

———— 1992. *Secrets of Life, Secrets of Death: Essays on Language, Gender and Science*. New York: Routledge.

Freud, S. 1947. *Gesammelte Werke*. Frankfurt: Fischer.

References

Fujimura, J. H. 1987. "Constructing Doable Problems in Cancer Research: Articulating Alignment." *Social Studies of Science,* 17: 257–293.

——— 1996. *Crafting Science: A Sociohistory of the Quest for the Genetics of Cancer.* Cambridge, Mass.: Harvard University Press.

Fuller, S. 1988. *Social Epistemology.* Bloomington: Indiana University Press.

——— 1992. "Social Epistemology and the Research Agenda." In A. Pickering (ed.), *Science as Practice and Culture.* Chicago: University of Chicago Press.

Galison, P. 1987. *How Experiments End.* Chicago: University of Chicago Press.

——— 1989. "The Trading Zone: Coordination between Experiment and Theory in the Modern Laboratory." Paper presented at International Workshop on the Place of Knowledge, Tel Aviv and Jerusalem, May.

——— 1993. "An Image Falling through Space." Paper presented at the Davis Center Colloquium, Princeton University, April.

Galison, P., and B. Hevly (eds.). 1992. *Big Science: The Growth of Large-Scale Research.* Stanford: Stanford University Press.

Galison, P., and D. Stump (eds.). 1996. *The Disunity of Science.* Stanford: Stanford University Press.

Garfinkel, H. 1967. *Studies in Ethnomethodology.* Englewood Cliffs, NJ: Prentice Hall.

Gauthier, L. 1991. "Construction de représentations visuelles et organisation spatio-temporelle des ressources en astronomie." Unpublished doctoral dissertation, University of Montreal.

——— 1992. "Les habitus perceptuels des astronomes et leur role dans la production de la connaissance scientifique." *Information sur les Sciences Sociales,* 31(3): 419–443.

Geertz, C. 1973. *The Interpretation of Cultures.* New York: Basic Books.

——— 1983. *Local Knowledge: Further Essays in Interpretative Anthropology.* New York: Basic Books.

——— 1988. *Works and Lives.* Stanford: Stanford University Press.

——— 1993. "'Ethnic Conflict': Three Alternative Terms." *Common Knowledge,* 2(3): 54–65.

Geison, G. 1981. "Scientific Change, Emerging Specialities, and Research Schools." *History of Science,* 10: 20–40.

——— 1993. "Research Schools and New Directions in the Historiography of Science." *Osiris,* 8: 67–80.

——— 1995. *The Private Science of Louis Pasteur.* Princeton: Princeton University Press.

Gibbens, P. 1987. *Particles and Paradoxes.* Cambridge: Cambridge University Press.

Giddens, A. (ed.). 1974. *Positivism and Sociology.* London: Heinemann.

——— 1990. *The Consequences of Modernity.* Stanford: Stanford University Press.

———— 1991. *Modernity and Self-Identity*. Cambridge: Polity.

Giere, R. 1988. *Explaining Science: A Cognitive Approach*. Chicago: University of Chicago Press.

———— 1999. *Science without Laws*. Chicago: University of Chicago Press.

Gieryn, T. F. 1982. "Relativist/Constructivist Programmes in the Sociology of Science: Redundance and Retreat." *Social Studies of Science*, 12: 279–297.

———— 1983. "Boundary-Work and the Demarcation of Science from Non-Science: Strains and Interests in Professional Ideologies of Scientists." *American Sociological Review*, 48(6): 781–795.

———— 1994. "Objectivity for These Times." Paper presented at the Annual Meeting of the 4S Society, West Lafayette, October 1993.

Giesen, B. 1987. "Beyond Reductionism: Four Models Relating Micro and Macro Levels." In J. Alexander, B. Giesen, R. Münch, and N. Smelser (eds.), *The Micro-Macro Link*. Berkeley: University of California Press.

Gilbert, N., and M. Mulkay. 1984. *Opening Pandora's Box: A Sociological Analysis of Scientists' Discourse*. Cambridge: Cambridge University Press.

Gilbert, W. 1992. "A Vision of the Grail." In D. Kevles and L. Hood (eds.), *The Code of Codes*. Cambridge, MA: Harvard University Press.

Goffman, E. 1959. *The Presentation of Self in Everyday Life*. New York: Doubleday.

———— 1972. "The Neglected Situation." In P. P. Giglioli (ed.), *Language and Social Context*. Harmondsworth, Middlesex: Penguin.

———— 1981. *Forms of Talk*. Philadelphia: University of Pennsylvania Press.

Gooday, G. 1991. "'Nature' in the Laboratory: Domestication and Discipline with the Microscope in Victorian Life Science." *British Journal of the History of Science*, 24: 307–341.

Gooding, D. 1989. "History in the Laboratory: Can We Tell What Really Went On?" In F. A. J. L. James (ed.), *The Development of the Laboratory: Essays on the Place of Experiment in Industrial Civilisation*. London: Macmillan.

Gooding, D., T. Pinch, and S. Schaffer (eds.). 1989. *The Uses of Experiment*. Cambridge: Cambridge University Press.

Grafton, A. 1997. *The Footnote: A Curious History*. Cambridge, MA: Harvard University Press.

Gregory, B. 1988. *Inventing Reality. Physics as Language*. New York: Wiley.

Griffith, B. C., and N. Mullins. 1972. "Coherent Social Groups in Scientific Change." *Science*, 177(4053): 959–964.

Habermas, J. 1970. *Zur Logik der Sozialwissenschaften*. Frankfurt am Main: Suhrkamp.

———— 1981. *Theorie des kommunikativen Handelns*. Frankfurt/M.: Suhrkamp.

Hacking, I. 1983. *Representing and Intervening*. Cambridge: Cambridge University Press.

References

———— 1992a. "The Disunified Sciences." In R. J. Elvee (ed.), *The End of Science?* Lanham: University of America Press.

———— 1992b. "The Self-Vindication of the Laboratory Sciences." In A. Pickering (ed.), *Science as Practice and Culture.* Chicago: Chicago University Press.

———— 1992c. "Statistical Language, Statistical Truth and Statistical Reason: The Self-authentification of a Style of Scientific Reasoning." In E. McMullin (ed.), *The Social Dimension of Science.* Notre Dame, IN: Notre Dame Press.

Hagendijk, R. 1990. "Structuration Theory, Constructivism and Scientific Change." In S. Cozzens and T. Gieryn (eds.), *Theories of Science in Society.* Bloomington: Indiana University Press.

Halter, H. 1983. "Das Spenderherz darf nicht sterben." *Spiegel,* 50(37), Dec. 12, p. 104.

Haraway, D. 1988. "Situated Knowledges: The Science Question in Feminism and the Privilege of Partial Perspective." *Feminist Studies,* 14: 575–609.

———— 1989. *Primate Visions: Gender, Race and Nature in the World of Modern Science.* New York: Routledge.

———— 1991a. *Simians, Cyborgs, and Women.* New York: Routledge.

———— 1991b. "A Cyborg Manifest to: Science, Technology and Socialist-Feminism in the Late Twentieth." In D. Haraway, *Simians, Cyborgs, and Women.* New York: Routledge.

Harding, S. 1990. "Feminism, Science, and the Anti-Enlightenment Critiques." In L. J. Nicholson (ed.), *Feminism/Postmodernism.* New York/London: Routledge.

———— 1991. *Whose Science? Whose Knowledge? Thinking from Women's Lives.* Ithaca, NY: Cornell University Press.

Hartsock, N. C. M. 1983. "The Feminist Standpoint: Developing a Ground for a Specifically Feminist Historical Materialism." In S. Harding and M. Hintikka (eds.), *Feminist Perspectives on Epistemology, Metaphysics, Methodology and Philosophy of Science.* Dordrecht: Reidel.

Hasert, F. J., et al. 1973. "Search for Elastic Muon-Neutrino Electron Scattering." *Physics Letters,* B46: 121–24.

Heelas, P., S. Lash, and P. Morris (eds.). 1996. *Detraditionalization: Critical Reflections on Authority and Identity.* Oxford: Blackwell.

Heilbron, J. L. 1992. "Creativity and Big Science." *Physics Today,* 45(11): 42–47.

Heilbron, J. L., and R. W. Seidel. 1989. *Lawrence and His Laboratory: A History of the Lawrence Berkeley Laboratory,* vol. 1. Berkeley: University of California Press.

Heintz, B. 1993. *Die Herrschaft der Regel: Zur Grundlagengeschichte des Computers.* Frankfurt am Main: Campus.

Henderson, K. 1991. "Flexible Sketches and Inflexible Data Bases." *Science, Technology and Human Values,* 16(4): 448–473.

———— 1993. "The Political Career of a Prototype: How Visual Representations Socially Organize Work, Workers, Their Collective Thought and Their Collective Product." Paper presented at the Workshop on Visualization, Princeton University, Shelby Cullon Davis Center, February.

Herrnstein Smith, B. 1991. "Belief and Resistance: A Symmetrical Account." *Critical Inquiry,* 18(1): 125–139.

———— 1997. *Belief and Resistance.* Cambridge, MA: Harvard University Press.

Hess, D. J., and L. L. Layne (eds.). 1992. *The Anthropology of Science and Technology: Knowledge and Society,* vol. 9. Greenwich: Jai Press.

Hessenbruch, A. 1992. "Balancing the Lab and the Non-Lab." Paper presented at the joint BSHS, HSS, and CSHS meetings, University of Toronto, July.

Hevly, B. 1992. "Reflections on Big Science and Big History." In P. Galison and B. Hevly (eds.), *Big Science: The Growth of Large-Scale Research.* Stanford: Stanford University Press.

Hicks, D., and J. Potter. 1991. "Sociology of Scientific Knowledge—A Reflexive Citation Analysis Or: Science Disciplines and Disciplining Science." *Social Studies of Science,* 21: 459–501.

Hilgartner, S. 1990. "Industrializing Genome Mapping: Skills and Scale in the Human Genome Project." Paper presented at the Conference "Rediscovering Skill," University of Bath, England, September 1990.

———— 1995. "The Human Genome Project." In S. Jasanoff, G. E. Markle, J. C. Petersen, and T. Pinch (eds.), *Handbook of Science and Technology Studies.* Thousand Oaks: Sage.

Hilgartner, S., and S. I. Brandt-Rauf. 1999. "Controlling Data and Resources: Access Strategies in Molecular Genetics." In P. David and E. Steinmueller (eds.), *A Productive Tension.* Stanford: Stanford University Press. Forthcoming.

Hirschauer, S. 1991. "The Manufacture of Bodies in Surgery." *Social Studies of Science,* 21(2): 279–319.

———— 1993. *Die medizinische Konstruktion von Transsexualität.* Frankfurt: Suhrkamp.

Hogan, B., F. Costantini, and E. Lacy. 1986. *Manipulating the Mouse Embryo: A Laboratory Manual.* Cold Spring Harbor, NY: Cold Spring Harbor Laboratory Press.

Holton, G. 1973. *Thematic Origins of Scientific Thought: Kepler to Einstein.* Cambridge, MA: Harvard University Press.

———— 1978. *The Scientific Imagination.* Cambridge: Cambridge University Press.

Horgan, J. 1994. "Particle Metaphysics." *Scientific American,* 270 (February): 71–78.

References

Hull, D. 1988. *Science as Process*. Chicago: University of Chicago Press.

Hut, P., and J. Sussman. 1987. "Advanced Computing for Science." *Scientific American,* 257(4): 136–145.

Hymes, D. 1964. "Introduction: Toward Ethnographies of Communication." In J. J. Gumperz and D. Hymes (eds.), *The Ethnography of Communication* (special issue of *American Anthropologist*), 66(6): 1–34.

Incandela, J. 1989. "A New Top Trigger for 1989." *UA2 pp Note,* No. 566, 10 March.

Jasanoff, S. 1990. *The Fifth Branch: Science Advisers as Policymakers*. Cambridge, MA: Harvard University Press.

Jenni, P. 1989. "Collider Experiments." *CERN-EP/89–51,* 7 April.

Jewson, N. D. 1976. "The Disappearance of the Sick-man from Medical Cosmology, 1770–1870." *Sociology,* 10: 225–244.

Johnson, B. 1980. *The Critical Difference*. Baltimore: Johns Hopkins University Press.

———— 1990. "Writing." In F. Lentricchia and T. McLaughlin (eds.), *Critical Terms for Literary Study*. Chicago: University of Chicago Press.

Jordan, K., and M. Lynch. 1992. "The Sociology of a Genetic Engineering Technique: Ritual and Rationality in the Performance of the Plasmid Prep." In A. Clarke and J. Fujimura (eds.), *The Right Tools for the Job: At Work in Twentieth-Century Life Sciences*. Princeton: Princeton University Press.

Judson, H. F. 1992. "A History of the Science and Technology behind Gene Mapping and Sequencing." In D. J. Kevles and L. Hood (eds.), *The Code of Codes: Scientific and Social Issues in the Human Genome Project*. Cambridge, MA: Harvard University Press.

Kahneman, D., P. Slovic, and A. Tversky. 1982. *Judgment under Uncertainty: Heuristics and Biases*. Cambridge: Cambridge University Press.

Keating, P., C. Limoges, and A. Cambrosio. 1999. "The Automated Laboratory: The Generation and Replication of Work in Molecular Genetics." In M. Fortun and E. Mendelsohn (eds.), *Practice of Human Genetics*. Dordrecht: Kluwer.

Kevles, D. J. 1987. *The Physicists: The History of a Scientific Community in Modern America*. Cambridge, MA: Harvard University Press.

Kevles, D., and L. Hood (eds.). 1992. *The Code of Codes: Scientific and Social Issues in the Human Genome Project*. Cambridge, MA: Harvard University Press.

Klein, P. 1994. "Technik als Passion. Zur Konstruktion von Einzigartigkeit." Unpublished M.A. thesis, Faculty of Sociology, University of Bielefeld.

Knorr, K. D. 1977. "Producing and Reproducing Knowledge: Descriptive or Constructive? Toward a Model of Research Production." *Social Science Information,* 16: 669–96.

Knorr Cetina, K. 1981. *The Manufacture of Knowledge: An Essay on the Con-*

structivist and Contextual Nature of Science. Oxford: Pergamon Press. (Revised German edition: *Die Fabrikation von Erkenntnis.* Frankfurt: Suhrkamp, 1984.)

────── 1991. "Epistemic Cultures: Forms of Reason in Science." *History of Political Economy,* 23(1): 105–122.

────── 1994. "Die Manufaktur der Natur oder: Die alterierten Naturen der Naturwissenschaft." In R. Wilke (ed.), *Zum Naturbegriff der Gegenwart.* Stuttgart: Stadt Stuttgart.

────── 1995. "How Superorganisms Change." *Social Studies of Science,* 25: 119–147.

────── 1997. "Sociality with Objects: Social Relations in Postsocial Knowledge Societies." *Theory, Culture and Society,* 14(4): 1–30.

────── 1998. "Epistemics in Society: On the Nesting of Knowledge Structures into Social Structures." Special Issue on "Sociology's Second Wind," Sociologie et Sociétés, 30(1): 37–50.

Kohler, R. 1994. *Lords of the Fly.* Chicago: University of Chicago Press.

Kornhauser, W. 1963. *Scientists in Industry.* Berkeley: University of California Press.

Krampen, M., K. Oehler, R. Posner, T. A. Sebeok, and T. v. Uexküll (eds.). 1987. *Classics of Semiotics.* New York and London: Plenum Press.

Krieger, M. 1992. *Doing Physics: How Physicists Take Hold of the World.* Bloomington: Indiana University Press.

Krige, J., and D. Pestre. 1986. "The Choice of CERN's First Large Bubble Chambers for the Proton Synchrotron." *Historical Studies in the Physical and Biological Sciences,* 16: 255–279.

Krohn, W., and J. Weyer. 1994. "Society as a Laboratory: The Social Risks of Experimental Research." *Science and Public Policy,* 21(3): 173–183.

Kuhn, T. S. 1962 (1970). *The Structure of Scientific Revolutions.* Chicago: University of Chicago Press.

Kutschmann, W. 1986. *Der Wissenschaftler und sein Körper.* Frankfurt: Suhrkamp.

Lachmund, J. 1997. *Der abgehorchte Körper. Zur historischen Soziologie der medizinischen Untersuchung.* Opladen: Westdeutscher Verlag.

Lakoff, G. 1987. *Women, Fire and Dangerous Things: What Categories Reveal about the Mind.* Chicago: University of Chicago Press.

Lamont, M. 1993. "The Supercollider, c'est moi." Comment on "How Superorganisms Change." Paper presented at the Colloquium on Credibility and Consensus in Scientific Communities, Shelby Cullon Davis Center for Historical Studies, April.

────── 1992. *Money, Morals, and Manners: The Culture of the French and the American Upper-Middle Class.* Chicago: University of Chicago Press.

References

Lash, S. 1988. "Discourse or Figure? Postmodernism as a 'Regime of Significa-tion.'" *Theory, Culture and Society,* 5: 311–336.

Lash, S., and J. Urry. 1994. *Economies of Signs and Space.* London: Sage.

Latour, B. 1987. *Science in Action.* Stony Stratford: Open University Press, and Cambridge, MA: Harvard University Press.

—— 1988. *The Pasteurization of France.* Cambridge, MA: Harvard University Press.

—— 1991. "Technology Is Society Made Durable." In J. Law (ed.), *A Sociology of Monsters: Essays on Power, Technology and Domination,* pp. 101–131. London: Routledge and Kegan Paul.

—— 1993. *We Have Never Been Modern.* Cambridge, MA: Harvard University Press.

Latour, B., and J. Johnson. 1988. "Mixing Humans with Non-Humans: Sociology of a Door-Opener." Special issue on Sociology of Science, L. Star (ed.), *Social Problems,* 35: 298–310.

Latour, B., and S. Woolgar. 1979. *Laboratory Life: The Social Construction of Scientific Facts.* Beverly Hills: Sage.

Lave, J. 1988. *Cognition in Practice: Mind, Mathematics and Culture in Everyday Life.* Cambridge: Cambridge University Press.

Law, J. (ed.). 1991. *A Sociology of Monsters: Essays on Power, Technology, and Domination.* London: Routledge and Kegan Paul.

Lenoir, T. 1992. "Practical Reason and the Construction of Knowledge: The Lifeworld of Haber-Bosch." In E. McMullin (ed.), *The Social Dimension of Science.* Notre Dame, IN: Notre Dame Press.

Lewin, B. 1990. *Genes IV.* Oxford: Oxford University Press.

Leydesdorff, L. 1993. "The Impact of Citation Behaviour on Citation Structure." In A. F. J. Van Raan (ed.), *Proceedings of the Joint EC/Leiden Workshop on Science and Technology Indicators.* Leiden: DSWO.

Leydesdorff, L., and O. Amsterdamska. 1990. "Dimensions of Citation Analysis." *Science, Technology and Human Values,* 15: 305–335.

Lipietz, A. 1992. *Towards a New Economic Order: Postfordism, Ecology and Democracy.* Oxford: Oxford University Press.

Livingston, E. 1986. *The Ethnomethodological Foundations of Mathematics.* London: Routledge and Kegan Paul.

Longino, H. E. 1990. *Science as Social Knowledge: Values and Objectivity in Scientific Inquiry.* Princeton: Princeton University Press.

Luckmann, Th. 1986. "Grundformen der gesellschaftlichen Vermittlung des Wissens: Kommunikative Gattungen." In F. Neidhardt et al. (eds.), *Kultur und Gesellschaft* (Special Issue 27 of the *Kölner Zeitschrift für Soziologie und Sozialpsychologie*). Opladen: Westdeutscher Verlag.

Luhmann, N. 1984. *Soziale Systeme.* Frankfurt am Main: Suhrkamp.

—— 1990. *Die Wissenschaft der Gesellschaft.* Frankfurt: Suhrkamp.

Lukes, S. 1989. "Making Sense of Moral Conflict." In N. L. Rosenblum (ed.), *Liberalism and the Moral Life,* pp. 127–142. Cambridge, MA: Harvard University Press.

Lynch, M. 1985. *Art and Artifact in Laboratory Science: A Study of Shop Work and Shop Talk in a Research Laboratory.* London: Routledge and Kegan Paul.

—— 1988a. "Sacrifice and the Transformation of the Animal Body into a Scientific Object: Laboratory Culture and Ritual Practice in the Neurosciences." *Social Studies of Science,* 18: 265–289.

—— 1988b. "The Externalized Retina: Selection and Mathematization in the Visual Documentation of Objects in the Life Sciences." *Human Studies,* 11: 201–234.

—— 1991. "Laboratory Space and the Technological Complex: An Investigation of Topical Contextures." *Science in Context,* 4: 81–109.

—— 1993. *Scientific Practice and Ordinary Action.* Cambridge: Cambridge University Press.

Lyotard, J.-F. 1984. *The Postmodern Condition.* Minneapolis: University of Minnesota Press.

MacCoun, R. 1989. "Experimental Research on Jury Decision Making." *Science,* 244: 1046–1049.

MacKenzie, D. 1981. *Statistics in Britain, 1865–1930.* Edinburgh: Edinburgh University Press.

—— 1990. *Inventing Accuracy: A Historical Sociology of Nuclear Missile Guidance.* Cambridge, MA: MIT Press.

Mansbridge, J. J. (ed.). 1990. *Beyond Self-Interest.* Chicago: University of Chicago Press.

Marcus, G. E. 1986. "Contemporary Problems of Ethnography in the Modern World System." In J. Clifford and G. E. Marcus (eds.), *Writing Culture.* Berkeley and Los Angeles: University of California Press.

Marcus, G. E., and M. M. J. Fischer. 1986. *Anthropology as Cultural Critique.* Chicago: University of Chicago Press.

Mark, R., and W. W. Clark. 1984. "Gothic Structural Experimentation." *Scientific American,* 251(4): 144–153.

Mars, F. 1998. "Wir sind alle Seher. Die Praxis der Aktienanalyse." Unpublished dissertation, Faculty of Sociology, University of Bielefeld.

Martin, B. R., N. Minchin, J. Skea, T. Peacock, D. Crouch, and J. Irvine. 1987. "The Assessment of Scientific Research: A Case-Study of CERN." *Interdisciplinary Science Reviews,* 12(1): 70–76.

Martin, E. 1991. "The Egg and the Sperm: How Science Has Constructed a Romance Based on Stereotypical Male-Female Roles." *Signs: Journal of Women in Culture and Society,* 16(3): 485–501.

—— 1992a. *The Woman in the Body: A Cultural Analysis of Reproduction.* Boston: Beacon Press.

References

—— 1992b. "The End of the Body?" *American Ethnologist,* 19(1): 121–140.

Maturana, H., and F. Varela. 1980. *Autopoeisis and Cognition: The Realization of the Living.* Dordrecht: Reidel.

Matza, D. 1969. *Becoming Deviant.* Englewood Cliffs: Prentice Hall.

Mayer, K. U. 1985. "Structural Constraints on the Life Course." *Human Development,* 29: 163–170.

McDonald, K. A. 1992. "Physicists in Large Collaborations Find That 'Big' Is Not Always Better." *Chronicle of Higher Education,* December 9.

Megill, A. (ed.). 1994. *Rethinking Objectivity.* Durham: Duke University Press.

Merleau-Ponty, M. 1945. *Phenomenologie de la perception.* Paris: Gallimard. (English translation: *Phenomenology of Perception.* London: Routledge and Kegan Paul, 1962.)

Merton, R. K. 1965. *On the Shoulders of Giants: A Shandean Postscript.* New York: Free Press. (Vicennial edition: New York: Harcourt Brace Jovanovich, 1985.)

—— 1973. *The Sociology of Science.* Chicago: University of Chicago Press.

Merz, M. 1998. "Der Ereignisgenerator als Objekt des Wissens: Computersimulation in der Teilchenphysik." In B. Heintz and B. Nievergelt (eds.), *Wissenschafts- und Technikforschung in der Schweiz: Sondierungen einer neuen Disziplin.* Zürich: Seismo.

Merz, M., and K. Knorr Cetina. 1997. "Deconstruction in a 'Thinking' Science: Theoretical Physicists at Work." *Social Studies of Science,* 27(1): 73–111.

Meyer, J. 1986. "The Self and the Life Course: Institutionalization and Its Effects." In A. B. Soerensen, F. E. Weinert, and L. R. Sherrod (eds.), *Human Development and the Life Course: Multidisciplinary Perspectives.* Hillsdale, NJ: Lawrence Erlbaum Assoc.

Meyer, J., and B. Rowan. 1991. "Institutionalized Organizations: Formal Structure as Myth and Ceremony." In P. J. DiMaggio and W. W. Powell (eds.), *The New Institutionalism in Organizational Analysis.* Chicago: University of Chicago Press.

Meyers, R. A. (ed.). 1990. "Elementary Particle Physics." In *Encyclopedia of Modern Physics,* 170–204. San Diego: Academic Press.

Miller, P., and T. O'Leary. 1994. "The Factory as Laboratory." *Science in Context,* 7(3): 469–496.

Mukerji, Ch. 1989. *A Fragile Power: Scientists and the State.* Princeton: Princeton University Press.

—— 1997. *Territorial Ambitions and the Gardens of Versailles.* Cambridge: Cambridge University Press.

Mulkay, M. 1979. *Science and the Sociology of Knowledge.* London: Allen and Unwin.

—— 1985. *The Word and the World: Explanation in the Form of Sociological Analysis.* London: Allen and Unwin.

Müller, K. H. 1994. "Virtuelle Laboratorien und Symbolsprachen." In R. Habich und K. H. Müller (eds.), *Sozialdaten und visuelle Kommunikation.* Berlin: Sigma.

Mullins, N., L. L. Hargens, P. Hecht, and E. Kick. 1977. "The Group Structure of Cocitation Clusters: A Comparative Study." *American Sociological Review,* 42: 552–563.

Nagel, E. 1956. *Logic without Metaphysics.* Glencoe, IL: Free Press.

Nagel, T. 1986. *The View from Nowhere.* New York: Oxford University Press.

Needham, R. 1963. "Introduction." In E. Durkheim and M. Mauss, *Primitive Classifications.* Chicago: University of Chicago Press.

Nelkin, D., and M. S. Lindee. 1995. *The DNA Mystique; The Gene as a Cultural Icon.* New York: Freeman.

Ophir, A., and S. Shapin. 1991. "The Place of Knowledge: A Methodological Survey." *Science in Context* 4(1): 3–21.

Otero, G. 1991. "The Coming Revolution of Biotechnology: A Critique of Buttel." *Sociological Forum,* 6(3): 551–565.

Park, D. 1988. *The How and the Why.* Princeton: Princeton University Press.

Parsons, T. 1947. "Introduction." In Max Weber, *The Theory of Social and Economic Organization.* New York: Free Press.

Penrose, R. 1993. "Nature's Biggest Secret." *New York Review of Books,* October 21, 1993.

Perrow, C. 1991. "A Society of Organizations." *Theory and Society,* 20: 725–762.

Pestre, D., and J. Krige. 1992. "Some Thoughts on the Early History of CERN." In P. Galison and B. Hevly (eds.), *Big Science: The Growth of Large-Scale Research.* Stanford: Stanford University Press.

Peterson, R. A. 1993 "Culture Studies through the Production Perspective: Progress and Prospects." Paper presented at the Annual Meeting of the American Sociological Association, August 19.

Pickering, A. 1984. *Constructing Quarks: A Sociological History of Particle Physics.* Chicago: University of Chicago Press.

—— 1991. "Objectivity and the Mangle of Practice." *Annals of Scholarship,* 8: 409–425.

—— (ed.). 1992. *Science as Practice and Culture.* Chicago: University of Chicago Press.

—— 1995. *The Mangle of Practice.* Chicago: University of Chicago Press.

Pinch, T. J. 1986. *Confronting Nature: The Sociology of Solar Neutrino Detection.* Dordrecht: Reidel.

Pinch, T. J., and W. E. Bijker. 1984. "The Social Construction of Facts and Artefacts: or How the Sociology of Science and the Sociology of Technology Might Benefit Each Other." *Social Studies of Science,* 14: 399–441.

Plothow-Besch, H. 1990. "The Standard Model Parameters: Review of Recent

References

Results on the Intermediate Vector Boson Production and Decay Properties at the CERN and FNAL p̄p Colliders." *CERN-PPE*, 90–168.

Polanyi, M. 1958. *Personal Knowledge: Towards a Post-Critical Philosophy*. London: Routledge and Kegan Paul.

Porush, D. 1985. *The Soft Machine: Cybernetic Fiction*. New York and London: Methuen.

Quinn, J. B. 1992. *Intelligent Enterprise: A Knowledge and Service Based Paradigm for Industry*. New York: Free Press.

Rabinow, P. 1996. *Making PCR: A Story of Biotechnology*. Chicago: University of Chicago Press.

Radcliffe-Brown, A. R. 1952. *Structure and Function in Primitive Society*. London: Cohen and West.

Rae, A. I. 1986. *Quantum Physics: Illusion or Reality?* Cambridge: Cambridge University Press.

Rammert, W., M. Schlese, G. Wagner, J. Wehner, and R. Weingarten. 1998. *Wissensmaschinen*. Frankfurt: Campus.

Restivo, S. 1983. *The Social Relations of Physics, Mysticism, and Mathematics*. Dordrecht: Reidel.

——— 1988. "Modern Science as a Social Problem." *Social Problems*, 35(3): 206–225.

——— 1992. *Science, Society and Values: Toward a Sociology of Objectivity*. Bethlehem: Lehigh University Press.

Rip, A. (ed.) 1995. *Managing Technology in Society*. London: Pinter.

Robertson, R. 1988. "The Sociological Significance of Culture: Some General Considerations." *Theory, Culture and Society*, 5: 3–23.

Rorty, R. 1991. *Objectivity, Relativism and Truth: Philosophical Papers*, vol. 1. Cambridge: Cambridge University Press.

Rose, H. 1986. "Beyond Masculinist Realities: A Feminist Epistemology for the Sciences." In R. Bleier (ed.), *Feminist Approaches to Science*. New York: Pergamon Press.

Rosenblum, N. 1989. "Pluralism and Self-Defense." In N. L. Rosenblum (ed.), *Liberalism and the Moral Life*, pp. 207–226. Cambridge, MA: Harvard University Press.

Rouse, J. 1987. *Knowledge and Power: Toward a Political Philosophy of Science*. Ithaca: Cornell University Press.

——— 1996. *Engaging Science: How to Understand Its Practices Philosophically*. Ithaca: Cornell University Press.

Rubbia, C. 1990. "The Universality of Science and International Collaboration." *Interdisciplinary Science Reviews*, 15(1): 12–16.

Rubbia, C., P. McIntyre, and D. Cline. 1976. In H. Faissner, H. Reithler, and P. Zerwas (eds.), *Proceedings of the International Neutrino Conference, Aachen*, p. 683. Braunschweig: Vieweg, 1977.

Rudwick, M. J. S. 1985. *The Great Devonian Controversy: The Shaping of Scientific Knowledge among Gentlemanly Specialists.* Chicago: University of Chicago Press.

Sachs, M. 1988. *Einstein versus Bohr.* La Salle: Open Court.

Sacks, H., E. A. Schegloff, and G. Jefferson. 1974. "A Simplest Systematics for the Organization of Turn-taking for Conversation." *Language,* 50: 696–735.

Schaffer, S. 1992. "Late Victorian Metrology and Its Instrumentation: A Manufactory of Ohms." In R. Budd and S. E. Cozzens (eds.), *Invisible Connections: Instruments, Institutions, and Science.* Bellingham, WA: SPIE Press.

Schatzki, T. 1996. *Social Practices: A Wittgensteinian Approach to Human Activity and the Soul.* New York: Cambridge University Press.

Schiebinger, L. 1993. "Why Mammals Are Called Mammals: Gender Politics in Eighteenth-Century Natural History." *American Historical Review,* 98(2): 382–411.

Seidel, R. 1992. "The Origins of the Lawrence Berkeley Laboratory." In P. Galison and B. Hevly (eds.), *Big Science: The Growth of Large-Scale Research.* Stanford: Stanford University Press.

Selleri, F. 1990. "Quantum Paradoxes and Physical Reality." In I. van der Merwe (ed.), *Quantum Paradoxes and Physical Reality.* Dordrecht, Boston, and London: Kluwer.

Serres, M. 1990. *Le Contrat Naturel.* Paris: Editions Francois.

Shapin, S. 1979. "The Politics of Observation: Cerebral Anatomy and Social Interests in the Edinburgh Phrenology Disputes." In R. Wallis (ed.), *On the Margins of Science: The Social Construction of Rejected Knowledge.* Sociological Review Monograph, no. 27. London: Routledge and Kegan Paul.

———— 1988. "The House of Experiment in Seventeenth-Century England." *Isis,* 79: 373–404.

———— 1994. *A Social History of Truth.* Chicago: University of Chicago Press.

Shapin, S., and S. Schaffer. 1985. *Leviathan and the Air-Pump: Hobbes, Boyle and the Experimental Life.* Princeton: Princeton University Press.

Shweder, R. A., and R. A. LeVine (eds.). 1984. *Culture Theory.* New York: Cambridge University Press.

Simmel, G. 1923 (1986). "Die Koketterie." In *Philosophische Kultur: Über das Abenteuer, die Geschlechter und die Krise der Moderne.* Berlin: Klaus Wagenbach.

Sismondo, S. 1993. "Some Social Constructions." *Social Studies of Science,* 23(3): 555–563.

———— 1996. *Social Knowledge: Constructivism, Realism, and the Politics of Science.* Albany: State University of New York Press.

Small, H. G. 1985. "The Lives of a Scientific Paper." In K. S. Warren (ed.),

Selectivity in Information Systems: Survival of the Fittest. New York: Praeger Science Publishers.

Smith, A. D. 1990. "Towards a Global Culture?" *Theory, Culture and Society,* 7: 171–191.

Smith, C. W. 1981. *The Mind of the Market: A Study of Stock Market Philosophies, Their Uses and Their Implications.* Totowa, NJ: Rowman and Littlefield.

Smith, C., and M. N. Wise. 1989. *Energy and Empire: A Biographical Study of Lord Kelvin.* Cambridge: Cambridge University Press.

Smith, D. 1987. *The Everyday World as Problematic: A Feminist Sociology.* Boston: Northeastern University Press.

Smith, R. W., and J. N. Tatarewicz. 1985. "Replacing a Technology: The Large Space Telescope and CCDs." *Proceedings of the IEEE,* 73(7): 1221–1235.

Soeffner, H.-G. 1992. *Die Ordnung der Rituale.* Frankfurt: Suhrkamp.

Spradley, J. P. 1979. *The Ethnographic Interview.* New York: Holt, Rinehart and Winston.

Star, S. L. 1989. *Regions of the Mind: Brain Research and the Quest for Scientific Certainty.* Stanford: Stanford University Press.

Stehr, N. 1994. *Arbeit, Eigentum und Wissen: Zur Theorie von Wissensgesellschaften.* Frankfurt am Main: Suhrkamp.

Storer, N. 1972. *The Social System of Science.* New York: Holt, Rinehart and Winston.

Suchman, L. A. 1987. *Plans and Situated Actions: The Problem of Human-Machine Communication.* Cambridge: Cambridge University Press.

Suppes, P. 1984. *Probabilistic Metaphysics.* Oxford: Blackwell.

Sutton, C. 1984. *The Particle Connection.* New York: Simon and Schuster.

Swidler, A. 1986. "Culture in Action: Symbols and Strategies." *American Sociological Review,* 51: 273–286.

Tarozzi, G., and A. van der Merwe (eds.). 1988. *Quantum Paradoxes.* Dordrecht, Boston, and London: Kluwer.

Taubes, G. 1986. *Nobel Dreams: Power, Deceit and the Ultimate Experiment.* New York: Random House.

Taylor, C. 1989a. *Sources of the Self.* Cambridge, MA: Harvard University Press.

———— 1989b. "Cross-Purposes: The Liberal-Communitarian Debate." In N. L. Rosenblum (ed.), *Liberalism and the Moral Life,* pp. 159–182. Cambridge, MA: Harvard University Press.

Thévenot, L. 1994. "Le régime de familarité. Des choses en personnne." *Genèsis,* 17: 72–101.

Tönnies, F. (1887) 1957. *Community and Society.* Trans. C. P. Loomis. East Lansing: Michigan State University Press.

Traweek, S. 1988a. *Beamtimes and Lifetimes: The World of High Energy Physics.* Cambridge, MA: Harvard University Press.

———— 1988b. "'Feminist Perspectives in Science Studies': Commentary." *Science, Technology and Human Values,* 13: 250–253.

———— 1992. "Border Crossing: Narrative Strategies in Science Studies and among Physicists in Tsukuba Science City, Japan." In A. Pickering (ed.), *Science as Practice and Culture.* Chicago: University of Chicago Press.

———— 1995. "Bodies of Evidence: Law and Order, Sexy Machines, and the Erotics of Fieldwork among Physicists." In S. L. Foster (ed.), *Choreographing History,* pp. 211–225. Bloomington: Indiana University Press.

Turkle, S. 1984. *The Second Self: Computers and the Human Spirit.* New York: Simon and Schuster.

———— 1995. *Life on the Screen.* New York: Simon and Schuster.

Turner, B. 1992. "Ideology and Utopia in the Formation of an Intelligentsia: Reflections on the English Cultural Conduit." *Theory, Culture and Society,* 9: 183–210.

Turner, S. 1994. *Social Theory of Practice: Tradition, Tacit Knowledge and Presuppositions.* Chicago: University of Chicago Press.

Turner, V. 1969. *The Ritual Process.* Chicago: Aldine.

Vaihinger, H. 1924. *The Philosophy of 'As if': A System of the Theoretical, Practical and Religious Fictions of Mankind.* New York: Harcourt, Brace and Co.

Watkins, P. 1986. *Story of the W and Z.* Cambridge: Cambridge University Press.

Watson, J. D. 1990. "The Human Genome Project: Past, Present, and Future." *Science,* 248 (4951): 44–49.

Watson, J. D., and F. H. C. Crick. 1953. "Molecular Structure of Nucleic Acid: A Structure for Deoxyribonucleic Acid." *Nature,* 171: 737–738.

Weber, M. 1947. *The Theory of Social and Economic Organization.* New York: Free Press.

Weinberg, S. 1992. *Dreams of a Final Theory.* New York: Pantheon.

Wimsatt, W. C. 1987. "False Models as Means to Truer Theories." In M. Nitecki and A. Hoffmann (eds.), *Neutral Models in Biology,* pp. 23–55. London: Oxford University Press.

Winner, L. 1993. "Upon Opening the Black Box and Finding It Empty: Social Constructivism and the Philosophy of Technology." *Science, Technology and Human Values,* 18(3): 362–378.

Wise, N. 1993. "Mediations: Enlightenment Balancing Acts, or the Technologies of Rationalization." In P. Horwich (ed.), *World Changes: Thomas Kuhn and the Nature of Science.* Cambridge, MA: The MIT Press.

Woolf, H. 1959. *The Transits of Venus: A Study of Eighteenth-Century Science.* Princeton: Princeton University Press.

Woolgar, S. 1985. "Why Not a Sociology of Machines? The Case of Sociology and Artificial Intelligence." *Sociology,* 19: 557–572.

References

Woolgar, S., and M. Ashmore. 1988. "The Next Step: An Introduction to the Reflexive Project." In S. Woolgar (ed.), *Knowledge and Reflexivity*. London: Sage.

Wulf, W. A. 1993. "The Collaboratory Opportunity." *Science,* 261 (13 August): 854–855.

Wuthnow, R. 1984. *Cultural Analysis: The Work of Pavel L. Berger, Mary Douglas, Michel Foucault and Jürgen Habermas*. London: Routledge and Kegan Paul.

——— 1992. *Vocabularies of Public Life: Empirical Essays in Symbolic Structure*. London: Routledge and Kegan Paul.

Wynne, B. 1982. *Rationality or Ritual? Nuclear Decision Making and the Windscale Inquiry*. London: British Society for the History of Science.

——— 1987. *Risk Management and Hazardous Wastes*. London and New York: Springer.

Zee, A. 1989. *Fearful Symmetry: The Search for Beauty in Modern Physics*. New York: Macmillan.

Zelizer, V. 1988. "Beyond the Polemics of the Market: Establishing a Theoretical and Empirical Agenda." *Sociological Forum,* 3: 614–634.

Zenzen, M., and S. Restivo. 1982. "The Mysterious Morphology of Immiscible Liquids: A Study of Scientific Practice." *Social Science Information,* 21(3): 447–473.

Zuckerman, H. 1967. "Nobel Laureates in Science." *American Sociological Review,* 32(3): 391–403.

——— 1977. *The Scientific Elite*. New York: Free Press.

——— 1988. "The Sociology of Science." In N. Smelser (ed.), *Handbook of Sociology*. Newbury Park: Sage.

Zuckerman, H., J. R. Cole, and J. Bruer (eds.). 1991. *The Outer Circle: Women in the Scientific Community*. New York: Norton.

Index

Accelerator (physics), 213
Acceptance, 65–66, 276n5
Ackerknecht, E. H., 29
Åkesson, T., 66
Aging. *See* Detectors, aging
Alberts, B., 139, 145, 150
ALEPH (experiment), viii, 75
Alexander, J., 9, 201, 247, 264n11
Alitti, J., 70
Alpha S, 53–54, 77, 166, 168
Alternate reality, 12, 250–251; object
    worlds, 244–245, 257
Amann, K., 19, 20, 37, 101, 140, 278n1
Amsterdamska, O., 167
Anderson, A. B., 295n8
Anderson, P. W., 273n3
Anthropomorphization, 283–286nn2,4
Apophantic theology, 64
Appadurai, A., 113
Appresentation, 100, 104, 198
Arnison, G., 64, 167, 265n18
Artificial intelligence, 218
ASCOT (experiment), 184, 196
Ashmore, M., 267n1
Astronomy, 27–28
ATLAS (experiment), vii, 15, 17, 20, 24,
    53, 56, 63, 67, 73, 114–115, 134, 160,
    163–164, 175, 180–190, 195–196,
    198–200, 202–204
Atrocity stories, 99, 107. *See also* Stories
Authorship (conventions), 166–168, 171,
    220, 255, 291n2; quarrels, 226, 231;
    rights, 256

Bach, M., 253
Background, 49–52, 59–60, 64, 67; as
    "enemy" in HEP experiments, 123–127
Bacteria, 142–143, 154
Bagnaia, P., 65, 265n18
Banner, M., 65
Barber, B., 28, 165
Barger, V. D., 50
Barnes, B., 29, 263n2
Beardsley, T., 140
Beck, U., 5, 166, 171, 246, 252
Bell, D., 5, 6
Benchwork: science, 81–82, 95, 144, 223;
    style, 84
Beniger, J. R., 5
Berger, P., 5
Bergmann, J., 108, 205
Biagioli, M., 218
Big Science, 82–83, 161–162
Bijker, W. E., 11, 263n1
Biological machine, 149–150, 153–156,
    158
Birth stage (of a collaboration), 193, 198,
    210, 214, 255, 258–259
"Blind" variation, 12, 81, 88, 91, 246;
    and natural selection, 81, 88, 91, 93,
    108–110, 230. *See also* Variation
Bloor, D., 263n2, 264n2
Boden, D., 175
Body, scientist's: acting, 95–97, 108; as
    black box, 99; experienced, 95, 99; sen-
    sory, 95–97, 108; as tool, 94–100. *See
    also* Embodiment

Boehme, G., 264n6
Bourdieu, P., 267n1
Bradney, P., 233
Brandt-Rauf, S. I., 84
Brown, R. H., 173, 269n1
Bruer, J., 29
Busch, L., 157
Buss, L., 166
Buttel, F., 157

Callon, M., 113
Calorimeter, 57–59
Cambrosio, A., 83, 146
Campbell, D. T., 81, 109, 158, 165, 263n1
Cantor, C.-R., 83
Care of the self, 47, 55–56, 60–61, 63, 93, 208, 252
Casper, M. J., 84
Cathedrals, 36
CDF (Collider-Detector at Fermilab), 15, 24, 75, 209, 239
Cells, 140, 143–144, 150, 151; cell lines, 143–145, 149, 151, 244
Center for Molecular Biology, 84
Centers: in molecular biology, 82–83
CERN (European Laboratory for Particle Physics), 13–25, 40, 42–43, 48, 50, 57, 59, 64, 67, 73–74, 114, 131–134, 160, 164, 166–167, 180, 182, 184, 187–188, 195, 199–200, 203, 206, 208, 211–213, 232, 239, 241, 245
Chubin, D. E., 290n9
Churchland, P. M., 23, 218, 276n4
Cicourel, A., 13, 55, 272n3
Clark, A., 36, 84
Classifications, 2, 11, 111–113, 139, 248, 250, 284–285nn2,4; primitive, 112–113, 126–128, 135–137
CLIC (CERN Linear Collider), 187–188
Clifford, J., 265n1
Cloning, 145–147, 150
Close, F., 161, 265n15
Closed universe (system), 46–47, 55
CMS (experiment), 25, 73, 187–188, 203
Cold Spring Harbor Laboratory, 141
Cole, J., 28
Cole, S., 28, 263n1
Coleman, J. S., 252
Collaborations, 4, 19, 23–25, 42–43, 74,

114, 131–132, 135, 159–162, 165, 167–169, 178, 181, 184–186, 193–194, 200, 204–205, 210–211, 215, 221, 239, 258–259; board, 185; forming, 194, 196, 258; meeting, 169, 197; in other areas, 295n8
Collaboratory, 23
Collective consciousness, 178–179
Collective responsibility and representation: in HEP experiments, 165, 168–170; self-representation, 266n1. See also Communitarianism; Distributed cognition
Collider, 18, 64, 114, 194, 213; experiments, 49–50, 74, 117; physics, 64
Collins, H. M., 11, 74, 99, 113, 218, 263n1, 272n3
Communitarianism, 4, 13, 25, 159–160, 165, 171, 178, 180–181, 185–188, 192–193, 195–196, 201, 213–216, 222, 236, 255–257, 259, 290–293nn1,5; versus individuation, 246; and superorganisms, 249–250
"Community without Unity," 291–292nn1,2
Comparative optics (approach), 4, 19, 22
Computer simulation. See Simulation
Confidence pathways, 159, 201–202, 204, 209, 214
Consensual culture (of HEP), 296n2
Consensus formation, 258–260
Construction, 3, 11, 32, 127, 147, 190, 229, 256, 274n3
Contests of unfolding, 196–198
Convoluting, 48, 71, 75–78, 252
Cooperation (in molecular biology), 234–237
Corlett, W., 165, 291n1
Corporate actors, 294n7
Corrections, 65–67
Coulter, J., 173
Cozzens, S., 290n9
Crane, D., 247
Crawford, R., 82
Crick, F. H. C., 153
Culture, 2, 5, 8, 80, 127, 246–252, 257, 271–272n3, 274n4; culturalist description, 24; as practice, 2, 8–10, 247; as symbolic, 247–251. See also Epistemic cultures

Index

Daston, L., 162, 201, 264nn7,12
DELPHI (experiment), viii
Dennett, D., 7
Detectors, 18, 24–25, 47, 53–59, 64–65,
    76–77, 111–130, 136, 195, 221, 245,
    259; aging, 57–59, 116; design, 215; ex-
    perts, 177; idiosyncracies, 117–118,
    120; histories, 62, as moral beings, 116,
    119–120; as physiological beings,
    113–114, 116–117, 121, 123, 136, 250;
    as social beings, 111, 116–118, 120
Differences, instituted in lab, 44–45. *See
    also* Reconfiguration
Differentiation theory, 246
DiLella, L., 15, 114
DiMaggio, P., 172, 247, 264n11
Discourse, 203, 250, 254, 294–295nn6,7;
    local, 212, 222; as medium in HEP ex-
    periments, 173–181, 190
Disenchantment, 248
Distributed cognition, 25, 165, 173–174,
    180, 242. *See also* Collective responsi-
    bility and representation
Disunity of science, 3–4
DNA (deoxyribonucleic acid), 139,
    142–143, 145, 147–150, 152–153,
    155–157
Dobbin, F., 247, 264n11
Doctoral students, 230–231
Douglas, M., 111, 285n4
Downey, G. L., 263n1
Dreyfus, H. L., 99, 218, 249
Dreyfus, S. E., 99, 218
Drucker, P. F., 5, 6, 172, 242
Dual organization (in molecular biology),
    216, 224–226, 238
Dumont, J.-P., 265n1
Dupré, J., 3
Durkheim, E., 111, 178, 247, 293n6

EAGLE (experiment), 184, 196, 202
ECFA (European Committee on Future
    Accelerators), 164, 187–188
Edge, D., 27, 166
Efficiency, 61, 65–67, 76, 119; logic of,
    247, 276n5
"Eigensinnig," 280–281n3
Embodiment: of action, 98; of lab and pro-
    ject by leader, 237–238; of skills, 221
Enchantment, 250–251

Enculturation of natural objects, 28
Epistemic cultures, 1–2, 8, 24, 29, 46, 80,
    93, 213, 241–242, 246–247, 249, 252,
    257; machineries, 3, 10, 159; practices,
    79; resources, 74; strategy, 55, 70. *See
    also* Culture
Epistemic subjects, 11–12, 25, 32, 159,
    217, 255–256; collective in HEP, 168;
    individual, erasure of, 165–166, 171,
    178, 236, 291–292nn1,3, 295n1; indi-
    vidual in molecular biology, 167; pro-
    curer of collective and dispersed
    knowledge, 178, 185
Errors, 65, 93; in contrast to uncertain-
    ties, 276–277n7; statistical, 67; system-
    atic, 67–68, 276–277n7
Ethnographer, 23, 140, 177
European Laboratory for Particle Physics.
    See CERN
Exchange relationships, 255; practices,
    256
Experiential register, 81, 93–94, 104, 246
Experiment, 3, 26, 32–34, 38–43, 53, 56,
    72, 93, 130, 221, 244
Experimental high energy physics. *See*
    HEP (experiments)
Experts, 34, 129, 134–135
Expert systems, 1–2, 6–8

Faulkner, R. F., 295n8
Fermilab, 13, 239
Feyerabend, P., 263n1
Fiction, 249–251, 257
"Filling in the test tube," 103–105
Fine, A., 290n9
Fischer, M. M. J., 267n1
Footnotes, 270n
Footprints, 41, 50
Forsythe, D., 263n1
Foucault, M., 29, 56, 138, 166, 297n3
Fox Keller, E., 144, 153, 268n1
Fragmentation, 76
Framing, 47–48, 71–74, 252
Freud, S., 39, 40
Fujimura, J., 37, 83, 84, 146, 154
Fuller, S., 290n9

Galison, P., 3, 16, 17, 48, 59, 76, 114,
    161, 162, 163, 264nn7,12, 273n3,
    274n3

Garfinkel, H., 13
Gauthier, L., 28
Geertz, C., 10, 13, 239, 248, 251, 264n4, 269n1, 285n4
Geison, G., 145, 239, 266n1
Gender, 232–233
Genetic code, 20
Genetic engineering, 157
Genome project, 81–83
Gibbens, P., 16
Giddens, A., 6, 7, 264n4
Giere, R., 26, 45, 264n5
Gieryn, T. F., 44, 157, 246, 263n1, 264n13, 290n9
Giesen, B., 201
Gilbert, N., 106, 197
Gilbert, W., 82
Goffman, E., 13, 175, 269n1, 285n4, 297n3
Gooday, G., 289n6
Gooding, D., 26, 263n1
Gossip, 200, 202, 250; circles, 201, 204; technical, 202–205, 207–208
Grafton, A., 270n1
Gregory, B., 16, 127
Griffith, B. C., 29
Groups, in HEP experiments, 181–186

Habermas, J., 5, 248, 264n4
Hacking, I., 3, 9, 33, 37, 209, 290n9
Hagendijk, R., 263n1
Halter, H., 97
Haraway, D., 29, 130, 158, 252, 267n1, 268n1, 269n1
Harding, S., 268n1
Hartsock, N. C. M., 268n1
Hasert, J. F., 161
Heelas, P., 248
Heilbron, J. L., 161, 162, 163, 266n1
Heintz, B., 263n1
Henderson, K., 263n1
HEP (experiments), 4, 12–13, 14, 17, 20, 33, 40–42, 46, 48, 53, 55, 63, 65, 68–69, 76, 79–80, 82, 100, 104, 112–114, 131, 135–136, 159, 163–164, 166, 168, 171, 173, 178, 181, 186, 192, 195, 202, 216–217, 220, 222, 234, 236–240, 242, 244–246, 250–251, 254, 256–258, 260
Herrnstein Smith, B., 263n1, 269n1
Hess, D. J., 263n1

Hessenbruch, A., 45
Hevly, B., 114, 160, 163, 264n7
Hicks, D., 167
Higgs Mechanism, 14–15, 24–25, 167, 258
Hilgartner, S., 81, 82, 83, 84
Hirschauer, S., 96, 218
Hogan, B., 141
Holton, G., 127, 166
Hood, L., 81, 82, 83, 153, 163, 173
Horgan, J., 277n9
Horizontal links, in organization of HEP experiments, 172
Hull, D., 263n1
Human genome project. See Genome project
Hut, P., 34
Hymes, D., 175, 205

Impression management, 296–297n3
Incandela, J., 72
Individuation, 171, 180, 186, 237–238, 245–246, 254, 259. See also Epistemic subjects; Scientific person
Inscriptions, 41; devices, 90
Institutes (physics), 211–212, 254; meeting, 212
Internally referential system, 2, 47, 63
Intervening, 9, 41, 93. See also Technology of intervention

Jasanoff, S., 290n9
Jenni, P., 265n15
Jewson, N. D., 29
Johnson, J., 113, 269n1
Joking relationships, 225, 232–233
Jordan, K., 37, 83, 84, 146
Judson, H. F., 138

Kahneman, D., 34
Kaleidoscope, 136
Keating, P., 83, 146
Kevles, D. J., 17, 81, 82, 83, 153, 163, 173
Klein, P., 114
Knorr, K., 11, 26, 263n1
Knorr Cetina, K., 11, 17, 20, 26, 72, 74, 101, 113, 240, 242, 258, 263n1, 264nn8,9,12,14
Knowledge: cultures, 21; machineries, 3. See also Machinery

Index

Knowledge societies, 1–2, 5–8, 25, 241, 242–246, 249–252
Kohler, R., 131, 140
Kornhauser, W., 242
Krampen, M., 80
Krieger, M., 263n1
Krige, J., 160, 268n1
Krohn, W., 5, 263n1, 264n6
Kuhn, T. S., 263n1, 264n6
Kutschmann, W., 94

L3 (experiment), 164
Laboratope, 278n, 288n
Laboratories: bench, 36, 42; small, 81–82; within laboratories, 244
Laboratorization, 30
Laboratory: leaders, 97, 216–217, 222–224, 227–233, 237–239, 255–256; as nursery, 85; practice, 13, 27, 95, 106, 127; processes, 45–46; protocols, 86, 88, 278–279n2; as repertoire of expertise, 225–226, 229–230; science, 30, 34; as structural form, 242–244; as toolshop, 85
Lachmund, J., 29, 30, 45
Lakoff, G., 111
Lamont, M., 247, 264n11
Large Hadron Collider. See LHC
Lash, S., 6, 269n1
Latour, B., 11, 26, 29, 41, 113, 128, 145, 223, 263n1, 264nn2,9
Lave, J., 263n1
Law, J., 263n1
Layne, L. L., 263n1
Leaders, 180, 222–223, 236, 254, 256. See also Laboratory leaders; Spokespersons
Lenoir, T., 263n1
LEP (experiments), viii, 20, 22, 42, 70, 73, 75, 167, 180, 187, 239; committee, 185
LeVine, R. A., 264n11
Lewin, B., 145, 148, 156
Leydesdorff, L., 167
LHC (Large Hadron Collider), 15, 25, 73, 160, 187–188, 239
Lifeworld, 217, 219–221, 256
Limen, 63
Liminal epistemology/knowledge, 12, 47, 64, 68–69, 80, 93, 106, 252, 257; and approach, 56, 63, 65, 67, 74, 246

Liminal phenomena, 63, 65, 69, 73, 252, 273n3
Limit analysis, 70, 168, 258
Limoges, C., 83, 146
Lindee, M. S., 290n9
Lipietz, A., 172
Livingston, E., 263n1
Longino, H. E., 290n9
Loss of the empirical, 4
Luckmann, Th., 175, 205
Luhmann, N., 202
Lukes, S., 158
Lynch, M., 11, 13, 26, 37, 83, 84, 86, 87, 88, 101, 146, 251, 263n1, 264nn9,10
Lyotard, J.-F., 5

MacCoun, R., 34
Machinery: empirical, 12, 24, 46; of knowing, 2, 5, 9; of knowledge construction, 2–3, 5, 11; social, 12, 24, 216; technological, 12, 24
Machines, 4, 113–114, 136, 156–158, 201, 213, 266n1; biological, 149–150, 153–156; cellular, 149; self-reproducing, 156. See also Molecular machines
MacKenzie, D., 29, 263n1, 264n2
Mammalian embryology, 141
Management by content, 159, 165, 171–173, 179–186, 192, 242–243, 293n5
Mansbridge, J. J., 165
Marcus, G. E., 265n1, 267n1
Mark, R., 36
Mars, F., 244
Martin, B. R., 264n7
Martin, E., 94, 263n1
Maturana, H., 47
Matza, D., 170
Mauss, M., 111
Max Planck Institutes, 18, 84, 199, 222
Mayer, K. U., 202
McDonald, K. A., 265n17
Meaninglessness of measurement, 47, 52–54, 65
Mediating device, 55
Meetings (in HEP experiments), 174–175, 197, 211
Megill, A., 201
Merleau-Ponty, M., 29, 94
Merton, R. K., 29, 51

Meyer, J., 172, 202, 204, 247
Meyers, R. A., 264n15
Merz, M., 17, 76
Microinjection, 151
Miller, P., 263n1
Mixtures (of physics components), 76–77
Model systems, 25, 149, 156, 244, 251
Modernization theory, 7
Moieties, 212
Molecular biology (as seen by physicists), 275n4
Molecular genetics, 65, 153
Molecular machines, 138, 149. *See also* Machines
Monitoring, 60–62, 105, 116, 130
Monte Carlo (simulation), 54–55, 67, 76–78, 122, 125–126, 130. *See also* Simulation
Mouse, 86–89, 100, 140–143, 145, 151–155, 244; wild mouse, 142
Müller, K. H., 246
Mukerji, Ch., 29, 264n11
Mulkay, M., 27, 106, 197, 264n2, 266n1, 272n3
Mullins, N., 29, 166

Nagel, E., 253, 264n3, 265n1
"Narcissistic ethnography," 267n1
Natural selection, as strategy in experimental work, 12, 81, 88, 91–93
"Nature," 287–290nn1–9
Needham, R., 111
Negative knowledge, 46, 64–65, 70
Negative epistemics, 65, 80, 93
Nelkin, D., 290n9
Nightmares (in HEP experiments), 170
Nobel Prize, 18, 132, 134, 167, 240, 259, 297n4
Noise, 49, 52, 64, 73

Object-oriented classifications, 128
Object-oriented epistemics, 79
Object-oriented management. *See* Management by content
Object-oriented mechanisms, 189, 243
Object-oriented organization, 171–172
Object-oriented processing, 84
Object, 12, 31, 37–39, 41, 43, 48, 72, 84–86, 101, 113, 122, 128–129, 136, 149, 172, 190, 206, 220–221; -centered

relationships, 194, 196, 218, 220, 221, 242; centering, 195; circuits, 173, 194, 196; and knowledge, 194; levels, 244, 251; malleability of, 26, 79–81; natural, 28; proximity with, 165, 172, 182, 184, 243; world, 172, 251
O'Leary, T., 263n1
Ontologies: actor-based, 215; individuating, 238; of instruments, 3, 12; interaction-based, 215; of laboratory, 222, 256; machine, 245; notion of, 252–260; of objects, 149, 244; of subjects, 127, 171, 203, 214
Operating theater, 218–219
Ophir, A., 13
Order: forms of, 13, 254, 257; actorial, 193, 201, 209; communitarian superordering, 193; natural orders, 28–29, 32, 40, 44; orderings, 13, 192, 246, 254; social orders, 28–30, 32, 44, 214, 250
Organisms, 4, 87, 114, 118, 121, 123, 136, 138, 140, 142–145, 148, 151, 154, 157; as production sites, 144–145
Organization: notion of, 242
Organizational philosophies, 203–204
Otero, G., 157

Park, D., 16
Parsons, T., 293n5
Particle Physics Experiments Division, 16
Penrose, R., 264n15
Perrow, C., 172, 252
Person, 238; person-centered, 242. *See also* Epistemic subjects; Individuation; Scientific person
Perspectival realism, 4
Pestre, D., 160, 268n1
Peterson, R. A., 247
Phages, 142, 148
Phantasmatic objects, 48, 248
Phillips, R. J. N., 50
Physicists (as symbionts), 126–135; conjunction with objects, 129, 131, 135
Physics theory, 14–17, 273n3
Pickering, A., 9, 11, 17, 26, 29, 50, 88, 263n1, 264nn2,7,9,12, 273n3, 280n3
Pinch, T. J., 11, 263n1
Plasmids, 142–143, 146, 148
Plothow-Besch, H., 68
Polanyi, M., 218

Index

Porush, D., 158
Postdocs, 133, 167, 227–230
Post-industrial, 6
Post-romantic communitarian structures.
  See Communitarianism
Potter, J., 167
Powell, W., 172, 247
Practice, 8–11, 13
Production: devices, 145, 147; machines,
  151, 153; mass production, 154; pro-
  gram, 62–63; systems (sites), 138,
  144–145, 147–149, 154–156
Proximity with objects, 172, 182, 184
Psychoanalysis, 39–40, 109

Quinn, J. B., 5

Rabinow, P., 249, 263n1
Radcliffe-Brown, A. R., 232
Rae, A. I., 16
Rammert, W., 263n1
Reconfiguration, 12–13, 26, 28–33, 35,
  40, 42–45, 113, 127, 135–138, 157,
  214, 218–220, 222, 253–254, 269n1,
  284n2
Reconstruction, 49, 55
Reflexive modernization, 6
Reflexivity as instrument of knowing, 25
Resistance, 236, 279–283nn3,1,
  286–287n5
Restivo, S., 11, 26, 201, 263n1, 264n2,
  290n9
Rip, A., 263n1
Risk-taking, as strategy, 230–231
Robertson, R., 247
Rorty, R., 290n9
Rose, H., 268n1
Rosenblum, N., 252
Rouse, J., 264n10, 290n9
Rowan, B., 172, 204, 247
Rubbia, C., 17, 18, 167, 187, 188, 259
Rudwick, M. J. S., 263n1

S1-Digestion, 103–104
Sachs, M., 16
Sandbox, 33–34
Scenic descriptions, 102
Schaffer, S., 29, 33, 131, 162, 263n1,
  264n12
Schatzki, T., 264n10

Schedules, 175, 189–191
Schiebinger, L., 94
Scientific person, 217, 220–221, 237–239,
  254, 256. See also Epistemic subjects;
  Individuation
Seidel, R. W., 161, 162, 163, 172, 173
Self-analysis, 56, 65, 79
Self-description, 60–62, 252
Self-enclosed system, HEP as, 51–52
Self-knowledge, 173, 178, 259, 294n6
Self-observation, 60–63, 252
Self-organization, 179–180, 209
Self-other-things, 29, 32, 40, 127, 136
Self-referential epistemics, 65, 80
Self-understanding, 56–63, 76, 91–93,
  105, 109–110, 121, 128, 164, 220,
  249, 252, 271–272n3
Selleri, F., 16
Serres, M., 113
Service (in molecular biology laborato-
  ries), 234–236
Shapin, S., 13, 29, 33, 43, 45, 131,
  263nn1,2, 264n12
Shweder, R. A., 264n11
Sign(s), 95, 100–101, 104, 106, 248, 251;
  processes, 80; processing of, 46–50, 52
Simmel, G., 232
Simulation, 13, 34–35, 41, 49, 65,
  121–122, 125–126, 156, 195, 198, 245,
  249–250
Sismondo, S., 263n1
Sister experiment, 25, 42, 73–74, 187,
  203, 292n2
Skills, 218
Slovic, P., 34
Small, H. G., 167
Small lifeworld. See Lifeworld
Smearing, 49, 51–52, 55, 64, 90
Smith, A. D., 5
Smith, C., 162, 243
Smith, D., 268n1
Smith, R. W., 27
Social authority (mechanisms), 189, 191,
  243–244, 250
Sociology of science, 290n9
Soeffner, H.-G., 264n4
Spokespersons, 134, 208, 222
Spradley, J. P., 265n19
SSC (Superconducting Supercollider), 15,
  24–25, 160, 188, 240

Standard model, 15
Standpoint, 268n1
Star, S. L., 263n1
Status report, 175–178
Stehr, N., 5
Storer, N., 29
Stories, 106–109, 173, 178
Structural form, 214, 242
Structure functions, 16, 68, 76
Stump, D., 3
Suchman, L. A., 263n1
Superconducting Supercollider. *See* SSC
Superordering, 13
Superorganisms, 4, 130, 249
Suppes, P., 3
Surveillance, 60. *See also* Monitoring; Self-observation
Sussman, J., 34
SUSY (supersymmetric particles), 15, 69–70
Sutton, C., 18, 264n7, 265n15, 273n3
Swidler, A., 247, 264n11
Symbiosis, 129–130
Symbolic (re)classifications and repertoires, 111–114, 127–128, 138

Tacit knowledge, 99
Tarozzi, G., 16
Tatarewicz, J. N., 27
Taubes, G., 165, 264n7
Taylor, C., 165, 252
Technology: of correspondence, 33, 35; of intervention, 33, 37, 41, 93, 95; of representation, 33, 47
Territorial vs. temporal topologies, 238–240, 250
Theory (physics), 54, 68–69, 76–77
Thévenot, L., 113
Tönnies, F., 165
Top quark, 15, 24, 167–168
Total institution, HEP lab as, 213
Transcriptional control mechanisms, 18–19
Transitory object-states, 37
Traweek, S., 17, 106, 129, 232, 263n1, 264n12, 268n1, 273n3
Trust, 23, 128, 130–133, 171, 202–203; cohorts of, 208; as selection mechanism, 133–136
"Truth will out" device, 197

Turkle, S., 113, 158, 284n3
Turner, B., 252
Turner, S., 264n10
Turner, V. 63
Tversky, A., 34
Two-tier system of social organization, 38. *See also* Dual organization

UA1 (experiment), 15, 17–18, 25, 48, 50, 61, 73–74, 164, 167, 187, 203, 239
UA2 (experiment), vii, 15, 17, 19–20, 24, 48, 50–51, 53, 56–57, 59, 61–63, 65–67, 69, 73–75, 114, 117–120, 123, 134, 160, 166, 168–170, 175–177, 180–183, 187, 203, 207, 209–210, 215, 239; "Future UA2," 187
Underlying event, 49, 51, 64, 73
Understanding, in molecular biology, 91, 93. *See also* Self-understanding
Underwater telescope, 44
Unfolding, 47, 60, 71–72, 196–201, 244, 252, 259, 297n3. *See also* Contests of unfolding
Unity of science, 3
Urry, J., 6

Vaihinger, H., 251
van den Daele, W., 264n6
van der Meer, S., 18
van der Merwe, A., 16
Varela, F., 47
Variation: in molecular biology, 91–92, 109–110, 230; in physics, 92. *See also* "Blind" variation
Vector bosons, 14, 50, 52, 64
Vienna Circle, 3
Viruses, 142–143, 154
Visual scripts, 101, 106, 109

Watkins, P., 264n7
Watson, J. D., 81, 153
Weber, M., 244, 247, 293n5
Weinberg, S., 14, 268n1
Weyer, J., 5, 263n1
Wimsatt, W. C., 251
Winner, L., 263n1
Wise, N., 55, 162, 263n1
Woolf, H., 162
Woolgar, S., 11, 26, 41, 114, 263n1, 264n9, 267n1

Index

Workshop, 37
Wulf, W. A., 23
Wuthnow, R., 111, 264n11
Wynne, B., 263n1, 290n9

Yearly, S., 113

Zee, A., 16
Zelizer, V., 264n11
Zenzen, M., 11, 26, 263n1
Zuckerman, H., 28, 29, 263n1